T0223082

Lecture Notes in Artificial Intelligence 1365

Subseries of Lecture Notes in Computer Science
Edited by J. G. Carbonell and J. Siekmann

Lecture Notes in Computer Science

Edited by G. Goos, J. Hartmanis and J. van Leeuwen

Springer
Berlin
Heidelberg
New York
Barcelona
Budapest
Hong Kong
London
Milan
Paris
Santa Clara
Singapore
Tokyo

Munindar P. Singh Anand Rao
Michael J. Wooldridge (Eds.)

Intelligent Agents IV

Agent Theories, Architectures, and Languages

4th International Workshop, ATAL'97
Providence, Rhode Island, USA
July 24-26, 1997
Proceedings

 Springer

Series Editors
Jaime G. Carbonell, Carnegie Mellon University, Pittsburgh, PA, USA
Jörg Siekmann, University of Saarland, Saarbrücken, Germany

Volume Editors

Munindar P. Singh
North Carolina State University, Department of Computer Science
Raleigh, NC 27695-7534, USA
E-mail: singh@ncsu.edu

Anand Rao
Australian Artificial Intelligence Institute
171 La Trobe Street, Melbourne, Victoria 3000, Australia
E-mail: anand@aaii.oz.au

Michael J. Wooldridge
Queen Mary and Westfield College, University of London
Department of Electronic Engineering
London E1 4NS, UK
E-mail: m.j.wooldridge@qmw.ac.uk

Cataloging-in-Publication Data applied for

Die Deutsche Bibliothek - CIP-Einheitsaufnahme

Intelligent agents IV : agent theories, architectures, and languages ;
4th international workshop ; proceedings / ATAL'97, Providence,
Rhode Island, USA, July 24 - 26, 1997. Munindar P. Singh ... (ed.). -
Berlin ; Heidelberg ; New York ; Barcelona ; Budapest ; Hong Kong
; London ; Milan ; Paris ; Santa Clara ; Singapore ; Tokyo : Springer,
1998
  (Lecture notes in computer science ; Vol. 1365 : Lecture notes in
  artificial intelligence)
  ISBN 3-540-64162-9

CR Subject Classification (1991): I.2, D.2, C.2.4, F.3

ISSN 0302-9743
ISBN 3-540-64162-9 Springer-Verlag Berlin Heidelberg New York

© Springer-Verlag Berlin Heidelberg 1998
Printed in Germany

Typesetting: Camera ready by author
SPIN 10631861   06/3142 – 5 4 3 2 1 0   Printed on acid-free paper

Preface

Intelligent agents are one of the most important developments in computer science in the 1990s. Agents are of interest in many important application areas, ranging from human-computer interaction to industrial process control. The ATAL workshop series aims to bring together researchers interested in the core aspects of agent technology. Specifically, ATAL addresses issues such as theories of agency, software architectures for intelligent agents, methodologies and programming languages for realizing agents, and software tools for applying and evaluating agent systems. One of the strengths of the ATAL workshop series is its emphasis on the synergies between theories, infrastructures, architectures, methodologies, formal methods, and languages.

Seventy-six papers were submitted to the ATAL-97 workshop, from seventeen countries. After stringent reviewing, twenty papers were accepted for full presentation and an additional five for short presentation. After the workshop, these papers were revised on the basis of comments received both from original reviewers and from discussions at the workshop itself. This volume contains these revised papers.

The technology of intelligent agents and multi-agent systems is beginning to migrate from research labs to software engineering centers. As the rate of this migration increases, it is becoming increasingly clear that we must develop principled techniques for analyzing, specifying, designing, and verifying agent-based systems. Without such techniques, agent technology will simply not realize its full potential. Consequently, the ATAL-97 program emphasized *methodologies* for agent systems. Besides several papers on methodologies, the program also featured two panels, one specifically on methodologies and one on agent programming languages. Another highlight of the 1997 program was three invited talks by leading exponents of agent research:

THEORIES	Les Gasser	Theories of Agents and Multi-Agents
ARCHITECTURES	Kurt Konolige	Connecting Software and Physical Agents
LANGUAGES	Danny Lange	Java — Just What Mobile Agents Need?

It is both our hope and our expectation that this volume will be as useful to the agent research and development community as its three predecessors have proved to be. We believe that ATAL and the *Intelligent Agents* series of which this volume is a part play a crucial role in a rapidly developing field, by focusing specifically on the relationships between the theory and practice of agents. Only through understanding these relationships can agent-based computing mature and achieve its widely predicted potential.

November 1997

Munindar P. Singh (Raleigh, USA)
Anand S. Rao (Melbourne, Australia)
Michael J. Wooldridge (London, UK)

Workshop Organization

Organizing Committee

Munindar P. Singh (GENERAL/AMERICAS CHAIR)
North Carolina State University, USA

Anand Rao (ASIA/PACIFIC-RIM CHAIR)
Australian AI Institute, Australia

Michael Wooldridge (EUROPEAN CHAIR)
Queen Mary and Westfield College, UK

David Kinny (METHODOLOGIES TRACK CHAIR)
Australian AI Institute, Australia

Nicholas R. Jennings Queen Mary and Westfield College, UK

Jörg P. Müller Zuno Ltd, UK

Program Committee

Ron Arkin	(USA)	Pete Bonasso	(USA)
Hans-Dieter Burkhard	(Germany)	Cristiano Castelfranchi	(Italy)
John-Jules Ch. Meyer	(Netherlands)	Keith Decker	(USA)
Ed Durfee	(USA)	Jacques Ferber	(France)
Klaus Fischer	(Germany)	Michael Fisher	(UK)
Stan Franklin	(USA)	Fausto Giunchiglia	(Italy)
Piotr Gmytrasiewicz	(USA)	Afsaneh Haddadi	(Germany)
Henry Hexmoor	(USA)	David Kinny	(Australia)
Kurt Konolige	(USA)	Sarit Kraus	(Israel)
Yves Lespérance	(Canada)	James Lester	(USA)
Charles Rich	(USA)	Jeff Rosenschein	(Israel)
Wei-Min Shen	(USA)	Carles Sierra	(Spain)
Devika Subramanian	(USA)	Kurt Sundermeyer	(Germany)
Katia Sycara	(USA)	Milind Tambe	(USA)
Mario Tokoro	(Japan)	Jan Treur	(Netherlands)

Additional Reviewers

Massimo Benerecetti	Frances Brazier	Bruno Caprile	Rosaria Conte
Marco Daniele	Joeri Engelfriet	Rino Falcone	Petra Funk
C. M. Jonker	Ralf Kühnel	Jürgen Lind	Serafini Luciano
Rina Schwartz	Luciano Serafini	Steven Shapiro	David Tremaine
Pascal van Eck	Gero Vierke		

Contents

Introduction

Like its three predecessors [2, 3, 1], this volume of the *Intelligent Agents* series focusses on the relationships between the theory and practice of intelligent autonomous agents. To this end, the volume is divided into six sections, reflecting the major current research and development trends in the intelligent agents field. Section I focusses on *methodologies* for agent systems — principled techniques for designing and implementing agent systems. Section II focusses on *architectures and infrastructures*: the papers in this section describe software architectures and techniques for building effective multi-agent systems. Section III focusses on *coordination*, which has long been recognised as an issue of importance in the multi-agent systems community. Section IV focusses on *formal methods* for agent systems, a particular strength of the ATAL workshop series. Section V focusses on the *theoretical foundations* of agent systems, and finally, Section VI focusses on *architectures and methodologies*.

Section I: Methodologies

Marcel Schoppers and Dan Shapiro develop an approach that gives equal importance to user-centric evaluation criteria on the one hand, and agent-centric or developer-centric criteria on the other. This parity is crucial for developing robust methodologies for designing agent-based systems, especially those applied where user-centric criteria, such as safety, cannot be ignored.

Considering agent construction as a special case of object-oriented design (OOD), *Joanna Bryson and Brendan McGonigle* observes that previous approaches, especially in robotic agents, have usually not been accompanied by methodologies for their application. This has limited their applicability to whatever can be achieved through *ad hoc* construction of agents. Using OOD enables the exploitation of traditional software techniques such as polymorphism and inheritance.

The language-action perspective as developed by Winograd and colleagues applies insights from speech act theory to understand and analyze interactions in human organizations. *Egon Verharen* et al apply the same conceptual approach to develop an architecture of agents in information applications. Their architecture yields the increased flexibility needed for modern applications in open information environments.

Van Parunak et al define synthetic ecosystems as multiagent systems consisting of a large number of simple agents that can, however, participate in complex interactions. They argue that synthetic ecosystems are beneficial in several industrial applications, including those to do with manufacturing. They then propose an approach for the design of such systems, including important steps toward a methodology.

Section II: Architectures and Infrastructure

Rina Schwartz and Sarit Kraus consider the problem of allocating data among a number of self-interested data servers. They develop a mechanism for optimal allocation of data in this environment. They model the servers as agents with individual preferences and not subject to any central control. Unlike traditional competitive market pricing, this approach works in settings where each product (data item) has exactly one instance.

Arvind Bansal et al apply traditional distributed systems techniques to agent systems. They consider the problem of fault tolerance of agents. Fault tolerance is increasingly important as agents are applied in critical domains. The proposed approach saves the state of each agent with other agents in the system. When the agent recovers from a crash, its state is reconstructed from the dumps taken at the other agents. This approach builds on research into logical clocks and potential causality.

Munindar Singh considers the problem of coordinating the actions of agents that are heterogeneous — with differing designs — and autonomous. These agents relinquish their autonomy to some extent in order to coordinate with other agents. The agents are modeled as small skeletons showing their actions or events that are visible to other agents, and which are relevant for coordination. This approach takes specifications in a temporal logic and converts them into guards on the individual events that can then be executed in a distributed manner.

Sylvia Coradeschi and Lars Karlsson introduce an approach for building reactive but coordinated agents. Their approach defines behaviors as canned scripts or decision-trees, which are specified along with their expected resources and priority. Agents coordinate in real-time, not through communications, but by identifying their team's tactics and knowing the roles they play in those tactics.

Section III: Coordination Planning and Monitoring

Jaeho Lee and Ed Durfee develop structure circuit semantics (SCS) which makes explicit the semantics of plans, otherwise left implicit in the underlying plan interpreter. It adapts GRAFCET, a formalism of the Petri net family, to capture the operational semantics of plans. This approach analyzes plans of different agents to detect and avoid potential deadlocks.

The robust execution of multiagent plans requires the ability on the part of each agent to detect failures and recover from them. *Gal Kaminka and Milind Tambe* develop an approach for failure detection and recovery based on social comparison theory. Social comparison theory, introduced in the 1950s, involves an agent comparing its behavior to that of other agents in a bid to identify discrepancies or to learn from them. Kaminka and Tambe consider classes of agents, such as the teammates of the given agent, from which the learning can be the most effective.

Coalitions promise an intuitive way to combine agents so as to improve the quality of the tasks they perform. However, determining suitable coalitions in nontrivial. Traditional, game-theoretic, approaches are centralized and intractable. *Onn Shehory* et al propose some well-argued simplifications and extensions with which an alternative approach can be defined. Their approach is practicable for systems involving dozens of agents, which cover many cases of practical interest.

Section IV: Formal Methods

Mark d'Inverno et al formally specify the behaviour of a Procedural Reasoning System (PRS) — a class of systems based on the BDI model of practical reasoning. They provide an abstract model of an idealised system and define the key data structures and the operations that manipulate these structures. The specification is undertaken in Z, a well-known formal specification language.

While a number of papers in the past have examined particular agent languages, very few have compared different languages with respect to developing the same system. *Marco Mulder* et al perform such a comparative study of two of the well known languages for agent modelling — Concurrent METATEM (a multi-agent programming language based on the METATEM paradigm of executable temporal logic), and DESIRE (a compositional specification framework for intelligent systems). The comparison is carried out with respect to the PRS agent architecture: the authors show how the main features of the PRS family of architectures can elegantly be expressed in both Concurrent METATEM and DESIRE.

Carles Sierra et al describe a general framework for negotiation in which agents exchange proposals backed by arguments. These arguments summarise the reasons why the proposals should be accepted. The paper uses a business process management example to illustrate the main concepts of argumentation-based negotiation. The primary contribution of the paper is in providing a formal integration of two well-known threads of reasoning — agent-based negotiation and argumentation-based reasoning.

The Knowledge Query and Manipulation Language (KQML) is a widely used language and protocol for communication between agents. Although the language has been around for a few years, there have to date been no serious attempts at giving a semantic description of it. *Yannis Labrou and Tim Finin* rectify this problem by providing a detailed semantics for three key KQML performatives.

Section V: Theories

Koen Hindriks et al propose an abstract agent programming language with a well defined semantics based on transition systems. The language combines both logic programming and imperative programming constructs. It allows users to write practical reasoning rules that provide a mechanism for goal revision. The approach has both theoretical and practical merit and helps to bridge the gap between theory and practice in this area.

Frank Dignum and Rosaria Conte address the issue of autonomous goal formation. The authors consider goal formation through behavioural conformity and goal conformity. An alternative mechanism of goal formation through the adoption of norms is also discussed. General rules for goal formation are formally expressed and applied to the social domain.

Cristoph Jung and Klaus Fischer present the COOP calculus, a language for concurrent, continuous inference processes as a means of bridging the gap between theory and practice in hybrid architectures of intelligent agent systems. Term rewriting calculus is used as the basis for specifying the semantics. The language can also be viewed as an extension of the hybrid system INTERRAP used for designing intelligent agents.

Frédéric Koriche provides a formal framework for modeling tractable reasoning in resource bounded agents that have very large, inconsistent and uncertain sets of knowledge. The paper proposes a model checking approach and a stepwise procedure for improving approximate answers and allowing their convergence to the correct answer.

Ho Ngoc Duc proposes an approach to formalizing resource-bounded agents by combining epistemic logic with complexity analysis. Such an approach considers how long an agent will need to compute the answer to a certain query. The paper once again provides a mechanism for bridging idealistic theories with existing practical agents.

Section VI: Architectures and Methodologies

Marian Nodine and Amy Unruh discuss inter-operability issues in multi-agent systems, with particular reference to the InfoSleuth project at MCC. In particular, they discuss the desirability of using common communication languages with a standardised set of speech acts, and a *service ontology* defining the "nouns" and "adjectives" that agents can refer to. In addition to these basic components, Nodine and Unruh describe *conversations*, which are rather like protocols for cooperation.

Walter Van de Welde et al describe the *competition for attention* paradigm for agent-based multi-media applications. The competition for attention paradigm is based on the currently popular paradigm of *push technology*, where users are pro-actively provided with information and other services. However, Van de Welde et al point out that unmodified use of push will almost certainly lead to "information overload", and that a solution is for agents to *compete* for user's attention. They describe an implementation of the approach in the WWW site for the Brussels-based Ecran film festival.

Carlos Iglesias et al continue the theme of methodologies for agent-based systems developed at previous ATAL workshops, by developing a methodology for agent system development based on the well-known Common KADS methodology for knowledge-based system construction. The methodology results in the generation of seven models, describing the various aspects of the system. The methodology is illustrated by means of a simple travel agency case study. Like Iglesias and colleagues, *Rune Gustavsson* also describes an approach to designing multi-agent systems based on the Common KADS methodology.

R. Scott Cost et al describe TKQML — an interpreted programming language for building agent systems based on the TCL (Tool Control Language) scripting language. TQML, as its name suggests, supports messaging in the KQML communication language. TKQML allows rapid prototyping of multi-agent systems, and allows the use of all Tcl/Tk facilities for building GUI front ends.

November 1997

Munindar P. Singh (Raleigh, USA),
Anand S. Rao (Melbourne, Australia), and
Michael J. Wooldridge (London, UK)

References

1. J. P. Müller, M. Wooldridge, and N. R. Jennings, editors. *Intelligent Agents III (LNAI Volume 1193)*. Springer-Verlag: Berlin, Germany, 1995.
2. M. Wooldridge and N. R. Jennings, editors. *Intelligent Agents: Theories, Architectures, and Languages (LNAI Volume 890)*. Springer-Verlag: Berlin, Germany, 1995.
3. M. Wooldridge, J. P. Müller, and M. Tambe, editors. *Intelligent Agents II (LNAI Volume 1037)*. Springer-Verlag: Berlin, Germany, 1996.

Panel: Methodologies for Multi-Agent Systems

David Kinny
Australian Artificial Intelligence Institute
171 LaTrobe Street, Melbourne, Victoria 3000, Australia
dnk@aaii.com.au

Jan Treur
Department of Mathematics and Computer Science
Vrije Universiteit Amsterdam
De Boelelaan 1081a, 1081 HV Amsterdam, the Netherlands
treur@cs.vu.nl

Les Gasser
Information Technology and Organizations Program
National Science Foundation
4201 Wilson Blvd, Arlington, VA 22230, USA
lgasser@nsf.gov

Steve Clark
Industrial Technology Institute
2901 Hubbard Rd, Ann Arbor, MI 48106-1485, USA
sjc@iti.org

Jörg Müller
ZUNO Ltd.
International House, Ealing Broadway, London W5 5DB, UK
jpm@zuno.com

Abstract. Multi-Agent Systems technologies are migrating from research labs to software engineering centres. If these technologies are to realize their potential, it will become increasingly important to develop and employ methodologies, accessible to software engineers, for specifying, analysing, designing, and verifying multi-agent systems. The panelists, who represented a broad range of approaches and experience in MAS theory and practice, addressed the following questions.

- What can we learn from existing software and knowledge engineering methodologies, such as object-oriented approaches? How can they be adapted and extended to apply to agent-based systems?
- How should MAS design and specification methodologies address the proliferation of MAS architectures and application environments? Is there any prospect of generic approaches? How important are efforts to standardize various aspects of MAS technology?
- What techniques and tools are needed to support agent-oriented design and development?
- What approaches, formal and practical, will allow us to verify and diagnose large-scale MAS applications? What can we learn from related domains, such as real-time and distributed systems?

Designing Embedded Agents to Optimize End-User Objectives

Marcel Schoppers* and Daniel Shapiro†

* Robotics Research Harvesting
PO Box 2111, Redwood City, CA 94063
marcels@netcom.com

† Dept of Engineering Economic Systems
Stanford University, Palo Alto, CA 94304
dgs@leland.stanford.edu

Abstract. We formulate the design of discrete-state stochastic control systems as optimizing a performance objective specified in user-oriented terms, i.e. terms that need not be perceivable by the controller or agent being designed. This addresses a user acceptance issue: while agent designs (control algorithms) are limited to distinctions about state supported by artificial perception systems, end users want to evaluate performance using terms such as safety, opportunity, and throughput.[1] We elucidate a feedback from evaluation to agent design via a sensitivity analysis, obtaining the gradient of a time-averaging objective function w.r.t. state transitions influenced by the agent. This gradient leads to a methodology for iteratively improving a system's performance, as perceived by others.

1 Motivation

Although users of artificial agents have a tremendous need to place guarantees on agent behavior, the topic of validation methodology is relatively under-explored. The empirical standard is to expose an agent to a large body of test cases, iteratively eliminating bugs and refining agent behavior while time and money last. The underlying performance criteria are often informal, contributing to a debatable guarantee. Verification approaches such as automated plan synthesis depend crucially on formal domain models (which are known to be inaccurate) and the availability of complete specifications (goal sets) that define desired behavior. The net result is that we are far more able to prove numerical properties of our algorithms than to validate the discrete behavior of our artifacts.

We submit that the difficulty of such validation problems stems from the need to compare reference frames: agents, designers, and users model the world in very different terms and apply qualitatively different criteria to measure success. For example, the agent (as an automaton) can only characterize the world within the limitations of its perception system, e.g. as a set of moving shapes, activated contact sensors and the like, with consequent restrictions on its decisions and

---

[1] This work was supported in part by NASA contract 9-19040.

behavior. The agent's engineers evaluate that behavior in terms of their own vastly superior perceptions and background knowledge, and care about such things as mechanical wear, throughput, and possible failure modes. As much as the engineers' concerns differ from anything the agent can compute, they also diverge from the interests of end users (think of bad VCR interfaces, and of pretty, but inconvenient kitchens). Users are typically motivated by questions of domain performance, convenience, and safety.

This paper introduces a design and validation methodology which explicitly addresses the need to compare reference frames. We consider a robot with a limited perceptual base that operates via a reactive loop, and an end-user whose success criteria are based on a qualitatively distinct perception of salient state. Our methodology solves the following problems:

#1 What is the mapping from robot-perceived states to human-perceived states?
#2 What is the expected utility of the robot process, expressed in end-user terms?
#3 What change to the robot's actions will best improve the end-user's received utility?

We define the mapping from robot- to human-perceived states as a probabilistic relation given a set of simultaneous observations, and ask the end-user to assign a constant utility to each user-perceived state. Next, we assume (and can compute) a predictive model of robot-perceived state, such as a Markov model. This allows us to average the end-user utility over possible futures and over time. We then derive the gradient of the expected end-user utility with respect to tunable elements of the agent's behavior. This yields a mathematical framework for evaluating and incrementally improving, the design of an artifact per human-held criteria. We submit that this expression of the validation problem is more formal than exhaustive testing and more natural than existing verification procedures.

This paper develops the necessary mathematics, and includes a walk-through of the proposed methodology in the context of a simplified NASA problem, namely the creation of a robot for space rescue. We conclude with a discussion of open issues, relevant work, and future directions.

2 Mathematics

2.1 Formalization

Our approach considers a control system, e.g. that of a robot. The robot's perceptions, including the states of its sensors and effectors and its own internal data, must be mapped into a set of mutually exclusive states S_r (mnemonic for "states perceivable by robot controller"). The number of states must be finite.

For simplicity we assume that, despite the uncertainty inherent in any real sensor suite, the agent declares itself to be in one particular state at any time. This might be the state deemed most likely in a probability distribution, or the process might indeed be fully observable. This single-state assumption is often made in discrete-state agents, which can't respond to 70% chance of rain by bringing 70% of an umbrella – the agent must act as if it's going to rain, or not. While such a single-state assumption is not crucial for our approach, it makes for a more intuitive exposition and removes an ambiguity.

Similarly for a human evaluator, observing the robot and its environment, there will be another set of states. These must be a mutually exclusive set S_e (mnemonic for "states perceivable by the evaluator"). For each state the evaluator must assess a single, constant, desirability value, and this value must depend only on the state, not on whatever comes before or after it. Clearly, the definitions of the evaluator's states will be driven by the evaluator's wish to assess different values at different times. The evaluator may however declare her belief to be any probability distribution over S_e, in which case the assessed value must be the corresponding expectation over the state's values.

S_e and S_r may be very large sets, but this does not impact the feasibility of our approach, which is intended for off-line, design-time use. (Even for $|S_r| = 10^6$ states our approach is well computable.) Further, since the evaluator need not guess at the robot's inner workings, S_e may be a much smaller set than S_r.

2.2 The Observer-Robot Relation

Toward our goal of improving robot performance as evaluated by a human observer, we need to express performance as a function of the evaluator's states, which are themselves a function of robot behavior. This means we need to derive a probability distribution over S_e for each robot state $r_j \in S_r$.

Let $p(e_i|r_j)$ denote the probability that the evaluator perceives state e_i *given* that the controller perceives state r_j. Also let $p_t(r_j)$ be the probability that the controller perceives state r_j at time t. Then by Bayes' Rule, $\sum_j p(e_i|r_j)p_t(r_j)$ is the probability that the evaluator perceives state e_i at time t.

This calculation can be written in matrix notation as follows. With $|S|$ denoting the cardinality of set S, we define a matrix $\mathbf{P}$ of size $|S_e| \times |S_r|$ whose entries are $P_{ij} = p(e_i|r_j)$. Also let $\mathbf{r}_t$ denote the vector $[p_t(r_1), p_t(r_2) \ldots p_t(r_n)]$, which is a probability distribution over the controller-perceivable states. Then we obtain $\mathbf{e}_t = \mathbf{P}\,\mathbf{r}_t$ as the probability distribution, corresponding to $\mathbf{r}_t$, over the evaluator-perceivable states. Because $\mathbf{P}$ predicts the state the evaluator will perceive, as a function of the state the controller perceives, we call $\mathbf{P}$ the *evaluator prediction matrix*.

It remains only to find the actual contents of $\mathbf{P}$. From a simulation instrumented with some extra code, and at given instants of time t, we can simultaneously collect the state estimate vectors computed by the controller ($\mathbf{r}_t$) and by the evaluator ($\mathbf{e}_t$). These may identify single states, or give probability distributions over the respective state sets. Finally we compute $\mathbf{P}$ as the solution to the explicit minimization problem:

$$\min_{\mathbf{P}} \sum_t \| \mathbf{e}_t - \mathbf{P}\,\mathbf{r}_t \|^2 \quad s.t. \quad \sum_w \mathbf{P}_{wk} = 1 \tag{1}$$

where the column sum constraint guarantees $\mathbf{P}$ transforms all of the probability mass in a given robot state into *some* evaluator state. We obtain the following solution (after some algebra):

$$\mathbf{P} = \left[\sum_t \mathbf{e}_t \mathbf{r}_t^T\right] \left[\sum_t \mathbf{r}_t \mathbf{r}_t^T\right]^+ \tag{2}$$

The first bracketed term of this equation is an $e \times r$ matrix, while the second is $r \times r$, making $\mathbf{P}$ $e \times r$, as desired. (We use the pseudo-inverse, denoted by $^+$, in place of the true inverse since the second term is clearly singular.) This solution guarantees that $\mathbf{P}$ is unique and that its columns are probability vectors, via the following argument: since $\mathbf{e}_t \mathbf{r}_t^T$ and $\mathbf{r}_t \mathbf{r}_t^T$ are products of probability vectors, both $\sum_t \mathbf{e}_t \mathbf{r}_t^T$ and $\sum_t \mathbf{r}_t \mathbf{r}_t^T$ are non-negative matrices. $\sum_t \mathbf{r}_t \mathbf{r}_t^T$ is also symmetric, with non-negative eigenvalues. The (pseudo)inverse of a such a matrix has non-negative eigenvalues and thus non-negative elements as well. $\mathbf{P}$ is therefore non-negative because it is the product of two non-negative matrices. Since the pseudo-inverse operator is unique, $\mathbf{P}$ is unique, non-negative, and its columns sum to 1 by virtue of the minimization constraint. QED.

Note that $\mathbf{P}$ always exists, but may be more or less informative. $\mathbf{P}$ is an identity matrix when robot and observer states are perfectly correlated, but it has constant rows when a change in belief about robot state has no impact on the estimate of evaluator state. This situation might apply if the robot and observer are on different planets.

2.3 Behavior Model Construction

To compute the expected system performance as seen by the evaluator, we use the evaluator prediction matrix $\mathbf{P}$ to map controller-perceived states into evaluator-perceived states, and calculate the system's expected behavior as perceived by the controller. For this first implementation of our methodology, we are temporarily assuming that the robot process is Markovian (possibly with hidden states). The mathematics of Markov processes is well understood, and there is a burgeoning literature on estimating the structure of Markov processes from observations, see the references in [3]. As it is trivial to make an agent's control software report the agent's perceptions of internal and external state, and thus to estimate the process's transition matrix, this paper limits discussion of the agent's behavior model to showing that the standard mathematics is indeed piecewise differentiable. See e.g. [5] for an introduction to Markov chain analysis. Here we need only the following paragraph of standard theory:

A "closed communicating class" (CCC) is a set of states that collectively function as a trap: once the process has entered a CCC it can never get out. For each CCC_i the transition matrix $\mathbf{R}$ has a left eigenvector with eigenvalue 1, i.e. $\mathbf{x}_i \mathbf{R} = \mathbf{x}_i$. Rewriting the eigen-equation as $\mathbf{0} = \mathbf{x}_i (\mathbf{I} - \mathbf{R})$ we see that the eigenvectors span the null space of $(\mathbf{I} - \mathbf{R})$, and hence can all be efficiently identified with one Singular Value Decomposition. Every state having a nonzero entry in any eigenvector having $\lambda = 1$ is a member state of some (one) CCC.

Knowing which states are in CCCs, we can re-number the states so that those occurring in CCCs come first, thus yielding a transition matrix in canonical form:

$$\mathbf{R}' = \begin{bmatrix} \mathbf{C} & \mathbf{0} \\ \Delta & \mathbf{A} \end{bmatrix}$$

where $\mathbf{C}$ covers transitions within CCCs, $\mathbf{A}$ covers transitions between transient states, and Δ covers transitions from transient states into CCCs. We can now compute the "fundamental matrix" $\mathbf{F} = \sum_{n=0}^{\infty} \mathbf{A}^n = (\mathbf{I} - \mathbf{A})^{-1}$, wherein F_{ij} is the expected number of times the Markov process will occupy transient state j when started in transient state i; and thence the matrix $\mathbf{T} = \mathbf{F}\,\Delta$ wherein T_{ij} is the probability of entering a CCC at state j when started in transient state i.

To automatically extract the transition matrix $\mathbf{R}$ from simulation traces, we assume that the controller can be instrumented with code that outputs the current controller-perceived state, as described previously. With the states identified and the possible transitions being explicit in the simulation trace, the only remaining problem is to calculate, for each state, the probabilities of transitioning to its successor states. This is a trivial calculation but for the possibility of non-stochastic behavior, e.g. a state that always transitions to itself exactly 5 times, then transitions to somewhere else. Non-stochastic behavior indicates the existence of a "hidden variable" such as a counter. An accurate Markov model must incorporate the hidden variable by modelling the repeating state as a sequence of distinct model states. We plan to use the "instance-based state identification" algorithm reported in [6], which uses state sequence observations (in addition to probability information) to automatically identify hidden variables.

2.4 The Performance Objective

We now order the human observer's subjective utilities as a vector $\mathbf{u}$, and hence predict the observer's instantaneous evaluation (at time n) as a function of the robot's initial state (distribution) $\mathbf{r}$: $\mathbf{u}^T \mathbf{P} (\mathbf{R}^T)^n \mathbf{r}$ for $n \geq 0$.

We choose an objective function that averages the (human-perceived) utility of the robot's behavior over possible futures and over time:

$$f(i) = \mathbf{u}^T \mathbf{P} \left(\frac{1}{N} \sum_{n=0}^{N} (\mathbf{R}^T)^n \right) \mathbf{r}$$

where N is a number of state transitions, possibly infinite. We choose this function for three reasons. First, we are especially interested in the design and validation of autonomous agents which act to maximize the value of an un-ending future. While goal-directed planners may tolerate arbitrarily bad outcomes that precede a goal, and ignore arbitrarily bad outcomes that follow it, an agent pursuing a time-averaged criterion behaves better in both cases. Second, time-averaged evaluation is quite general. It can be reduced to goal-directed behavior, and to shortest-path behavior, by giving all states equal utility except for one (goal) state of higher utility. Third, the above objective can be evaluated both for finite and infinite life-times, as we show next.

Rewriting the objective function $f(i)$ in terms of the canonical form $\mathbf{R}'$ of the transition matrix (see the previous subsection), and permuting the columns of $\mathbf{P}$ to match the new state numbering, we find, using $(\mathbf{R}'^T)^n = (\mathbf{R}'^n)^T$:

$$f(i') = \mathbf{u}^T \mathbf{P}' \, \frac{1}{N} \begin{bmatrix} \sum\limits_{n=0}^{N} \mathbf{C}^n & \mathbf{0} \\[2ex] \sum\limits_{m+n=0}^{N-1} (\mathbf{A}^m \Delta \mathbf{C}^n) & \sum\limits_{n=0}^{N} \mathbf{A}^n \end{bmatrix}^T \mathbf{r}',$$

$$\rightarrow \mathbf{u}^T \mathbf{P}' \begin{bmatrix} \Lambda & \mathbf{0} \\[1ex] \mathbf{F}\Delta\Lambda & \frac{1}{N}\mathbf{F} \end{bmatrix}^T \mathbf{r}', \qquad N \rightarrow \infty. \qquad (3)$$

The submatrixes have straightforward interpretations. The ith row of the upper submatrix $[\Lambda \; \mathbf{0}]$ gives steady-state occupancy frequencies when the process is started in state r_i in a CCC. Similarly, since $\mathbf{F}\Delta = \mathbf{T}$, the ith row of the lower submatrix $[\mathbf{F}\Delta\Lambda \; \frac{1}{N}\mathbf{F}]$ gives expected steady-state occupancy frequencies when the process is started at *transient* state r_i.

To evaluate a non-terminating process we focus on the steady-state behavior, namely the behavior inside CCCs as given by the left-hand submatrixes of Equation 3, since in the limit of infinite time, the time-averaged occupancy frequency of transient states (the right-hand submatrixes) is 0. To evaluate a terminating process we simply reverse the foregoing bias by focusing on the right-hand submatrixes of Equation 3, with $\Lambda = \mathbf{0}$. (Note that "goal" states must precede termination to be included in the evaluation).

If we wish $f(i')$ to give some weight to both steady-state and transient behavior, we can evaluate $f(i')$ exactly as written for some finite choice of N. With more efficiency but less confidence, we can also evaluate the steady-state and transient behaviors separately as described above, and return a weighted sum.

2.5 Gradient: ∇f

To show that our objective function is not only evaluable but also useful to guide agent design, we must provide an effective method for making agents optimize the objectives. To this end we show that it is possible to compute ∇f, the gradient vector of f with respect to the agent's internal state transition probabilities.

We obtain the elements $\frac{\partial f(i)}{\partial R_{kl}}$ by constructing a perturbation matrix $\tilde{\mathbf{R}}$ whose entries are zero but for $\tilde{R}_{kl} = \epsilon$. We write $^\epsilon f(i)$ for the perturbed evaluation (using $\mathbf{R} + \tilde{\mathbf{R}}$ in place of $\mathbf{R}$). Thus we obtain:

$$\frac{\partial f(i)}{\partial R_{kl}} = (\mathbf{u}^T \mathbf{P}) \left(\frac{1}{N} \sum_{n=1}^{N} \sum_{m=0}^{n-1} (\mathbf{R}^m)_{ik} ((\mathbf{R}^{n-(m+1)})_{l*})^T \right) \qquad (4)$$

$(\mathbf{R}^m)_{ik}$ is the probability that the process will be in state k, and be affected by the perturbation, at time m. $(\mathbf{R}^{n-(m+1)})_{l*}$ gives occupancy probabilities for states after l (down-stream from the perturbation) at time n. $\sum_m$ thus computes the expected effect of the perturbation on all trajectories of length n, and $\sum_n$ averages the evaluation to time N.

Eq 4, with its high powers of potentially large (but sparse) matrixes, is not recommended for computation. We isolate the gradient of the *transient* behavior by putting $\mathbf{R}$ into canonical form $\mathbf{R}'$, extracting the transient submatrix $\mathbf{A}$, computing $\mathbf{F} = \sum_{m=0}^{\infty} \mathbf{A}^m = (\mathbf{I} - \mathbf{A})^{-1}$, and thus simplifying Eq 4 to get

$$\frac{\partial f(i)}{\partial R_{kl}} = \mathbf{u}^T \mathbf{P}'(\mathbf{F}_{l*})^T \mathbf{F}_{ik} / t \qquad (5)$$

where $\mathbf{P}'$ is $\mathbf{P}$ with its columns permuted to match the new state numbering. Since t scales all the gradient elements it is arbitrary. This simplification can be computed with one Singular Value Decomposition, one matrix inversion, and a few vector products. Because $\mathbf{I} - \mathbf{A}$ is very sparse, this computation can be made very fast: nearly linear in the number of states. The gradient for terminating processes of 100 states can be computed in 0.007 sec; for 10^6 states it takes 28 sec to 50 mins (on an old Sparc 2), depending on process structure.

The gradient for steady-state performance is work-in-progress.

2.6 Total Derivatives

The gradient gives crucial information for optimizing the design of the controller, specifically by focusing attention on the transition probabilities the end-user would most want changed. However, we are not free to change them arbitrarily. Our use of a Markov model imposes the constraints

$$\sum_m R_{km} = 1, \quad \text{and} \quad \sum_m \frac{dR_{km}}{dR_{kl}} = 0. \qquad (6)$$

To satisfy these constraints the iterative improvement process must be concerned with the total derivatives

$$\frac{df(i)}{dR_{kl}} = \sum_m \frac{\partial f(i)}{\partial R_{km}} \frac{dR_{km}}{dR_{kl}}. \qquad (7)$$

Other constraints arise from the physics of the underlying sensors and effectors, and from the economics of changing the agent design: not all conceivable improvements are feasible. Hence the revealed optimization problem is to maximize f subject to reality constraints. As usual, the optimal agent design will occur either at a boundary point of the physics constraints, or at a bliss point where the total derivatives are zero.

3 A Worked Example

The following example comes from a domain of considerable interest to NASA: a robot whose task is to rescue an astronaut adrift in space. A simplified version of the robot might be cognizant of four states: #1 astronaut has been sighted far away, #2 robot is standing-off the astronaut, #3 astronaut has been attached, and #4 astronaut has been released into the Shuttle. The actions performed in these states are: #1 navigating to an arm's length from the astronaut, #2 matching the astronaut's motion and then grappling him, #3 navigating back to the Shuttle and releasing the astronaut, and #4 deactivating the robot. Along the way, things can go wrong, like bumping the astronaut before matching his motion, or "dropping" him on the way back. A possible state diagram is shown in Fig 1a, with transition probabilities on the arcs. Since we choose to regard this "process" as terminating at a goal state, we cast it as the transient part of a Markov chain, and plan to use Eq 5. To be included in the evaluation, the goal state must be transient, so we have it transition into a new terminal state, shown shaded. The resulting transition matrix $\mathbf{R}$ appears in Fig 1b. $\mathbf{A}$ is the upper-left 4×4 part of $\mathbf{R}$, and $\mathbf{F} = (\mathbf{I} - \mathbf{A})^{-1}$ appears in Fig 1c.

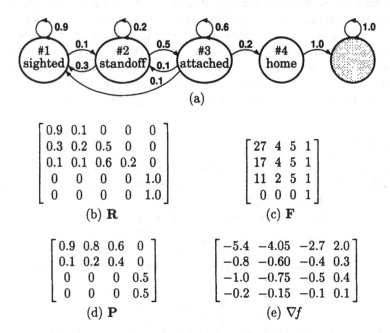

(a)

$$\begin{bmatrix} 0.9 & 0.1 & 0 & 0 & 0 \\ 0.3 & 0.2 & 0.5 & 0 & 0 \\ 0.1 & 0.1 & 0.6 & 0.2 & 0 \\ 0 & 0 & 0 & 0 & 1.0 \\ 0 & 0 & 0 & 0 & 1.0 \end{bmatrix}$$

(b) $\mathbf{R}$

$$\begin{bmatrix} 27 & 4 & 5 & 1 \\ 17 & 4 & 5 & 1 \\ 11 & 2 & 5 & 1 \\ 0 & 0 & 0 & 1 \end{bmatrix}$$

(c) $\mathbf{F}$

$$\begin{bmatrix} 0.9 & 0.8 & 0.6 & 0 \\ 0.1 & 0.2 & 0.4 & 0 \\ 0 & 0 & 0 & 0.5 \\ 0 & 0 & 0 & 0.5 \end{bmatrix}$$

(d) $\mathbf{P}$

$$\begin{bmatrix} -5.4 & -4.05 & -2.7 & 2.0 \\ -0.8 & -0.60 & -0.4 & 0.3 \\ -1.0 & -0.75 & -0.5 & 0.4 \\ -0.2 & -0.15 & -0.1 & 0.1 \end{bmatrix}$$

(e) ∇f

Fig. 1. Astronaut rescue, robot & evaluation models.

The observer cares about (S) has the astronaut been returned to the Shuttle, and (H) is he harmed, yielding 4 observer states. This categorization emphasizes that the end-user is unconcerned with details of the retrieval, but does consider harm, which the robot cannot measure. The observer says that a return is worth $+10$, harm is worth -5, thus giving us an explicit value function, and assigning the following values:

$\neg S\&\neg H$ 0, $\neg S\&H$ -5, $S\&\neg H$ 10, $S\&H$ 5,

and these constitute the $\mathbf{u}$ (utility) vector in Eq 5.

Simultaneous sampling of robot and observer states, followed by application of Eq 2, yields the observer $\mathbf{P}$ matrix of Fig 1d, whose columns map the robot states of Fig 1a into probability distributions over the observer states just listed (in the given order). The observer appears to believe that each stage of the rescue increases the probability of harm. This might be explained by elapsed time, or by the robot itself doing harm on contact, but explanations are not essential. Multiplying out $\mathbf{u}^T \mathbf{P}$ yields the expected utility of *robot* states to the end-user:

$$-0.5, \quad -1.0, \quad -2.0, \quad 7.5 \ .$$

Finally, assuming the robot starts in state #1 and taking $t = 100$, Eq 5 yields the gradient elements. Fig 1e shows them arranged as a matrix with $\nabla f_{kl} = \frac{\partial f(1)}{\partial R_{kl}}$.

Before we can identify the most helpful changes we must recall that these are only partial derivatives where we want the total derivatives given by Eq 7. In other words, when considering which robot transition to make more likely we must also ask, at the expense of which other transition in the same row? The total derivative is the difference of those gradient elements. Thus it turns out that the largest net benefit accrues at $\nabla f_{14} - \nabla f_{11} = 7.4$ utils/step, going directly from being outbound to having returned, without any potential delays and harms. Impossible! The best realistic change is at $\nabla f_{34} - \nabla f_{31} = 1.4$, increasing the probability of the return transition by reducing the probability that the astronaut will have to be chased down again. This might be achieved by simply increasing the strength of the robot's grasp. The next best change is at $\nabla f_{12} - \nabla f_{11} = 1.35$, spending less time in the approach state. (Notice that $\nabla f_{12} < 0$, but a larger R_{12} can still yield better performance.) All other changes are much less significant.

How much can $R_{34} - R_{31}$ and $R_{12} - R_{11}$ be changed, and at what cost? Whether and how to proceed are project management decisions. Nevertheless, our approach has identified *what* is most worth improving.

4 Summary and Discussion

While most of this paper has developed mathematical foundations, its purpose has been to articulate a novel design and validation methodology for discrete-state embedded agents. We constructed an objective function over ongoing robot behavior by means of user-held criteria, and then derived the gradient ∇f with respect to perturbations of state transition probabilities deep within the agent model. Availability of ∇f led to the following design and validation methodology:

1. Derive the evaluator state prediction matrix $\mathbf{P}$ as above, and obtain $\mathbf{u}$, the vector of subjective utilities for the evaluator/user-defined states.
2. Use ∇f to identify influential state transition probabilities in the Markov model of agent behavior, as well as whether to increase/decrease them.
3. Change the indicated state transition probabilities by redesigning the agent. ($\mathbf{P}$ need not be re-computed as long as design optimization changes only the state transition probabilities.)
4. Repeat from step 2 until...

Since the physical and financial constraints on the system's design may not be represented mathematically at design time, final validation will require an explicit decision that each of the remaining opportunities to improve total system performance is not worth the cost. The cost may be monetary, or may result from a performance tradeoff.

Reliance on the gradient of the objective function has several implications. Obviously, the numerator (the objective function) must be at least piecewise differentiable w.r.t. something the robot can influence. This requirement comes to apply to each of

(a) the expectation of robot state occurrence probabilities/counts,
(b) the mapping from robot- to user-perceived states,
(c) the mapping from user states to values, and
(d) the manner of reducing all possible futures down to a single number.

(b) and (c) will usually be linear and trivially differentiable. We adopted a Markov model of robot state for (a), and evaluated a time-averaged utility for (d), thus achieving differentiability. The important point here is that those choices are not essential to our approach: any other choices that satisfy the differentiability requirement would do.

The gradient's other implication is from its denominator: only continuous parameters of the robot's behavior can be candidates for improvement. We cannot evaluate the net benefit/loss that might accrue from choosing an entirely different reaction to a given state, or from enlarging the set of robot states, e.g. by allowing the robot to perceive a new distinction. We can however evaluate whether or not existing states should ever be entered.

Our only assumptions about the human observer are that we can sample his/her state simultaneously with that of the robot, and of course that the observer can define a set of mutually exclusive states with associated (constant) values. In short, there is no requirement on the human observer's state sequence (e.g. that it be Markovian) nor is there any restriction on the observer's utility function. Moreover, the human observer is allowed to be arbitrarily uncertain, and may declare that s/he is experiencing any probability distribution over observer-defined states (provided of course that the value assessed for such uncertainty is a probabilistic weighting over the values of the base states).

While we have calculated ∇f w.r.t. state transition probabilities inside the robot, closing the design loop requires us to know how those transition probabilities depend on concrete parameters in the robot's perception and action subsystems. Such parameters might include thresholds on subjective belief, such that certain conditions are accepted as true iff the threshold is exceeded; or motion parameters that make actions more or less likely to succeed. To compute ∇f w.r.t. such a parameter χ requires the derivatives $\frac{dR_{kl}}{d\chi}$ which are of course application dependent and hence beyond our reach. Given such derivatives, however, the corresponding augmentation of Equation 4 is trivial:

$$\frac{df(i)}{d\chi} = \frac{df(i)}{dR_{kl}} \frac{dR_{kl}}{d\chi}.$$

5 Related Work

Our work is intended as a contribution to the methodology of agent design. While methodological questions have received little formal attention, every agent architecture makes some (possibly implicit) commitment to design strategy. Just in this volume, [1] represents agent components via C++ class hierarchies and advocates an object oriented design approach; [8] highlights agent commitments and implicitly advocates a methodology for constructing agent societies based on the orderly exploration of contract nets. The work by [7] on agents with provable epistemic properties may be closest to ours in feel: it suggests that end-users identify crucial domain contraints (e.g., that vases remain on tables), and derives a satisficing agent (cast as a reactive controller) via a proof process. This work shares our interest in relating agent-held distinctions to user-held observations of the world, but it lacks a representation of expected utility and therefore any explicit guidance for an iterative improvement process.

Reinforcement learning methods [3] suggest an alternate methodology for optimizing agents w.r.t user-held success metrics: reward the agent for good behavior and let a credit assignment algorithm adjust the agent's internal structure. This approach addresses the iterative refinement problem, but uses search over possible attributions (through time) in place of the tighter focus provided by our explicit gradient calculation.

Decision theoretic planning algorithms [2] [4] seek to define utility maximizing agents as an *a priori* proof problem. This work addresses the core issue of design optimality, but is currently limited to small domains. These efforts also side-step the issue that utility is naturally defined in user-held terms (the algorithms currently evaluate the utility of agent-recognized states), and once again employ search (over goals and actions) in place of the more focused attention supplied by a gradient calculation. Finally, decision theoretic planning systems (as paper exercises) lack a reality check on the plans they produce. In contrast, our methodology employs end-user observations to construct a state correspondence mapping; this feedback ensures that the end-user optimizes real world performance, versus the predicted performance of an agent model.

References

1. J. Bryson. Agent architecture as object oriented design. In this volume.
2. D. Draper, S. Hanks & D. Weld. Probabilistic planning with information gathering and contingent execution. Proc Int'l Conf on AI Planning Systems 1994, 31–36.
3. L. Kaelbling, M. Littman & A. Moore. Reinforcement learning: a survey. JAIR 4, 1996, 237–285.
4. N. Kushmeric, S. Hanks & D. Weld. An algorithm for probabilistic planning. AI Journal 76:1, 1995, 239–286.
5. D. Luenberger. *Introduction to Dynamic Systems – Theory, Models and Applications*, chapter 7. Wiley & Sons, New York, 1979.
6. R.A. McCallum. Hidden state and reinforcement learning with instance-based state identification. *IEEE Trans SMC (B)* 26:3, 1996, 464–473.
7. S. Rosenschein & L. Kaelbling. The synthesis of digital machines with provable epistemic properties. Theoretical Aspects of Reasoning Conf 1986, 83–98.
8. E. Verharen, F. Dignum & S. Bos. Implementation of a cooperative agent architecture based on the language-action perspective. In this volume.

Agent Architecture as Object Oriented Design

Joanna Bryson and Brendan McGonigle

Laboratory for Cognitive Neuroscience and Intelligent Systems, Edinburgh University
Edinburgh EH8 9JZ, UK
Joanna.Bryson@ed.ac.uk

Abstract. Improving the development of agent intelligence requires improving the mechanisms of that development. This paper explores the application of an established software methodology, object-oriented design, to agent development in two ways. We present a distributed agent architecture, Edmund, and describe first its own object-oriented structure. Then we relate the methodology for developing agent behaviors under Edmund. We explain how this methodology exploits key aspects of object-oriented design, particularly the development of the class hierarchy, as a prototype for agent design.

1 Introduction

The history of computer science, like that of mathematics, has clearly demonstrated that tools and methodologies are not only useful but necessary for advancing through stages of complexity. Human problem solving seems to have finite limits in the level of complexity one mind can encompass. A powerful representation or language can reduce the cognitive load by encapsulating and condensing well understood elements of a problem. Similarly, a methodology is a tool that provides rules for decomposing a problem into manageable sections.

Methodology is particularly important in the design of reactive systems, because the reactive approach to intelligent agent research depends entirely on the hand-coding of the agent's behavior [36]. Our laboratory operates on the hypothesis that the most likely way to replicate the natural phenomena of intelligence is through careful design [22]. This implies that building on and expanding design methodologies is a necessary component of research into artificial intelligence.

This paper describes one of the architectures, Edmund, under development in our laboratory as a platform for cognitive modeling. Edmund was developed under object-oriented design (OOD), and the design methodology developed for using Edmund is similar to OOD. Because the agent community is examining OOD as a design tool, we present both Edmund's control architecture and accompanying methodology as an exemplar.

2 Edmund

Edmund can be thought of as an agent architecture in two senses. First, it is designed to run the intelligence of an autonomous mobile robot, an agent in the strong sense of the term. Second, it serves to structure a library of behaviors, which are themselves implemented as objects. To some extent, any behavior-based architecture could be described as a multi-agent system, but most constituent behaviors, though independent and executing in parallel, are too simple to describe as agents. Edmund's Nomad Robot Library (ENRL), however, is decomposed along lines not of behavior, but of capability. Thirty-two sensing and action primitives for the architecture are based on methods from five classes. Each class is based on a knowledge-set representing attributes of the external world or the robot's mechanism. These might be considered agents in the weaker sense of semi-autonomous software units with state, monitoring aspects of the world and responding to queries.

Edmund is the result of an attempt to scale the behavior-based artificial intelligence (BBAI) approach to building intelligent systems without resorting to hybrid symbolic / reactive architectures such as 3T [3] or PRS [13]. During development, Edmund has evolved commonalities with these architectures which we review briefly Section 6. It addresses three problem areas in BBAI, the first being control structure. Strict parallelism provides insufficient bias for action selection and goal persistence. Tyrrell demonstrates that this is particularly true in non-hierarchical machines such as Maes [20], but suggests it is even a problem with his own hierarchy-based spreading activation approach [32]. Animal intelligence appears to provide sequencing primitives for both representation and action [23, 31]. At the same time, rigidly connected structures as in Brooks' subsumption architecture [4] or even as constructed by Firby's RAPs [10] overly constrain behavioral flexibility. Subsumption architecture fixes goal prioritization in a linear order. RAPs constructs tree structures not suited to the continuous, nonterminating processes of life-like agents; processes including language [11]. Edmund's architecture addresses the selection bias problem by providing structures for both parallel and sequential control components. It addresses the flexibility issue by providing a parallel reactive drive structure, each element of which allows for chaining or looping sub-structures. Edmund's control is discussed in the architecture section below.

The second problem area we address is the need for specialized, modularized learning. In BBAI, learning tends to be either nonexistent, as in strictly reactive systems [4], or fairly homogeneous, with each behavior having a generic learning capability [28, 2]. Often it is monolithic, as in systems that employ reinforcement learning, genetic algorithms, or neural networks to supervise control. Vertebrate brains have specialization both by organs and regions within organs for storing relevant state, whether that state is fairly transient computations of perceptual or motor information or longer term skills and information [6]. BBAI systems with specialized learning or state elements (such as [21, 16]) have been successful, but no principled system for supporting multiple state elements with varying representations has been developed. Edmund addresses this with object-oriented behavior libraries, described in Section 4 below.

Finally, a crucial element to scaling is programmability. Since behavior-based architectures (and most actively used agent architectures) are essentially hand coded, their complexity is highly dependent on the methodological support for the software designers. We consider developing a methodology for programming agents under Edmund as important as developing its architecture. To facilitate development under Edmund we offer a development methodology based on the established methodology of object oriented design (OOD). Methodology is discussed in Section 5.

Sense	A perceptual primitive returning a value.
Act	A primitive affecting the external world or internal state, including perception.
Trigger	A sequence of primitives executed atomically, for selecting actions. Should have no impact external to agent.
Lap	An action pattern, a sequence of primitives which may have external impact. The L is for "learnable", not yet implemented.
Competence	A prioritized set of Laps or other Competences and their triggers. Includes a goal lap that, if successfully triggered, indicates completion.
Drive	A type of competence (may also contain Drives) that runs its components in parallel. Generally has no goal.

Fig. 1. The classes composing the Edmund architecture.

3 The Architecture

3.1 Elements

The Edmund architecture classes are as specified in Figure 1. The classes may be divided into two sets, primitives and collections. Primitive actions and senses are the interface to the behavior library code, which will be discussed in the next section. Collections provide bias through control structure for determining appropriate and coherent ordering of the primitives. This ordering of primitives into control structures via collective classes is specified in script files. Behavior libraries are specific to a platform, they provide the agent's fundamental behaviors and perceptions. Scripts specify specific tasks or persona. Figure 2 shows an example control structure for navigation on a symmetric mobile robot. Section 4.1 describes the behavior library.

The collective classes are described in detail below, but roughly their tasks are the following. Action sequences provide persistence and reduce the combinatorics of action selection by encoding skills in a canonical way. During execution they maintaining state specifying which element of a skill is currently being executed, and thus which element should be next. Competences are essentially reactive plans, much like triangle tables [25]. Drives are similar to competences but may have several elements in some state of execution at the same time, they provide scheduling and priority between parallel tasks for the robot. Like action sequences, competences and drives maintain attentional state while the program is executing.

Edmund was written under object-oriented design primarily to exploit inheritance and polymorphism: a collective class does not need to know the type of an element it contains, merely when to execute it. Edmund also extends the class/object idiom to the instances of its classes. There may, for example, be multiple occurances of a single primitive occuring in different control contexts, that is, in different LAPs. Within an action sequence, a sense primitive serves as a conditional to check whether the sequence should continue. Consequently, scripts always associate senses with tests, which are in turn stored in the sense instance when it is incorporated into a LAP. Different instances of the same sense may be associated with different tests in different laps.

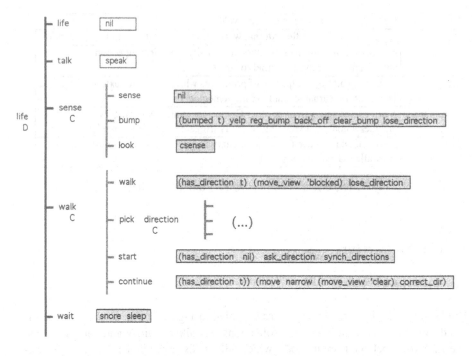

Fig. 2. A simple control heirarchy with no loops. This controls a navigating mobile robot. Priorities are not shown, but initial priority is ordered from top to bottom. Drives are labeled **D**, Competences **C**. Senses are paired with test values, unpaired primitives are Acts.

3.2 Reactivity

Edmund's reactiveness comes from two sources. First, on execution a competence checks the trigger of each of its elements to find the highest priority element that can run. No assumptions are made about the outcome of an action sequence; the environment is always resampled for selecting the next element. Second, drives allow the execution of multiple competences or actions in parallel. Although the program only attends to a single drive component at a time, each component maintains state while the other components are being attended to. Consequently, their execution proceeds as if in parallel, via coarse-grained time slicing. In the library described below, primitive acts often give commands to parallel hardware systems and do not wait for a result, so true parallelism from the perspective of the robot is achieved.

The continuous sampling of the environment through triggers results in a form of active perception. Competences that are currently active and have priority will be the ones executing their components' triggers, thus extra time and attention is given to seeking information relevant in the current context.

Which drive component receives attention is determined by priority level. The priorities can be "habituated"; scripts may specify a penalty per execution and a recovery rate per second. In drives, this allows for allocation of attention resources via best-effort scheduling. Competence elements may also habituate, though normally with no recovery. This allows for alternative solutions of similar priority to be tried, and for competences to guarantee failure after a certain number of attempts. Competences fail if none of their elements can be triggered.

When the top drive or competence has determined where its attention lies, that element is executed. Since drives and competences can be nested, an architecture like this might become highly unreactive due to a long chain, or worse, a loop of components calling each other. Edmund solves this problem by not fully preserving a stack. Competences don't attend to other competences, but rather shift the attention currently allocated to themselves. Assume a drive $D = (C_a, C_b, L_c, \ldots)$ where competence $C_a = (L_1, L_2, C_3, \ldots)$. If C_a's arbitration selects C_3 as the highest priority triggerable element, then C_a flags itself for replacement. The next time D fires, it contains $(C_3, C_b, L_c, \ldots)$. Thus the the activation tree is never deeper than the deepest drive plus three (a competence, a lap, and a primitive). In practice, we have yet to nest drives, and doubt that they should need to be nested more than two layers.

This chaining of attention guarantees reactivity, but might fail to provide coherent behavior or persistence. A competence that is an element of another's list might reasonably be described as a subgoal. Once a subgoal has completed, shouldn't its parent continue? Edmund addresses this issue in the drives. A drive not only keeps track of the processes to which it is currently attending, but also has a default process for each element. The default starts if that drive element is triggered with no other active process, for example, at start up. Thus if a competence completes, the drive returns attention to the root of the tree that brought it to that competence in the first place. If the context is the same, then attention will return to the parent competence. If the context has changed, some other behavior may now be more appropriate. A competence can terminate by failing to execute any of its elements or by succeeding to trigger its goal element.

3.3 Biological Plausibility

Edmund is designed to be a platform for running psychologically and ethologically based models of intelligence. We have attempted to make it neurologically plausible. Behavior sequences are supported in the natural intelligence literature as described in Section 2. Competences are not directly supported, but could exist as sets skills that are collectively stimulated to varying degrees in a particular context, similar to priming in spreading activation networks [24]. Similar action selection mechanisms have been postulated by [14].

Drives allow the simulation of parallel activity in non-cortical parts of the brain. For example areas of the forebrain such as the amygdala operate on separate channels of sensor input and can interrupt cortical activity by providing independent activation, while elements of the hindbrain maintain metabolic event scheduling independent of cortical sensing and activation [6].

The perpetuation of activation and its chaining through competences as described above is related to the problems of binding and attention, issues which are receiving a great deal of attention in neuroscience at the moment. See for example [33, 29].

Direction	For moving and detecting motion-relevant information, knows current and preferred directions. Instances correspond to faces of the robot.
PMem	Perceptual Memory, a short list of recent combined sensor readings. The main source of sensing. No significant instances.
Bump	Provide information about local "invisible" obstacles. Instances represent collision points.
Wave	Detect people waving at sonar (a source of communication).
DpLand	Decision point landmarks, the basis for navigating (vs. wandering.) Instances represent choice points and the decisions made there.

Fig. 3. The classes composing the Edmund's Nomad Robot Library (ENRL).

4 The Behavior Library

4.1 Structure

The functions and state on which the sensing and action primitives depend are located in platform-dependent behavior libraries. So far two libraries have been constructed, one for using visual routines theory in a blocks world simulating (as in [34, 7]), and the other for a Nomad 200 mobile robot. This paper focuses on Edmund's Nomad Robot Library (ENRL), which is the more recent work.

The Edmund architecture's only interface to its libraries are function pointers that are passed to its primitives on loading. A library routine might consist entirely of calls to underlying hardware or software routines provided by the agent's platform. The Nomad provides primitive actions and senses, but these are at a lower level of abstraction than is actually useful for the control scripts. The behaviors that *are* needed cluster naturally by shared resources and functions. Consequently, ENRL is also of object-oriented design, with the classes based around these clusters. See Figure 3 for examples.

One of the resources shared between behaviors is memory, or state. This can be anything from very short term (< 1 second) perceptual memory, for things like "sanitizing" sonar readings, to long term memory, for tasks like map learning. Often different but related forms of state are stored as class and instance variables for a single class. For example, when an obstacle is encountered via the robot's bumpers, an instance of Bump may record its approximate coordinates, while a Bump class variable refers to the list of all currently remembered Bumps.

The primitives for detecting collisions (using bumper state information provided on the Nomad platform), storing instances (using similarly provided odometric information), recalling and pruning information from memory are all based on methods in the Bump class. The information (except for that provided directly by the Nomad) is not computed automatically, but only on demand when relevant primitives are called from the control structure. Nevertheless, as mentioned in Section 2, behavior library elements are designed to represent different areas of a modular (but not fully encapsulated) memory structure like the brain. This corresponds roughly to Dennett and Kinsbourne's [8] multiple drafts hypothesis of awareness . There is no single continuous stream or record

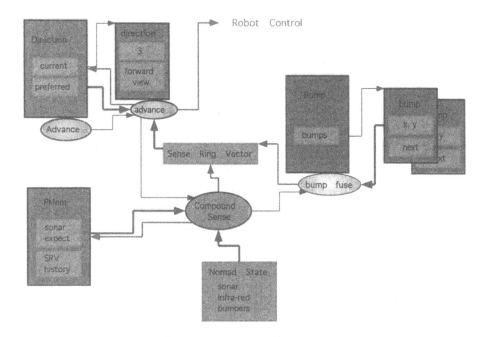

Fig. 4. The state supporting the Direction library function **advance**.

of information; what is perceived is in a continuous state of flux, and only resolves to a snapshot when attended to.

4.2 A Sample Behavior

This section describes one of the elements of ENRL, Direction, as an example of the nature the library. This example will also be referred to in the following section on methodology. Direction is largely responsible for the familiar task of low-level navigation and obstacle avoidance. The behaviors necessary for motion are based on its methods, though these in turn refer to information and methods from the perceptual classes. Figure 4 illustrates the classes involved in the Direction member function *advance*, and their flow of information. The behavior is described below.

There are 16 instances of Direction correlating to the 16 faces of the Nomad, each with a sonar and an infra-red sensor (see Figure 5). An Act primitive, **move**, calls *advance* on whichever instance of Direction the robot is currently pursuing. There were initially two subclasses of Direction to include an additional 16 directions on the axis between two faces, but in experiments these proved unnecessary for smooth trajectories and were removed to simplify the code.

Advance works as follows. The current Direction instance computes a new velocity for translation, based on the room it has to maneuver. It also computes a velocity for rotation, based on the difference between the robot's current steering angle θ_r, and the Direction's own orientation, θ_d. The formulae are based on power curves, making the

Fig. 5. The Nomad 200 robot on which ENRL has been developed. In this picture it is encountering a desk — the surface is too low for the sonar sensors to detect when proximate, and the leg too dark for the infra-red sensors, so the robot must learn about the desk with its bumpers.

robot's trajectories fluid and natural[1]. *Advance* directs the Nomad to move at these velocities, then finishes by choosing a new current direction if obstacle avoidance is called for.

Advance is an example of how an apparently continuous action can be sliced appropriately for an architecture based on discrete steps. Operating on the Nomad robot, ENRL results in smooth, continuous motion. In fact, high level drive attention is being switched between motion, sensing the external world, and checking and reporting battery level. Motion is also expressed as a competence, and that competence routinely

---

[1] The steering rate is $k_2 e^{-k_1 \frac{1}{\sqrt{\theta_c}}}$ where the k_1 (26) adjusts the slope of the exponential, k_2 (450) adjusts the scale of the result, and θ_c is the difference between θ_r and θ_d, adjusted for the nearest direction of rotation. The translation velocity is $k_2 e^{-k_1 \frac{1}{\sqrt{dist}}}$ where k_1 (5) is as above, k_2 (100) is the maximum velocity in tenths of an inch per second, and $dist$ is the nearest obstacle in the direction of motion also in tenths of an inch.

move	(A)	`Direction::current->advance()`
narrow	(A)	`if (Direction::current - Direction:: pref > 4)` `{lose-dir && fail}`
move-view	(S)	`Direction::current->state()`
correct-dir	(A)	`Direction::correct-to-pref()`

Fig. 6. The interface between the library and the control script. Left are the motion primitives in the action sequence **move** in Figure 2. Right is the corresponding code using member functions from Figure 4.

checks the triggers for starting and terminating motion before choosing the case of continuing motion, executing **move**. In Nomad's commercial simulation, the calls to *advance* do appear as discrete events, because the commands cannot be performed by separate hardware systems as they are on the real Nomad.

4.3 The Use of State

Advance requires a great deal of state and sensing capabilities which are reused in other primitive behaviors. To begin with, choice of speed and direction are determined by the perceived space surrounding the robot. This is represented by an array of 16 values representing the distance in inches from the robots faces to the nearest obstacle. This perceptual array is a construction regularly updated with information from sonar, infra-red and bump sensors. Information from the sonars is not taken directly, because sonars often give false readings. Sonar values are based on a perceptual memory of previous values and rates of change – sudden changes may not be believed for nearly half a second, then they just as suddenly replace the old value in the perceptual memory. This approach is consistent with human perception [8]. Bumps require a quite different, more persistent form of perceptual memory since, in order to be useful, they need to influence behavior by being avoided for some time, possibly even a minute, after impact. Consequently PMem sonar memory is stored in a fixed size array, while Bumps are stored in instances indexed off a class variable and trimmed as a special process.

In addition to these perceptual classes, Direction itself stores state as class variables recording which direction is currently being pursued, and which direction was actually intended or preferred. Another Act primitive, **correct-dir**, tries to move the current direction closer to the preferred one. This is typically called in scripts where the robot is to display persistence in direction, as part of an action sequence with **move** after a Sense primitive shows the robot is not avoiding any obstacles. Other state in Direction includes state in the instances that specifies a distorted window on the perceptual array mentioned above, for which elements are relevant (and how relevant) to forward motion. The Nomad can pass through doorways only a few inches wider than itself, but will stop four inches in front of most obstacles.

5   Methodology

Much of the variety of approach in autonomous agent architectures reflects variety in the underlying theories of intelligence. Ideally, our agents should provide us with platforms for testing and developing such theories. However, our only perspective for viewing and comparing the behavior of our agents superimposes our ability to program on top of our underlying theories. As a result, methodology is an inextricable part of intelligent agent research.

The thesis of this paper is that a good architecture should encourage and facilitate a particular methodological approach. In the previous section we described the implementation of Edmund, which exploited some aspects of object-oriented design to organize state and behavior into logical units. The implementation was explicitly in an object-oriented language, C++. This section describes the development of behavior under Edmund. This requires the co-evolution of the control scripts that specify *when* a behavior is expressed, and the behavior libraries, which describe *how* that behavior expresses itself. We now use object-oriented design (OOD) as an *analogy* — as a basis for Edmund's own methodology.

Behavior-based systems and OOD both exploit modularity and encapsulation to manage complexity. The following subsection discusses how that modularity is established. Other issues of methodology appear at the end of the section.

5.1   Class Hierarchies and Behavior Decomposition

One of the key problems of behavior-based design is *behavior decomposition*, the problem of determining what the fundamental elements of behavior are. Because Edmund separates the flow of control state from that of perception, the decomposition problem is also redescribed. The designer needs to determine whether a behavior should be encoded as a competence, a sequence, or as a primitive supported in the behavior library.

The methodology we recommend is iterative, similar to that of OOD. One of the main principles of OOD is rapid prototyping. The design process is first boot-strapped by a combination of analysis and intuition. The process described in [27] for multi-agent systems would be adaptable for both object-oriented systems and to some extent Edmund. Once an initial decomposition has been reached, the class hierarchy is evolved as the classes of objects are developed and tested.

In OOD, the importance of the hierarchy is to simplify development and reduce replication of code by having basic classes defined whose instances would have the standard requirements of functionality. For objects that require more specialization, subclasses are created that add functionality or attributes. There are standard situations that indicate when a hierarchy needs to be adjusted. Two classes that replicate code indicate the need for the creation of a common super class. If some object needs half the functionality of a class then this indicates a need for dividing a class into a parent and child, so that the object may inherit only from the parent. A parent class with a single child is an opportunity to collapse structure unless instances of the parent actively use methods overwritten in the child. Too much multiple inheritance, the frequent need to inherit from several classes from different parts of the hierarchy, may indicate bad fundamental hierarchy decomposition and a need to start over.

We take as given that rapid prototyping and the design-test cycles are the only means for developing finished robot behavior. In creating Edmund, we have tried to design a platform for developing complex behavior. Ideally, the behavior library should provide reliable, robust elements of behavior, while the control scripts provide flexible ways for expressing that behavior at times suited to the situation and task. To bootstrap, we organize the libraries along the lines of function and adaptive state requirements[2].

We have also been developing heuristics for determining how to develop the decomposition while developing the behavior. To begin with, we favor more simple elements. A primitive is preferred to an action sequence, a sequence to a competence. However, if for some script only part of a primitive behavior is required, then that primitive is broken down into elements, which are typically expressed in a sequence to replicate the former behavior. Similarly, if a sequence sometimes needs to contain a cycle, or often does not need some of its elements to fire, then it is really a competence.

A competence may be thought of, and designed, as a sequence of behaviors that might need to be executed in a worst-case scenario. The ultimate (last) element is the highest priority element of the competence, the penultimate the second highest and so on. Triggers on each element determine whether that element actually needs to fire at this instant. If a competence is actually deterministic, if it nearly always actually executes a fixed path through its elements, then it should be changed into a sequence.

For complex tasks such as those involving manipulation, one of the most difficult part of programming Edmund is guaranteeing correct behavior from the competences. (See the next section for a discussion of leveraging formal languages for Edmund scripts.) One way a competence can flag a need for incremental change in decomposition is by relying on large numbers of triggers. Perception should be handled at the behavior library level, it should be a skill. A large number of triggers should be converted into a single perceptual test. A perception so central to a competence may well be useful for other elements of behavior as well.

A simple example of these techniques can be drawn from the development of the motion primitives **move** and **correct-dir** mentioned in Section 4.2. **Move** initially behaved as it does now, but as part of developing a behavior for reliable segments for a simple map-learning routine it was extended to correct the direction of travel. This invalidated an old script "wander," which changed directions without concern and was useful for herding the robot into desired areas. The new **move** was therefore broken into elements which included a cleaner version of its previous self, and **correct-dir**. These elements are now run as a Lap in the map-building scripts. (See Figure 2.)

5.2 Other Issues of Methodology

Another related methodological problem and technique is developing the scheduling for Edmund in dynamic situations. Scheduling in Edmund is inexact. Too many things may be scheduled per second with no direct indication they are failing to execute. This is to some extent an artifact of the reactive nature of the system — we expect some events and behaviors to arrest the attention of the agent.

---

[2] Bryson [5] has suggested earlier that adaptivity requirements serve as good indicators for behavior decomposition.

An initial schedule for Edmund can be computed with the help of simple bench-marking, facilities for which are built into the control program. These help determine the constraints on the number of elements run per second, which allows estimates for rate at which varying numbers of drives can be executed. On the Nomad, for example, sensing is fairly expensive and limits the number of cycles for the architecture to about 340Hz. However, if the robot stops moving and reduces its sense sample rate, the cycle rate increases by an order of magnitude. This suggests that the robot should engage in phased periods of activity, for example switching between sense-intensive work like exploration and compute-intensive work like map learning. This strategy is found in most mammals (e.g. [35]), and is facilitated by the Edmund drive system. We are developing a navigation system based on this for the robot have modeled such behavior in simulation.

Correcting scheduling problems can also be done incrementally; switching elements between competences and drives can also occur at the control script level. Elements in drives can be scheduled the most reliably. However, an element which is only required in a particular context may waste cycles if it is scheduled as a drive. A Lap for handling bumps was initially added into the competence for motion, "walk", but this overlooked the fact some Laps in walk were long and the bumpers would not be checked between their elements once triggered. Consequently, "bump" was moved to the top level drive. On the other hand, a perceptual routine for watching for landmarks was successfully moved into "walk" since it was only needed in the context of motion, and could rely on perceptual memory if it was called less frequently.

6 Discussion: Related and Future Work

In describing his subsumption architecture, Brooks [4] states that development must begin from the bottom up, with each layer being fully tested before the next is added, so that at every level one is only debugging that level and its interface to the working sublayers. Although we consider this a good working principle, in our experience it is not easy to determine that layers are either fully or correctly implemented before other layers that need them have been added. Certainly evolution does not leave primitive brain organs completely untouched, but reuses them creatively [18].

Unlike Brooks, we do not expect layers will necessarily be fully or correctly implemented before moving to the next one. If as the project progresses problems are discovered in early levels, earlier scripts exercising only those levels can be used to test that redevelopment does not damage earlier behavior. The scripting facility also allows for easily switching elements between competences and drives. Our work has more in common with the multi-layered architectures that are currently dominating mobile robotics [1], such as [12, 15, 3]. However, we place more intelligence and learning in what corresponds to the lower, reactive level in these systems. We take the lesson from biology that learning and memory are a part of perception [6, 23], and from Brooks that perception and action must be tightly linked.

We are currently reviewing better established architectures. If we can model the essential elements of our approach in a system that provides better tools for development and analysis, we feel we should exploit these programming benefits. One obvious candidate is PRS, discussed extensively in this volume (for example [9, 17]). However, there would be a problem with implementation at the level of perception and belief. Edmund's beliefs consist of what is currently reported by its senses, combined with its perceptual memory and built-in biases. Moreover, for a real embodied system the entire sensory world cannot be attended to at once. PRS with its uniform sense cycle and rule-based belief libraries would not seem particularly suited to active or selective perception.

On the other hand, there could be a fairly direct mapping of competences to plan library and drives to goals, (though note the loss of scheduling, which relates to the perception points above.) Edmund could be said to keep track of its intentions through its system of control attention. Certainly Edmund's scripts can be described in formal languages such as Robot Schemes (RS) [19] or Structured Circuit Semantics (SCS) [17]. To borrow the formalism of SCS, an action sequence is simply a list of atomic actions (where Senses combined with their test are considered to be primitive actions, as are Acts) and a competence could be expressed as a do first. (Competences are also very similar to Nilsson's Teleo-Reactive programs [26].) Although the primitive actions change behavior slightly over time because of their learning, all of these systems have to be robust to unreliable behavior in actions, so these languages might still be used to assist in checking competences for internal cycles or deadlocks. Edmund might then also more easily "plug in" to multi-agent coordination systems such described in [17, 30]. The perception of having a flexible or inevitable action currently blessed by a coordinator [30] could be worked into the action selection routines.

There is a similar imprecise mapping of PRS back into Edmund, which may be useful if only insofar as the development of PRS agents might also exploit this sort of iterative design. So far, nearly all PRS-type architectures use hand-built plans for their plan libraries. Presumably these plans as well need to take into account their appropriate level of implementation.

Another possible direction for Edmund, however, is toward a less rigorously categorized system. In ENRL the object metaphor, particularly encapsulation, breaks down in relation to sensing. This is not surprising given that external to the robot, information is flowing in streams. Senses filter and, in the case of digital systems, segment this information. Many areas of animal brains, both cortical and subcortical, fuse information from multiple senses. In fact, very few animal behaviors are independent of sensory context. Pitch detection, time sense, and intentional learning and recall all show strong context dependency [6]. Encapsulation violations in the object library amount to methods or even functions calling for information from multiple classes. OOD methodologies address the problems of interdependencies by limiting and documenting the points of interface.

These OOD methodologies have been directly transferable to ENRL. It is possible, however, that the control structure itself may need to be fused with the perception and action units. We are currently exploring the use of episodic memory for tasks involving search of multiple contingencies, such as principled (directed) navigation. This may involve treating learned patterns like drives or competences, with associated patterns of habituation or inhibition.

7 Conclusion

This paper has presented an agent architecture, Edmund, as a demonstration of an inter-action between object-oriented and agent design. We suggest that an agent architecture can serve as a guideline to application development. We also suggest object-oriented design methodologies such as encapsulation, specified interfaces, and evolving hierar-chies are useful in creating a reusable library of behaviors for a particular application domain. If intelligence is to be achieved by design, it will necessarily be a learning experience for the designer. The programming of intelligent agents requires not only principled structure and approach, but also methodological support.

Acknowledgments

Edmund has benefited from discussions with many people, particularly Ian Horswill, Leslie Kaelbling, Brendan McGonigle, and Will Lowe. This paper has benefited from extensive comments by Will Lowe, John Hallam and Rob Ringrose.

References

1. Special issue: Software architectures for hardware agents, 1997.
2. J. S. Albus. The NIST real-time control system (RCS): an approach to intelligent systems research. *Journal of Experimental & Theoretical Artificial Intelligence*, 9(2/3), 1997.
3. R. P. Bonasso, R. J. Firby, E. Gat, D. Kortenkamp, D. P. Miller, and M. G. Slack. Experi-ences with an architecture for intelligent, reactive agents. *Journal of Experimental & Theo-retical Artificial Intelligence*, 9(2/3):237–256, 1997.
4. Rodney A. Brooks. A robust layered control system for a mobile robot. *IEEE Journal of Robotics and Automation*, RA-2:14–23, April 1986.
5. Joanna Bryson. The reactive accompanist: Adaptation and behavior decomposition in a music system. In Luc Steels, editor, *The Biology and Technology of Intelligent Autonomous Agents*. Springer-Verlag, 1995.
6. Niel R. Carlson. *Physiology of Behavior*. Allyn and Bacon, Boston, 5 edition, 1994.
7. David Chapman. Penguins can make cake. *AI Magazine*, 10(4):51–60, 1989.
8. Daniel C. Dennett and Marcel Kinsbourne. Time and the observer: The where and when of consciousness in the brain. *Brain and Behavioral Sciences*, 15:183–247, 1992.
9. Mark d'Inverno, David Kinny, Michael Luck, and Michael Wooldridge. A formal specifica-tion of dMARS. In this volume.
10. James Firby. An investigation into reactive planning in complex domains. In *Proceedings of the National Conference on Artificial Intelligence (AAAI)*, pages 202–207, 1987.
11. James Firby. Personal communication, 1995.
12. Erann Gat. *Reliable Goal-Directed Reactive Control of Autonomous Mobile Robots*. PhD thesis, Virginia Polytechnic Institute and State University, 1991.
13. M. P. Georgeff and A. L. Lansky. Reactive reasoning and planning. In *Proceedings of the Sixth National Conference on Artificial Intelligence (AAAI-87)*, pages 677–682, 1987.
14. David W. Glasspool. Competitive queuing and the articulatory loop. In J. Levy, D. Bairaktaris, J. Bullinaria, and P. Cairns, editors, *Connectionist Models of Memory and Language*. UCL Press, 1995.

15. Henry H. Hexmoor. *Representing and Learning Routine Activities*. PhD thesis, State University of New York at Buffalo, December 1995.

16. Ian Horswill. Visual architecture and cognitive architecture. *Journal of Experimental & Theoretical Artificial Intelligence*, 9(2/3):277–293, 1997.

17. Jaeho Lee and Edmund Durfee. On explicit plan languages for coordinating multiagent plan execution. In this volume.

18. Peter J. Livesey. *Evolutionary Processes*, volume 1 of *Learning and Emotion: A Biological Synthesis*. Lawrence Erlbaum Associates, Hillsdale, NJ, 1986.

19. Damion M. Lyons. Representing and analyzing action plans as networks of concurrent processes. *IEEE Transactions on Robotics and Automation*, 9(3), June 1993.

20. Pattie Maes. How to do the right thing. A.I. Memo 1180, MIT, Cambridge, MA, 1989.

21. Maja J. Mataric. Integration of representation into goal-driven behavior-based robots. *IEEE Journal of Robotics and Automation*, 8(3):304–312, June 1992.

22. Brendan McGonigle. Incrementing intelligent systems by design. In Jean-Arcady Meyer and Stuart Wilson, editors, *From Animals to Animats*, pages 478–485, Cambridge, MA, 1991. MIT Press.

23. Brendan McGonigle and Margaret Chalmers. The ontology of order. In Les Smith, editor, *Piaget: A Critical Assessment*. Routledge, 1996.

24. J. H. Neely. Semantic priming effects in visual word recognition: A selective review of current findings and theories. In D. Besner and G. W. Humphreys, editors, *Basic Processes in Reading: Visual Word Recognition*, chapter 9. Lawrence Erlbaum Associates, 1991.

25. Nils Nilsson. Shakey the robot. Technical note 323, SRI International, Menlo Park, California, April 1984.

26. Nils Nilsson. Teleo-reactive programs for agent control. *Journal of Artificial Intelligence Research*, 1:139–158, 1994.

27. Van Parunak, John Sauter, and Steve Clark. Specification and design of industrial synthetic ecosystems. In this volume.

28. Miles Pebody. Learning and adaptivity: Enhancing reactive behaviour architectures in real-world interaction systems. In F. Moran, A. Moreno, J.J. Merelo, and P. Chacon, editors, *Advances in Artificial Life (Third European Conference on Artificial Life)*, pages 679–690, Berlin, Germany, 1995. Springer-Verlag.

29. W. A. Phillips and W. Singer. In search of common cortical foundations. *Brain and Behavioral Sciences*, forthcoming.

30. Munindar Singh. A customizable coordination service for autonomous agents. In this volume.

31. Jun Tanji. Involvement of motor areas in the medial frontal cortex of primates in temporal sequencing of multiple movements. In R. Caminiti, K-P Hoffmann, F. Lacquaniti, and J. Altman, editors, *Vision and Movement: Mechanisms in the Cerebral Cortex*, volume 2, pages 126–133. Human Frontier Science Program, Strasbourg, 1996.

32. Toby Tyrrell. *Computational Mechanisms for Action Selection*. PhD thesis, University of Edinburgh, 1993. Centre for Cognitive Science.

33. Christoph von der Malsburg. Binding in models of perception and brain function. *Current Opinion in Neurobiology*, 5:520–526, 1995.

34. Steven D. Whitehead. Reinforcement learning for the adaptive control of perception and action. Technical Report 406, University of Rochester Computer Science, Feb 1992.

35. Matthew Wilson and Bruce McNaughton. Reactivation of hippocampal ensemble memories during sleep. *Science*, 261:1227–1232, 29 July 1994.

36. Michael Wooldridge and Nicholas R. Jennings. Intelligent agents: Theory and practice. *Knowledge Engineering Review*, 10(2), 1995.

Implementation of a Cooperative Agent Architecture Based on the Language-Action Perspective

Egon M. Verharen*, Frank Dignum†, and Sander Bos‡

* Infolab, Tilburg University
Tilburg, POBox 90153, 5000 LE, the Netherlands
E.M.Verharen@kub.nl

† Fac. of Maths & Comp. Sc., Eindhoven University of Technology
Eindhoven, POBox 513, 5600 MB, the Netherlands
Dignum@win.tue.nl

‡ Fac. of Maths & Comp. Sc., Eindhoven University of Technology
Eindhoven, POBox 513, 5600 MB, the Netherlands
A.J.Bos@stud.tue.nl

Abstract. In this paper the architecture and implementation of Cooperative Information Agents (CIA) is described. Taking a language-action perspective to the design of CIAs allows for the specification of obligations and authorizations, and results in the separation of tasks (things the agent must do) and contracts (mutually agreed commitments to the course of communication). The architecture describes the functional components of a CIA: task manager (responsible for managing the agenda), contract manager (managing and negotiating contracts), communication manager (responsible for all external communication), and service execution manager (managing the execution of actions). The prototype agents show how a formal logical theory for communicating agents can be used as a sound basis for an actual implementation.

1 Introduction

Traditionally an information system (IS) was considered as one central database and a set of users accessing the database through application programs or directly via an SQL interface. Today, ISs are connected to each other and have to be accessible using electronic networks and EDI, while still maintaining their autonomy. Complete integration of the various resources might not be possible for technical or organizational reasons, hence the growing reliance on interaction between systems. This led to the paradigm of cooperative information systems (CIS) introduced in [16]. For systems to be able to cooperate they must have an intelligent interface that can cope with all types of requests and eventualities. A CIS actively maintains its information; it can communicate with other systems and reason about the information that it contains. It might decide to search for information that it needs by inquiring for it from other CISs if it knows that it does not contain the information itself, preferably in ways it negotiates with (and lays down in contracts with) those other systems. It can respond more intelligently to messages explaining why a request does not have an answer, or propose alternatives.

And it can negotiate about which requests it is willing to respond to and which requests will have no effect. For this purpose the CIS should contain a task module that plans the tasks the CIS has to fulfill. A *task* is a meaningful unit of work assigned to an agent. Performing the task often involves initiating communication transactions. However, the task's specification and updates thereof do concern the agent in question only, whereas changes in the possible transactions (involving other agents) can only be made by consent of those agents. For that reason, we make a distinction between task and contract, where the contract corresponds to the agreements between agents and the task draws on this potential for fulfilling an agent's goal. We refer to an autonomous CIS with tasks and contracts as a *Cooperative Information Agent* (CIA).

In our approach we place much more emphasis on the communication and negotiation between CIAs than takes place in occasional contacts. Because the abilities of the CIA to communicate and negotiate take an important place we claim that the influence of *linguistics* for these systems should go beyond that of a natural language interface. We use a language-action perspective [10] (based on the speech act theory as developed by Searle [17, 18] and Habermas [12]) to describe the communication itself and guide the architecture. In contrast to traditional data-flows the language-action perspective emphasizes what agents (human or automated) *do* while communicating and how communication brings about a coordination of their activities. The focus is on language as action, and the speech act is the basic unit of communication. We view a CIA as a kind of normative system, in which the coordination of activities is governed by making commitments, described by obligations and authorizations of the communicating agents. An obligation is the result of a commitment to perform a certain act and authorizations restrain or allow the commitment to and operation of an act (including doing other communicative acts). Because a CIA must be able to reason about its tasks, contractual obligations and the information that it possesses we think it is crucial that there is an underlying formal theory in which the agents can be described (including the communication). We have described this theory in a multi-modal logic (see e.g. [4, 19, 20]). In this paper we focus on the way this theory is used, in concepts such as authorization relationships between agents and how obligations (resulting from tasks and contracts) are dealt with. The agents do not contain theorem provers that derive new knowledge from the knowledge they possess and the communication they have. However, the way that the agents act is conform to the axioms that hold for the underlying logic.

This paper describes a (conceptual) architecture for CIAs, that integrates much of our previous work ([20, 5, 6]), and its implementation. The structure of this paper is as follows. In section 2 the CIA architecture is presented. In section 3 its implementation is described. Section 4 presents an example of a CIA specification and the resulting agent, and section 5 gives some conclusions and areas for further research.

2 Architecture

In figure 1 we show the (global) architecture of a CIA (its main functional modules and their interaction) as we use it. Although the components are similar to the ones in other agent architectures described in the literature (e.g., the general architecture of a social agent in [13] and the TAEMS architecture [2]) both the structure and working

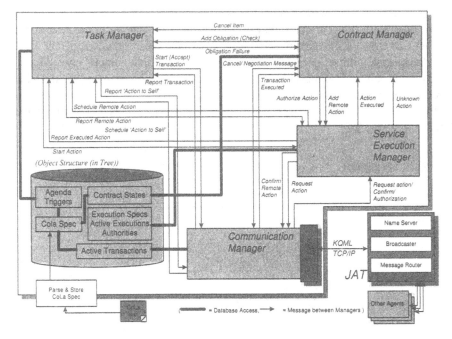

Fig. 1. General CIA architecture

of the components, based on our communication-oriented approach, is distinct. In the rest of this section we will give a short overview of the most important features of the components in this architecture.

The CIA consists of a number of functional modules, each responsible for one of the agents' main activities: task management, contract management, communication and interaction, and execution of services.

Each agent has an *agenda* containing the actions to be performed by the agent, instantly or at some designated time. The agenda is derived from the *obligations* of the agent. The agent can add new items to the agenda (typically done on the request of another agent) and can reason about them. Obligations can be the result of the (sub)task of the agent, but can also follow from the contract (see below). Items can be removed from the agenda by performing actions or by violating an obligation. In the latter case usually some compensatory action has to be performed. Maintaining the agenda is the primary task of the task manager, which therefore is the central module of the agent.

The pro-active behavior of a CIA is determined by the tasks the CIA defined in *CoLa* (Communication and Coordination Language) during the specification of the agent.

The agent performs *actions* and *transactions*. Actions can be performed by the agent itself (executed and monitored by the *service execution manager*) without interaction with other agents. Transactions are actions that involve communication with other agents. The basic building blocks of transactions are the speech acts. Agents communicate with each other by sending KQML messages. The communication is initiated and monitored by the *communication manager*. Transactions are used in a *contract* describing the commitments between two agents. The contract also specifies what should happen in case of a violation of one of the obligations, or cancellation by one of the agents, possibly leading to other obligations described by another transaction in the contract, and triggering a "contingency" plan, describing what should happen in order to get the subtask fulfilled. Both agents have direct access to the contracts between them. The *contract manager* monitors the contracts that a CIA is involved in and decides what steps to take when a contract is breached.

In the next subsections the working of the different managers is described in more detail.

2.1 Task Manager

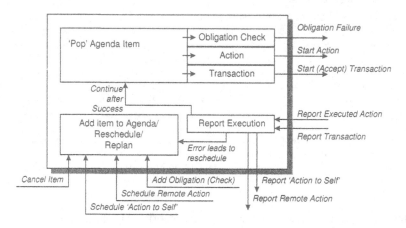

Fig. 2. Task Manager

The *task manager*'s main function is managing the agenda. The execution model of the task manager is as follows: when a task is called or a goal is established, the task manager devises a plan to fulfill the goal or perform the task. The plan consists of a number of subtasks with precedence relations and alternatives (see section 3.3). The subtasks are put on the agenda in the right order (the task manager schedules the items on the agenda in an order based on their constraints and deadlines). It then tries to perform all subtasks, backtracking when a task fails or an exception occurs. In case of an action the service execution manager is notified, in case of a transaction control is transferred to the communication manager. A special kind of action is the obligation check in which the task manager evaluates the knowledge bases (history) to see if another agent has fulfilled its obligation. If the check fails the contract manager is notified.

Special attention should be paid to cancellations of both actions and transactions. In case of a cancellation a contingency plan, that can be specified separately, can be triggered. A notorious problem with contingencies is that later (dependent) subtasks may already have completed, but their result have become obsolete. Whether they have to be retried or not depends on what kinds of results they have produced. A contingency plan consists of a set of *results* that come about by certain subtasks and can become invalidated by other subtasks. When this occurs, a task can be triggered to repair the damage. This task can make use of the fact that all the essential results obtained so far (and not invalidated) are explicit. For example, if a hotel-reservation is dependent on an airline-reservation, and the flight is canceled, the contingency plan can try to repair the damage by trying another airline. Only if that fails the hotel- reservation has to be canceled (independently, there can be a sanction on the party canceling, as specified in the contract).

2.2 Communication Manager

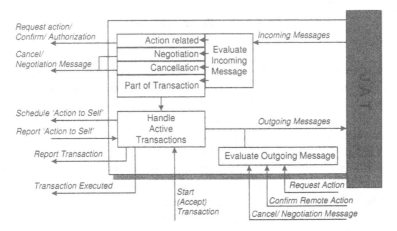

Fig. 3. Communication Manager

The *communication manager* handles all external communication of a CIA. When it receives a request for executing a transaction it constructs a communication plan (based on possible deadlines and constraints on the order of messages specified in the transaction). It handles all incoming messages, routing them to the appropriate managers.

We do not assume that the CIAs follow a fixed communication protocol. Therefore we need a rich communication language in which also the intent of each message is clear. This is achieved by basing the messages on the theory of speech acts (Searle [17, 18]). Using speech acts we can model existing protocols that are often used, e.g., the Contract Net Protocol, or the protocol from the ADEPT framework [15] as is done in [3]. However, the CIA can also react when other agents do not follow the same protocol. Communication through the Java Agent Template (JAT) takes place by sending KQML packages. However, we only use our own defined KQML performatives for our communication language which have a clearly defined semantics in the underlying logic (unlike some standard KQML performatives (see also [1] and the FIPA proposal [9])).

2.3 Service Execution Manager

The *service execution manager (SEM)* manages the local actions. It may also handle simple exceptions within the services (usually when the service can be restarted). The

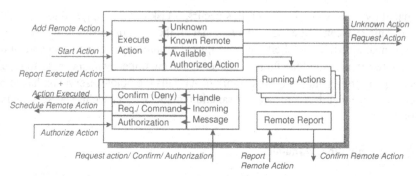

Fig. 4. Service Execution Manager

SEM also manages the services the CIA can give to other CIAs. That is, it checks whether the other agents are authorized to request the service. It maintains a database with information about services the CIA can provide itself and also services provided by other CIAs. In this way it assists the task manager in the execution of tasks that the CIA cannot perform itself but has to request from others.

The SEM distinguishes three authorization relationships: *power* (which is a fixed institutional relationship, allowing an agent to command the execution of a service); *authority* (which must be granted explicitly and disappears after use or some time. For example authority to demand payment for delivered products); and *charity* (or *peer* relationship, where an agent can only request the execution of a service and no guarantee is given on the execution). If no relationship with the other agent is recorded, the contract manager is notified to negotiate the execution of the service.

2.4 Contract Manager

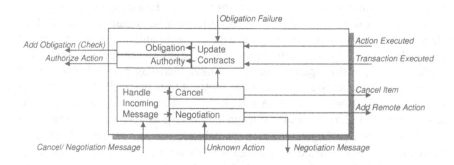

Fig. 5. Contract Manager

The agreements about the interactions between the CIAs are described in the contracts. In our framework, contracts conceptually specify obligations between different parties about services provided to each other. If a particular service is not being fulfilled, it is possible to reason about this violation and take a remedial action without forcing the whole task to abort. A contract describes the authorized communication be-havior among providers and receivers of services. If the provider does not adhere to the obligation it is the job of the contract manager to impose the violation policies.

The contract manager also negotiates contracts with other agents. At the moment only a simple form of Contract Net negotiation is implemented, but other negotiation strategies can be incorporated.

Contracts are specified by Petri-nets. If interaction proceeds as planned the contract manager only notifies the task manager to add obligation checks to the agenda. In case of a violation (or any other event that causes the entrance of a failure place in the contract, e.g. in case of a cancellation) the contract is examined and the task manager is notified to add the appropriate obligations to the agenda.

3 Implementation

In this section some of the aspects of implementation are described. Several sources of information are used by all parts of the CIA. The loaded CoLa specification is stored as a whole in an object-structure with a schema similar to the CoLa specification. This object-structure acts as input to and reference for the rest of the agent. The 'real-world knowledge' of the agent and the history of events, which is important for determining the truth-value of conditions and deadlines, is also used throughout the CIA. This data is stored as a number of linked objects in a list.

3.1 Java Agent Template

The basis of the CIA implementation is the Java Agent Template (JAT) [11]. The JAT offers basic agent functionality, its agents are non-mobile and can exchange any type of information. The CIA is running as an interpreter (message-handler) in the JAT, and is initialized when the JAT starts.

The CIA Implementation uses only the low-level (KQML) communication of the JAT, not the more advanced features. Sending and receiving of messages is done through just two primitives in the CIA, making it easy to replace the JAT with another commu-nication system.

The central router mostly serves as an 'agent-name to address'-list maintainer, and accepts only sign-on/ sign-off messages, Internet address-queries based on agent names and requests for broadcasting a message. There is no such thing as a 'Facilitator' (see e.g. [8]) in our implementation to support the agents functionality, the agents are mostly truly autonomous.

3.2 Tableau Decomposition

As described in e.g. [19, 14], the order in which 'action-items' (transactions, messages, local actions) in the CIA may take place are specified using constraints in Propositional Temporal Logic. This logic extends the simple Propositional Logic by adding the oper-ators SOMETIMES, NEXT, ALWAYS and BEFORE.

A graph is created of all possible paths of item orderings allowed by the constraints. To determine this dependency graph the Tableau Decomposition method is used, which is explained in detail in [14]. A small and contrived example of a dependency graph for three items ('a', 'b' and 'c'), and two constraints on those items,

```
a BEFORE (b OR c), b BEFORE c
```

is shown in figure 6. The constraints that identify the nodes are placed below them. The

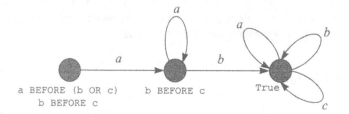

Fig. 6. A small example of a dependency graph

created graphs are used in two different ways in the CIA. The task manager uses them to create the agenda and the communication manager uses them to determine which actions can be performed immediately and which actions must wait. This is explained in more detail in the next sections where some implementation issues of these modules are described.

3.3 Task Manager

The information stored by the task manager all relates to the Agenda, which formally stores 'the obligations of the agent, a set of deontic temporal constraints'. Informally, the agenda specifies everything the agent has to do (and when). In practice, there are three types of items on the agenda: Actions, transactions and obligation checks. The obligation checks are performed for the contract manager. Actions and transactions may originate from tasks, local actions in transactions, violations of contracts and authorized actions executed for other agents. So, even though local actions are executed by the execution manager they are also reflected on the agenda!

All these items may have a deadline specified, which is used to order the agenda-items. All items are scheduled in the order of their deadlines, with the additional constraint that all items related to one task must be placed in their original order (the order of the current plan for that task). When an item of a task is being executed the rest of the items of the same task are 'frozen'. All unfrozen items on the agenda may be executed, which means that items placed below frozen items may be executed immediately.

When a task is called a complete path leading to the (specified) goal is selected in the plan graph created for the task. If a path in the graph ends without reaching a goal the path is backtracked looking for an alternative path which ends in a goal-state. Once a path leading to a goal has been found the items on this path are placed on the agenda in sequence. If execution of one of the items fails it might be possible to find another path using an alternative in the graph for the failed item, or to backtrack from that point looking for a new path to a goal. Contingency actions may be specified for executed items that have become obsolete because of backtracking.

There is also a lists of triggers. Triggers are items which are waiting for events, after which they perform some kind of action (on the agenda). Deadlines may be specified for the triggers. There are different kinds of triggers:

- A trigger is created to handle the report send by managers when they have finished processing an action/ transaction. Activation of the trigger may lead to either routing the report to another manager that was responsible for placing the item on the agenda, unfreezing the remainder of a task or causing a replan of the task (if the item failed).
- Obligation checks must not be placed on the agenda immediately, but only when the obligation's deadline has passed.
- Tasks may have a precondition, in which case they will only be scheduled when the precondition is activated.

3.4 Communication Manager

The communication manager uses the graphs created from the transaction specifications to determine the possible entries of communication. When a transaction starts the communication manager examines which messages (and local actions) may be executed initially, by examining a path leading to a desired state. All the items that can be reached on a path to a goal without entering messages which are send by the partner in the transaction (the plan-graph also stores which side initiates each item) or a local action (which has to be completed before the transaction may proceed) may be selected and executed. When an agent receives new messages related to an active transaction (or a local action related to an active transaction is completed) it recreates the path in the plan-graph from the history of the transaction. If the path cannot be recreated, the other agent did not keep to the constraints and the transaction fails. Otherwise it may be that the agent can continue the transaction based on the newly added events (if it is allowed to select new items on a continuing path to the goal) or that it must wait. Because the execution of local actions and the transmitting of messages is final, backtracking is not used for the transaction graphs.

For each running transaction information such as a reference to the specification and plan graph, instantiated deadlines and a message history is stored.

When messages are part of a transaction the transaction-name and a unique identifier are put in each message in order to be able to determine the 'conversation' to which they belong. (Not all messages are part of transactions! The most notable are cancellations.) When a transaction starts, one agent must initiate the transaction and one agent must accept it. To alleviate the synchronization of this process, messages belonging to unresolved transactions are buffered for a limited amount of time at the receiving end, waiting for the task manager to deliver the corresponding acceptance.

4 Example

To give an idea of the actual CIA-implementation an example specification for an agent is given concerning the well-known case of booking a business trip [7]. We also included some screenshot of the running agent that results from this specification.

4.1 Example Specification

This section describes some of the more important fragments of the CoLa specification used for the travel agent. The complete specification of all four agents of the business-trip example can be found on the CIA WWW-page:

```
http://machtig.kub.nl/egon/CIA/
```

In the business-trip example there are four (types of) agents, the user, the travel- agent, the airline and the hotel. We will focus on the travel agent here, which communicates with all the other agents. The travel agent is called upon by the user agent with the request for a trip. The travel agent then books a flight and reserves a hotel based on the user's wishes. The accompanying CoLa specification consists of three parts, the tasks of the travel agent, specifications of the transactions and specification of the contracts.

Travel Agent Tasks The main task of the travel agent, 'plan trip', consists of accepting a request from the user, booking the flight and the hotel, notifying the user of the arrangements and making sure the user pays.

```
task plantrip
subtasks:  accept(booktrip);
           T.flightreservation(klm);
           hotelreservation;
           T.bookedtrip(trip);
           T.payment;
```

There are several constraints on the order in which these actions may be performed; initially the user will ask the travel agent to generate a trip through a 'booktrip'- transaction, while finally the user must pay for his trip.

```
constraints:
        accept(booktrip) BEFORE (hotelreservation OR
                            T.flightreservation(klm));
        T.flightreservation(klm) BEFORE
                            T.bookedtrip(trip);
        hotelreservation(klm) BEFORE T.bookedtrip(trip);
        T.bookedtrip(trip) BEFORE T.payment;
goal = T.payment
```

During execution of the task several results are created. The task-specification can contain information on how results are created, and what events have what effect on them.

```
dependencies: "trip" depends-on "ticket"
  (create fail update);
contingency:  result "ticket" created-by plantrip
                closed-by  T.betaling
                updated-by T.changeflight
                invalidated-by A.skip_it
                compensated-by A.removedb(ticket)
              end-result;
```

In the 'plantrip' task 'hotelreservation' is defined as a sub-task, which must reserve a room at the Sheraton or the Hilton (with a preference for the Sheraton).

```
task hotelreservation
subtasks: T.hotelreserve(sheraton);
T.hotelreserve(hilton);
goal = T.hotelreserve(sheraton) [2] XOR
       T.hotelreserve(hilton)   [1]
end-task;
```

Travel Agent Transactions One of the simpler transactions is the one which initiates the communication between the agents. The user requests the travel agent to reserve a trip, the travel agent then either starts a new reservation and sends a confirmation or refuses.

```
transaction booktrip
agents:  t: travelagent;  u: user;
         t can send messages:
             A.reserve(trip) to self;
             confirm(A.reserve(trip)) to u;
             assert(refuse-to(A.reserve(trip))) to u;
         u can send messages:
             request(A.reserve(trip)) to t;
         constraints:
             request(A.reserve(trip)) BEFORE
               (A.reserve(trip) XOR
                 assert(refuse-to(A.reserve(trip))));
             A.reserve(trip) BEFORE
                 confirm(A.reserve(trip));
goal = confirm(A.reserve(trip))
exit = assert(refuse-to(A.reserve(trip)))
end-transaction;
```

Travel Agent Contracts One of the contracts specified is used between the travel agent and the airline. It consists of three states. The contract is activated once the 'flightreservation' transaction is completed. Then, if the flight is performed the contract reaches the acceptance state, but if the flight is canceled a fine must be paid first.

```
contract flight
agents:    a: airline;    t: travelagent;
clauses:
      S1: obl(a, A.fly)
      in: T.flightreservation(klm)
      goal: A.fly => S2
      exit: cancel("flight") => S3
      end S1;

      S2: acc(t)
      in: A.fly, T.payfine
      end S2;

      S3: obl(a, T.payfine)
      in: cancel("flight")
      deadline: T.payfine << NOW + 14 days
      goal: T.payfine => S2
      end S3;
end-contract;
```

The above specification is a textual representation of the Petri-net definition of the contract, which is omitted due to space limitations.

4.2 Screenshot running agent

In figure 7 a screenshot can be seen of the actual CIA- implementation. At the center right the main control window of the travel agent is shown, with display windows for the agent's state around it.

The messages in the main window show that the travel agent has parsed its specification and initialized correctly, and has been started and stopped. The buttons at the top of the window allow for several general actions (one of which is the unprepared cancellation of realized actions and transactions), while the buttons at the bottom allow the user to view several aspects of the state of the agent. All of these windows have been opened in the screenshot.

The state-windows show that the agent has been running for a while. All items placed on the agenda (shown left) belong to the same task and are all frozen. This is because the travel agent is currently working on the transaction 'booked trip' of the same task, as can be seen in the communication window (top right). The communication window also shows that the travel agent has send and received messages to and from the user agent and the airline, according to several executed transactions. For instance, in the fourth message the airline has asserted a flight- schedule to the travel agent. This flight-schedule has since been stored in the travel agent's database (bottom right), in which you can also see the trip[1] the travel agent has created for the user (in the example, the hotel-reservation has been created by the travel agent itself). The flight

---

[1] 'reis' means trip in the Dutch language

Fig. 7. Screenshot of example CIA

has been selected by a local 'check' action, which is one of the actions executed by the agent (the 'Actions'-window at the bottom left). In the 'Contracts'-window (top middle) one can see the flight-contract is still in its initial state.

5 Conclusion

In this paper we have given an impression of the architecture and implementation of Cooperative Information Agents based on the language-action perspective. Important elements that come back in the implementations are the use of speech act theory for the communication between agents and especially the commitments and obligations following from the communication. Another important aspect from the agent architecture is the distinction between tasks and contracts. This distinction gives advantages in the case of failure of tasks or cancellations of results.

Future research should include the scalability of this prototype. Also some aspects such as the negotiation protocol and conversation rules are now only present in their most simple form and should be upgraded to more realistic formats.

References

1. P. Cohen and H. Levesque. Communicative Actions for Artificial Agents. In *Int. Conf. on Multi-Agent Systems*, pages 65–72, 1995.
2. K. Decker and V. Lesser. Task environment centered design of organizations. In *AAAI Spring Symp. on Computational Organization Design*. Stanford, 1994.
3. F. Dignum. Social Interactions of Autonomous Agents: Private and Global Views on Communication. In P.-Y. Schobbens, editor, *Proc. of 3rd workshop of the ModelAge Project*, Sienna, Italy, 1997.
4. F. Dignum and B. van Linder. Modeling Rational Agents in a Dynamic Environment: Putting Humpty Dumpty Together Again. In J.L. Fiadeiro and P.-Y. Schobbens, editors, *Proc. of 2nd workshop of the ModelAge Project*, pages 81–92, Sesimbra, Portugal, 1996.
5. F. Dignum and H. Weigand. Communication and Deontic Logic. In R. Wieringa and R. Feenstra, editors, *Information Systems, Correctness and Reusability*, pages 242–260, Singapore, 1995. World Scientific.
6. F. Dignum and H. Weigand. Modeling Communication between Cooperative Systems. In J. Iivari et. al., editor, *Proc. of CAISE'95*, pages 140–153, Berlin, 1995. Springer-Verlag.
7. A. Elmagarmid. *Database Transaction Models for Advanced Applications*. Morgan Kaufman, 1992.
8. T. Finin, R. Fritzson, D. McKay and R. McEntire. KQML: a language and protocol for knowledge and information exchange. In M. Klein et. al., editor, *Distributed AI - 13th Int.l. WS*, pages 99–103, Menlo Park, CA., 1994. AAAI Press.
9. Fipa. *http://drogo.cselt.stet.it/fipa/index.htm*.
10. F. Flores and J.J. Ludlow. Doing and speaking in the office. In G. Fick et. al., editor, *DSS: Issues and Challenges*, pages 95–118, New York, 1980. Pergamon Press.
11. R. Frost. The jat. *http://cdr.stanford.edu/ABE/JavaAgent.html*.
12. J. Habermas. *The Theory of Communicative Action: Reason and the Rationalization of Society, Volume One*. Beacon Press, Boston, 1984.
13. B. Moulin and B. Chaib-draa. An overview of distributed artificial intelligence. In H. O'Hare and N. Jennings, editors, *Foundations of DAI*, pages 3–55, New York, 1996. John Wiley and Sons Inc.
14. A.H.H. Ngu, R.A. Meersman and H. Weigand. Specification and verification of communication for interoperable transactions. In *Int.l. Journal of Intelligent and Cooperative Information Systems, vol. 3, no. 1*, pages 47–65, 1994.
15. T. Norman, N. Jennings, P. Faratin and E. Mamdani. Designing and Implementing a Multi-Agent Architecture for Business Process Management. In M. Wooldridge J. Mueller and N. Jennings, editors, *Intelligent Agents III - Proceedings ATAL-96*, pages 149–162, 1996.
16. M. Papazoglou. *An organizational framework for intelligent cooperative IS*. IJICIS-1(1), 1992.
17. J.R. Searle. *Speech Acts*. Cambridge University Press, 1969.
18. J.R. Searle and D. Vanderveken. *Foundations of illocutionary logic*. Cambridge University Press, 1985.
19. E.M. Verharen. *A Language-Action Perspective on the Design of Cooperative Information Agents*. PhD thesis, Katholieke Universiteit Brabant, 1997.
20. E.M. Verharen and F. Dignum. Cooperative Information Agents and Communication. In M. Klusch, editor, *Proc. of the 1st Int.l. WS on CIAs*, Berlin, 1997. Springer-Verlag.

Toward the Specification and Design of Industrial Synthetic Ecosystems

Van Parunak, John Sauter, and Steve Clark

Industrial Technology Institute
PO Box 1485
Ann Arbor, MI 48106
{van, john, sjc}@iti.org

Abstract. Many agent-based systems rely for their effectiveness on the intelligence of individual agents, and interaction among agents is required simply to coordinate these individually complex decisions. Specification and design methods for such systems focus on the internal architecture of individual agents. An alternative approach, "Synthetic Ecosystems," uses relatively simple agents and draws heavily on the dynamics of the interaction among these agents as well as their internal processing to solve domain problems. The specification and design of such systems must include not only the individual agents, but also the structure and dynamics of their interaction. This paper briefly defines and motivates the Synthetic Ecosystems approach and outlines some techniques that have proven useful in specifying and designing them.

1   Introduction

Jennings and Campos [10] summarize the history of agent-based systems design in two phases: a reductionist period that focused on top-down analysis of system issues at the expense of agent autonomy, and a constructionist period in which the focus of design attention moves to the individual agent. They argue cogently that this second approach does not adequately provide for socially coherent behavior. To remedy this shortcoming, they propose a social level in the architecture of individual agents that supports socially rational actions, just as Newell's knowledge level immediately beneath it supports individual rationality. This approach builds social coherence on individual rationality. The methodology presented in [8] is based on this view.

In recent years, there has been growing interest in systems of agents that do not possess even the usual mechanisms of individual rationality (such as models of self, the environment, and other agents), and yet exhibit social coherence [5; 4; 25]. These "synthetic ecosystems" are inspired by social behavior in non-humans, often insects. [19] formalizes such systems, identifies a number of their characteristics, and argues that they follow naturally from the notion of an agent as a bounded process immersed in an active environment.

The relative simplicity and directness of such agents and their match to emerging technologies for distributed shop-floor control make them attractive candidates for early industrial deployment. However, such deployment depends critically on the availability of a design methodology that can be taught, so that development of agent systems can move out of the laboratory and into widespread industrial practice [17].

Like the approach of [10], it must provide for social coherence. Unlike their approach, it cannot rely primarily on explicit coordinating decisions by the agents, but must take a broader view of the structure of the overall community and its dynamics.

We have synthesized an approach to designing industrial-strength ecosystems based on techniques that we have used successfully in a number of development projects. Although detailed case studies are beyond the scope of this paper, examples and illustrations are drawn from these experiences. Table 1 outlines the four kinds of activity in our overall approach: initial conceptual analysis, human role-playing to test the basic kinds of agents and their relation to one another, computerized simulations to explore the emergent properties of the system under realistic numbers of agents and interchanges; and selection of deployment technologies on the basis of the dynamic information gathered from the simulations.

This discussion of *how* we design agents (also [1]) is orthogonal to the questions of *what* needs to be designed (individual agents, their organization, and mechanisms for coordination, as in [2]) and *why* one would choose the synthetic ecosystem approach [19]. Methodologies that focus on *what* needs to be designed have many useful tools and models that are compatible with the techniques presented here, often even if they are originally intended for individually rational agents. A rich set of seven fairly formal models may be found in [9]. [11] splits the problem into the external viewpoint (agent classes and interactions, compatible with our approach) and the internal viewpoint, which facilitates the development of individually rational agents. A pragmatic presentation of an agent methodology that is very compatible with synthetic ecosystems is [20].

Table 1: Activities in Designing Multi-Agent Systems

Technique	Focus	Supporting Analysis	Answers
Conceptual Analysis	Components		• What system-level behavior do we want? • What kinds of agents do we think we might need to get it? • How should they behave?
Role-Playing	Architecture (Kinematics)	Speech-Acts & Dooley Graphs	• How do our proposed agents interact with one another in an organization? • What low-level behaviors are needed?
Computer Simulation	Behavior (Dynamics)	Nonlinear mathematics	• What kind of behavior emerges from realistic numbers of agents and interchanges?
Implementation Design	Platforms and Tools		• How can I instantiate this design in a deployable system?

Between any two of these activities, there is a good deal of iteration. Role-playing may send us back to the drawing board to rethink what agents are needed and what they should do individually. Computer simulation may uncover a need for a revised organizational structure that requires more role-playing, while implementation design may raise further questions that require additional simulation. Still, there is a rough time ordering of these activities, in that conceptual analysis is the first to begin and implementation design is the last to complete.

This paper focuses on the first and second of these activities. Section 2 discusses Conceptual Analysis, Section 3 outlines how to role-play a multi-agent system, and Section 4 briefly summarizes the place of Dooley Graphs and computer simulation in analyzing the results of the first two activities. Although we do not consider formal verification of synthetic ecosystem behavior, [26] takes a step in that direction.

2   Conceptual Analysis

Conceptual analysis gives us our initial vision of what the system as a whole will do (expressed both in abstract terms and as role-playing cases), what agents will be involved, and how they will behave. At this point, the overall system behavior can be specified with a fair amount of detail, since it comes from the overall system requirements, but the identity and behavior of the agents themselves are only initial guesses, guided by general principles of good agent design (drawn from [19] and discussed more fully there).

2.1   Define Desired System Behavior[1]

We begin by identifying the requirements for which the system is being constructed. In conventional systems, we would then proceed to design these behaviors top-down, and the required system behaviors thus specify the outer envelope of the accessible system behaviors. In agent-based systems, these requirements are used to evaluate the adequacy of the emergent behavior of the collection of agents, and thus guide the refinement of individual behaviors.

At a high level, desired system behavior may be of several kinds. We may want the system to maintain some set of state variables in a specified relationship with one another, thus exhibiting *homeostasis*. The system may be a *transducer* that needs to

---

[1]   System behavior is only one of a broad set of requirements that need to be taken into account in designing a system. Other requirements include interface constraints, performance constraints, operating constraints, life-cycle constraints (e.g., maintainability), economic constraints, and political constraints. [21] offers a helpful summary. A complete design method for agent-based systems needs to take account of all these issues. For starters, we are concentrating on the functional requirements, those that concern the behavior of the system.

convert specified stimuli into corresponding responses. Or we may want the system to *learn* over time in response to its experience.

At least two criteria are involved in a good behavioral specification.

- It should be specific enough to know if we succeed in achieving it. A qualitative specification is usually adequate for role-playing, but we need a quantitative one to support simulation. For example, in a process control environment, "homeostasis" by itself is too vague. "Balance temperature and pressure" is OK for role-playing. For simulation, we need to specify the quantitative link desired between pressure and temperature.

- It should be relevant to system architecture as opposed to other system variables. For example, the system behavior "Have tooling available when needed" might be better addressed by buying more tools rather than expecting magic from agents. Better specifications for this example include: "Get high-value parts through the system first"; "Identify relative scarcity of tool types"; "Reduce overall tool idleness."

The design team needs a concise statement of the problem to be solved and the constraints that must be observed. For example:

- What is the desired overall system behavior?
- What can be varied in the effort to achieve this behavior?
- What must not be touched?
- What approach is currently taken to solving the problem?
- Why is a new solution being contemplated? (Are there obvious shortcomings of the current solution? Is a change needed that is beyond the scope of the current solution?)

These questions are not intended to be exhaustive, but simply to indicate the kind of information that should be summarized in the preparatory documents.

2.2   Identify Agents

The next step is to decompose the system into pieces that will become our agents. In this initial phase, the engineer is guided by a body of "good practice" that will grow as the result of experiences such as ours. This activity focuses roughly on the "agent model" of [2]. We have found linguistic case analysis a useful tool in developing the initial partition of the system. The candidate agents identified in this way are then reviewed against design principles that appear to be followed in naturally occurring agent systems.

2.2.1   Case Analysis for Agent Identification

One widely-used technique for identifying objects in an object-oriented systems analysis [22] is to extract the nouns from a narrative description of the desired system behavior. We use a refinement of this approach, based on linguistic case theory [6; 3]. The basic idea is that each verb has a set of named slots that can be filled by other items, typically nouns. Each slot describes the semantic role of its filler with respect to the verb. Thus the case role of a noun captures basic behavioral differences among entities in the domain.

Instead of the case names used by linguists (which are too general for our purposes, and in the case of "Agent" might lead to unfortunate confusion), we define a set that is appropriate for the domain we are treating. For example, in discrete manufacturing, we can describe what happens in a factory in a series of sentences of the form, "Joe oversaw Unit Process 12 on Part 25 from Acme Supplies, using Mill 32, Cutter 86, and Part Program 19, producing Part 26 for US Army Order 22." The essential components of such a sentence, and the case labels by which we might refer to them, are:

Unit Process ("Unit Process 12").—The unit process is the level below which manufacturing ceases to be a discrete activity. The Manufacturing Studies Board of the National Academy of Sciences distinguishes five basic types of unit processes: Mass-Change, Phase-Change, Structure-Change, Deformation, and Consolidation [15]. An instantiation of a Unit Process in space and time (e.g., the specific instance of heat treating performed in Oven 18 at 14:32 3 May 1993) is an Operation.

Resource ("Mill 32," "Cutter 86," "Part Program 19").—The linguist's Instruments; the "tools" that are needed to perform an Operation (an instance of the Unit Process), including machines, material handling devices, energy, tooling, fixtures, gauges, part programs, and documentation. Those aspects of the machine operator that are required to complete a unit process are best modeled as a Resource as well. Other aspects of humans are covered in the Manager category.

Manager ("Joe").—This is the human responsible for the Operation. In an automated factory, it becomes the plant manager. Automated representatives watch for things like chaos, performance metrics, energy consumption, and cash flow.

Part ("Part 25," "Part 26").—The inputs (Materials) and outputs (Products) for a Unit Process. There may be more than one input (in assembly) or output (in disassembly, or sawing up bar stock, or injection molding of a tree of parts). Between Unit Processes, Parts are in the custody of material handling operations such as transport and storage mechanisms. Like other Unit Processes, material handling changes characteristics of a part (its age and location). However, these changes do not alter the part functionally, and the part number (identifying its type) does not change across a material handling operation (as it does across other Unit Processes). Thus we make Parts responsible for their own material handling, and permit them to acquire necessary Resources just as Unit Processes do in order to move from one Unit Process to another.

Customer ("US Army Order 22").—The linguistic Beneficiary; the one who benefits from the execution of the work. The Customer represents a single purchase decision, or order. This cohesion is necessary in order to let the system handle each unit in a purchase separately (for processing simplicity) and yet be able to identify different parts that will all be made or not made based on the same purchase decision (so that we can take advantage of economies of scale).

Supplier ("Acme Supplies").—Another variety of Beneficiary, this time the one from whom the input material is purchased.

The case analysis does not provide a finished system design, but does give an initial set of agents and agent types (from the linguistic roles) that lends itself to discussion among the developers and has proven to be very robust in terms of covering the issues that need to be addressed. In the example, some questions were raised by linguistic case analysis alone but were answered in role playing, such as:

1. Is there a separate agent for each of several identical Resources?

2. Is there one Manager agent for each human with a manager role, or for each management function, or for each Operation?

3. Does a Part agent represent an individual part, a lot containing many parts, or a type of part? Should there be both Part Instance and Part Type agents?

Space does not permit discussing the resolution of these particular questions in this paper.

2.2.2   Principles for Validating Candidate Agents

To complete the preliminary decomposition, these categories are reviewed and possibly revised against overall system requirements and general principles (for example, those in [19], used here).

Thing vs. Function.—Classical software engineering techniques condition many systems designers toward "functional decomposition." This approach is unprecedented in naturally occurring systems, which divide agents on the basis of distinct entities in the physical world rather than functional abstractions. Our experience supports this principle. Each functional agent needs detailed knowledge of many of the physical entities being managed, and so when the physical system changes, the functional agent needs to change as well. However, it is often possible to endow physically defined agents with generic behaviors from which the required functionality will emerge, for widely varying overall populations of agents. In most cases, deriving agents from the nouns in a narrative description of the problem to be solved yields things rather than functions.

Legacy systems and watchdogs are two exceptions to this principle. Most agent applications in the near future will be incremental additions to existing systems, and will need to interface with legacy programs, some of which will be functionally oriented. For example, a shop-floor control system will need to interface with a factory-wide MRP system that is doing classical scheduling. As in the CIDIM application of ARCHON [27], we encapsulate the legacy program as an agent. Though the MRP system is functionally defined, as a legacy program it is a well-defined "thing" and so deserves agenthood. By using it as a link to other system information rather than as a main source of functionality, we can ensure that it does not dominate the system, and pave the way for its eventual replacement.

Functional agents are sometimes needed as watchdogs. Some system states may not be perceivable at the level of an individual agent, and yet may be necessary to ensure overall system safety or performance. A functional agent that simply monitors the behavior of a population of physical agents is not nearly as restrictive on future reconfiguration as one that does centralized planning and action. The most elegant designs do not rely on watchdogs at all, but if they are used, they should sense and raise signals but not plan or take action.

Small in Size.—Natural systems like insect colonies and market economies are characterized by many agents, each small in comparison with the whole system. Such agents are easier to construct and understand, and the impact of the failure of any single agent will be minimal. In addition, a large population of agents gives the system a richer overall space of possible behaviors, thus providing for a wider scope of emergent behavior. (Very roughly, system state space is exponential in the number of agents.) Ecological studies frequently find that the functioning of a biological system depends on minimum population levels much higher than one would suspect based on a naïve analysis of rates of reproduction, predation, and food consumption, because emergent properties essential to the community's survival are driven by the interaction of many entities. We expect that the same principle will hold true of artificial systems.

Keeping agents small often means favoring specialized agents over more general ones, using appropriate aggregation techniques. For example, rather than writing a single agent to represent a complete manufacturing cell, consider an agent for each mechanism in the cell (e.g., one for the fixture, one for the tool, one for the load-unload mechanism, one for the gauging station).

Decentralized.—Natural systems do not reflect the kind of centralization that often appears in artificial systems. For example, a market economy achieves superior distribution of goods compared with attempts at central economic control. We can hypothesize several reasons for this tendency. A central agent is a single point of failure that makes the system vulnerable to accident. It can easily become a performance bottleneck. More subtly, it tends to attract functionality and code as the system develops, pulling the design away from the benefits of agents and regressing to a large software artifact that is difficult to understand and maintain.

Centralization can sometimes creep in when designers confuse a class of agents with individual agents. For example, one might be tempted to represent a bank of paint booths as "the paint agent," because "they all do the same thing." Certainly, one would develop a single class (in the object-oriented sense of the word) for paint-booth agents, but each paint booth should be a separate instantiation of that class.

Diversity and Generalization.—Natural communities of agents balance diversity (which enables them to monitor an environment much larger than any single agent) with generalized mechanisms (enhancing their interaction with one another and reducing the need for task-specific processing). For example, pheromones enable insects not only to map out paths to food sources, but also to coordinate nest construction. The class inheritance mechanisms of the object-oriented platforms on which we construct agents are an excellent support for comparable generalization across the agents we build, but experience shows that the hard part is identifying appropriate generalizations in the first place. Early designs typically multiply differences among agents unnecessarily, while later refinements can make more effective use of the power of inheritance.

2.3 Hypothesize Agent Behaviors and Message Types

With a candidate set of agents in hand, we define their individual behaviors and the classes of messages they can exchange. At this point in the design, these behaviors must be considered hypothetical. There exists no algorithm to compute from desired system behaviors to the individual agent behaviors that will yield the system behaviors. Some behaviors (even most) may be straightforward and obvious, but there will always be subsystems where only simulation of example agent behaviors (first in role-playing, later on a computer) can tell us when we have the right behaviors

There are many multiagent communication and coordination methods [14] and many methodologies to address them. [24] separates protocol specification and design, and distributed coordination from internal agent design. [13] presents an automatic, dynamic coordination method for individually rational agents that could just as well be used as an analysis tool by human designers of individually simpler agents. The activities described in this section most closely relate to development of the "cooperation model" and aspects of the "organizational model." of [2], and of the "coordination model" and "communication model" of [9].

2.3.1 Method

At this point in our design, our main concern is with identifying the decisions each agent needs to make and the other agents with which it needs to make them, rather than on the details of each agent's internal reasoning. Table 2 is an example of the information we gather at this point, in the case of a simple automotive supply chain. All agents in this example are of the same type. Since the focus of the role-playing is on the interaction dynamics of the system rather than the individual decision-making of the agents, it is often sufficient to flip one or more coins to select among possible alternative actions. By treating a penny, a dime, a nickel, and a quarter as successively higher bit positions, up to 2^4 alternatives can be represented. The entries in the "Stimulus" and "Response" columns identify some of the classes of messages or interactions that will be needed.

Table 2: High-Level Behavioral Design for a Simple Supply Chain

Agent Type	Stimulus	Behavioral Question	Mechanism in Role-Play	Response
Supplier-Consumer		What parts can I manufacture?	Predefined Constant: PartA; PartB	
Supplier-Consumer	Incoming RFQ	1. Do I have capacity to honor this RFQ?	Flip a coin; if Tails, ask your competitors to help	RFQ to Competitors
		2. Assuming I CAN do the work, do I WANT to bid?	Flip a coin	
		3. Are the inputs I need available?	Ask your suppliers	RFQ to Suppliers
		4. What should I charge per piece?	Roll a die	Send bid to customer
Supplier-Consumer	Incoming Bid	Which bid shall I accept?	Flip a coin for each incoming bid until one comes up Heads.	Purchase Order to successful supplier; rejection to others

2.3.2 Principles

The following principles from [19] pertain to agent dynamics and interactions.

Concurrent Planning and Execution.—Traditional systems alternate planning and execution. For example, a firm develops a schedule each night for its manufacturing operations the next day. The real world tends to change in ways that invalidate advance plans. Natural systems do not plan in advance, but adjust their operations on a time scale comparable to that in which their environment changes. Watch out for suggested behaviors that involve extensive up-front planning.

Currency.—Naturally occurring multi-agent systems often use some form of currency to achieve global self-organization. The two classical examples are the flow of money in a market economy, and the evaporation of pheromones in insect communities. These mechanisms accomplish two purposes. They provide an "entropy leak" that permits self-organization (reduction of entropy) at the macro level without violating the second law of thermodynamics overall, and they generate a gradient field that agents can perceive and to which they can orient their actions, thus becoming more organized. Wherever possible, artificial agent communities should include such a currency. It should have three characteristics [12]:

1. It should establish a gradient across the space in which the agents act, either as a potential field or as an actual flow.

2. The agents should be able to perceive it and orient themselves to this gradient.

3. The agents' actions should reinforce the gradient (positive feedback).

Local Communication.—Agents need to limit the recipients of their messages as much as possible. Wherever possible, instead of "broadcast X," seek to define more precisely the audience that needs to receive the message.

Information Sharing.—Agents often need to share information across both time and space. ("Learning" thus becomes a special case of information sharing.) Three approaches are available [7]. Classical AI learning is ontogenetic, taking place within a single agent during the course of its existence. Phylogenetic mechanisms such as genetic programming can improve the behavior of a species of agents over successive generations. Sociogenetic mechanisms that construct markers in the environment can enable an agent community as a whole to learn even if individual agents are not modified. Each mechanism places different requirements on the behavior of the agents in the system. Phylogenetic learning is not nearly as demanding as the ontogenetic mechanisms developed in classical AI, and sociogenetic mechanisms can be even simpler.

3 Role-Play the System

With agents identified and tentative behaviors described, we can experiment with the emergent behavior of selected subsystems by having people play the roles of the various agents. Such a rehearsal does not show the full dynamic behavior that would be expected from a complete population of agents operating at computer speed, but does validate the basic behaviors needed and provides a basis for defining some internal details of computerized agents. Where computer agents supplement the activity of human operators, the role-playing exercise also helps capture the techniques, knowledge, and rules that the humans have been using to ensure that the computer agent augments this behavior appropriately.

3.1 Select Subsystems and Scripts for Role Playing

In our experience, a large proportion of the individual behaviors for most of the agents will be fairly obvious. This empirical result is fortunate, since role-playing a complete system as small as 50 or 100 agents can be slow, tedious, and inconclusive. To explore the emergent behaviors of the system in regions that are not obvious, we focus on subsystems of a dozen or so agents where we are least comfortable about the match between individual and system behaviors.

In addition to selecting these subsystems for role-playing, we need several scripts of the desired system behavior. For example, if we seek a system with homeostasis, we need to identify the state variables that can independently change, the range of variation that they can expect, and the corresponding corrections needed in other variables. These scripts guide the role-playing activities. Because of the time and effort constraints of role-playing, they will sample the overall space of desired system behaviors only sparsely, and should be chosen to explore widely separated regions of this space.

3.2 Assign Agents to People

A separate person should represent each agent in the subsystem identified in the conceptual analysis phase. When there are many more agents than people available, it may be necessary for a single person to handle a complete class of agents. In this case we need to distinguish carefully between the behavior of the agent class and what a single agent of that class can know. Agents, even those of the same class, do not have automatic access to one another's variables, and people representing them in a role-play need to be careful not to "leak" information among them.

An important characteristic of synthetic ecosystems is that the environment is not necessarily passive, but may have state and processes associated with it [19]. It differs from an agent in that it is unbounded. In addition to the agents proposed for the system being engineered (the "system agents"), a person should be assigned to play the role of the environment manipulated by the system. The environment raises external conditions as called for in the script, receives actuator outputs from the system agents, and integrates these outputs into their overall effect on the environment, thus monitoring the system's ability to achieve the required changes. The facilitator can represent a simple environment. When the environment is more complicated, its representative may need to do more extensive reasoning, and should be separate from the facilitator.

The primary responsibility of participants in the role-playing is to figure out the rules that should guide the behavior of the agent for which they are responsible. The structure of the conversation among agents will emerge naturally from the interaction, and can be retrieved by post-hoc analysis, but the internal rules need to be developed by the participants themselves.

3.3 Record Actions

To support later analysis, we capture all actions that agents (both system and environment) take external to themselves. These actions may be either speech acts (messages to other agents) or non-speech acts (influences on the environment). The agents record these actions on cards that are then given to the participant representing the receiving agent (for a message) or the environment (for a physical action). Each card records five pieces of information, in addition to the actual content of the message:

• The identity of the sending agent
• The identity of the receiving agent
• The time the card is sent
• The identity of the agent whose card stimulated this one
• The time that the card stimulating this one was sent

This information enables reconstruction of the thread of conversation among the agents. The time entries are a useful way to determine the order in which messages are generated. Ideally, one could assign a unique sequence number to all cards, but the task of maintaining such a number across all participants is burdensome and prone to error. By placing a digital desk clock in view of all participants, it is easy to maintain an unambiguous ordering of the cards that permits reconstruction of the conversation.

3.4   Facilitate the Interactions Among Agents

A facilitator who is not one of the agents should oversee the execution of each script. There are three phases in this responsibility.

Initiate.—The facilitator announces that a new script is starting. If the facilitator and environment are not the same person, the facilitator makes sure the correct script drives the environment.

Run.—While the participants are running the script, the facilitator has the following responsibilities:

- If the facilitator is doing double duty as the environment agent, simulate exogenous inputs to the system and account for the effect of outputs.

- Act as "postman" to carry message cards between agents.

- Watch for possible cross-talk between agents ("Isn't your action based partly on what B said a few moments ago to C? Should you have been included on the distribution for that message?")

Debrief.—After completion of a script, the facilitator helps participants synthesize important conclusions from the session. Here are several examples that we can identify at the outset. There may be others.

- What operational decisions could not be resolved locally? These point to the need for a partial redesign to make them local, or if none can be found, functional "watchdog" agents.

- What state information does each agent need to maintain?

- How complex do agents need to be? One way to get a first cut at this is to see how succinctly participants can write down a description of the decision processes for their agents.

- Are participants conscious of internal state shifts?

3.5   Graph the Conversations

Agent- and object-oriented methodologies have many ways of modeling conversations, e.g. [16]. We have found that Enhanced Dooley Graphs [18] are a useful tool to analyze conversations in agent-based systems. Each node in the graph represents an agent in a role. A given agent may appear at different nodes if it takes on different roles in the course of the conversation. These roles are good candidates for units of behavior that can often be reused across an agent community. Thus they provide a first-level decomposition of individual agents into behaviors, and guide the initial coding of the system.

4   Further Analysis

Brainstorming and role-playing are flexible, creative ways to explore possible agent designs, but their results need to be checked before implementation begins, especially in architectures (such as synthetic ecosystems) that rely so heavily on emergent behavior. We have found simulation an indispensable tool. It enables the designer to observe and evaluate the emergent behavior of the entire community, and to test how the behavior seen in a limited role-play scales up to a full population of agents. The growing acceptance of genetic methods in industry opens the door for using simulation to grow agents, avoiding the need to program them manually. The code of the simulated agents can serve as a detailed design for the final implementation.

The transition from design to implementation is the selection of the deployment platforms and tools that will be used in the fielded system. Sometimes these choices are known at the outset. In other cases, the results of the earlier steps of design may guide implementation design, as when simulation studies show that the required level of performance requires agents to execute on separate processors. Applicable either to simulated or implemented systems, [23] offers a quantitative method to guide effort in improving the performance of individual agents; perhaps it could be extended to multiagent systems as well.

In the discrete manufacturing example of Section 2.2.1, Operation originally was defined as a particular instance of a Unit Process in space and time. Operation was an agent type through the first design iteration, but detailed implementation-level design showed that the Operation was composed of behaviors that shared high-volume data with Unit Processes and behaviors that shared high-volume data with Resources. Unexpectedly, these two sets of behaviors were separable with relatively low-bandwidth communication. In the actual implementation, there was no Operation agent per se. The Operation became a "virtual agent," occupying a conceptual place in the architecture but with all of its behaviors migrated to Unit Processes and Resources.

5　Summary

Agents in synthetic ecosystems tend to be simpler than those in architectures that support explicit agent cognition, and much of the desired system behavior emerges from the interactions of the agents rather than being computed explicitly within individual agents. Our approach to designing synthetic ecosystems thus pays special attention to exploring these interaction dynamics, relying heavily on role playing and computer simulation to explore and refine the system-level behavior of the agent community.

6　References

1.　J. Bryson. Agent Architecture as Object Oriented Design. In this volume.

2.　B. Burmeister. Models and Methodology for Agent-Oriented Analysis and Design. In *Proceedings of the Workshop on Agent-Oriented Programming and Distributed Systems (KI'96)*, 1996.

3. W.A. Cook. Case Grammar: Development of the Matrix Model. Washington: Georgetown University, 1979.

4. A. Drogoul. When Ants Play Chess (Or Can Strategies Emerge from Tactical Behaviors?) In C. Castelfranchi and J.-P. Müller, editors, *From Reaction to Cognition: Selected Papers, Fifth European Workshop on Modelling Autonomous Agents in a Multi-Agent World (MAAMAW '93)*, pages 13-27, 1995.

5. J. Ferber. *Les systèmes multi-agents: vers une intelligence collective.* Paris: InterEditions, 1995.

6. C.J. Fillmore. The Case for Case Reopened. *Studies in Syntax and Semantics* 8:59-81, 1977.

7. D. Fogel. *Evolutionary Intelligence.* IEEE Press, 1995.

8. R.E. Gustavsson. Multi Agent Systems as Open Societies. In this volume.

9. C.A. Iglesias, M. Garijo, J.C. González, and J.R. Velasco. Analysis and Design of Multiagent Systems using MAS-CommonKADS. In this volume.

10. N.R. Jennings and J.R. Campos. Towards a Social Level Characterization of Socially Responsible Agents. *IEEE Proceedings, Software Engineering* 144(1):11-25, 1997.

11. D. Kinney, M. Georgeff, and A. Rao. A Methodology and Modelling Technique for Systems of BDI Agents. In W. Van de Velde and J.W. Perram, editors, *Agents Breaking Away: Proceedings of MAAMAW '96*, pages 56-71. Berlin: Springer, 1996.

12. P.N. Kugler and M.T. Turvey. *Information, Natural Law, and the Self-Assembly of Rhythmic Movement.* Lawrence Erlbaum, 1987.

13. J. Lee and E.H. Durfee. On Explicit Plan Languages for Coordinating Multiagent Plan Execution. In this volume.

14. M. Lejter and T. Dean. A Framework for the Development of Multiagent Architectures. *IEEE Expert*, December, 47-59, 1996.

15. NASMSB. *Unit Manufacturing Processes: Issues and Opportunities in Research.* Washington, DC: National Academy Press, 1995.

16. M.H. Nodine and A. Unruh. Facilitating Open Communication in Agent Systems: the InfoSleuth Infrastructure. In this volume.

17. H.V.D. Parunak, Workshop Report: Implementing Manufacturing Agents. Sponsored by the Shop Floor Agents Project of the National Center for Manufacturing Sciences in conjunction with PAAM'96, Westminster Central Hall, London, UK, 25 April 1996. http://www.iti.org/~van/paamncms.ps

18. H.V.D. Parunak. Visualizing Agent Conversations: Using Enhanced Dooley Graphs for Agent Design and Analysis. In *Proceedings of ICMAS'96*, pages 275-282, 1996.

19. H.V.D. Parunak, Go to the Ant: Engineering Principles from Natural Multi-Agent Systems. *Annals of Operations Research*, forthcoming. Also http://www.iti.org/~van/gotoant.ps

20. M.J. Pont and E. Moreale. *Towards a Practical Methodology for Agent-Oriented Software Engineering with C++ and Java*. Technical Report 96-33, Leicester University Department of Engineering, Dec. 1996.

21. G.C. Roman. A Taxonomy of Current Issues in Requirements Engineering. *IEEE Computer*, April, 14-22, 1985.

22. J. Rumbaugh, M. Blaha, W. Premerlani, F. Eddy, and W. Lorensen *Object-Oriented Modeling and Design*. Englewood Cliffs: Prentice Hall, 1991.

23. M. Schoppers and D. Shapiro. Designing Embedded Agents to Optimize End-User Objectives. In this volume.

24. M. Singh. A Customizable Coordination Service for Autonomous Agents. In this volume.

25. L. Steels and R. Brooks, editors. *The Artificial Life Route to Artificial Intelligence: Building Embodied, Situated Agents*. Hillsdale: Lawrence Erlbaum, 1995.

26. J. Treur and M. Willems. Formal Notions for Verification of Dynamics of Knowledge-Based Systems. In M. Ayel and M.C. Rousset, editors, *Proceedings of the European Symposium on the Validation and Verification of Knowledge-Based Systems, EUROVAV'95*, pages 189-199. Chambéry: ADERIAS-LIA, 1995.

27. T. Wittig, editor. *ARCHON: An Architecture for Multi-Agent Systems*. New York: Ellis Horwood, 1992.

Bidding Mechanisms for Data Allocation in Multi-Agent Environments *

Rina Schwartz* and Sarit Kraus*†

* Department of Mathematics and Computer Science,
Bar-Ilan University, Ramat-Gan, 52900 Israel
{schwart,sarit}@macs.biu.ac.il

† Institute for Advanced Computer Studies,
University of Maryland, College Park, MD 20742

Abstract. We propose a bidding mechanism for data allocation in environments of self-motivated data servers with no common preferences and no central controller. The model considers situations where each server is concerned with the data stored locally, but does not have preferences concerning the exact storage location of data stored in remote servers. We considered situations of complete, as well as incomplete, information, and formally proved that our method is stable and yields honest bids. In the case of complete information, we also proved that the results obtained by the bidding approach are always better than the results obtained by the static allocation policy currently used for data allocation for servers in distributed systems. In the case of incomplete information, we demonstrated, using simulations, that the quality of the bidding mechanism is, on average, better than that of the static policy.

1 Introduction

In this paper, we consider the problem of determining the location of data items in a distributed information system, where the information servers are self-motivated and each one is trying to maximize its own utility.

A specific example of a distributed knowledge system is the Data and Information System component of the Earth Observing System (EOSDIS) of NASA [7], which supports archiving and distribution of data at multiple and independent data centers (called DAACs). The current policy for data allocation in NASA is static: each DAAC specializes in specific topics. When new data arrive at a DAAC, it checks if the data are relevant to its topics, and if so, it uses other criteria, such as storage cost, to decide whether or not to accept the data and store it in its database. If the data is not relevant to the DAAC, it may forward it to another DAAC whose topics seem more relevant.

In this paper, we propose the use of a bidding mechanism as a solution method for the data allocation problem in environments where the servers are self-motivated and have no common preferences and no central controller.[2] In addition, a server is

---

* This material is based upon work supported in part by NSF under Grant No. IRI-9423967. Rina Schwartz is supported by the Israeli Ministry of Science.

[2] Previous work on file (data) allocation in distributed systems (e.g., [3]) considers systems where a central decision maker exists, which tries to maximize the performance of the overall system. This assumption is not valid today in many cases, when the objective is to distribute information among self-motivated servers.

concerned about the data stored locally, but does not have preferences concerning the exact storage location of data stored in remote servers. According to our approach, the location of each data unit will be determined using a bidding mechanism, where the server bidding the higher price for obtaining the data will actually obtain it.[3] This approach yields an efficient and fair solution, its implementation is simple, and the bidders are motivated to offer efficient prices.

Bidding has been used previously in Distributed Artificial Intelligence (DAI) in the contract net framework [12]. Agents in the contract net environment decompose their tasks to subtasks and subcontract them to other agents, using bidding. Extensions of the contract net for environments with self-motivated agents were proposed in [9]. Mullen and Wellman [6] proposed a market price model for decisions about establishing mirror sites in a network. They suggested competitive-market pricing of the transportation price (when no mirror site is established) and the price of establishing mirror sites. However, the competitive approach is not useful in our environment since it is applicable only in environments in which it is possible to produce more than one item of each product type, and in our environment each data item is unique.

A bidding mechanism is suggested by [8] for an automated negotiation environment, where phone companies compete to serve as carriers for long distance phone calls, with dynamic prices. In particular, they propose the use of *Vickrey's sealed bidding scheme* [13]. In this kind of auction, each bidder submits one bid, in ignorance of the other bids, and the highest bidder pays the amount of the second-highest bid and wins. In this paper, we have implemented a sealed bidding scheme for the data allocation problem in distributed knowledge environments. We have specified the rules of the bidding in the case of data allocation and suggested strategies for the servers.

In the following, we will describe the data allocation problem and suggest a utility function which characterizes the servers' preferences. Then we will suggest a bidding protocol, which is a dominant strategy mechanism [5]. We will also consider the incomplete information case, where each server has information only about past usage frequency of local data, and we suggest how it can estimate its utility from other data items (new or remote ones) in order to bid efficiently for them. We will discuss the servers' performance in the complete information case, as well as in the incomplete information case.

2 Environment Description

We consider an environment in which there is a set of several (more than two) information servers, denoted by SERVERS, connected by a communications network. The information stored in each information server is clustered in datasets.[4] Each dataset is characterized by a set of keywords and contains a large number of documents.[5] The set

---

[3] Only one copy of each dataset is allowed, since the datasets considered are extremely large, and it is not efficient to allow multiple copies of a dataset. However, if the datasets are small it is possible to extend the model to allow multiple copies of each dataset.

[4] A dataset corresponds to a *cluster* in information retrieval, and to a *file* in the file allocation problem.

[5] A document corresponds to a 'granule' in EOSDIS.

of datasets in the system in a given time period is denoted by DS.

In this paper, we consider an information system where each client retrieves information directly from the server in which it is stored, and s/he pays this server for the retrieved information. Therefore, in our environment, a server is concerned only with the datasets stored in its local databases, and is indifferent to the exact location of datasets not stored locally. The environment we consider changes dynamically. New datasets arrive frequently, and usage frequency of old datasets changes over time. The servers have to determine the location in which each new dataset will be stored and they are also able to change the location of old datasets. Since the datasets considered are very large, each dataset can be stored only in one server, and it is forbidden for a server to store a dataset unless it has become its legal "owner." Conflicts among the servers may arise when two or more servers would like to store the same dataset locally.

In a centralized system, a solution for such a problem is simple: the location of each dataset will be determined so as to maximize the profits of the entire system. But a dataset allocation which is beneficial for the entire system may be non-beneficial for some of the servers. In our case, where each server has its own interests, the servers will follow the centralized solution only if it is beneficial to them. Thus, any proposed protocol must be fair and consider the preferences of all the servers in order to be accepted by the designers of the servers. Moreover, if there is incomplete information about the usage of datasets, then the centralized solution is not applicable, since nobody has enough information in order to compute this solution.

In all the situations which we considered, the servers are uncertain about the future usage of the datasets. First, we have considered a symmetric environment with *complete information*, where all the servers have the same knowledge about the past, and they have the same expectations about the future usage of each dataset by clients located in each area, but they do not know the actual future usage. Then, we have considered an asymmetric environment with *incomplete information*, where each server knows the past usage only of the datasets stored locally, but can only partially estimate the past usage of datasets stored by other servers.

3 Utility Functions

In this section, we will describe the components of the utility derived by a server from storing a dataset. Recall that each server receives queries from clients and answers them by sending back documents which belong to a datasets located in its databases. The clients pay the server a *query_price* per document that is retrieved as an answer to a query. We assume that there is a monetary system in the environment which is used for this payment, as well as for other payments described below.

The cost of sending a document to a client depends on the virtual distance between the client and the server. It is measured in terms of delivery time, which plays an important role in loaded systems in which the documents are very large (e.g., images). The function *distance* specifies the virtual distance between any two servers. For simplicity, we assume that each client is located in a geographical area of one of the servers, and in order to compute the distance between server i and a client which is located in the geographical area of server j, we use the distance between servers i and j. The term *answer_cost* specifies the cost for a server providing a client from another area with one document over one unit of distance.

Another important factor of the utility function is the usage of this dataset by clients. $Usage : SERVERS \times DS \mapsto R^+$ is a function which associates with each server and dataset the number of documents belonging to this dataset which will be requested by clients located in the geographical area of that server, during one time period (e.g., one week, one month, etc.). In addition, we denote by *storage_cost* the cost of storing locally one data unit for one time period [6] and the function *dataset_size* specifies the size of each dataset in data units. Each server calculates the utility it obtains from a dataset location, given its estimation of the expected query flows related to this dataset. Note that *storage_cost* and *answer_cost* are common to all the servers, and this is known to all servers. The following attribute defines the utility (or loss) for a server in one time period from one dataset stored in it, when its usage is known.

Attribute 3.1 *The profits which server s expects to obtain from storing dataset ds locally for one time period are as follows:*

$$V_s(ds) = -storage\_cost * dataset\_size(ds) + \sum_{s' \in SERVERS}(usage(s', ds) * (query\_price - distance(s, s') * answer\_cost)).$$

V_s considers the costs and benefits due to queries which are obtained at one time period, and also the storage cost which is expected to be paid at each time period (e.g., using the disk space).

The following attribute defines the profits P_s which server s expects to obtain from storing one dataset over time. We assume that there is a monetary system in which each server is able to borrow any required amount of money at the current interest rate r. Using this interest rate, P_s is evaluated as the net present value (NPV) of future income from queries related to the dataset, computed w.r.t. the interest rate r. The NPV is used in financing systems in order to find the value of an investment. It is computed by discounting the cash flows at the firm's "opportunity cost" of capital [2]. We will use the same term for finding the value of a dataset storage, considering the dataset as a possible investment.

Attribute 3.2 *The profits which server s expects to obtain from a dataset ds located in loc from time 0 until time N, given V_s, is as follows:*

$$P_s(ds, loc) = \begin{cases} \sum_{t=0}^{N} \frac{V_s(ds)}{(1+r)^t} & loc = s \\ 0 & otherwise. \end{cases}$$

where r is the interest rate, and N is the number of periods during which the environment exists. If the environment is considered to exist forever, then $N = \infty$. In this case,

$$P_s(ds, loc) = \frac{V_s(ds) * (1 + r)}{r}.$$

---

[6] For simplicity, we assume that storage space is not restricted.

The function above specifies the net present value of the profits flow accepted by server s related to dataset ds, assuming that ds will be stored in loc indefinitely. In subsection 5.5 we will discuss the expected profits for situations where old datasets can be reallocated.

We denote by $U_s(ds, loc)$ the utility which a server s obtains from a dataset ds which is stored in location loc. In order to evaluate U_s, the server will consider the expected profits as well as the risk involved in obtaining these profits. Such a risk is involved in both the complete and the incomplete environments which we consider in this paper, since in both cases, *usage* is only estimated, and the server is not sure about the value of a dataset, since the queries flow is not certain and thus the payments due to queries are not certain. If s is risk neutral, i.e., its utility is determined only regarding its expected profits [4], then its utility function is the same as its expected profits, and $U_s(ds, loc) = P_s(ds, loc)$. Otherwise, if s is risk averse, then the uncertainty involved in future queries flows will influence the utility it derives from storing the dataset, so U_s will be risk adjusted in order to consider the element of uncertainty involved in its expected profits [2], i.e., $U_s(ds, loc) < P_s(ds, loc)$. Similarly, if s is risk prone, then $U_s(ds, loc) > P_s(ds, loc)$. In the following sections, unless explicitly written, we assume risk neutral servers.

4 The Trading Mechanism

Bidding sessions are carried on during predefined time periods. When new datasets arrive, they are stored in a temporary buffer until the next bidding session, when their location will be decided upon. Each server is represented by an automated agent, which participates in the bidding session. In the rest of the paper we will use a server and its agent interchangeably.

Each server is responsible for the datasets it stores, and the initial responsibility for each new dataset is determined according to a static policy: the server with the areas of interest closest to a new dataset will be responsible for it.[7] At the beginning of a bidding session, each agent broadcasts an announcement for each new dataset it is responsible for, and also for some of its old local datasets. An announcement of the availability of a dataset by agent $s \in$ SERVERS, denoted as the contractor, indicates that agent s would like to *sell* this dataset.

In the next step of the bidding session, for each announcement and for each agent $s' \in$ SERVERS, such that s' is not the contractor which has made the announcement, s' sends a *sealed bid* to the contractor. A bid contains the price, in standard currency, which s' is willing to pay the contractor in order to store the dataset made available in the announcement in s' (i.e., to *buy* the dataset.) If it does not want to buy this dataset, it will bid a negative price, which indicates how much it would like the contractor to pay it, in order for it to agree to store this dataset locally. All the bids must be sent up until a predefined deadline. The contractor of each dataset collects all the bids related to this dataset up to the deadline.

---

[7] The initial owner can be determined by the source of the information, which will direct the dataset to the server with the nearest topics

In the third step of the bidding session, which is called the awarding step, the winner of each announcement is determined by its contractor. For each announcement, the winning agent will be the agent with the highest bid, but the price it pays will be determined according to the second highest bid. The price paid is based on *Vickrey's sealed bidding*, and the bidding of true values is a dominant strategy in this protocol. That is, for each dataset, the best bidding strategy for each agent is to bid a price which is equal to its utility from storing this dataset, and this is independent of the other bids [13].

In the awarding step, each agent will broadcast an award message for all announcements it made in the first step. In this message, it will include the "winner" of the dataset, which is the highest bidder, the price it has to pay, as well as the agent that sent the second-highest bid.[8] If the second bid is less than the utility the contractor derives from storing the dataset of the announcement by itself, or if there is only one bidder (which is a rare event, since all servers are supposed to send a bid for each dataset), then the contractor will continue to store the dataset locally (or obtain it, if the dataset is new).

The agents are assumed to be self-interested, and each one tries to maximize its own utility. In order to do so, it is able to borrow money at the current interest rate r. Thus, the agents do not need any initial budget.

We suggest that bidding for different datasets will take place simultaneously, since if the usage of different datasets is correlated (when they include similar keywords), then a server may update its expectations according to its knowledge about the bids of the other servers for the previous datasets.

In our protocol, there is no need to synchronize the announcements and awarding messages of different datasets. Simultaneous announcement of awards is not necessary, since we assume that the utility from one dataset location is independent of the location of other datasets. The simultaneous bidding is also unnecessary, since as we will show below, the dominant strategy for each bidder is to bid its true value, and this holds also if it has information regarding the other bids.

5 Attributes of the Bidding Protocol

In this section we will describe some of the attributes of the bidding protocol. We will prove that it is a dominant strategy mechanism, and we will present a strategy that enables an agent to choose datasets to announce when the announcement process is costly.

5.1 Details of the Protocol

In the following, we present the costs and concepts related to the bidding process. The function *contractor* specifies for each dataset its current "owner", which will be its contractor during the bidding session. For an old dataset, this is the server where it is currently stored, and for a new dataset, this is the server which is responsible for this

---

[8] Specifying the agent that sent the second-highest bid in the award message prevent the auctioneer from overstating the second highest bid [10].

dataset (as explained in section 4). The function *move_cost* associates with a dataset, *ds*, and a server the cost for the server *contractor*(*ds*) to move the dataset from it to the specified server. If the dataset is new, then it is stored in the temporary buffer, and *contractor*(*ds*) has no costs involved in moving it, so *move_cost* is 0. The function *obtain_cost* associates with a dataset and a server, the cost for the server to move a dataset to its location from the server *contractor*(*dataset*), if it is an old dataset, or from the temporary buffer otherwise. Relocating datasets is costly both to the sender and the receiver, since we take into consideration the communication time required on both sides in order to reallocate a dataset. But, allocating a dataset in its initial location causes costs only to the buyer, since it receives the dataset from the temporary buffer, but doesn't use the contractor's resources, since it is not the sender in that case. Finally, we denote by *price_suggested(b,ds)* the price suggested by bidder *b* for dataset *ds*.

After a contractor announces a dataset, each server sends the contractor a bid concerning this dataset. Sending a bid is free (all the costs related to the process of bidding for a dataset are covered by its contractor). Thus, in general, each agent will send a bid for any dataset that is announced. The contractor for each dataset collects all the bids related to this dataset until a predefined deadline occurs. Then it has to decide whether to move the dataset, and if so, where to move it to. The function *move*(*ds*) will associate "true" with a dataset *ds*, if the agent *contractor*(*ds*) can beneficially move the dataset to another server, given a set of bids, and "false," otherwise. Further discussion on *move*(*ds*) appears below. If the contractor decides to move the dataset, it must abide by the following regulations of our bidding protocol. Deviation from this protocol is revealed immediately and yields a penalty. The following attribute defines the winner of a dataset, as determined by the protocol proposed here.

Attribute 5.1

$$
winner(ds) = \begin{cases} argmax_{bidder \in SERVERS} & move(ds) = true \\ price\_suggested(bidder, ds) - \\ move\_cost(ds, bidder) \} \\ \\ none & otherwise. \end{cases}
$$

If there is more than one bidder with the same maximal value of
$price\_suggested(bidder, ds) - move\_cost(ds, bidder)$, then the contractor will select one of them (arbitrarily) to be the *winner*, and the other will be considered to be the bidder with the second best bid.

The price paid by the winning agent (if it exists) is the second best bid, w.r.t. the net suggested price. That is, if the dataset is new, then the final price will be precisely the amount of the second best bid, and if the dataset is old and already stored by the contractor, then the final price will be the second best price, deducting the costs of moving the dataset to the bidder of the second best price, but including the costs of moving the dataset to the winner. Our protocol is different from the basic bidding protocol [13], since we include the payments of the relocation costs in the protocol, and thus the desired properties of the bidding mechanism should be proved for this modified protocol.

Attribute 5.2 *The price which will be paid by the winning agent is:*

> $price(ds)=$
> $second\_max_{bidder \neq contractor(ds)} \{price\_suggested(bidder, ds) -$
> $move\_cost(ds, bidder) \mid bidder \in SERVERS\} + move\_cost(ds, winner).$

As mentioned above, the contractor must specify the winner, the second price and the agents which offered the second price in its awarding message, and there is a high penalty for revealed lies. It is easy to show that if there is a penalty for revealed lies, then the contractor would follow the regulation above. It will not be motivated to specify a price higher than the second price in its awarding message, since such a lie can be revealed immediately by the agent that is specified by the contractor as the sender of the second price. It would also not be motivated to specify a lower price, since this would never be beneficial for it.

5.2 Bidding Strategies

Given the above regulations in the bidding protocol, and given a set of bids, the contractor will decide whether or not to move an old dataset, i.e., whether $move(ds)$ is true or false. We suggest that the contractor move a dataset if the utility it is able to derive from selling it is more than the utility it can derive from continuing to store the dataset, (if there is only one bidder, then the dataset will not be moved). Note that this is not part of the regulations, but is the best strategy for a self-motivated contractor if it must choose the price and the winner, as described above.

Attribute 5.3 *Situations in which it is beneficial for the contractor to move ds, are:*

> $move(ds)=true$ if
> $|bidders| > 1$ and $second\_max\{price\_suggested(bidder, ds) -$
> $move\_cost(ds, bidder) \mid bidder \in SERVERS\} \geq$
> $U_{contractor(ds)}(ds, contractor(ds)).$

In the following lemma we state that the winning agent will derive a nonnegative utility from obtaining the dataset.

Lemma 1. *If there is a winner of an announcement, and if it is chosen as specified in attribute 5.1 and is paid price(ds) as specified in attribute 5.2, then if the winner's bid was exactly equal to its utility from obtaining the dataset, it will have a nonnegative utility from "buying" the dataset, deducting the price it should pay.*

Proof. Denote by *winner* the winning agent, by *second* the agent with the second offer, and by *ds* the dataset being considered. Suppose the winner offered exactly the utility it will derive from obtaining the dataset. Then, the utility which the winner will derive obtaining *dataset* is exactly $price\_suggested(winner, ds)$. The price it will have to pay is: $price\_suggested(second, ds) - move\_cost(ds, second) + move\_cost(ds, winner)$. By definition,
$price\_suggested(second, ds) - move\_cost(ds, second))$ is lower or equal than the chosen $price\_suggested(winner, ds) - move\_cost(ds, winner))$.

Thus, $price\_suggested(second, ds) - move\_cost(ds, second) +$
$move\_cost(ds, winner) \leq price\_suggested(winner, ds)$. □

Now we will state that each agent's bid will be equal to its utility from obtaining the dataset, for each dataset.

Lemma 2. *In a protocol where the best bidder wins and pays the second price as specified in attributes 5.1 and 5.2, each bidder will bid its utility from storing this dataset, deducting the cost of obtaining it. i.e.,*

$$price\_suggested(bidder, ds) = U_{bidder}(ds, bidder) - obtain\_cost(ds, bidder).$$

Bidding the real utility is the dominant strategy, and the proof is similar to that of the Vickrey auction [13]. However, in our case, the winner incurs expenses related to obtaining the dataset, and the contractor incurs expenses related to moving the datasets to the winner (costs of resources needed for the move). Thus, the price paid by the winner is different than the second price, as described in attribute 5.2. Another difference is that, in our case, the contractor itself has its own interests and preferences and has the ability not to move a dataset if the offers it receives are too low, as described in attribute 5.3. These changes cause the proof to be slightly different from the original. Using the above lemmas we have proved the following theorem.

Theorem 3. *If bidding is free, then the allocation reached by the bidding protocol always yields better or equal utility for each server than does using the static policy. The utility function of each server is evaluated according to its expected profits from the allocation.*

In summary, the protocol which we suggest can be implemented in a distributed system in which no central controller exists: its implementation is stable and will ensure satisfactory results. However, even though bidding the true utility of obtaining the dataset is a dominant strategy, it may be beneficial for the first and second bidders to cooperate based on an agreement negotiated between them prior to the bidding, so that the second bidder will bid a lower price, and the first bidder - the winner - will pay a reduced amount. That is, bidding the true utility is not in a strong Nash equilibrium [1], since there may be a subgroup of agents which can gain when they deviate together from the suggested strategies. If communication during the bidding process is forbidden, then the servers will not be able to cooperate. In situations where cooperation may occur, if there is complete information, then should the agents cooperate, the same winner will be chosen per dataset (as in the case of honest reports), so that the bidding process will result in the same allocation, but the gains will be distributed differently among the agents.[9] In situations of incomplete information, the "winner" is not known before the bidding begins, and in order to lower prices cooperation among bidders is not stable, since an agent may agree to bid a low price and then bid a higher one in order to obtain the dataset for itself.

---

[9] Note, however, that if there is complete information, a simple protocol which enforces bidding the expected utility can be used.

5.3 Estimating Usage

In our environment, the storage costs and answer costs of the servers are common knowledge, but the servers may have asymmetric information about the past usage volume of the clients, and thus the agents will have an asymmetric and uncertain information about the future usage of datasets. Each agent knows only the past usage of its local datasets, so it will estimate the future usage of these datasets for each geographical area, using its knowledge of the past usage. Estimating the future usage of new datasets and datasets located in remote servers is more difficult, since the agent has no knowledge regarding their past usage. In order to accomplish this, the agent will use information about the datasets' contents. Each dataset is characterized by several keywords, and each query consists of keywords. When a query is handled, the server saves the information about the query, including the keywords which the query contains, i.e., the agent saves the past usage of each area for each keyword and each local dataset.

When an estimation about a new or remote dataset is required, the agent uses the information it has about the keywords' past usage and computes the expected usage of the dataset according to the keywords it is familiar with. The future usage of a new dataset by each geographical area can also be estimated according to the past usage of similar datasets, when their similarity is measured according to the keyword contents.

For simplicity, we assume that the clients form their queries according to keywords and that each query is sent to all the datasets containing that keyword. Under these assumptions, an agent can determine the usage frequency of a new or remote dataset ds for a given area to be the sum of the usage frequency of all the keywords contained in ds. If it does not have data about a keyword which is associated with ds, i.e., no local dataset contains this keyword, then it can use the average usage frequency of all the keywords for the unknown value.

Formally, suppose that there where T time periods before the current bidding session, $key\_usage(area, key)$ indicates the volume of usage of key in different queries of clients located in the area of $server$ in the previous time periods, $dataset\_usage(area, ds)$ indicates the volume of usage of ds by $area$ in the previous time periods, and $exp\_usage_s(area, ds)$ indicates the expectations of agent s about the usage of ds by $area$; then

$$exp\_usage_s(area, ds) = \begin{cases} dataset\_usage(area, ds)/T & \text{contractor(ds)=s} \\ & \text{and is\_old(ds)} \\ \sum_{key \in ds} key\_usage(area, key)/T & otherwise. \end{cases}$$

A more complex learning schema may be considered in order to estimate the future usage of datasets for situations where queries are formed differently, when keywords are related, etc., but we leave this for future work. After estimating the future usage of a dataset, the agent can compute its expected utility from obtaining the dataset, according to the utility function we presented above and w.r.t. the risk involved, as described in Section 3.

5.4 Choosing Datasets

Another issue related to the bidding protocol is how an agent should choose a beneficial set of datasets to announce for bidding. If there is no cost associated with dataset announcement and bidding, then each agent will announce all its datasets, including all its old datasets. However, the announcements can be expensive, due to costs of time and communication. Alternatively, the bidding protocol can limit the number of datasets which an agent can announce, for environments with a large number of datasets. In such cases, each agent will have to select carefully which datasets to announce.

In order to estimate *exp_announcement_profit*, which denotes the profits the agent expects to obtain from an announcement, the agent has to estimate which prices it will receive as bids. According to lemma 1, the price which each agent will offer is equal to its utility from storing the dataset, deducting the cost for obtaining the dataset. Thus, in order to decide which dataset to announce, an agent has to estimate the expected utility of the other agents and to compute the expected price it will obtain. The next attribute defines the profit which the agent expects to derive from an announcement. In particular, the expected profit includes the payments which are expected to be obtained forselling the dataset (*expected_price(ds)*), deducting the utility from continuing to store the dataset and the cost of moving the dataset to the new location. If the profit from moving the dataset is negative, then the contractor will continue to store the dataset, and, in this case, the profit of the announcement is zero.

Attribute 5.4 *The expected profit from announcing a dataset ds:*

$exp\_announcement\_profit \ (ds) =$
$$max\{0, expected\_price(ds) - move\_cost(ds, expected\_winner(ds)) - U_{contractor(ds)}(dataset, contractor(ds))\}.$$

If the contractor is risk neutral, it will announce only those datasets which the expected profit of announcing them exceeds the cost of the announcing process. If there is a limit on the number of the announcements, it will announce the datasets with the highest expected profits. If the contractor is risk averse, then it will consider in its evaluation the risk involved in the expected price it will obtain, and the risk involved in its expected profits from retaining the dataset.

As described above, in order to determine *expected_price(ds)* and to compute *exp_announcement_profit(ds)*, the agent, s, needs to estimate the prices of ds which would be offered by the bidders. The price offered by a bidder $\hat{s}$ depends on its utility function ($U_{\hat{s}}$), which takes into consideration its expectations of the usage of dataset ds by other servers.

Thus, in order to evaluate the expected profit of announcing a dataset, the potential contractor needs to estimate the function *expected_usage$_{\hat{s}}$(s, ds)*. If the agent does not have information about $\hat{s}$'s estimation, we propose that it should use its own estimation of the expected usage, which is computed as specified in Section 5.3, as the estimation of $\hat{s}$, i.e., we will assume that *expected_usage$_{\hat{s}}$ = expected_usage$_s$*. If the agent knows which keywords appear in $\hat{s}$'s datasets, it can estimate *expected_usage$_{\hat{s}}$* by using only the keywords that appear both in its own datasets and in $\hat{s}$'s datasets. This may lead to a better estimation of the other agent's beliefs.

5.5 Utility Function - Relocation Case

In Section 3 we defined the profits which a server expects to obtain from storing a dataset indefinitely. However, there is a possibility that at some future time, the dataset will be moved to another server. This could happen if its owner announces it, and is offered compensation which is at least equivalent to the expected profit obtained while continuing to store the dataset. In such cases, when evaluating the expected profits of the server for storing a dataset, we have to take into consideration both the costs and benefits associated with this dataset, and the price it expects to receive for this dataset in the future, if it is sold. Formally, the profits that server s expects to derive from obtaining dataset ds, at time t, are as follows:

$$P_s(ds, s, t) = V_s(ds) + max\{P_s(ds, s, t+1),$$
$$expected\_price_{t+1} - move\_cost(ds, expected\_winner(ds))$$
$$+P_s(ds, remote \neq s, t+1)\}/(1+r).$$

where r is the interest rate, $expected\_price_{t+1}$ denotes the payments expected to be obtained from selling the dataset at time $t+1$. $move\_cost(ds, expected\_winner(ds))$ denotes the cost of moving the dataset from the winner at time t to $expected\_winner(ds)$; and, $P_s(ds, remote \neq s, t+1)$ specifies the profits the server expects to obtain from not storing the dataset at time $t+1$.

The profits that a server expects to obtain from not storing the dataset at time t are composed of a profit of 0 at the current time period, but it has to take into consideration the possibility of obtaining this dataset in the future. Formally, we state that

$$P_s(ds, remote \neq s, t) =$$
$$max\{P_s(ds, s, t+1) - expected\_price_{t+1} - obtain\_cost(ds, s),$$
$$P_s(ds, remote \neq s, t+1)\}/(1+r).$$

However, if the agents believe at time t that in time $t+1$ their expectations of the usage at time $t+1$ will be the same as their current expectations of the usage at time $t+1$, they also believe that no reallocation will be done at time $t+1$, i.e., $U_s(ds, s, t+1) > expected\_price_{t+1} - move\_cost(ds, expected\_winner(ds)) + U_s(ds, remote \neq s, t+1)$ and then we get that $U_s(ds, s, t) = V_s + U_s(ds, s, t+1)/(1+r)$. Expanding this formula, we get that $U_s(ds, s, t) = V_s + \frac{V_s}{1+r} + \frac{V_s}{(1+r)^2} + ... + \frac{V_s}{(1+r)^N}$, which is the utility function defined in Section 3.

The same assumptions will also simplify $P_s(ds, remote \neq s, t)$, since if the agents believe that they will not significanlty change their expected usage of the datasets in the future, then they also believe that datasets will rarely be relocated. Thus, we assume, for simplicity, that the utility for s of storing a dataset on a remote server is 0.

We leave for future research the formulation of the explicit formulas of the general case, where an agent at time t may believe that some of the agents will have a different expectation at time t+1.

6 Experimental Evaluation

In order to test the bidding techniques and compare them with other approaches, we designed and implemented a simulation of our servers' environment. In comparing the performance of the approaches, we used a measurement which excluded the payments of users for their queries and the storage costs, since the total values of these costs do

	vcost ratio	CU	CI
static	*	0.22266	*
bidding	0.7375	0.22255	1.0683
optimal	0.6798	0.45966	43.289

Table 1. Bidding in Complete Information Situations.

not depend on a specific allocation. So their influence on the sum of the servers' utilities does not depend on a specific allocation. In particular, we denote by $vcosts(alloc)$ the variable costs of an allocation which consists of the transportation costs due to the flow of queries. Formally, given an allocation, its variable cost is defined as follows:

$$vcosts(alloc) = \sum_{ds \in DS} \sum_{s \in SERVERS} usage(s, ds) * distance(s, alloc(ds)) * answer\_cost.$$

The actual measurement we use is denoted by $vcost\_ratio$ – the ratio of the variable cost of the bidding mechanism (or another mechanism, as specified below) and the variable cost of the static allocation. The efficiency of the bidding technique increases as $vcost\_ratio$ decreases.

First we tested the bidding mechanism where the agents have complete information about each other and about the environment. In particular, all the agents have the same estimation of future usage of datasets, but are still uncertain about the actual future usage. In such cases, a first bid protocol can be used too, since no server can lie. However, we check the results of the second bid protocol, in order to evaluate the loss of using a second bid protocol w.r.t. using the first bid protocol. We compared three different methods: static allocation, an optimal allocation using a central algorithm which maximizes the sum of all the servers' utilities, and our bidding mechanism.

In Table 1 we present the results of 50 runs of randomly generated environments, with 200 old datasets and 20 new ones, in environments where the relocation of old datasets is seldom beneficial since the size of the datasets is very large. The second column (vcost ratio) in Table 1 specifies the average of $vcost\_ratio$ of the new datasets and the datasets which were reallocated. This measurement excludes the costs of old datasets not moved in that environment. The third column (CU) indicates the average of the relative dispersion of the utility due to the new datasets and the ones that were moved among the agents (std util/mean util). The last column (CI) specifies the average of the relative dispersion of the added benefit of the new datasets and the old ones that were moved. The variable costs obtained via the bidding mechanism were better than the static policy results, but were not as good as the results obtained by the central optimization algorithm.

We observed that the only case in which the bidding mechanism and the central optimization algorithm located datasets differently were for datasets in which their contractor's utility of storing them locally was higher than its utility of selling them according to the second price, but lower than its utility of selling them according to the first price, causing the contractor to prefer not to sell them. This effect is caused by the use of the second-price bidding. However, the bidding mechanism has an advantage since, in any

	vcost ratio	CU	CI
static	*	0.218161	*
bidding	0.791596	0.217939	1.56416
centralized	0.68908	0.441369	41.1896
optimal	0.685007	0.45565	42.3611

Table 2. Bidding in Incomplete Information Situation.

situation, it guarantees each server a utility which is at least the utility it could obtain via the static policy. We notice that the bidding mechanism yields a lower dispersion of the utility among the agents, w.r.t. the central algorithm. That is, maximizing the sum of utilities by the central algorithm yields a higher dispersion, with some agents unsatisfied with the results. This was prevented, however, by the monetary system of the bidding mechanism, which causes the dispersion of the utilities while using the bidding mechanism to be lower and similar to that of the static allocation.

In the second set of experiments we introduced incomplete information concerning the future usage of the datasets, (i.e., the agents didn't know the mean usage by clients in each area of each dataset) and asymmetric information about past usage. To simulate such situations, we implemented a system in which queries are sent according to keyword frequency to the servers. First, the mean usage of each keyword by each geographical area is randomly generated. Then the queries generator sends queries, such that the number of queries concerning a given keyword sent from a specified geographical area is generated using Poisson distribution, with the specified mean usage. Each server receives queries related to its own datasets and maintains the statistical information for estimating the future use. However, it has no knowledge about the queries which were sent to the other servers.

We assume that each agent knows the keywords of the datasets located in the other servers. Based on the queries sent to it w.r.t. these keywords, the agent estimates the usage of the other datasets, as described in section 5.3. Thus, as the number of keywords in the system increases while the number of datasets is kept fixed, each server has less information about the usage frequency of datasets (since there are keywords that the agent does not have in its datasets) and incomplete information in the system increases.

In Table 2 we present the results obtained from a simulation of 50 randomly created environments where there was some incomplete information in the system (the mean error of the expectations was 13%). We compared the results obtained by the static allocation, the bidding allocation, the centralized allocation which is obtained when maximizing the sum of servers' utilities using all the information stored by all the servers, and the optimal allocation found by a centralized algorithm which also maximizes the sum of servers utilities but has the real usage frequency. We see that the bidding allocation succeeds in reducing the average variable costs of a server, although there is a gap between its performance and the performance of the centralized allocations. This gap was caused since each server had only partial information about the future usage of datasets. However, the bidding mechanism obtained a much lower standard deviation than the centralized alternatives. We also carried out a set of simulations to test the effect of the amount of incomplete information in the system on the bidding performance, by varying the number of keywords while keeping the number of datasets fixed. As would be expected, we found that *vcost_ratio* decreases (i.e., the level of improvement w.r.t. the static allocation increases) as there is more information.

7 Conclusion

This paper presents a bidding protocol for the data allocation problem in multi-agent environments. For complete information, we have formally proved that bidding yields efficient and fair results. For situations in which the agents have incomplete information, we ran simulations, and the results of the bidding approach were, on the average, better than those of the static policy.

In environments in which each server cares about the exact location of each dataset, even when such a location is remote, a bidding protocol is not beneficial, since the server's agent cannot influence the location of such a dataset. For such environments, we suggest elsewhere [11] using the strategic model of alternating offers as a solution method, enabling each agent to influence the decision of the exact location of each dataset, even without storing it locally. We showed, however, that bidding is better than strategic negotiations in the environments considered in this paper.

References

1. B.D. Bernheim, B. Peleg, and M.D. Whinston. Coalition-Proof Nash Equilibria I: Concepts. *J. of Economic Theory*, 42, 1:1–12, 1987.
2. T. E. Copeland and J. F. Weston. *Financial Theory and Corporate Policy*. Addison-Wesley publishing company, 1992.
3. X. Du and Fred J. Maryanski. Data allocation in a dynamically reconfigurable environment. In *Proc. of the IEEE Fourth Int. Conf. Data Engineering*, pages 74–81, Los Angeles, 1988.
4. S. French. *Decision Theory: An Introduction to the Mathematics of Rationality*. Ellis Horwood Limited, 1986.
5. D. Fudenberg and J. Tirole. *Game Theory*. MIT Press, Cambridge, Ma, 1991.
6. T. Mullen and M. Wellman. A simple computational market for network information services. In *Proc. of the First International Conference on Multiagent Systems*, pages 283–289, California, USA, 1995.
7. NASA. EOSDIS Home Page. http://www-v0ims.gsfc.nasa.gov/v0ims/index.html, 1996.
8. J. S. Rosenschein and G. Zlotkin. *Rules of Encounter: Designing Conventions for Automated Negotiation Among Computers*. MIT Press, Boston, 1994.
9. T. Sandholm. An implementation of the contract net protocol based on marginal cost calculations. In *Proc. of AAAI-93*, pages 256–262, 1993.
10. T. W. Sandholm. Limitations of the vickrey auction in computational multiagent systems. In *International Conference on Multiagent Systems (ICMAS-96)*, pages 299–306, Kyoto, Japan, 1996.
11. R. Schwartz and S. Kraus. Negotiation on data allocation in multi-agent environments. In *Proc. of AAAI-97*, pages 29–35, Providence, Rhode Island, 1997.
12. R.G. Smith and R. Davis. Negotiation as a metaphor for distributed problem solving. *Artificial Intelligence*, 20:63–109, 1983.
13. William Vickrey. Counterspeculation, auctions, and competitive sealed tenders. *J. of Finance*, 16:8–37, 1961.

Distributed Storage of Replicated Beliefs to Facilitate Recovery of Distributed Intelligent Agents

Arvind K. Bansal[*], Kotagiri Ramohanarao[†], and Anand Rao[††]

[*]Department of Mathematics and Computer Science
Kent State University, Kent, OH 44242, USA
arvind@mcs.kent.edu

[†]Department of Computer Science
University of Melbourne , Parkville, Victoria 3052, Australia
rao@cs.mu.oz.au

[††]Australian Artificial Intelligence Institute
Level 6, 171 La Trobe Street, Melbourne, Victoria 3000, Australia
anand@aaii.oz.au

Abstract

We address the problem of recovering the state of an agent after a hardware/software failure of the system. We address the replication and reincarnation sub-problems of agent recovery under certain assumptions. An algorithm for distributed storage of replicated beliefs is provided and its correctness is proved formally. This algorithm allows the reincarnation of multiple crashed agents in a system of distributed autonomous intelligent agents. The scheme uses replication and distributed storage in the immediate neighboring agents, and uses distributed logical clocks to preserve the causality and to terminate retransmission.

Key-words: Distributed fault tolerance, Multi-agent system, Recovery, Reliability

1 Introduction

The past few years has seen a rapid explosion of systems built using the agent-oriented paradigm [8, 9, 15]. Increasingly, these systems are being embedded into safety-critical applications, such as, air-traffic management, telecommunications network management, and intensive-care monitoring. Agent based systems either carry out critical tasks autonomously or assist humans in critical decision-making activity in these applications. In either case, the need for robustness and a quick recovery from hardware and/or software faults becomes critical. In spite of its importance, the complexity of the task has meant that the problem has not received sufficient attention in the agent-oriented research community. This paper redresses this imbalance by examining in greater detail the problem of *agent recovery*: recovering the state of an agent after a major crash or failure.

---

[*] Address for correspondence

Although the agent recovery problem shares similarities with other related problems of database recovery and process recovery in distributed systems, there are significant differences as well. We explore some of these differences below.

First, the agents continuously sense the external environment and based on their internal mental state take certain actions that affect the environment. The effects of these external actions cannot be undone. Also, agents lack a clear notion of a transaction that can be used to log changes to its internal state onto a permanent store. In other words, rolling back to a previous state is much harder in agents than in conventional databases.

Second, the agents themselves are embedded in a continuously changing environment and often interact with other agents and/or humans to carry out a variety of tasks. As a result, even if a failed agent was capable of being recovered in a finite time, the recovered agent would still be out-of-step with the external environment, as there is a high likelihood that the external environment and the other agents have changed significantly during this period. These differences require us to modify existing techniques and adapt it for agent recovery.

Given the complexity of the agent recovery problem it is useful to split the problem into its constituent sub-problems. The agent recovery problem can be split into three simpler sub-problems:

1. the *replication* problem or the problem of replicating the state of an agent at other nodes in a distributed network, so that the agent can be rebuilt when a system failure occurs;
2. the *reincarnation* problem or the problem of building the state of a crashed agent from the replicated information across the distributed network; and finally
3. the *assimilation* problem or the problem of the agent "catching-up" with the external environment, by reaching a state which could be considered a state where it would have been, had it not crashed.

In this paper, we consider the replication and reincarnation problems. Although we do not address the assimilation problem, an application developer can write agent-oriented programs in such a way that goals which are yet to be satisfied are re-established and tried under the new conditions. Depending on the time-criticality of the application such a solution may be adequate. However, the problem of providing fault tolerant recovery in a non-stop real-time system is quite complex. We believe that the research presented in this paper will certainly help in providing a practical fault-tolerant systems.

Before we proceed with the solution for the agent recovery problem, we briefly describe system of agents under consideration, assignment of agents to machines, and *crash* or *failure* of an agent.

The agents we have in mind are Belief-Desire-Intention (BDI) agents. BDI agents [8] are autonomous software entities that sense a continuously changing environment and based on their internal mental state take certain actions which affect their external environment. The primary distinguishing feature of a BDI agent is its mental state - comprising the mental attitudes of *beliefs*, *desires*, and *intentions* that represent information, motivational, and deliberative components, respectively. In addition, these agents are programmed by writing *plans* that specify how to achieve desires in certain situations. A practical realization of such BDI agents is dMARS (distributed Multi-Agent Reasoning System) agent-oriented development environment that has been used to build a number of practical applications [15]. The multi-agent environment dMARS allows the specification and execution of multiple BDI agents which cooperate with each other to solve a problem. The architecture allows multiple agents to be assigned to a single operating system process, and spawns multiple processes to run on a single machine.

Given a generic agent architecture which allows multiple agents to run simultaneously on a single machine, one can envisage at least three different types of crashes or system failures (see Figure 1): single agent crash, multiple non-neighbor crashes, multiple neighbor crashes.

Single agent crash implies that a reincarnated agent fully recovers before another agent crashes. After the crash of an agent, its belief and vaults (needed to store the beliefs of the neighboring agents) are lost. To facilitate the recovery, the agent's beliefs are distributed in the vaults of the neighbors and the secondary storage of the neighbors. To recover the vaults, fault tolerance and check-pointing are needed during the storage of beliefs. After the full recovery, there is no loss in the belief system.

Multiple non-neighbor crash is treated as multiple isolated single agent crashes. Since none of the crashed agent store the beliefs of other crashed agents in their vaults, each one of them can be recovered fully in a concurrent manner.

Multiple neighbors crashes suffer from the problem of information loss since the neighbors share mutually part of the each other's beliefs. To avoid information loss, belief replication has to ensure that multiple neighboring vaults are sent the same belief.

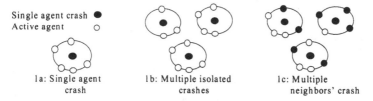

Single agent crash ●
Active agent ○

1a: Single agent crash 1b: Multiple isolated crashes 1c: Multiple neighbors' crash

Fig. 1. Different types of crashes

In this paper, we consider single agent and multiple non-neighbor crashes. With such a crash the loss of an agent results in a temporary loss of some of the functionality of the overall system. As long as the situation does not deteriorate to a state where multiple neighboring agents are failing at the same time, the agents can be reincarnated at other nodes, and can be integrated with the rest of the system to facilitate the reliable execution of the overall system. After reincarnation, an agent has no knowledge of the tasks (or intentions) that were being executed at the time of crash, has no knowledge of the neighboring agents which initiated new tasks, and has no knowledge of the agents with whom it had to communicate. In addition, the state of agents would have changed between the time of crash and time of recovery: beliefs would have altered, and some of the tasks being executed at the time of crash would not be needed. Under these restrictions, we examine the solutions for the problem of agent recovery.

A naive solution of periodically sending messages to neighboring agents informing them of one's own belief state will not provide the desired behavior. For example, assume that an agent A sent a message at Time 1 to its neighboring agent B that A's position is (10, 10) on an X-Y axis, and the agent A sent another message at Time 3 to the agent B that A's position is (11, 10). Depending on how the agent B processes the messages one might end-up with different results. To avoid this problem one can insist that the agent B updates based on its local clock, i.e., process the messages in the order that they arrive.

However, this solution is also inadequate since order of processing based on arrival does not preserve the order of events. Consider the situation where there are three neighboring agents A, B, and C, each sending their belief state (which includes the position of itself and other agents) to their neighbors. In such a situation it is possible that an agent, say B, receives a message from A that its new position is (11, 10) followed by another message from C that A's position is (10, 10). Processing these messages according to its local clock can result in agent B incorrectly recording that agent A's position is (10, 10).

To overcome these problems each agent needs to maintain a distributed logical clock [7] and update the beliefs based on their causal ordering, not just their local clock. In this paper, we discuss the distributed storage of replicated beliefs of a crashed agent to facilitate recovery. Beliefs are time-stamped and are replicated at the neighboring agents. In addition, to reduce the overhead of communication between agents, the time-stamped beliefs are piggybacked on existing messages. The scheme assumes that replicated beliefs are check-pointed periodically to facilitate fast recovery by the agents.

The major contributions of this paper are twofold. First, to the best of our knowledge, this is the first time that causality and replication used in the recovery of distributed transaction processing and fault tolerant computing systems [2] have been applied for the recovery of distributed intelligent agents. Compared to direct acknowledgment based schemes, this mechanism provides fault tolerance in the case of signal loss. Second, the agent recovery mechanism proposed here allows for reincarnation of an agent on any node in the network independent of the crash of a node. Third, we also use the messages at the application level for transmitting the belief updates, and use time-stamp comparison of the messages at application level to ascertain the storage of the belief updates in the neighbors.

2 Background

In this section, we describe distributed logical clocks and their application to ensure causality, and introduce the notations and definitions.

In a heterogeneous network different machines have different physical clocks. These clocks have different values at the same absolute instance. As a result communication delay causes the same event to be recorded at different times and the causality of events can not be guaranteed. Logical clocks [5] are needed to maintain the order of distributed events. The schemes are based upon associating a logical clock - count of events - associated with each agent and transmitting a vector of logical clocks [7] among agents. The vector of clocks are piggybacked with every message from one agent to the another. Upon the receipt of a vector clock instance from another agent, the local vector clock is updated by taking the *least upper bound* of the common logical clocks from two vector-clock instances. Events are time stamped by the current value of the vector clock in an agent. Causality between the events is established by using partial order between the time-stamps. A vector clock instance precedes another vector clock instance if all the logical clocks in the first instance precede or equal the corresponding logical clocks in the second instance, and there exists at least one logical clock in the first instance which precedes the corresponding logical clock in the second instance. Two events are concurrent in the absence of partial ordering between the corresponding vector clock instances.

In this paper, we denote vector clock as a sequence of integers within angular brackets < ... >. An unknown logical clock instance (or a vector clock instance) is denoted by the bottom symbol "⊥". We define two important notions: least upper bound of tuples (lub), and greatest lower bound of tuples (glb), which we use throughout this paper to update the value of vector clocks. The definition of *lub* and *glb* are as follows:

$$lub(<a_1, ..., a_n>, <b_1, ..., b_n>) = <max(a_1, b_1), ..., max(a_n, b_n)> \qquad (1)$$
$$lub(<a_1, ..., a_n>, \perp) = <a_1, ..., a_n>$$
$$lub(\perp, <a_1, ..., a_n>) = <a_1, ..., a_n>$$

$$glb(<a_1, ..., a_n>, <b_1, ..., b_n>) = <min(a_1, b_1), ..., min(a_n, b_n)> \qquad (2)$$
$$glb(<a_1, ..., a_i, ..., a_n>, \perp) = <a_1, ..., a_i, ..., a_n>$$
$$glb(\perp, <a_1, ..., a_i, ..., a_n>) = <a_1, ..., a_i, ..., a_n>$$

$$max(a, \perp) = a; \quad max(\perp, b) = b; \quad max(a, b) = a \ if \ a > b \ otherwise \ b \qquad (3)$$

$$min(a, \perp) = a; \quad min(\perp, b) = b; \quad min(a, b) = a \ if \ a < b \ otherwise \ b \qquad (4)$$

Example 1

Let us consider Figure 2. There are three communicating agents: A_1, A_2, and A_3. The belief updates are marked by filled circles, and the transmission of messages from a agent to another are marked by arrows. The direction of the arrows is from the originator of a message to the destination of the message. The triples inside the angular brackets denote the: I_{th} field in a vector-clock instance represents the number of preceding belief updates for the agent A_i ($0 < I < 4$). A message from the agent A_1 increments the vector clock of the agent A_2 from $<0, 1, 0>$ to $<1, 1, 0>$ (least upper bound of $<1, 0, 0>$ and $<0, 1, 0>$); a message from the agent A_3 increments the vector clock of the agent A_2 from $<1, 1, 0>$ to $<1, 1, 1>$ (least upper bound of $<1, 1, 0>$ and $<0, 0, 1>$); a message from the agent A_2 increment the vector clock of the agent A_1 from *<2, 0, 0>* to *<2, 1, 1>* (least upper bound of *<2, 0, 0>* and *<1, 1, 1>*); a message from the agent A_2 increments the vector clock of the agent A_3 from *<0, 0, 2>* to *<1, 1, 2>* (least upper bound of *<0, 0, 2>* and *<1, 1, 1>*); and a message from the agent A_1 increments the vector clock of the agent A_3 from *<1, 1, 2>* to *<2, 1, 2>* (least upper bound of *<1, 1, 2>* and *<2, 1, 1>*). The partial ordering of instances of vector clock maintains the causality.

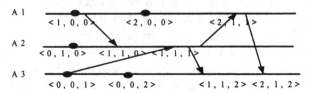

Fig. 2. Causality in logical clocks

2.1 Notations

We denote least upper bound by *lub;* greatest lower bound by *glb;* for all by $\forall$; existence by $\exists$; logical conjunction by $\wedge$, logical disjunction by $\vee$, composition of two functions by $\bullet$; a vector within a pair of angular brackets $< \ldots >$; a tuple between a pair of parenthesis (...), and logical clock pair within the curly brackets $\{ \ldots \}$[1], a logical clock instance by t_i; projection of i_{th} sub-field of a tuple by Π_i; composition $\Pi_i \bullet \Pi_j$ by $\Pi_i\Pi_j$; agent-ids by italicized upper case English alphabet *A, B, C, D*; a vector clock by the capital Greek alphabet Γ, a vector clock of a generic agent D by Γ^D; an instance of a vector clock by Γ_1; a logical clock of a generic agent *A* by $\Pi_A(\Gamma)$; I_{th} element of vector clock by $\Pi_I(\Gamma)$; precedence by the symbol "$\prec$"; "precedes or equal to" by the symbol "$\preceq$"; and concurrency of two clocks by the symbol "$\|$". We use natural language and syntax structure of C like languages to explain the algorithms.

3 Modeling Multi-agents System

In this section, we briefly describe the modeling of agents and the notion of distributed clocks in a multi-agents based system.

Although we are primarily interested in BDI agents [8, 9] the solutions proposed in this paper are generic enough to be applied for autonomous agents that communicate with each other using messages. The only requirement of these agents is that they capture the state of the external environment as a set of beliefs. We assume that agents communicate with each other using four primitive types of messages: *ask, reply, tell,* and *ack* (acknowledgment) messages. A *tell* message is unidirectional in nature; *ask* and *reply* messages are complementary; and *ack*

---

[1] We use curly brackets instead of pair of parenthesis just for better comprehension. Both have the same meaning.

message is a receipt of *ask, reply*, and *tell* messages. At any point in time, multiple agents are executing their programs; updating their beliefs; cooperating with each other through ask-reply message pairs, tell messages, and ack messages; and interacting with the environment through sensors to collect information and through actuators to control the environment.

The message connectivity between agents is modeled by an agent connectivity graph (A-graph). An A-graph is a weighted graph[2]: Agents are represented as nodes, and the possibility of a message transfer from one agent to the other is represented by an edge. The weight of an edge is the number of occurrences of message commands between two agents. The presence of an implicit ack message for every ask, reply, and tell implies a symmetrical edge A_iA_j for every edge A_jA_i. The total weight of an edge is given by (*occurrences of tell-messages from A_i to A_j + occurrences of ask-messages from A_i to A_j + occurrences of reply messages from A_i to A_j + occurrences of tell-messages from A_j to A_i + occurrences of ask messages from A_j to A_i + occurrences of reply messages from A_j to A_i*). An agent is a *neighbor* of another agent if there is an edge between the corresponding nodes.

In an agent based system, a *logical clock* is an incremental count of events within an agent. An event is either a *belief update event* or a *message event*. In a *belief update event*, a belief is updated, i.e., added, deleted, or modified. A *message event* is either an ask, tell, reply, or ack message. A *vector clock* Γ is of the form $<\gamma_1, ..., \gamma_i..., \gamma_n>$ where each γ_i is a pair of the form (*agent-id, logical-clock*). Each logical-clock is a pair of the form {*belief update count, message count*}. *A belief update count* is incremented after each assertion, deletion, or modification of a belief in an agent. A *message count* is incremented before each message is sent to a neighboring agent. We assume that events in the same agent are ordered resulting into monotonicity in logical clocks. We separate the belief update count from the message count as they are handled differently at the time of recovery.

We denote the set of logical clocks that have been altered between *two consecutive instances* of a vector clock by Δ. We denote the agent-id of the I_{th} element in a vector clock instance Γ by $\Pi_I^1(\Gamma)$ and the I_{th} logical clock by $\Pi_I^2(\Gamma)$. From this we denote the belief update count of the logical clock of an agent I by $\Pi^b\Pi_I^2(\Gamma)$ and the message count of the logical clock of an agent I by $\Pi^m\Pi_I^2(\Gamma)$. We denote belief update precedence by the symbol $\prec_b$, and message precedence by the symbol $\prec_m$, "belief count precedes or equals to" by the symbol $\preceq_b$ and "message count precedes or equals to" by the symbol "$\preceq_m$".

There are two types of precedence relations between instances of the same logical clock: belief precedence and message precedence. A *belief precedence* is based on partial order between the belief update counts and *message precedence* is based on partial order between message counts.

---

[2] Although, we do not make use of these weights in this paper, they are useful in providing a probabilistic interpretation of agent failure. This is beyond the scope of this paper.

Given two instances t_i and t_j of the same logical clock, $t_i \prec_b t_j$ if $\Pi^b(t_i) <$ $\Pi^b(t_j)$, and $t_i \prec_m t_j$ if $\Pi^m(t_i) < \Pi^m(t_j)$. For example, $\{1, 3\} \prec_b \{2, 3\}$ and $\{1, 3\} \prec_m \{1, 4\}$. An instance of a logical clock precedes another instance of the same clock if $t_i \prec_b t_j \wedge t_i \preceq_m t_j$ or $t_i \prec_m t_j \wedge t_i \preceq_b t_j$. Due to the monotonicity property in logical clocks, it is impossible to have two instances t_i and t_j such that $t_i \prec_b t_j$ and $t_j \prec_m t_i$.

Given two instances Γ_i and Γ_j $(i \neq j)$ of a vector clock, $\Gamma_i \prec \Gamma_j$ if $\exists k$ ($\Pi_k^2(\Gamma_i)$ $\prec \Pi_k^2(\Gamma_j)) \wedge \forall l(\Pi_l^2(\Gamma_i) \preceq \Pi_l^2(\Gamma_j))$. For example, consider an agent graph where an agent A is connected to another agent B, and the agent B is connected to the agents A and C. The vector clock has three fields: one field for every logical clock. For example, $<(A, \{1, 1\}), (B, \{2, 4\}), (C, \{2, 5\})> \prec <(A, \{2, 2\}), (B, \{2, 4\}), (C, \{2, 5\})>$ since $\{1, 1\} \prec \{2, 2\}$ in the agent A, and other two logical clocks in the agents B and C are equal.

Two events are concurrent if the above conditions are not satisfied. For example, $<(A, \{4, 6\}), (B, \{3, 4\}), (C, \{1, 5\}), (E, \{4, 3\})> \parallel <(A, \{3, 5\}), (C, \{6, 7\}), (D, \{4, 5\}), (E, \{10, 3\})>$ since the logical clock instances $\{4, 6\}$ (in the first vector) $\succ \{3, 5\}$ (in the second vector) for the agent A and $\{1, 5\}$ (in the first vector) $\prec \{6, 7\}$ (in the second vector) for the agent C. This situation violates the condition that all the logical clock instances of a vector-clock precede or equal ($\preceq$) the corresponding logical clocks of the other vector-clock. Similarly, $<(A, \{4, 6\}), (B \{3, 4\}), (C, \{6, 7\}), (E, \{4, 3\})> \parallel <(A, \{4, 6\}), (C, \{6, 7\}), (D, \{4, 5\}), (F, \{10, 3\})>$ since no logical clock instance in either of the vector clocks strictly precedes the corresponding logical clock instance in the other vector clock.

4 Distributed Storage and Recovery

In this section, we describe a scheme to distribute the replicated beliefs in the neighbors, using causality to control the transmission of replicated beliefs. We also describe an algorithm for the transmission of replicated beliefs to neighbors.

4.1 Distributed Storage of Replicated Beliefs

Each agent holds a secure vault to store the transmitted beliefs for each of its neighbors. These vaults are updated dynamically after a message from the corresponding neighbor is received. A *neighboring vault* is a set of 5-tuples of the form (*agent-id of origin, birth clock, old-belief, nature of update, new-belief*) where *agent-id* identifies the neighboring agent requesting the update; *birth clock* is an instance (of origination) of the vector clock of the originating agent; and nature of update specifies the action to take. An update could be *assert, retract,* or *modify*. The vault in an agent is periodically check-pointed. We require that the vault be check-pointed immediately after a recovery. The advantage of check pointing is that number of belief updates are reduced during recovery since check-pointing retains the latest belief updates.

4.2 A Brief Overview of the Belief Recovery Process

If the secondary storage used by the crashed agent is reachable during the recovery process to reincarnate an agent, then the check-pointed beliefs and the check-pointed vaults related to the neighbors are restored; the check pointed replicated beliefs of the crashed agent in the neighbors' secondary storage are restored; and the remaining subset of beliefs is restored from the distributed vaults. In the absence of secondary storage used by the crashed agent, the problem becomes complex since check pointed beliefs and the vaults in the crashed agent are lost. The use of fault tolerance to ensure that multiple neighbors get the same replicated beliefs in their vaults is beyond the scope of this paper.

4.3 Belief Replication and Transmission

A replicated belief update is stored in at least one of the vaults in the neighboring agents. Belief updates are time-stamped and retransmitted through the following messages to neighboring agents. Retransmission mechanism uses piggybacking on one of the implicit messages - *ask, reply, tell,* or *ack* - until piggybacked clock instance on one of the received messages ensures that the replicated beliefs have been received by one of the neighbors. The sending agent increments its message-count before sending the message; incrementing the clock and sending the message constitute an atomic action. Each agent keeps track of the last clock transmitted to the neighbor and the last clock received from each of its neighbors. It sends Δ to reduce the communication overhead [7]. The overall clock instance is re-built at the destination. The neighboring agent, receives the updated belief and stores the transmitted belief updates. The agent then increments its vector clock. We require that storing the belief and updating the vector clock constitute an atomic action. The value of a vector-clock instance and the notion of causality is used to control the retransmission of replicated beliefs as described in the following section.

4.4 Belief Storage and Acknowledgment

The belief updates are sent by any of the four types of messages: ask, reply, tell and ack which results in sixteen pair combinations for sending the belief updates and receiving back a vector-clock instance acknowledging the receipt of the update in the corresponding neighbors. However, the edges in the A-graph limit the use of different combinations. There are two scenarios for the transmission of belief updates and the acknowledgment that it has been received by one of the neighbors:

1. The agent A_i's neighbor A_j $(i \neq j)$ which received the belief update sends one of the four messages to the agent A_i, and the agent A_i receives the message before receiving any other agent's message which received a message from A_j after A_j received A_i's message.

2. The agent A_i's neighbor A_j $(i \neq j)$, received the belief update, and sends a message to a neighbor A_k $(i \neq k, j \neq k)$. Before A_i receives a message from A_j, A_i receives a message which succeeds (by causality) the message from A_j to A_k.

The update in the neighboring vault is ascertained by comparing the received clock instance with a *last update acknowledged marker* (*LUA marker*). A *LUA marker* is an instance of an agent's vector clock which marks the birth of the last belief update which has been stored in one of the neighbors' vault. Every agent has its own LUA marker.

4.5 An Algorithm for Retransmission of Belief Updates

As shown in Figure 3, a queue of 5-tuples (*birth-time, agent-id, old-belief, update-type, new belief*) is maintained in each agent to retransmit the belief updates. At any time, all the beliefs updated between the interval of the current LUA marker and the current value of the agent's vector clock are transmitted to one of the neighbors (see Figure 3). A LUA marker is updated to received-clock instance if LUA marker $\prec$ received-clock instance, and all the messages with birth-time $\preceq$ the new LUA marker are removed from the queue.

Example 2

Let us consider a strongly connected A-graph with three agents A, B and C. Consider a case in the agent A when the P_A^2(LUA marker) of the agent A = $\{1, 1\}$. After the assertion of each belief the agent A increments its belief update count by 1. The boxes in the queue in Figure 3 show the belief updates stored in the outgoing queue, and the pairs in the bottom line of Figures 3a and 3b and 3c give P_A^2(birth-time) associated with each belief update. Let us assume that the messages are transmitted to the agent B when the logical clock instance for the agent A is $\{4, 1\}$. Before transmission the message count of the logical clock is incremented by 1, and the logical clock instance of the agent A gets updated to $\{4, 2\}$, and the belief-updates (in the outgoing queue of the agent A) with P_A^2(birth time) $\{2, 1\}$, $\{3, 1\}$, $\{4, 1\}$ are transmitted to B. The next re-transmission occurs when the logical clock instance is $\{5, 2\}$, and the agent A sends a message to the agent C. Before re-transmission the message-count is incremented by 1, the logical clock instance for the agent A at the time of re-transmission becomes $\{5, 3\}$, and the belief updates with P_A^2(birth time) $\{2, 1\}$, $\{3, 1\}$, $\{4, 1\}$, $\{5, 2\}$ are transmitted to the agent C. Note that the belief updates with P_A^2(birth time) $\{2, 1\}$ and $\{3, 1\}$ and $\{4, 1\}$ are being re-transmitted to one of the neighbors. Figure 3a shows a snapshot of this instance.

Figure 3b shows a snapshot after the belief updates with P_A^2(birth-time) $\{2, 1\}$, $\{3, 1\}$, $\{4, 1\}$, $\{5, 2\}$ have been transmitted to the agent C, and the current logical clock has been updated to $\{7, 3\}$ after two more belief updates. Figure 3b also depicts a snapshot when an incoming tell-message is received from the agent B. The Δ (received-clock instance) sent from B to A is <(A, $\{4, 2\}$), (B, $\{3, 2\}$)>. Upon receipt of the message, the LUA marker of the Agent A has been updated to <(A, {*4, 2*}), (B, {3, 2})>, and the belief updates (in the agent A) with P_A^2(birth time) {*2, 1*}, {*3, 1*}, {*4, 1*} have been deleted from the outgoing messages queue. The snapshot after the deletion of the messages is shown in Figure 3c.

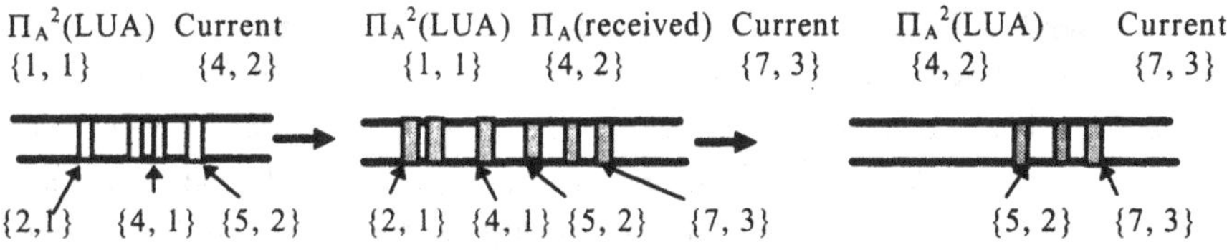

3a: Message retransmission 3b: Message received 3c: LUA marker update

Fig. 3. Belief re-transmission and LUA marker update

From the above description it should be reasonably straightforward to arrive at an algorithm for retransmitting updated beliefs. The algorithm is given in Figure 4.

Algorithm Belief-retransmission-and-LUA-update;

Input: 1. A queue Q of replicated beliefs in an agent *A*;
2. A vector-clock instance C_i for an agent *A*;
3. The LUA marker for an agent *A*;

Output: 1. An updated queue Q of the replicated beliefs;
2. The vector clock instance C_{i+1} for the agent *A*;
3. The modified LUA marker for the agent A;

{1.Receive the next message. Build the full received-clock instance from Δ;
2.If ((Π_A^2(LUA-marker) $\prec_m$ Π_A^2(received-clock instance)) &&
(LUA-marker $\prec$ received-clock instance)) {
3. LUA-marker = received-clock instance;
4. Delete the beliefs from Q with birth-time $\prec$ LUA-marker;}
5. Agent's vector-clock C_{i+1} = *lub*(received-clock instance, C_i);}

Fig. 4. An algorithm for retransmission

To prove the correctness of the algorithm, namely, that the belief updates of an agent A will be stored in at least one of its neighbors we need to prove the following theorem.

Theorem: The transmitted beliefs between the interval LUA marker and the logical clock preceding the Π_A^2(received clock instance) of an agent *A* are stored in at least one of the neighbors iff (Π_A^2(*LUA marker*) $\prec_m$ Π_A^2(*received-clock instance*)) ∧ (*LUA marker* $\prec$ *received-clock instance*).

Proof: Let us consider an A-graph, without loss of generality, which contains three agents A, B, and C such that the agents A and B are neighbors, the agents B and C are neighbors, and there is a path from the agent C to the agent A other than through the agent B.

We first prove that if the vault update is done in a neighbor B of an agent A then the condition is true. After the vault update, the neighbor B updates its vector clock Γ^B to new value lub(current value of Γ^B, clock instance received from A). The neighbor B sends at least one message. The $\Pi^m\Pi_B{}^2(\Gamma^B)$ is incremented by 1. If the message is directly sent back to the agent A then there is no problem since the logical clock of B has been updated and incremented such that LUA marker of A $\prec$ vector clock instance sent by A $\prec$ value of the current instance of Γ^B. If the message is sent from B to another agent C ($C \neq A$) and there is a path from C to A in the A-graph then all the agents in the path will at least increment the message-count in their logical clocks by at least one before A gets the acknowledgment.

We now prove that if the condition is true then vault update is done. The proof is by contradiction. Let us assume that there is a case $(\Pi_A{}^2(LUA\ marker) \prec_m \Pi_A{}^2(received\text{-}clock\ instance)) \wedge (LUA\ marker \preceq received\text{-}clock\ instance)$ but the corresponding beliefs with the belief update count $\Pi^b\Pi_A{}^2(birth\text{-}time) \leq \Pi^b\Pi_A{}^2(received\text{-}clock\ instance)$ have not been stored in any of the neighboring vaults. The logical-clock instance $\Pi_A{}^2(received\text{-}clock\ instance)$ can only be incremented by A. Thus, at least one of the neighbor received a later value of the logical clock of A. A later instance of logical clock of A is only piggybacked in the messages sent after the LUA marker. Thus at least one of the neighbors got the message with the time-stamp $\Pi^m\Pi_A{}^2(received\text{-}clock\ instance)$. Due to monotonic property in the logical clock instances, if $\Pi_A{}^2(birth\text{-}time) \prec_m \Pi_A{}^2(received\text{-}clock\ instance)$ then $\Pi_A{}^2(birth\text{-}time) \preceq_b \Pi_A{}^2(received\text{-}clock\ instance)$. Hence, all the beliefs with the belief update count $\Pi^b\Pi_A{}^2(birth\text{-}time) \leq \Pi^b\Pi_A{}^2(received\text{-}clock)$ have been received by one of the neighboring agents. The operation of receiving the message and storing the message in the vault are atomic. Hence the update has been done. A contradiction.∎ QED

Complexity: Let us say that the size of the message queue is M, the number of neighboring agents are upper bounded by N. Thus the clock-size of each agent is bounded by N. The overall complexity is guided by the binary-search of an N-tuple clock in a message queue of size M, and to delete all messages before the LUA marker. The overall complexity is O(NlogM + M). We delete the details due to the space limitation.

4.6 Complexity of Handling Multiple Neighbors Crash

Failure from a multiple neighbors crash is a dynamic property. and a probabilistic model can be used to estimate the overall loss of information for an agent in a multiple neighbor crash scenario. The estimated loss is:

$$\sum_{m=0}^{m=r}(m/k)\binom{K}{m} \Bigg/ \binom{n-1}{m} \times p^{(m+1)}(1-p)^{n-m-1}$$

where m is the number of failure, k is the average number of neighbors of an agent, r is the maximum number of failed agents at a time, n is the number of agents in the system, and p is the probability of failure of an agent.

It can be shown in the probabilistic model that providing fault tolerance by re-transmitting extra number of messages to different neighbors can alleviate the problem of multiple neighbor crashes. The upper bound on the number of re-transmissions to different neighbors can be derived for a specific failure rate. The need for providing fault tolerance increases with the failure rate. The need for extra fault tolerance increases the re-transmission and message logging overheads on the agents. However, the probabilistic model is outside the scope of this paper.

5 Related Works

The work on distributed fault tolerant computing, replication of facts for fault tolerant distributed transaction processing, and the use of vector of distributed logical clocks has been well researched [1, 2, 6, 7, 13]. However, to the best of our knowledge, this is the first attempt to apply distributed logical clocks to ensure reliability in intelligent agents. Indeed, this paper uses the results from distributed computing and database recovery. However, the problem is more complex in agent-based systems as the agents are autonomous and interact continuously (in a non-stop fashion) with a changing environment.

Our scheme of storing the replicated beliefs in immediate neighbors keeps the overhead low which is necessary to satisfy a realistic time interaction of humans with agent based systems. The proposed scheme does not use any additional message (other than *implicit ask, reply, tell*, and *ack* messages) between the agents, and make use of vector clock comparison to ascertain the belief-updates.

Specifically, this work is different from standard distributed operating and database system due to its use of application level messages: *ask, reply, and tell* messages instead of low level acknowledgments. Unlike other schemes, we use clock comparisons for the acknowledgment of messages; and message can come from any neighbor if clocks satisfy causality.

Related work is also being done in the application of group communications to the transaction level processing [10]. Our scheme of establishing reliability by storing the beliefs in neighbors is different from the scheme of establishing reliability of group communications. Group communication is at a lower level while our scheme is at the application level. We use neighborhood as a group and reincarnate crashed agents to provide reliability, while group communication approaches use majority scheme [2, 10] and group based integrity to provide fault tolerance. Group communication schemes have additional communication overhead due to the distribution of the processes in the same groups on different nodes.

Other work to provide message acknowledgment [14] suffer from the problem of synchronization and loss of acknowledgment due to loss in communication. Our scheme is free from any problem of synchronization and data loss since the acknowledgment is based upon clock comparison. Such a clock comparison provides implicit fault tolerance against any data loss during communication. However, we believe that reliability will benefit from fault tolerance and group communication at lower level [10].

The work on social comparison of agents [3] uses comparison of trace of events of an agent with the trace of similar agents. This scheme is suitable to correct deviations when there are multiple similar agents, and does not address the issue of recovery when the agents crash.

The work on customizable coordination system [12] provides a high level declarative specification of interaction between agents. It will be very interesting to integrate the low level messages generated in this scheme with our scheme of distributed logical clock comparison to provide application level fault tolerance.

6 Conclusion and Future Work

In this paper, we have described a scheme for reliable intelligent distributed agents. The scheme benefits from previous research on fault tolerance distributed computing and recovery in distributed transaction processing, and the use of causality based on vector of logical clocks. The scheme uses partial ordering of clocks, comparison of vector clocks for the acknowledgment of update, piggybacking on existing messages, and storage of replicated beliefs in immediate neighbors to reduce the overhead of communication during storage and recovery.

The assumption of mapping one agent per processor will be relaxed in future. The notion of uniform connectivity will be relaxed using static and dynamic analysis of the behavior of agents. We aim to address the problem of non-neighborhood crashes, provide a probabilistic interpretation of failure, and enhance the scheme to address dynamic message transfer behavior between agents.

Acknowledgments

This first author was supported in part by the Australian Federal Government funded program of Cooperative Research Center for Intelligent Decision Systems during his sabbatical to The University of Melbourne. The authors acknowledge Michael Georgeff, Andrew Worsley, and Andrew Hodgson at the Australian Artificial Intelligence Institute for useful discussions.

References

[1]   D. Agarwal and A. Malpani, "Efficient Dissemination of Information in Computer Networks," *The Computer Journal*, 34:6, 1991, pp. 534 - 541.

[2]   P. Jalote, "Fault Tolerant Distributed Computing," *Prentice Hall*, 1993.

[3] G. Kalinka and M. Tambe, "Social Comparison for Failure Detection and Recovery," In this volume.

[4] D. Kinny, M. Georgeff, J. Bailey, D. B. Kemp, and K. Rammohanarao, "Active Databases and Agent Systems," *Proceedings of the Second International Rules in Database Systems Workshop, RIDS95,* Athens Greece, 1995.

[5] L. Lamport, "Time, Clock, and the ordering of Events in a Distributed Systems," *Communications of the ACM,* 21:7, 1978, pp. 558 - 565.

[6] H. V. Leong and D. Agrawal, "Using Message Semantics to Reduce Rollback in Optimistic Message Logging Recovery Schemes," *Proceedings of the 14th International Conference on Distributed Computing Systems,* 1995

[7] M. Ranyal and M. Singhal, "Capturing Causality in Distributed Systems," *Communications of the ACM,* February 1996, pp. 49 - 56.

[8] A. S. Rao and M. P. Georgeff, "Modeling Rational Agents Within a BDI-Architecture," *Proceedings of the Second International Conference on Principles of Knowledge Representation and Reasoning,* San Mateo, CA, USA, Morgan Kaufaman publishers, 1991.

[9] A. S. Rao, "AgentSpeak(L): BDI Agents Speak Out in a Logical Computable Language," in *Agents Breaking Away,* editors, Van de Velde, W. and Perram, J. W. Lecture Notes in Artificial Intelligence, LNAI 1038, Springer-Verlag, 1996

[10] A. Scheiper and M. Ranyal, "From Group Communications to Transactions in Distributed Systems," *Communications of the ACM,* 39:4, 1996, pp. 84 - 87.

[11] F. B. Schneider, "Implementing Fault Tolerant Services using the State Machine Approach, a tutorial," *ACM Computing Surveys* 22: 4, 1990, pp. 299-319.

[12] M. P. Singh, "A Customizable Coordination Service for Autonomous Agents," In this volume.

[13] J. Wuu and A. J. Bernstein, "Efficient Solutions to the Replicated Log and Dictionary Problems," *Proceedings of the 3rd ACM Symposium of Principles of Distributed Computing,* ACM Press, New York, 1984, pp. 233 - 242.

[14] A. R. Worsely and A. Hodgson, "dMARS Fault Tolerant Communications, Reliable Messaging Use Cases," *Internal Report,* The Australian AI Institute, Carlton, Victoria 3053, Australia, February 1995.

[15] M. Wooldridge and N. R. Jennings, " Intelligent Agents: Theory and Practice," *The Knowledge Engineering,* Publisher: Springer Verlag, Volume 890, 1995

A Customizable Coordination Service for Autonomous Agents

Munindar P. Singh*

Department of Computer Science
North Carolina State University
Raleigh, NC 27695-7534, USA

singh@ncsu.edu

Abstract. We address the problem of constructing multiagent systems by coordinating autonomous agents, whose internal designs may not be fully known. We develop a customizable coordination service that (a) takes declarative specifications of the desired interactions, and (b) automatically enacts them. Our approach is based on temporal logic, and has a rigorous semantics and a naturally distributed implementation.

1 Introduction

Open information environments are heterogeneous, distributed, dynamic, large, and frequently comprise autonomous components. For these reasons, they require solutions that marry artificial intelligence (AI) and traditional techniques to yield extensibility and flexibility. Agents are a result of this marriage. Currently, many agent approaches are centralized in a single agent. However, centralization has obvious shortcomings in accommodating the above properties of open environments. Consequently, there has been increasing interest in multiagent systems [11, 19], which can yield the benefits of intelligent agency while preserving openness and scalability.

What sets multiagent systems apart from single agents is that they require the agents to behave in a coordinated manner—agents must follow some protocol even to compete effectively. Therefore, the designer of a multiagent system must handle not only the application-specific aspects of the various agents, but also their interactions with one another. Current approaches to constructing multiagent systems offer no special coordination support to the designer, who must manually ensure that the (potentially autonomous) agents interact appropriately. This can lead to unnecessarily rigid or suboptimal designs, wasted development effort, and sometimes to the autonomy of the agents being violated. We believe it is the difficulty of constructing effective coordination that has led many researchers and practitioners to the centralized approaches.

To alleviate this problem, we propose that coordination be separated into a distinct service. The service would be responsible for delivering the desired coordination. This presupposes that the service takes declarative specifications of the desired interactions,

---

* Munindar Singh is supported by the NCSU College of Engineering, the National Science Foundation under grants IRI-9529179 and IRI-9624425, and IBM corporation.

and include the functionality to enact them. This service should be customizable, because each application has its own requirements for coordination. This service should be minimally intrusive so as to preserve the autonomy of the participating agents. Such a service would help improve designer productivity. It would also help improve system efficiency by optimizing and enacting the desired coordination in a changing environment, potentially generating a different execution each time.

This is the kind of service we have developed. It mediates between the infrastructure and the application-specific components. It includes functionality to specify the desired coordination, translate them into low-level "events," and schedule them through passing appropriate messages among agents. The low-level events correspond to the agents' significant (external) transitions. Capturing the specifications of the coordination explicitly enables us to flexibly execute them, thereby maintaining the key properties of interactions across different situations. Thus a programmer can create a multiagent system by defining (or reusing) agents, and setting them up to interact as desired. Managing the coordination requires knowledge only of the agents' external events that feature in the interactions.

Our service enhances techniques from workflow and relaxed transaction scheduling in databases. It is rigorous, being based on temporal logic. It includes abstractions for (a) a semantics of events in a multiagent system and (b) message passing to implement control and data flow [9]. Our approach is distributed and requires only limited knowledge of the agents' behavior.

As we show in section 3, our formal language is quite simple. Simplicity and rigor are both crucial: a service should be easy to use and highly reliable. Intuitively, this service is analogous to truth maintenance systems (TMSs), which are immensely successful because of their simplicity, and enable design of complex systems. Similarly, we do not expect our service to replace more sophisticated approaches [6, 19], but to facilitate their robust implementation.

Section 2 motivates and presents our conceptual approach. Section 3 describes our algebra for specifying interactions and uses it to formalize an example from section 2, as well as the contract net protocol (CNP). Section 4 shows how the service operates. Section 5 reviews the pertinent literature.

2 A Coordination Service

Although our approach is generic, we consider information search applications for concreteness. In such applications, agents cooperate to perform combinations of tasks such as resource discovery, querying heterogeneous databases, and information retrieval, filtering, and fusion. Our running example follows.

Example 1. Consider a ship on the high seas. Suppose an engine spare-part, a valve, runs low in the ship's inventory. This can lead the maintenance engineer to a search for information: Are such valves available at the next sea-port to be visited? Intuitively, she must access the bridge to find the next sea-port, query a directory of suppliers, and call up the suppliers at the next sea-port. ∎

Consider a multiagent approach that uses information agents for each resource [11]:

Example 2. The search of Example 1 involves querying the bridge agent for the next port, querying a directory agent to find suppliers in the next port, and mapping over the list of suppliers to ask each of their agents about the desired valve. One positive response is enough, but additional responses improve reliability and help optimize other criteria, e.g., the price. ∎

Clearly, since the directory and suppliers are autonomous, so must their agents be. However, the agents must be coordinated to carry out the search.

2.1 Agent Events and Skeletons

There are two aspects of the autonomy of agents that concern us. One, the agents are designed autonomously, and their internal details may be unavailable. Two, the agents act autonomously, and may unilaterally perform certain actions within their purview. We assume that the designer has some limited knowledge of the agents' designs. This knowledge is in terms of their externally visible actions, which are potentially significant for coordination. We call these the significant *events* of the agent. We consider four kinds of events, which have different properties with respect to coordination. Events may be

- *flexible*, which the agent is willing to delay or omit
- *inevitable*, which the agent is willing only to delay
- *immediate*, which the agent is neither willing to delay nor omit
- *triggerable*, which the agent is willing to perform based on external request.

The first three categories are mutually exclusive; each can be conjoined with trigger-ability. Intuitively, immediate events are those that the agent performs unilaterally. We do not have a category where an agent will entertain omitting an event, but not delaying it, because unless the agent performs the event unilaterally, there must be some delay in receiving a response from the service.

It is useful to view the events as organized into a *skeleton* to provide a simple model of an agent for coordination purposes. This model is typically a finite state automaton. Although the automaton is not used explicitly by the coordination service during execution, it can be used to validate specified coordination requirements. The set of events, their properties, and the skeleton of an agent depends on the agent, and is application-specific. The coordination service is independent of the exact skeletons or events used in a multiagent system. Although traditional database approaches, e.g., [4], are limited to loop-free skeletons, which correspond to single-shot queries or transactions, we place no such restrictions here. Example 3 discusses two common skeletons in information search.

Example 3. Figure 1 shows two skeletons that arise in information search. The left skeleton is suited for agents who perform one-shot queries. Its significant events are *start* (accept an input and begin), *error*, and *respond* (produce an answer and terminate). The right skeleton is suited for agents who filter a stream or monitor a database. Its significant events are *start* (accept an input, if necessary, and begin), *error*, *end of stream*, *accept* (accept an input, if necessary), *respond* (produce an answer), *more* (loop back to expecting more input). In both skeletons, the application-specific computation

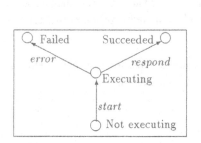 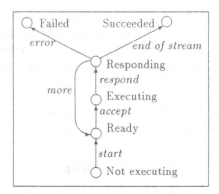

Fig. 1. Example Skeletons: (l) Simple querying agent; (r) Information filtering agent

takes place in the node labeled "Executing." We must also specify the categories of the different events. For instance, we may state that *error, end of stream*, and *respond* are immediate, and all other events are flexible, and *start* is in addition triggerable. ∎

2.2 Architecture of the Service

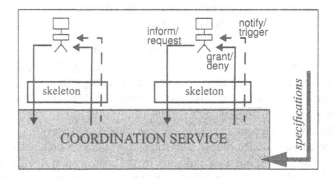

Fig. 2. The coordination service, logically

Figure 2 shows how the service interacts with agents. The agents *inform* it of the immediate events that have happened unilaterally and *request* permission for inevitable and flexible events, which it may control; The service *grants* or *denies* permissions, *notifies* the agents, or *triggers* more events. It can delay inevitable events; delay or deny flexible events; and trigger triggerable events. Any necessary reasoning on intermediate results for decision-making is carried out through application-specific subtasks.

Although we logically view the service as lying beneath each agent, it is *not* a separate entity in the implementation! It is distributed across the significant events of each agent. The following sections show how events exchange messages whose content and direction are automatically compiled.

3 Formalizing Coordination

We formalize interactions in an event-based linear temporal logic. $\mathcal{I}$, our specification language, is propositional logic augmented with the *before* ($\cdot$) temporal operator. The literals denote event types, and can have parameters. A literal with all constant parameters denotes an event token. *Before* is formally a dual of the more conventional "until" operator. Crucially, $\mathcal{I}$ can express a remarkable variety of interactions, yet be compiled and executed in a distributed manner.

The syntax of $\mathcal{I}$ follows. Ξ includes all event literals (with constant or variable parameters); $\Gamma \subseteq \Xi$ contains only constant literals. A *dependency* is an expression in $\mathcal{I}$. A *workflow*, $\mathcal{W}$, is a set of dependencies.

Syntax 1. $\Xi \subseteq \mathcal{I}$

Syntax 2. $I_1, I_2 \in \mathcal{I} \Rightarrow I_1 \vee I_2, I_1 \wedge I_2, I_1 \cdot I_2 \in \mathcal{I}$

Like for many process algebras, our formal semantics is based on traces, i.e., sequences of events. Our universe is $\mathbf{U}_{\mathcal{I}}$, which contains all consistent traces involving event tokens from Γ. Consistent traces are those in which an event token and its complement do not occur, and in which event tokens are not repeated. $[\![\,]\!] : \mathcal{I} \mapsto \wp(\mathbf{U}_{\mathcal{I}})$ gives the denotation of each member of $\mathcal{I}$. The specifications in $\mathcal{I}$ select the acceptable traces—specifying I means that the service may accept any trace in $[\![I]\!]$.

Let constant parameters be written as c_i etc.; variables as v_i etc.; and either variety as p_i etc. $e[c_1 \ldots c_m]$ means that e occurs appropriately instantiated.

Semantics 1. $[\![e[c_1 \ldots c_m]]\!] = \{\tau \in \mathbf{U}_{\mathcal{I}} : e[c_1 \ldots c_m] \text{ occurs on } \tau\}$

$\bar{e}$ refers to the complement of e. Since $[\![\,]\!]$ yields sets of traces, complementation is stronger than negation in other temporal logics. Intuitively, $\bar{e}[c_1 \ldots c_m]$ is established only when it is definite that $e[c_1 \ldots c_m]$ will never occur. This is crucial in the correct functioning of our service. Complemented literals are included in Ξ and need no separate syntax or semantics rule.

$I(v)$ refers to an expression free in variable v. $I(v ::= c)$ refers to the expression obtained from $I(v)$ by substituting every occurrence of v by c. Variable parameters are effectively universally quantified by:

Semantics 2. $[\![I(v)]\!] = \bigcap_{c \in C} [\![I(v ::= c)]\!]$

$I_1 \vee I_2$ means that either I_1 or I_2 is satisfied. $I_1 \wedge I_2$ means that both I_1 and I_2 are satisfied (in any interleaving). $I_1 \cdot I_2$ means that I_1 is satisfied before I_2 (thus both are satisfied).

Semantics 3. $[\![I_1 \vee I_2]\!] = [\![I_1]\!] \cup [\![I_2]\!]$

Semantics 4. $[\![I_1 \wedge I_2]\!] = [\![I_1]\!] \cap [\![I_2]\!]$

Semantics 5. $[\![I_1 \cdot I_2]\!] = \{\tau_1 \tau_2 \in \mathbf{U}_{\mathcal{I}} : \tau_1 \in [\![I_1]\!] \text{ and } \tau_2 \in [\![I_2]\!]\}$

Section 4.2 presents a set of equations, which enable symbolic reasoning on $\mathcal{I}$ to determine when a certain event may be permitted, prevented, or triggered.

3.1 Specification

Our language allows a variety of relationships to be captured. We now consider some common examples. These assume that we are given events e, f, and g in different agents. The events all carry parameter tuples, but we don't show them below to reduce clutter. (We assume that $\cdot$ (before) has precedence over $\vee$ and $\wedge$, and $\wedge$ has precedence over $\vee$.) Some of these relationships are then applied on our running example.

R1. e is required by f. If f occurs, e must occur before or after f: $e \vee \overline{f}$

R2. e disables f. If e occurs, then f must occur before e: $\overline{e} \vee \overline{f} \vee f \cdot e$

R3. e feeds f. f requires e to occur before: $e \cdot f \vee \overline{f}$

R4. e conditionally feeds f. If e occurs, it feeds f: $\overline{e} \vee e \cdot f \vee \overline{f}$

R5. Guaranteeing e enables f. f can occur only if e has occurred or will occur: $e \wedge f \vee \overline{e} \wedge \overline{f}$

R6. e initiates f. f occurs iff e precedes it: $\overline{e} \wedge \overline{f} \vee e \cdot f$

R7. e and f jointly require g. If e and f occur in any order, then g must also occur (in any order): $\overline{e} \vee \overline{f} \vee g$

R8. g compensates for e if f doesn't happen: $(\overline{e} \vee f \vee g) \wedge (\overline{g} \vee e) \wedge (\overline{g} \vee \overline{f})$

The above (and similar) relationships can capture different coordination requirements. For example, R3 suggests an enabling condition or a data flow from e to f. R8 captures requirements such as that if an agent does something (e), but another agent does not match it with something else (f), then a third agent can perform g—which might restore consistency by undoing e. Notice that R7 and R8 involve events of three agents.

Example 4 formalizes Example 2. Here, x denotes the unique id of the information search through which the various instantiations of the relevant computations in the agents are tied together. tup is a variable bound to a tuple. sup is a variable bound to a supplier. v indicates the availability of the desired valve. Subscripts s, r, and a respectively denote *start*, *respond*, and *accept* events.

Example 4. Assume five types of agents corresponding to different functions: B to the bridge, D a directory lookup, Q the main queries (there is one agent for each supplier), M to map over the responses of D, and F to fuse the results. M takes a single input at start. Thus, B, D, and the Qs are information agents, and M and F are task agents [19]. Assume all agents except M have skeletons as in Figure 1(l) with D returning a tuple response containing a list of suppliers and Q being invoked on each of its members. M has a skeleton as in Figure 1(r). M is started with tuple tup of suppliers, and initiates a query to each supplier agent. This yields:

D1. $B_r[x\ port]$ feeds $D_s[x\ port]$

D2. $D_r[x\ tup]$ feeds $M_s[x\ tup]$

D3. $M_r[x\ sup]$ initiates $Q_s^{sup}[x]$

D4. $M_{eof}[x]$ initiates $F_s[x]$

D5. $Q_r^{sup}[x\ v]$ conditionally feeds $F_s[x]$. ∎

3.2 Contract Net Protocol

Our approach applies well to higher-level coordination protocols, such as the CNP [5]. Briefly, the CNP begins when the manager sends out a request for proposals (RFP); some potential contractors respond with bids; the manager accepts one of the bids and awards the task. Much of the required reasoning is application-specific, e.g., who to send the RFP to, whether to bid, and how to evaluate bids.

Example 5. Since all agents can play the role of manager or contractor, we assume that all have the same significant events. Any agent because of internal reasons can perform the $A_{rfp}[m\ t\ c]$ event. Here m is the manager id, t is the task id, and c is a potential contractor—there will be a separate event for each c. (Multicasts can also be captured.) This involves the following dependencies:

D6. $A_{rfp}[m\ t\ c\ \text{info}]$ initiates $A_{think}[c\ t\ m\ \text{info}]$
D7. $A_{bid}[c\ t\ m\ \text{bid}]$ conditionally feeds $A_{eval}[m\ t\ c\ \text{bid}]$
D8. $A_{award}[m\ t\ c\ \text{task}]$ initiates $A_{work}[c\ t\ m\ \text{task}]$.

D6 means that the receiving agents think about the RFP and autonomously decide to bid or not bid. If not, they exit the protocol. If they continue, D7 kicks in. The manager now autonomously evaluates bids, leading to an award on one of them, which triggers the work, because of D8. ∎

4 Scheduling

One of our requirements is that the coordination service be as distributed as possible, which presupposes that the events take decisions based on local information. Our approach requires (a) determining the conditions, i.e., *guards*, on the events by which decisions can be taken on their occurrence, (b) arranging for the relevant information to flow from one event to another, and (c) providing an algorithm by which the different messages can be assimilated.

4.1 Temporal Logic

Intuitively, the guard of an event is the weakest condition that guarantees correctness if the event occurs. Guards must be temporal expressions so that decisions taken on different events can be sensitive to the state of the system, particularly with regard to which events have occurred, which have not occurred but are expected to occur, and which will never occur. The guards are compiled from the stated dependencies; in practice, they are quite succinct.

T, the language in which the guards are expressed, captures the above distinctions. Intuitively, $\Box E$ means that E will always hold; $\Diamond E$ means that E will eventually hold (thus $\Box e$ entails $\Diamond e$); and $\neg E$ means that E does not (yet) hold. $E \cdot F$ means that F has occurred preceded by E. For simplicity, we assume the following binding precedence (in decreasing order): $\neg$; $\cdot$; $\Box$ and $\Diamond$; $\wedge$, $\vee$.

Syntax 3. $\Gamma \subseteq T$

Syntax 4. $E, F \in T \Rightarrow E \vee F, E \wedge F, E \cdot F, \square E, \diamond E, \neg E \in T$

The semantics of T is given with respect to a trace (as for I) *and* an index into that trace. This semantics characterizes progress along a given computation and uses it to determine the decision on each event. Our semantics has important differences from traditional linear temporal logics [7]. One, our traces are sequences of events, not of states. Two, most of our semantic definitions are given in terms of a pair of indices, i.e., intervals, rather than a single index. For $0 \leq i \leq k$, $u \models_{i,k} E$ means that E is satisfied over the subsequence of u between i and k. For $k \geq 0$, $u \models_k E$ means that E is satisfied on u at index k—implicitly, i is set to 0. $\Lambda \triangleq \langle \rangle$ is the empty trace.

A trace, u, is *maximal* iff for each event, either the event or its complement occurs on u. $U_T \triangleq$ the set of maximal traces. We assume $\Xi \neq \emptyset$; hence, $\Gamma \neq \emptyset$. Semantics 6, which involves just one index i, invokes the semantics with the entire trace until i. The second index is interpreted as the present moment. Semantics 8, 9, 11, and 12 are as in traditional formal semantics. Semantics 13 and 14 involve looking into the future. Semantics 7 and 10 capture the dependence of an expression on the immediate past, bounded by the first index of the semantic definition. Semantics 10 introduces a nonzero first index.

Semantics 6. $u \models_i E$ iff $u \models_{0,i} E$

Semantics 7. $u \models_{i,k} f$ iff $(\exists j : i \leq j \leq k$ and $u_j = f)$, where $f \in \Gamma$

Semantics 8. $u \models_{i,k} E \vee F$ iff $u \models_{i,k} E$ or $u \models_{i,k} F$

Semantics 9. $u \models_{i,k} E \wedge F$ iff $u \models_{i,k} E$ and $u \models_{i,k} F$

Semantics 10. $u \models_{i,k} E \cdot F$ iff $(\exists j : i \leq j \leq k$ and $u \models_{i,j} E$ and $u \models_{j+1,k} F)$

Semantics 11. $u \models_{i,k} \top$

Semantics 12. $u \models_{i,k} \neg E$ iff $u \not\models_{i,k} E$

Semantics 13. $u \models_{i,k} \square E$ iff $(\forall j : k \leq j \Rightarrow u \models_{i,j} E)$

Semantics 14. $u \models_{i,k} \diamond E$ iff $(\exists j : k \leq j$ and $u \models_{i,j} E)$

4.2 Calculating Guards

Since the guards must yield precisely the computations that are allowed by the given dependencies, a natural intuition is that the guard of an event covers each computation in the denotation of the specified dependency. For each computation, the guard captures how far that computation ought to have progressed when the guarded event occurs, and what obligations would remain to realize that computation. We term this reasoning *residuation* and notate it by an operator $/ : I \times \Xi \mapsto I$, which is not in I or T. Roughly, given a dependency D and event e, D/e gives the residual or "remnant" of D after e occurs.

Interestingly, / can be computed symbolically. We propose a set of equations exists using which the "residual" of any dependency with respect to an event can be computed. These equations require that the expressions be in a form such that there is no $\wedge$ or $\vee$ in the scope of the $\cdot$ (CNF is one such form). Such a representation exists, because of the distribution laws validated by the semantics of $\mathcal{I}$. Because of this restriction, in the equations below, D is a sequence expression, and E is a sequence expression or $\top$ (the latter allows us to treat an atom as a sequence, using $f \equiv f \cdot \top$). $\Gamma_E \triangleq \{e : e \text{ or } \bar{e}$ occurs in $E\}$. (We define $\bar{\bar{e}}$ as e.) We set the denotation of any sequence $e_1 \cdot \ldots \cdot e_n$ in which (for $i \neq j$) $e_i = e_j$ or $e_i = \bar{e_j}$ to the empty set; we assume such sequences are reduced to 0.

Equation 1. $0/e = 0$

Equation 2. $\top/e = \top$

Equation 3. $(E_1 \wedge E_2)/e = ((E_1/e) \wedge (E_2/e))$

Equation 4. $(E_1 \vee E_2)/e = (E_1/e \vee E_2/e)$

Equation 5. $(e \cdot E)/e = E$, if $e \notin \Gamma_E$

Equation 6. $D/e = D$, if $e \notin \Gamma_D$

Equation 7. $(e' \cdot E)/e = 0$, if $e \in \Gamma_E$

Equation 8. $(\bar{e} \cdot E)/e = 0$

We define guards as below. These cases cover all the syntactic possibilities of $\mathcal{I}$. Importantly, our definition distributes over $\wedge$ and $\vee$: using our normalization requirement, each sequence subexpression can be treated separately. Thus the guards are succinct for the common cases, such as the relationships of section 3.1.

Definition 1. The guards are given by the operator $G : \mathcal{I} \times \Xi \mapsto \mathcal{T}$:
(a) $G(D_1 \vee D_2, e) \triangleq G(D_1, e) \vee G(D_2, e)$;
(b) $G(D_1 \wedge D_2, e) \triangleq G(D_1, e) \wedge G(D_2, e)$;
(c) $G(e_1 \cdot \ldots \cdot e_i \cdot \ldots \cdot e_n, e_i) \triangleq \square e_1 \wedge \ldots \wedge \square e_{i-1} \wedge \Diamond(e_{i+1} \cdot \ldots \cdot e_n)$;
(d) $G(e_1 \cdot \ldots \cdot e_n, e) \triangleq \Diamond(e_1 \cdot \ldots \cdot e_n)$, if $\{e, \bar{e}\} \not\subseteq \{e_1, \bar{e_1}, \ldots, e_n, \bar{e_n}\}$;
(e) $G(e_1 \cdot \ldots \cdot e_i \cdot \ldots \cdot e_n, \bar{e_i}) \triangleq 0$;
(f) $G(0, e) \triangleq 0$;
(g) $G(\top, e) \triangleq \top$.

Example 6. We compute the guards for the events in R2 as follows:

- $G(R2, e) = \Diamond \bar{f} \vee \square f$.
- $G(R2, \bar{e}) = \top$.
- $G(R2, \bar{f}) = \top$.
- $G(R2, f) = (\Diamond \bar{e} \vee (\neg e \wedge \Diamond e))$, which equals $\neg e$ under the semantics of $\mathcal{T}$.

Thus $\bar{e}$ and $\bar{f}$ can occur at any time. However, e can occur only if f has occurred or will never occur. Similarly, f can occur only if e has not yet occurred (it may or may not occur in the future). ∎

4.3 Scheduling with Guards

Execution with guards is straightforward. When an event e is attempted, its guard is evaluated. Since guards are updated whenever an event mentioned in them occurs, evaluation usually means checking if the guard evaluates to $\top$. If e's guard is satisfied, e is executed; if it is 0, e is rejected; else e is made to wait. Whenever an event occurs, a notification is sent to each pertinent event f, whose guards are updated accordingly. If f's guard becomes $\top$, f is allowed; if it becomes 0, f is rejected; otherwise, f is made to wait some more. Example 7 illustrates this. The correct disablement interpretation of R2 also requires setting the categories of the events appropriately, which we lack the space to discuss.

Example 7. Using the guards from Example 6, if f is attempted and e has not already happened, f's guard evaluates to $\top$. Consequently, f is allowed and a notification $\Box f$ is sent to e (and $\bar{e}$). Upon receipt of this notification, e's guard is simplified from $\Diamond \bar{f} \vee \Box f$ to $\top$. Now if e is attempted, it can happen immediately.

If e is attempted first, it must wait because its guard is $\Diamond \bar{f} \vee \Box f$ and not $\top$. Sometime later if $\bar{f}$ or f occurs, a notification of $\Box \bar{f}$ or $\Box f$ is received at e, which simplifies its guard to $\top$, thus enabling e. Events $\bar{f}$ and $\bar{e}$ have their guards equal to $\top$, so they can happen at any time. ∎

Abstractly, given a workflow, our evaluation technique *generates* traces as follows. We sloppily write generation as $\mathcal{W} \rightsquigarrow u$ and define it as $(\forall i : i \leq |u| \Rightarrow \mathcal{W} \rightsquigarrow_i u)$, where $\mathcal{W} \rightsquigarrow u_i \triangleq (\forall j : 1 \leq j \leq i \Rightarrow u \models_{j-1} G(\mathcal{W}, u_j))$. From this we obtain the following correctness result, which states that precisely those traces are generated that are in the denotation of the stated dependencies. A rigorous formalization is available in [18].

Theorem 2. $\mathcal{W} \rightsquigarrow u$ iff $(\forall D \in \mathcal{W} : u \models D)$. ∎

Assimilating Messages The above result establishes correctness abstractly without regard to how it is determined whether $u \models_{j-1} G(\mathcal{W}, u_j)$ for a trace u and an index j. Our approach computes $\models_{j-1}$ incrementally as much as possible. Events produce notifications, which are incrementally assimilated by the recipients, leading to simplification of their guards. The operator $\div$ captures the assimilation process. This operator embodies a set of "proof rules" to reduce guards when an event occurs or is promised.

When the dependencies involve sequence expressions, the guards can end up with sequence expressions, which indicate ordering of the relevant events. In such cases, the information that is assimilated into a guard must be new. This is because the stability of events is in tension with ordering. If $e_1 \cdot e_2$ is specified, we wish to refer to the first occurrences of e_1 and e_2—otherwise, we would end up allowing $\langle e_2 e_1 \rangle$, and thereby $e_1 \cdot e_2$ would be violated. For this reason, the updates in those cases involve $\neg$ expressions, which are not ordinarily sent as messages. These are discussed as prohibitory relationships below.

Theorem 3 means that the operator $\div$ preserves the truth of the original guards. The receipt of a message, no matter how delayed, cannot cause any violation. In other words,

Old Guard G	Message M	New Guard $G \div M$
$G_1 \vee G_2$	M	$G_1 \div M \vee G_2 \div M$
$G_1 \wedge G_2$	M	$G_1 \div M \wedge G_2 \div M$
$\Box e$	$\Box e$	$\top$
$\Box \overline{e}$	$\Box e$ or $\Diamond e$	0
$\Diamond e$	$\Box e$ or $\Diamond e$	$\top$
$\Diamond \overline{e}$	$\Box e$ or $\Diamond e$	0
$\Box(e_1 \cdot e_2)$	$\Box e_1 \wedge \neg e_2$	$\Box e_2$
$\Box(e_1 \cdot e_2)$	$\Box e_2 \wedge \neg e_1$	0
$\Box(e_1 \cdot e_2)$	$\Box \overline{e_i}$ or $\Diamond \overline{e_i}, i \in \{1, 2\}$	0
$\Diamond(e_1 \cdot e_2)$	$\Box e_1 \wedge \neg e_2$	$\Diamond e_2$
$\Diamond(e_1 \cdot e_2)$	$\Box e_2 \wedge \neg e_1$	0
$\Diamond(e_1 \cdot e_2)$	$\Box \overline{e_i}, i \in \{1, 2\}$	0
$\neg e$	$\Box e$	0
$\neg \overline{e}$	$\Box e$ or $\Diamond e$	$\top$
G	M	G, otherwise

Table 1. Assimilating Messages

no spurious traces are generated by our assimilation process. We can also show that all of the original traces are still generated.

Theorem 3. $(\exists k \leq j : u \models_k M$ and $u \models_j G \div M) \Rightarrow u \models_j G.$ ∎

Mutual Constraints Among Events By the above, if the events send the appropriate notifications, we can compute the semantics of $\mathcal{T}$ incrementally. But in some situations potential race conditions and deadlocks can arise. To ensure that the necessary information flows to an event when needed, the execution mechanism should be more astute in terms of recognizing and resolving mutual constraints among events. This reasoning is essentially encoded in terms of heuristic graph-based reasoning. Although we believe we can handle the interesting cases, pathological cases can arise that cannot be easily handled without assistance from a human designer.

Prohibitory Relationships During guard evaluation for an event e, subexpressions of the form $\neg f$ may need to be treated carefully. We must allow for situations where the message announcing f occurrence could be in transit when $\neg f$ is evaluated, leading to an inconsistent evaluation. A message exchange with f's actor is essential to ensure that f has not happened and is not happening—essentially to serialize the execution where necessary.

Example 8. Following Example 6, f should not occur unless we can be sure that e has not occurred. ∎

This is a *prohibitory* relationship between events, since e's occurrence can possibly disable f (depending on the rest of the guard of f). Prohibitory messages can be avoided if the disabler is made responsible for preserving the correct order of execution—in our approach this can always be done, except when the disabler is an immediate event.

Promissory Relationships If the guard on an event is neither $\top$ nor 0, then the decision on it can be deferred. The execution scheme must be enhanced to prevent mutual waits in situations where progress can be consistently made.

Example 9. Consider $W = \{R1, R2\}$. $G(W, e) = \Diamond f \wedge \neg f$ and $G(W, f) = \Box e \vee \Diamond \overline{e}$. Roughly, this means that e waits for $\Diamond f$, while f waits for $\Box e$. ∎

The guards given in Example 9 do not reflect an inconsistency, since f is allowed to occur after e. This relationship is recognized during preprocessing. The events are set up so that when f is attempted, it *promises* to happen if e occurs. Since e's guard only requires that f occur sometimes, before or after e, e is then enabled and can happen as soon as it is attempted. When news of e's occurrence reaches f, f discharges its promise by occurring.

The correctness of these and other strategies for resolving mutual constraints can be established by recourse to the formal semantics of $\mathcal{I}$ and $\mathcal{T}$, and an associated formalization of the execution process.

5 Discussion

We presented a generic, customizable coordination service for building multiagent systems. Our approach hones in on the structure of the coordinating computations by avoiding low-level details. It can thus facilitate the design and enactment of coordinated behavior. Our approach introduces traditional scheduling ideas into an environment of autonomous agents without requiring unnecessary control over their actions, or detailed knowledge of their designs. In our present approach, the specifications are given when the multiagent system is constructed. If the specifications do not conflict with the autonomy of the agents, then they can be executed in a distributed manner. Determining the coordination requirements on the fly would be an important extension, and would be necessary when the coordination requirements are based on the agents' social commitments [17].

The relevant previous tools for developing multiagent systems are either not formal, are centralized or violate the autonomy of agents. AgenTalk [13] gives a programming environment, but no formal semantics. Kabanza [12] adapts a traditional temporal logic for synchronizing agent plans; his approach has a centralized scheduler and violates autonomy by requiring full knowledge of, and modifying, the agents' plans. Traditional temporal logic approaches do not apply here. Such approaches preclude encapsulation of the component computations as agents; they do not accommodate the notion of admissibility, which captures the knowledge of the scheduler; they (in the case of databases) are limited to single-shot transactions and not applicable to arbitrary, nonterminating, complex computations that characterize agents.

Sycara & Zeng [19] articulate many of the intuitions that we share, including the ultimate necessity of multiagent, versus single-agent, approaches. They show how agents need to be coordinated to collectively search or manage information in open environments. Oates *et al* [14] propose an approach for planning searches. However, their approach does not have an explicit representation of search patterns, and does not apply generically. The search techniques are captured as different search patterns in our approach. Decker & Lesser [6] present coordination algorithms in the generalized partial global planning framework. This work is both more and less ambitious than our work. It includes heuristics to reason about deadlines and coordination problems in various situations, but it does not provide a formal semantics. We believe that our approach can help encode their intuitions in a rigorous setting. Our approach complements the above, because they develop semantic representations, whereas our approach focuses on the activity management infrastructure itself.

There is also work on the lower-level aspects of providing robust infrastructures for implementing multiagent systems, e.g., [1]. We believe this work is important, and can in principle be used to support the kind of approach developed here.

High-level abstractions for agents have been intensively studied, e.g., [15]. Formal research on interactions among agents includes [8]. These approaches develop formal semantics, but do not give as precise an operational characterization. The present work has a formal semantics along with an operational interpretation. There has been much work on social abstractions for agents, e.g., [3]. We believe that the present infrastructure will facilitate the development of a computational treatment of the social constructs by capturing the mechanics of possible interactions in a succinct manner. Including mental and social abstractions into a generic executable system is an important open problem.

We prototyped our approach initially in an actor programming language. We are now reimplementing it with enhancements in Java. One of the enhancements being developed is being able to switch between TCP/IP and CORBA for the underlying functionality. CORBA is important, because it is becoming a de facto standard for lower-level functionality in distributed systems. It provides an event service with notifications and triggers [16], but not a coordination service of the sort we described.

References

1. Arvind K. Bansal, Kotagiri Ramamohanarao, and Anand Rao. Distributed storage of replicated beliefs to facilitate recovery of distributed intelligent agents. In this volume.
2. Alan Bond and Les Gasser, editors. *Readings in Distributed Artificial Intelligence*. Morgan Kaufmann, San Francisco, 1988.
3. Cristiano Castelfranchi. Commitments: From individual intentions to groups and organizations. In *Proceedings of the International Conference on Multiagent Systems*, pages 41–48, 1995.
4. Panos K. Chrysanthis and Krithi Ramamritham. Synthesis of extended transaction models using ACTA. *ACM Transactions on Database Systems*, 19(3):450–491, September 1994.
5. Randall Davis and Reid G. Smith. Negotiation as a metaphor for distributed problem solving. *Artificial Intelligence*, 20:63–109, 1983. Reprinted in [2].
6. Keith S. Decker and Victor R. Lesser. Designing a family of coordination algorithms. In *Proceedings of the International Conference on Multiagent Systems*, pages 73–80, 1995.

7. E. A. Emerson. Temporal and modal logic. In J. van Leeuwen, editor, *Handbook of Theoretical Computer Science*, volume B. North-Holland, Amsterdam, 1990.

8. Afsaneh Haddadi. Towards a pragmatic theory of interactions. In *Proceedings of the International Conference on Multiagent Systems*, pages 133–139, 1995.

9. Carl Hewitt. Viewing control structures as patterns of passing messages. *Artificial Intelligence*, 8(3):323–364, 1977.

10. Michael N. Huhns and Munindar P. Singh, editors. *Readings in Agents*. Morgan Kaufmann, San Francisco, 1997.

11. Michael N. Huhns, Munindar P. Singh, Tomasz Ksiezyk, and Nigel Jacobs. Global information management via local autonomous agents. In *Proceedings of the 13th International Workshop on Distributed Artificial Intelligence*, August 1994.

12. Froduald Kabanza. Synchronizing multiagent plans using temporal logic specifications. In *Proceedings of the International Conference on Multiagent Systems*, pages 217–224, 1995.

13. Kazuhiro Kuwabara. Meta-level control of coordination protocols. In *Proceedings of the International Conference on Multiagent Systems*, pages 165–172, 1996.

14. Tim Oates, M. V. Nagendra Prasad, and Victor R. Lesser. Cooperative information gathering: A distributed problem solving approach. TR 94-66, University of Massachusetts, Amherst, MA, 1994.

15. Anand S. Rao and Michael P. Georgeff. Modeling rational agents within a BDI-architecture. In *Proceedings of the International Conference on Principles of Knowledge Representation and Reasoning*, pages 473–484, 1991. Reprinted in [10].

16. Jon Siegel. *CORBA: Fundamentals and Programming*. Object Management Group and Wiley, New York, 1996.

17. Munindar P. Singh. Commitments among autonomous agents in information-rich environments. In *Proceedings of the 8th European Workshop on Modelling Autonomous Agents in a Multi-Agent World (MAAMAW)*, pages 141–155, May 1997.

18. Munindar P. Singh. Coordinating heterogeneous autonomous agents. TR 97-07, Department of Computer Science, North Carolina State University, Raleigh, July 1997. Available at www.csc.ncsu.edu/ faculty/ mpsingh/ papers/ mas/ coord-tr.ps.

19. Katia Sycara and Dajun Zeng. Multi-agent integration of information gathering and decision support. In *Proceedings of the European Conference on Artificial Intelligence*, pages 549–553, 1996.

A Behavior-Based Approach to Reactivity and Coordination: A Preliminary Report*

Silvia Coradeschi and Lars Karlsson

Department of Computer and Information Science
Linköping University, Sweden
silco@ida.liu.se, larka@ida.liu.se

Abstract. This paper gives a preliminary account of a system for developing autonomous agents operating in uncertain and rapidly changing environments. The decision-mechanism of an agent is specified in terms of behavior modules. Behavior modules specify what actions and submodules should be executed and under what conditions to fulfill some specific aims or purposes. Behavior modules can be executed simultaneously if they are compatible, allowing the agents to perform several tasks at the same time. The coordination between agents is mainly obtained through common tactics, strategies, and observations of actions of team members, rather than explicit communication. Agents act and coordinate with other agents depending on their roles.

1 Introduction

This paper is a preliminary report on an effort to develop means for specifying the behaviors of autonomous agents that combine reactivity to an uncertain and rapidly changing environment with commitment to long term courses of actions (behaviors). The system has initially been developed in the context of a cooperation project with Saab Military Aircraft with the aim to investigate the design of automated agents for air combat simulation [4]. It has also been used in a simulated soccer domain (RoboCup [7]) and we intend to use some of the ideas here developed in a project for the design of autonomous aircraft for traffic surveillance.

The basic assumptions are as follows. There are one or more agents capable of performing actions, receiving information from sensors and communicating. The agents might be organized in teams and solve tasks that require coordination. The execution of actions (for instance an aircraft making a turn) requires the use of some resources (for instance maneuvering system). Actions can be executed concurrently. Compatibility between actions is tested mainly by looking at the resources used.

The basic element of the decision-mechanism in our system is the concept of *behavior module*, which provides a degree of modularity and parallelism to the system. A behavior module specifies what actions and submodules should be executed and under what conditions to fulfill some specific aims or purposes. An important aspect of the system is that several behavior modules can be executed simultaneously, provided they

---

* This work has been supported by the Knut and Alice Wallenberg Foundation project *Information Technology for Autonomous Aircraft*.

are compatible. This allows the agent to accomplish several tasks at the same time. For example an airborne vehicle can at the same time follow a road and detect traffic jams along the road. Follow a road and detect a traffic jam can be specified as submodules of a module that has the task of checking the traffic and they can be activated at the same time by that behavior module if a road should be checked with respect to traffic jams. The emphasis on concurrency is one of the main differences between our system and systems as Soar [10] and dMARS [6]. In fact concurrent execution of tasks is not considered in Soar and in dMARS just one intention at a time is executing. Concurrency of behaviors is considered in Brooks' subsumption architecture [1] and in Payton [9]. However, the behaviors in our system differ from the behaviors in Brooks' and Payton's work as there is a central control of the behaviors and an internal representation of the world, and as behaviors can be invoked in a recursive manner. A work in this volume that has some similarity with our is Bryson's behavior-based approach to reactivity [2], although in a single-agent setting. Our work also has similarities with Firby's RAP system [5], but while in RAP the emphasis is in execution of sketchy plans, our system has a stronger emphasis on fast reactivity and concurrency in highly dynamic environments such as simulated air-combat and soccer.

In both the soccer domain and the air combat domain, coordination between agents is essential, but it cannot be achieved by mainly communication and negotiation due to the real-time constrains in these domains and the presence of hostile agents [8]. In our system coordination between agents is mainly obtained through common tactics and observations of actions of team members. In the present system we are not considering commitment between members of a team as in [11], but we plan to extend the architecture to take this aspect into account. In domains where the agents operate in team, what they do and how they coordinate with other agents is mostly determined by their roles in the team [3]. Our decision-mechanism is specified in term of roles and the agents will execute the behavior modules and actions that are proper to their roles.

2 Decision Mechanism

A behavior module is characterized by a priority, which indicates the importance of the module, a set of resources that are used, and a decision-tree which encodes what the module does. A decision-tree is a tree of hierarchically structured and prioritized decision rules. Each node is associated with a condition, and at the leaves there are actions or submodules, which will be considered candidates to be performed if the leaf is reached. The actions and submodules have priority values, which are computed dynamically. Furthermore, behavior modules and actions can be composed using for instance constructors for sequential and concurrent execution, choice and error handling.

To clarify the concept of main behavior module and behavior module, part of the main behavior module of an attacker is shown in Fig. 1. In the **attacker** module, the submodule **take ball** is started if there is an opponent that has the ball and it is near the attacker. Notice that once the **take ball** module is started, its further execution is independent of the conditions in the decision-tree that started it. If there is a teammate midfielder that has the ball the attacker will execute a **coordinated attack** module in order to coordinate an attack with him. Behavior modules can recursively initiate sub-

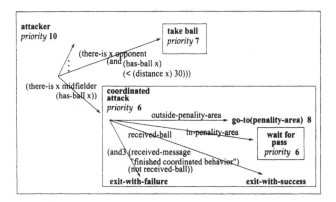

Fig. 1. Part of the main behavior module of an attacker. The decision-trees of the **wait for pass** and **take ball** behavior modules have been omitted due to lack of space.

modules and the same structure is repeated at several levels of the decision mechanism. The **coordinated attack** module for example contains a submodule **wait for pass** that the agent executes when he has positioned himself in the penalty area and waits for the midfielder to pass. As shown in the example, behavior modules have different complexities; they are used for specifying coordination and the behavior module proper of a role as attacker, but also for specifying simple routine such as waiting for the ball.

For each cycle of the decision mechanism, the decision-trees of all ongoing behavior modules are visited. This generates a number of actions and new behavior modules which are candidates to be performed. The selection of those that will actually execute is done based on priority values and compatibility, in competition with ongoing actions and behavior modules. Ongoing modules can be interrupted or suspended if they are outcompeted by new modules with higher priority. The handling of interruptions and failures of modules and actions is a central issue.

An important aspect that emerge in the specification of behaviors is the need for modularity, that is the internal specification of the behavior should not be visible in higher levels. In fact, roles and coordinated behavior modules can be specified independently of higher level modules of which they can be part. Also simple routines should be reusable in different modules. On the other hand, the actions and submodules selected in a behavior module will compete with all other active behavior modules and actions.

Behavior modules can terminate, successfully or unsuccessfully, or can be interrupted. A behavior module can have exiting conditions that are used to exit the module when it is successfully terminated and when the module cannot be continued and terminates with failure. A behavior module can be interrupted if an incompatible module with higher priority is selected or if an action selected in the module cannot be executed as it is incompatible with another selected action with higher priority. In this last case the module can be exited or not depending on whether the action is essential for the module.

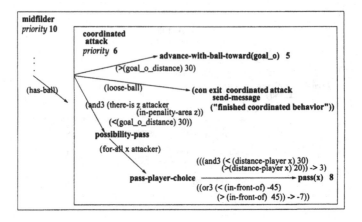

Fig. 2. Part of the main behavior module of a midfielder

3   Coordination and Roles

In both the soccer and the air combat domain teamwork is essential, but the possibility of communication, due to real time constrains and possibility of interception, is limited. Coordination is therefore obtained by common tactics and strategies learned and practised during training. Each agent knows the tactics of the team and his role in the tactics and tries to act according to this knowledge. In our approach the knowledge required for applying the tactics is coded in behavior modules and the observations of the situation and of the actions of other agents influence the decisions about which tactics to adopt. Explicit communication is performed through communication actions present in the decision tree of the behavior module. The message is stored in the state of the agent and will influence his future decisions.

Lets consider a simple example of coordination between an attacker and a midfielder, Fig.1 and Fig. 2. The coordinated behavior module can be started if the midfielder has the ball and it is terminated when the midfielder loses or passes the ball. The midfielder advances with the ball toward the opponents' goal and when he is near the opponents' goal and an attacker is in the penalty area he considers the possibility of passing the ball to an attacker among those that are in the penalty area (*for-all x attacker (in-penalty-area x)*). The preference to which player to pass is based on the distance of the player, and on the distance to the opponent goal. The attacker, if he is outside the penalty area goes to the penalty area, and when he is inside the penalty area waits for a pass.

What the agents do and how they coordinate with other agents is mostly determined by their roles in the team. A role is specified as a behavior module and when a role is assigned to the agent then the module specifying the role become the main module of the agent. A role-behavior module can in turn initiate role-specific submodules when some coordinated tactics is executed by a team of agents. For instance, if a soccer agent has the role of left-wing attacker and the team is executing a left-wing attack, then the agent will execute a behavior module that will make it position itself and play the ball according to its part in this tactics. Some issues that we are currently investigating are specialization and combination of roles (and of behavior modules in general), and how to specify tactics involving multiple agents in a concise and readable manner.

4 Summary

We have described a decision mechanism for autonomous agents based on behavior modules. Behavior modules specify what actions and submodules should be executed and under what conditions to fulfill some specific tasks. Several behavior modules can execute in parallel.

In the present system each agent has a main module that selects submodules depending on the tasks the agent is performing. We are currently developing a deliberative component of the system with predictive capabilities that can reason about goals and plans and that can monitor the execution of behavior modules. Coordination between agents is mainly obtained through common tactics and strategies and observations of actions of team members and are specified in terms of roles.

The system has been partially implemented and tested. We are now working in completing the implementation and in further testing.

References

1. R. A. Brooks. How to build complete creatures rather than isolated cognitive simulators. In K. VanLehn, editor, *Architectures for Intelligence*. Lawrence Erlbaum Associates, 1991.
2. J. Bryson. Agent architecture as object oriented design. In this volume.
3. S. Ch'ng and L. Padgham. Role organisation and planning team strategies. In *Proc. of the 20th Australian Computer Science Conference*. Sydney, Australia, 1997.
4. S. Coradeschi, L. Karlsson, and A. Törne. Intelligent agents for aircraft combat simulation. In *Proc. of the 6th Conf. on Computer Generated Forces and Behavioral Representation*. Orlando, FL, 1996.
5. R. J. Firby. The RAP language manual. Technical Report AAP-6, Univ. of Chicago, 1995.
6. M. P. Georgeff and F. F. Ingrand. Decision-making in an embedded reasoning system. In *Proc. of IJCAI'89*. Detroit, Michigan, 1989.
7. H. Kitano, M. Tambe, P. Stone, M. Veloso, S. Coradeschi, E. Osawa, H. Matsubara, I. Noda, and M. Asada. Robocup synthetic agent challenge 97. In *Proc. of IJCAI'97*. Nagoya, Japan, 1997.
8. J. E. Laird, R. M. Jones, and P. E. Nielsen. Coordinated behavior of computer generated forces in TacAir-Soar. In *Proc. of the 4th Conference on Computer Generated Forces and Behavioral Representation*. Orlando, FL, 1994.
9. D. W. Payton, D. Keirsey, D.M. Kimble, J. Krozel, and J. K. Rosenblatt. Do whatever works: a robust approach to fault-tolerant autonomous control. *Journal of Applied Intelligence*, 2:222–250, 1992.
10. P. S. Rosenbloom, J. E. Laird, A. Newell, and R. McCarl. A preliminary analysis of the Soar architecture as a basis for general intelligence. *Artificial Intelligence*, 47, 1991.
11. M. Tambe. Teamwork in real-world, dynamic environments. In *Proc. of the 2nd International Conference on Multi-agent Systems (ICMAS-96)*. Kyoto, Japan, 1996.

On Explicit Plan Languages for Coordinating Multiagent Plan Execution

Jaeho Lee* and Edmund H. Durfee†

* ORINCON Corporation
9363 Towne Centre Drive, San Diego, CA 92121, USA
jaeho@orincon.com

† Artificial Intelligence Laboratory, The University of Michigan,
1101 Beal Avenue, Ann Arbor, MI 48109, USA
durfee@eecs.umich.edu

Abstract. An agent coordinating with another agent needs a model of the other agent to promote cooperation or to avoid interference. Agent plans in their executable form, however, are not well suited for being reasoned over, particularly because the plans are meaningful only when they are interpreted along with the execution or operational semantics.

In this paper, we introduce Structured Circuit Semantics (SCS) and Grafcet Model of Agent Plans (GAP) to distill out explicit, transferable operational semantics for agent plans from embedded implicit semantics of plan specifications used by plan execution systems. We also present and demonstrate a closed-loop process of exploiting our model of agent plans to discover multiagent coordination requirements and then applying the coordination requirements back to the agent plans.

1 Introduction

An agent coordinating with another agent needs a model of the other agent to promote cooperation or to avoid interference. Generally, a model consists of both declarative information such as goals and beliefs, and procedural knowledge such as agents' plans. Agent plans in their executable form, however, are not well suited for being reasoned over, particularly because the plans are meaningful only when they are interpreted along with the execution or operational semantics.

We have developed Structured Circuit Semantics (SCS) and Grafcet Model of Agent Plans (GAP) to distill out explicit, transferable operational semantics for agent plans from embedded implicit semantics of plan specifications used by plan execution systems such as our University of Michigan Procedural Reasoning System (UM-PRS). While SCS makes explicit the directives to an interpreter, GAP makes explicit what behavior these directives elicit.

Our explicit, transferable semantics allows us to define what situations and transitions occur in plan executions, and to capture the dynamically evolving situation transitions in the course of multiagent plan execution. In turn, our classification of situations enables coordinating agents to find commitment conditions to avoid interference situations, or to promote cooperation.

In this paper, we present this closed-loop process of exploiting our model of agent plans to discover multiagent coordination requirements and then applying the coordination requirements back to the agent plans. First, we enumerate needed transferable semantics and present a language for representing the identified semantics. We then introduce a process model for defining semantic implications in an interpreter and present an algorithm to use the process model for multiagent coordination.

2 Structured Circuit Semantics

The realization that agents in dynamic, unpredictable environments should consider the evolving state of the environment when making decisions about which actions to take to pursue their goals has led to a plethora of systems for reactive plan execution, including Procedural Reasoning System (PRS) [5], Universal Plans [15], Teleo-Reactive Programs [13], and RAPs [4], among others.

Our implementation of PRS, which we call the University of Michigan Procedural Reasoning System [10], is a part of our initial effort to provide a conceptual framework to build agents populating such dynamic environments. UM-PRS has been successfully applied to various applications and has demonstrated that its representation and control scheme are powerful enough to be considered as a general reactive agent architecture [7, 1, 16, 3].

However, agent plans written for the UM-PRS plan execution system are not easily amenable to formal analysis mostly because the execution semantics of agent plans is not explicit, but implicit within the plan interpreter. Our development of Structured Circuit Semantics [8] is the next step toward formal analysis of the agent plans from the implementation of the UM-PRS plan execution system.

Our approach to the design of SCS has been to incorporate the most essential features of agent plans in a compact, yet rich, formal semantics to explicitly represent the control behavior of agents. A formal specification of plan execution semantics is essential for us to be able to generate a plan, reason about it, and communicate it among multiple agents.

Our SCS formalism extends the Circuit Semantics of Teleo-Reactive (T-R) Programs [12] to be powerful enough to encompass the representation of many agent plans, and to facilitate the development of our coordination process. Major design decisions in SCS include how to handle continuous actions and failures, and how to represent various agent behaviors such as nondeterministic behavior, best-first behavior, and persistent behavior. Metalevel reasoning and multiple threads of execution are also considered in the execution semantics.

The basic unit in Structured Circuit Semantics is an *action*, a_i. Every action is atomic; it is guaranteed to terminate within a bounded time and cannot be interrupted. Execution of an action usually changes the environment and/or internal state and returns either *success* or *failure*.

A *step* is defined recursively as follows. In the constructor descriptions below, a_i, S_i, K_i, U_i are actions, steps, conditions, and utility functions, respectively.

- a_i is a step composed of a single atomic action. An action returns either success or failure and so does the step.

- $(a_1; \cdots; a_n)$ is an atomic step composed of atomic actions. The step fails if any of the actions fails.
- do $\{S_1; S_2; \cdots; S_n\}$ is a step that specifies a group of steps that are to be executed sequentially in the given order. The overall do step fails as soon as one of the substeps fails. Otherwise it succeeds. do* $\{\cdots\}$ has the same semantics as do except that, whenever a substep fails, it retries that substep until it succeeds. Thus do* itself never fails. This constructor allows us to specify *persistent* behavior.
- do all $\{S_1; S_2; \cdots; S_n\}$ is a step which tries to execute all steps in parallel (at least conceptually). If the agent can do only one step at a time, it nondeterministically chooses among those as yet unachieved. If any one of the steps fails, the whole do all fails immediately. do* all is a variation of do all which tries failed substeps persistently, yet nondeterministically until all of them have succeeded.
- do any $\{S_1; S_2; \cdots; S_n\}$ is a step which selects nondeterministically one S_i and executes it. If that step fails, it keeps trying other actions until any of them succeeds. If every step is attempted and all fail, the do any step fails. do* any is a variation of do any which keeps trying any action including the already failed steps until any of them succeeds.
- do first $\{K_1 \to S_1; \cdots; K_n \to S_n\}$ is a step which behaves almost the same as a T-R program. That is, the list of condition–step pairs is scanned from the top for the first pair whose condition part is satisfied, say K_i, and the corresponding step S_i is executed. The energizing condition K_i is continuously checked (at the characteristic frequency) as in T-R programs. The difference is that, if a step fails, the whole do first fails. To persistently try a step with satisfied conditions even if it fails (as in T-R programs), the do* first constructor can be used.
- do best $\{K_1 [U_1] \to S_1; \cdots; K_n [U_n] \to S_n\}$ is a step which evaluates the expected utility U_i for each True K_i $(1 \leq i \leq n)$, and selects a step S_i which has the highest utility. If several steps have the highest utility, one of these is selected by the do any rules. The failure semantics is the same as that of the do any constructor. The do* best step is similarly defined.
- repeat $\{S_1; S_2; \cdots; S_n\}$ works the same way as do, but the steps are repeatedly executed to form an execution loop. The repeat* step is also similarly defined.

The do, do all, do any, do first, do best, repeat, and their *-ed constructors may have the following optional modifiers:

- while K_0 : specifies the energizing condition K_0 to be continuously checked between each atomic action. The associated step is kept activated only while K_0 is true. For example, do while K_0 $\{\cdots\}$ does the do step as long as K_0 is true. until K_0 is shorthand for while $\neg K_0$.
- when K_0 : specifies that the condition K_0 must be true before the associated step is started. That is, K_0 is only checked before execution, but not checked again during execution. unless K_0 is shorthand for when $\neg K_0$.
- on failure$\{S_1; S_2; \cdots; S_n\}$: specifies the *failure steps* to be taken when the associated step fails. The failure step is atomically executed until it completes or fails.

3 Operational Semantics of Agent Plans

Our next step, toward an explicit model of the operational semantics of SCS using the Grafcet model [2], complements our goal of developing explicit, clean semantics for both static agent plan descriptions and dynamic run-time plan executions. Explicit operational semantics permit us to define explicit run-time execution states of agents in terms of the *tokens* and *steps* in Grafcet, which in turn contribute to supporting explicit reasoning over dynamic agent behaviors. In multiagent reactive plan execution, explicit run-time state descriptions are especially essential for reasoning for effective coordination such as state-based forward simulation, and state reachability tests.

The Grafcet model, which is derived from Petri nets [6, 11], was first a specification method for discrete systems, but later became a graphical programming language based on the concept of steps and transitions. By connecting steps and transitions, concepts like sequentiality, multiple choice, and parallelism are very easy to express, and by means of some special instructions, functional and hierarchical designs can be achieved. We believe that the simple, clear semantics of the Grafcet specification of procedural agent behavior is best suited for effective reasoning about agent actions and plans.

3.1 Basic Elements of Grafcet

The basic elements of Grafcet are steps and transitions. A *grafcet*, then, is a graph having two types of nodes: steps and transitions.

- A *step* is represented by a square. Steps are similar to *places* in Petri nets. A black dot inside the step represents an active step. A double square represents an *initial* step which should be active when the system is started up. An *action* can be associated with the step and it is written in a rectangle to the right of the step (Figure 6). Actions are executed when the associated steps are activated.
- A *transition* is represented with a bar as shown in Figure 1. The transition symbol is preceded by a double bar when two or more links join the transition (Figure 1(b) and (d)) and followed by a double bar when two or more links leave the transition (Figure 1(c) and (d)). A *receptivity* is associated with each transition ($R_1, \cdots, R_4$ in Figure 1). The receptivities are logical conditions associated with the transitions. They describe a true/false condition that must be satisfied before the transitions can occur, or *fire*.

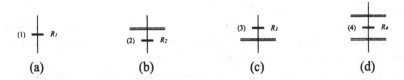

Fig. 1. Transitions

The rules for connecting steps and transitions are similar to those for Petri nets. A *directed link* always runs from a step to a transition or from a transition to a step. When two or more directed links join the same step, they can be grouped (Junction OR). When two or more directed links leave the same step, they can have a common departure point (Distribution OR).

3.2 Evolution of the State

An inactive step contains no tokens, and an active step contains one and only one token. The set of active steps at any given moment is called a *marking* and it defines the Grafcet *situation* at that moment. A Grafcet situation is thus represented by the set of active steps. The *evolution* of the Grafcet situation is carried out by the firing of transitions.

A transition is *fireable* if and only if the receptivity of the transition is true and all the steps preceding the transition are active. Firing of a transition inactivates all the steps upstream of the transition and activates all the steps downstream. The activation and inactivation operations are not separable and are simultaneously carried out. A firing has a *zero duration*.

A grafcet *evolves* according to the following rules: (1) All fireable transitions are immediately fired, (2) Several simultaneously fireable transitions are simultaneously fired, and (3) When a step must be simultaneously activated and inactivated, it remains active.

3.3 Grafcet for Agent Plans (GAP)

As we mentioned in the previous section, the Grafcet model has the necessary components to describe agent plans such as steps, actions, transitions, and receptivities. The Grafcet steps and actions correspond to the *steps* of SCS, and the Grafcet transitions and receptivities to the *conditions* of SCS. Additionally, by connecting steps and transitions, sequentiality, multiple choice, or parallelism can be represented easily. Grafcet, however, lacks explicit notions of atomicity and the failure of an action, energizing conditions, and modular nested specification of agent plans, which we have identified in the development of SCS (Section 2).

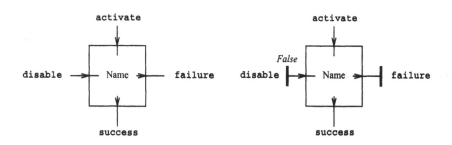

Fig. 2. GAP Module   **Fig. 3.** Module representation of a step

Grafcet for Agent Plans (GAP) is a natural extension to Grafcet. The GAP module shown in Figure 2 incorporates the notions of failure of actions and energizing conditions into the Grafcet step. Note that GAP does not extend the expressiveness of Grafcet, but provides a shorthand representation for agent plans. In other words, GAP modules can be translated into plain Grafcet representations. The `activate` input and `success` output of a module correspond to the normal Grafcet step input and output. Additionally, a module has the `disable` input and the `failure` output. Thus Grafcet steps can be represented using GAP modules as shown in Figure 3 where the `disable` input is never enabled and the `failure` output is always ignored.

Modules are activated only when the `activate` input has a token. Once a module is activated, the module *stays* activated until the associated step, if there is any, is completed with either a success or failure result, or the `disable` input has a token. When a module is inactivated, the token is passed to either the `success` or `failure` output depending on the execution result of the associated action.

The Grafcet definition of *fireable* transitions needs to be slightly modified to incorporate the power of the `disable` input and the `failure` output. A transition in GAP is *fireable* if and only if (1) the receptivity of the transition is true, (2) all the modules and steps preceding the transition are active, (3) the actions associated with the modules preceding the transition connected via `success` output are completed successfully or disabled, and (4) the actions associated with the modules preceding the transition connected via `failure` output are completed with failure.

3.4 GAP for SCS

SCS plans can be mechanically translated into GAP representations [9]. The translation basically involves extracting the operational semantics embedded in the interpreter of the SCS constructors. Each Grafcet representation for each SCS plan constructor forms a GAP module and the module can be nested into other modules exactly like the SCS constructors can be nested into other SCS constructors.

4 Model of Agent Plans for Multiagent Coordination

In the context of multiagent coordination, an operational model of agent plans is essential to be able to manifest the state description in which the agent is situated. The explicit state description also should be communicable to other agents. Our formal GAP model of agent behaviors allows agents to explicitly represent the current situation, systematically generate reachable situations to lookahead at, identify undesirable situations such as deadlock situations, and externalize the plan execution status to other coordinating agents for effective coordination. This explicit manifestation coupled with well-established formal analysis methods in Grafcet allows the agents to reach a better coordinated decision.

4.1 GAP for Multiagent Coordination

In the previous section, we mentioned that any SCS agent plan can be systematically translated into a GAP model, a notational extension to Grafcet. The implicit semantics hidden in the interpreter, a black box, is extracted and explicitly represented in the GAP model. Based on the GAP model of agent plans, we can now start to develop multiagent coordination methodologies. The GAP model of agent plans provides a means of introducing ideas of reachability analysis and model checking into multiagent coordination, where before the lack of formal operational semantics for complex AI plan execution systems would stand in the way. The analysis is based on an algorithm to generate a *situation transition diagram* from which we can reason about commitment conditions to avoid a deadlock situation among cooperative agents.

In short, our formal, explicit agent plan model opens up a new way to look at agent plans beyond declarative beliefs and goals, for effective multiagent coordination. In this section, we present a simplified example application of the GAP model of agent plans to demonstrate the general power of our model.

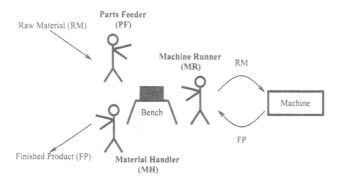

Fig. 4. A Workbench for three agents

The example scenario has three autonomous agents working in a product line around a shared workbench as shown in Figure 4. The agents want to keep the product line operating continuously. The PartsFeeder (PF) agent supplies raw materials, the MachineRunner (MR) agent produces finished product from the raw materials supplied by PF, and the MaterialHandler (MH) agent ships out the finished product. The shared workbench, however, can hold only one object, either a raw material set (RM) or a finished product (FP). Figure 5 shows SCS plans for the agents, and Figure 6 shows a corresponding, but simplified GAP model of the plans.

The manufacturers of PH, MR, and MH might be all different. The plans, thus, might have been generated independently of the other agents' plans. The plans now need to be checked to see if they would work correctly collectively.

4.2 Generating Situation Transition Diagrams

The GAP model of agent plans allows us to define precisely the situations where agent plans can lead, and the transitions between situations. A GAP *situation* consists of GAP markings and a state description expressed using predicates. In order to derive the

```
PF: repeat {
        wait until (Bench "empty");
        execute load "RM";
        wait until (Bench "RM"); }

MH: repeat {
        wait until (Bench "FP");
        execute unload "FP";
        wait until (Bench "empty"); }

MR: repeat {
        wait until (and (Bench "RM")
        (Machine "empty"));
        execute unload "RM";
        wait until (Bench "empty");
        execute load "FP";
        wait until (Bench "FP"); }
```

Fig. 5. SCS plans with a deadlock

situation transitions, we need one more piece of information to be added to the model. We need to know the *effects* of each action associated with each Grafcet step. In GAP, the effects are annotated at the bottom of each action as in Figure 6.

Figure 7 shows only important situation transitions for the purpose of explanation. A formal algorithm to generate the situation diagram is presented in [9]. Situation 0 is the initial situation with the initial marking, $< \{0\}, \{0\}, \{0\} >$ for the GAP model of agent plans.[1] The initial conjunctive state description, Bench(empty), Machine(empty), is assumed to be given.

The cycle of situation transitions through $1 \rightarrow 2 \rightarrow 3 \rightarrow 4 \rightarrow 1$ is a normal operation cycle of Load RM by PF, Unload RM and Load FP by MR, and Unload FP by MH. Situation 5 is a deadlock situation where no agent can proceed to change the situation. The deadlock situation is reached only from situation 3 when both PF's Load RM and MR's Load FP actions compete for the shared workbench and PF's Load RM action randomly occurs first. In this situation, FP cannot be handed off to MH. At the marking $< \{0\}, \{0\}, \{0\} >$ with the state Bench(RM), ¬Machine(empty), no transitions are fireable.

4.3 Commitment Decision

In the previous sections, we presented the GAP model and the situation transition diagram to demonstrate the ability to define the situations where agent plans will lead. Thus, the GAP model provides us with an essential foundation to reason about the actions and plans of the agents for multiagent coordination. In this section, we show how the situation transition diagram can be used to derive commitment decisions to avoid undesirable situations such as a deadlock or to promote desirable situations.

---

[1] In this example, the marking is a 3-tuple, one element for each agent.

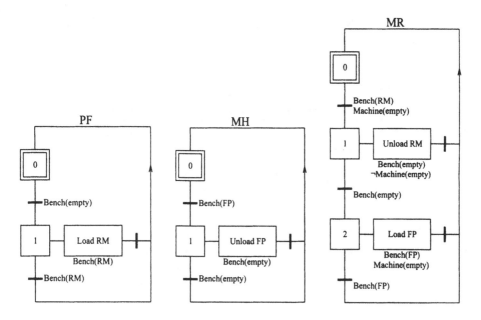

Fig. 6. GAP plans with a deadlock

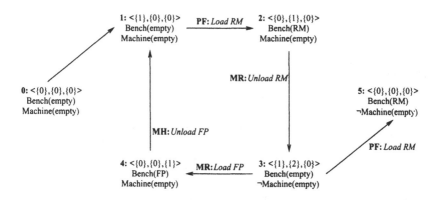

Fig. 7. Situation transitions with a deadlock

Situation 5 in Figure 7 is a deadlock situation where no agents can proceed to change the situation. The deadlock situation is reached only from situation 3 by PF's Load RM action. In order to avoid the deadlock situation, PF should not perform the Load RM action in situation 3. The question then is how to find the conditions under which PF should not perform the action.

In the situation transition diagram, PF performs a Load RM also in situation 1. Thus, we need to derive the conditions distinguishing the two situations: situation 1 where the Load RM is fine, and situation 3 where it is not. Table 1 lists the situations with the three relevant attributes, and the *classification* (deadlock or not) of the situation. In this simple classification problem, the two situations are classified easily on the

`Machine(empty)` attribute, but in general we can use *decision trees* [14] to solve general classification problems.

Situation	Attributes			Deadlock
	PF's Marking	Bench(empty)	Machine(empty)	
1	{1}	Yes	Yes	NO
3	{1}	Yes	No	YES

Table 1. Classification of situations

From the decision tree, we can identify the conditions to avoid the transition leading to the deadlock situation. That is, the condition for PF to perform the `Load RM` action without the consequent deadlock situation is `Machine(empty)`. PF now can *commit* to perform the `Load RM` action only when `Machine(empty)`, in addition to the original condition `Bench(empty)`, as shown in Figure 8.

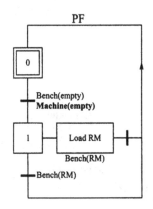

```
repeat {
    wait until (and (Bench "empty")
    (Machine "empty"));
    execute load "RM";
    wait until (Bench "RM");
}
```

Fig. 8. Commitment by PF

4.4 Alternative Commitment Decisions

While we currently follow and adopt the idea behind the algorithm for building decision-trees, there is plenty of room for further investigation of commitment decisions in the case of multiagent systems. In the domain of multiagent systems, the most important attribute might not be locally known to the decision-making agent, so that a sense of utility is involved to access the attribute. In the previous example, the chosen attribute (the only possible choice, in this simple case), `Machine(empty)`, is not local information to PF, but local to MR. PF thus needs to query MR every time before it performs `Load RM`.

In this section, we show a scenario where an agent finds the need to commit to an alternative course of actions to get out from an otherwise deadlock situation. Suppose that MH has two ways of removing the finished product to ship it out as shown in the GAP model of the new plan in Figure 9. One is to unload the finished product from the workbench (Unload FP), and another is to pick it up directly from MR (Pickup FP) without using the workbench. Also assume that the Pickup action can be activated only when MH expects majority profit (MajorityProfit(MH)).

```
repeat {
 do any {
  do when (Bench "FP") {
     execute unload "FP";
     wait until (Bench "empty");
  }
  do when (MajorityProfit "MH") {
     execute pickup "FP";
     wait until (Machine "empty");
  }}}
```

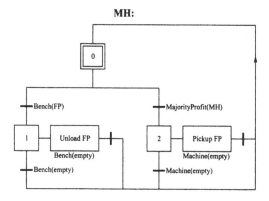

Fig. 9. Plans with alternatives

Under the default condition where MajorityProfit(MH) is initially false, the new plan still generates the same situation transitions as those in Figure 7. The solution to avoid situation 5, as previously discussed, could be costly in terms of ongoing communication overhead between PF and MR. Alternatively, suppose that the condition MajorityProfit(MH) is controllable. That is, the truth of the condition can be negotiated among agents to set it to an arbitrary value. Agents now can take advantage of MH's flexibility in handling the finished product to get out of the deadlock in situation 5.

The GAP model of agent plans and the corresponding situation transition diagram provide a systematic way to decide which conditions, if controllable, need to be satisfied to lead to desirable states. In situation 5, the three agents have the following conditions to be satisfied to move on.

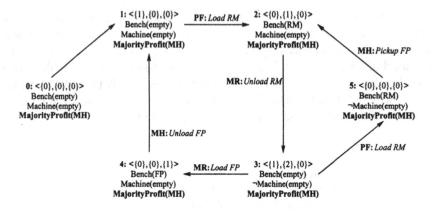

Fig. 10. Situation Transitions with alternatives

Agent	Condition
PF	Bench(empty)
MR	Bench(RM), Machine(empty)
MH	Bench(FP)
MH	MajorityProfit(MH)

In this table, MajorityProfit(MH) is the only controllable condition, and it enables MH's Pickup FP action to make the transition from (previously deadlock) situation 5 to the normal situation 2 as shown in Figure 10.

Agents thus have two coordination options. They could, at the outset, agree to MajorityProfit(MH) so that MH chooses Pickup FP directly from the machine, or they could constrain PF's Load RM action. Agents can decide between the communication cost to provide the non-local information to PF every time before PF performs Load RM, and the cost to provide MajorityProfit to MH with the one-time agreement.

5 Conclusion

This paper describes a complete process of multiagent coordination based on our SCS reactive agent plan execution semantics and the corresponding GAP model.

We started from our UM-PRS reactive plan execution system. Through applications to both physical robots and software agents, the representation and interpretation scheme of UM-PRS has been demonstrated to be sufficiently powerful for plan specification and execution in procedurally rich domains. This conceptual framework for building agents populating dynamic, unpredictable environments was used to identify the gap between reactive plan execution semantics, often implicit in the interpreter of the plans, and explicit, transferable semantics for multiagent coordination.

The problem of the embedded, implicit semantics of UM-PRS, inherited from PRS, prompted our development of Structured Circuit Semantics (SCS). SCS is an effort to bring out the embedded semantics from the interpreter using explicit, less interpreter-dependent plan constructors. SCS has been able to encapsulate the essential features of UM-PRS (and, we speculate, other plan execution systems) in a compact, yet rich formal semantics. SCS can handle continuous actions and failures, and can represent various agent behaviors such as nondeterministic behavior, best-first behavior, and persistent behavior.

Our explicit modeling of the operational semantics of SCS using the Grafcet model complements our goal of developing explicit, clean semantics for both a static agent plan description and dynamic run-time plan execution. Explicit operational semantics permit us to define explicit run-time execution states of agents in terms of *tokens* and *steps* in Grafcet, which in turn help support explicit reasoning over dynamic agent behaviors.

Our Grafcet for Agent Plans (GAP) allows us to define situations and systematically derive *situation transition diagrams* from SCS plans. From the situation transition diagram, situations can be classified as desirable or undesirable. A decision tree, then, can be used to classify conditions to avoid undesirable situations or to promote transitions to desired situations. Classifications of situations and the identification of necessary transitions can lead to agents' commitment decisions for coordination. The selected commitment decision can be mapped back to the GAP model and then SCS plans, closing the loop started from SCS plans. This closed loop completes our goal of realizing reactive, coordinating agents populating real dynamic environments.

References

1. William P. Birmingham, Edmund H. Durfee, Tracy Mullen, and Michael P. Wellman. The distributed agent architecture of the university of michigan digital library (extended abstract). In *AAAI Spring Symposium Series on Information Gathering from Distributed, Heterogeneous Environments*, March 1995.

2. René David and Hassane Alla. *Petri nets and Grafcet: tools for modelling discrete event systems*. Prentice Hall, 1992.

3. Edmund H. Durfee, Marcus Huber, Michael Kurnow, and Jaeho Lee. TAIPE: Tactical assistants for interaction planning and execution. In *Proceedings of the First International Conference on Autonomous Agents (Agents '97)*, pages 443–450, Marina del Rey, California, February 1997.

4. R. James Firby. Building symbolic primitives with continuous control routines. In James Hendler, editor, *Artificial Intelligence Planning Systems: Proceedings of the First International Conference*, pages 62–68, College Park, Maryland, June 1992. Morgan Kaufmann.

5. Francois F. Ingrand, Michael P. Georgeff, and Anand S. Rao. An architecture for real-time reasoning and system control. *IEEE Expert*, 7(6):34–44, December 1992.

6. Kurt Jensen. An introduction to the theoretical aspects of coloured petri nets. In J.W. de Bakker, W.-P. de Roever, and G. Rozenberg, editors, *A Decade of Concurrency: Reflections and Perspectives*, Lecture Notes in Computer Science Vol. 803, pages 230–272. Springer-Verlag, 1994.

7. Patrick G. Kenny, Clint R. Bidlack, Karl C. Kluge, Jaeho Lee, Marcus J. Huber, Edmund H. Durfee, and Terry Weymouth. Implementation of a reactive autonomous navigation system on an outdoor mobile robot. In *Association for Unmanned Vehicle Systems Annual National*

Symposium (AUVS-94), pages 233–239, Detroit, MI, May 1994. Association for Unmanned Vehicle Systems.

8. Jaeho Lee. On the design of structured circuit semantics. In *AAAI Spring Symposium on Lessons Learned from Implemented Software Architectures for Physical Agents*, pages 127–134, March 1995.

9. Jaeho Lee. *An Explicit Semantics for Coordinated Multiagent Plan Execution*. PhD thesis, University of Michigan, Ann Arbor, Michigan, January 1997.

10. Jaeho Lee, Marcus J. Huber, Edmund H. Durfee, and Patrick G. Kenny. UM-PRS: an implementation of the procedural reasoning system for multirobot applications. In *Conference on Intelligent Robotics in Field, Factory, Service, and Space (CIRFFSS '94)*, pages 842–849, Houston, Texas, March 1994.

11. Tadao Murata. Petri nets: Properties, analysis and applications. *Proceedings of the IEEE*, 77(4):541–580, April 1989.

12. Nils J. Nilsson. Toward agent programs with circuit semantics. Technical Report STAN-CS-92-1412, Department of Computer Science, Stanford University, January 1992.

13. Nils J. Nilsson. Teleo-reactive programs for agent control. *Journal of Artificial Intelligence Research*, 1:139–158, 1994.

14. Stuart J. Russell and Peter Norvig. *Artificial Intelligence : A Modern Approach*. Prentice Hall, 1995.

15. Marcel J. Schoppers. Universal plans for reactive robots in unpredictable environments. In *Proceedings of the Tenth International Joint Conference on Artificial Intelligence*, pages 1039–1046, Milan, Italy, 1987.

16. José M. Vidal and Edmund H. Durfee. Task planning agents in the UMDL. In *Proceeding of the 1995 Intelligent Information Agents Workshop*, 1995.

Social Comparison for Failure Detection and Recovery

Gal A. Kaminka and Milind Tambe
Computer Science Department and Information Sciences Institute
University of Southern California
4676 Admiralty Way, Marina del Rey, CA 90292
{galk, tambe}@isi.edu

Abstract. Plan execution monitoring in dynamic and uncertain domains is an important and difficult problem. Multi-agent environments exacerbate this problem, given that interacting and coordinated activities of multiple agents are to be monitored. Previous approaches to this problem do not detect certain classes of failures, are inflexible, and are hard to scale up. We present a novel approach, SOCFAD, to failure detection and recovery in multi-agent settings. SOCFAD is inspired by *Social Comparison Theory* from social psychology and includes the following key novel concepts: (a) utilizing other agents in the environment as information sources for failure detection, (b) a detection and repair method for previously undetectable failures using abductive inference based on other agents' beliefs, and (c) a decision-theoretic approach to selecting the information acquisition medium. An analysis of SOCFAD is presented, showing that the new method is complementary to previous approaches in terms of classes of failures detected.

1 Introduction

Agent behavior monitoring in complex dynamic environments is an important and well known problem, e.g., [3], [10]. This problem is exacerbated in multi-agent environments due to the added requirements for communication and coordination. The complexity and unpredictability of such dynamic environments causes an explosion of state space complexity, which inhibits the ability of any designer, human or machine (i.e., planners), to enumerate the correct response in each possible state. The agents are therefore presented with countless opportunities for failure, which could not have been anticipated. For instance, it is generally difficult to predict when sensors will return unreliable answers, communication messages get lost, etc.

The agents must therefore be responsible for autonomously detecting the failures, and for recovering from them. To this end, an agent must have information about the ideal behavior expected of it. This ideal can be compared to the agent's actual behavior to detect discrepancies indicating possible failures. Previous approaches to this problem (e.g., [3], [10], [15]) have focused on the designer or planner supplying the agent with redundant information, either in the form of explicitly specified execution-monitoring conditions, or a model of the agent itself which may be used for comparison. Indeed, monitoring explicit conditions on the agent's behavior have proved useful to us in initial stages of failure detection.

However, both of these approaches suffer from limitations which render them insufficient for failure detection in general:

1. *Information failures.* Both approaches fail where relevant information is unexpectedly unavailable. For instance, if a condition monitor depended on a sensor to provide verification, a failure of the sensor will render the monitor useless.

2. *Inflexibility.* Monitoring conditions in agent behavior can be too rigid in highly dynamic environments, as agents in complex environments must often adjust their behavior flexibly to respond to the actual circumstances they are in.

3. *Difficulty in scaling up.* Both approaches mandate that the designer supply redundant information, which entails further work for the designer, and encounters difficulties in scaling up to more complex domains. Model-based approaches require the designer to specify the agent design twice, in a sense: Once in designing the agent, and again in designing a self-model for simulation and comparison.

We propose a complementary novel approach to failure detection and recovery, which is unique to multi-agent settings. This approach, SOCFAD (Social Comparison for FAilure Detection), is inspired by ideas from *Social Comparison Theory* [9]. The key idea in SOCFAD is that agents use other agents as sources of information on the situation and the ideal behavior. The agents compare their own behavior, beliefs, goals, and plans to those of other agents, in order to detect failures and correct their behavior. The agents do not necessarily adapt the other agents' beliefs, but can reason about the differences in belief and behavior, and draw useful conclusions regarding the correctness of their own actions. This approach alleviates the problems described above:

1. It allows agents to overcome information failures, as relevant information may be inferred from other agents' behavior and used to replace or complement the agent's own erroneous perceptions.

2. It allows for flexibility in detecting failures, since the flexible, dynamic, behavior of other agents' is used as an ideal for comparison.

3. It doesn't require the designer to provide the agent with redundant information about itself (in the form of a model or conditions), utilizing instead other agents as sources of information.

One key general heuristic used in SOCFAD is application in a team context. In particular, teamwork or collaboration is ubiquitous in multi-agent domains. An important issue in SOCFAD is that the agents being compared should be *socially similar* to yield meaningful differences. By constraining SOCFAD to use team-members for comparison, we narrow down the search for socially-similar agents. Furthermore, by exploiting agent modeling (plan-recognition) techniques to infer team members' goals, SOCFAD enables efficient comparison without significant communication overhead. We also allow the agent to explicitly reason about *social roles* and *status*, so that it can compare itself only to agents that can provide it with meaningful information.

SOCFAD is implemented and discussed within the context of IFDARS (Integrated Failure Detection And Recovery System), a system provided to our agents for the purpose of failure detection and recovery. IFDARS integrates different failure detection and recovery techniques within a unified framework, allowing evidence from different failure detection modules to be combined and reasoned about explicitly.

An additional novelty in IFDARS is that it brings forth an assumption that is implicitly made with the other approaches: The model (or condition) provided by the designer is always correct (the *model-correctness assumption*). However, in social comparison, other agents act as the knowledge sources, and cannot be assumed to be correct at all times. In detecting failures by social comparison, the agents must reason not only about the actual differences found, but also about the possibility that the agent itself is not at fault, but its social role models. By making this assumption explicit, IFDARS recovery modules can utilize different information sources and parameterized biases to reason about the differences in a general way.

2 SOCFAD and IFDARS: Motivation

The motivation for our approach comes from our application domain which involves developing automated pilot agents for participation in synthetic multi-agent battlefield simulation environments [12]. The environment was commercially developed for military training, and is highly dynamic, complex, and rich in detail. In addition to the unpredictability of the environment, communications and sensors are unreliable, mission and task specifications may be incomplete, etc. These qualities present the agents with never-ending opportunities for failure, as anticipation of all possible internal and external states is impossible for the designer. Two examples may serve to illustrate: In the first, a team of three helicopters takes off from the home base and heads out towards their battle position. While two of the agents follow the mission plan, a single agent hovers in place at the starting position indefinitely, due to an unanticipated miscommunication of the mission specification. In the second example, a similar team of three agents arrives at a specified landmark position. One of the team-members, whose role is that of a scout, is to continue forward towards the enemy, identifying and verifying its position. The scout's team-mates are to wait for its return in the specified position, and indeed one agent correctly lands and waits. Due to unanticipated sensory failure, the remaining agent, which is also supposed to wait, does not detect the landmark marking the waiting point. Instead of waiting behind, it continues to fly forward with the scout, following it into the battlefield.

We have collected dozens of such failure reports over a period of a few months. While it is generally easy for the human designer to correct these failures once they occur, it is generally hard to anticipate them in advance. The failures occur despite significant development and maintenance effort -- given the complexity of the dynamic environment, predicting all possible states and all possible interactions is impossible.

These failures are not negligible. Rather, they are very obvious failures, usually due to unanticipated (by the human designer) circumstances, and generally catastrophic, completely prohibiting the agent in question from participating in the simulation. In the first example above, not only is the single agent stuck behind unable to participate in the simulation, but the remaining agents are unable to carry out the mission by themselves.

An underlying quality of many of these failures is that they are not specific to military procedures. Indeed, the domain experts expect some level of common sense handling of failures even in the most structured and strict military procedure. By exercising social common sense, an agent may at least detect that something may be wrong, even if it does not have knowledge of the military domains. Social clues, such as (in the examples above) noticing that team-mates are leaving while the agent is hovering in place, or that a team-member has landed while the team was flying in formation, would have been sufficient to infer that something may be wrong.

3 IFDARS

The *Integrated Failure Detection And Recovery System* (IFDARS) integrates different failure detection and recovery techniques, and allows for evidence from multiple sources to be combined and reasoned about explicitly (Figure 1).

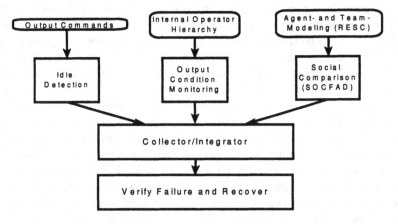

Figure 1. IFDARS Structure.

IFDARS uses three different failure-detection modules which all interface in a unified manner by generating '*interesting events*'--indications of possible failures (false positives are allowed). Events have *specificity*--they may be *generic*, i.e., general indications, not localized to a specific fault; or they may be *specific*-- indicating for instance that the aircraft may have a problem with its speed. To allow the system to reason about specific failure-detection modules, all events are tagged by the failure-detection module that generated them. Events have *weight* which indicates how important they are, and *certainty* that in fact a failure took place. Events may also be generated as a response to other events. For example, a continuing repetition of events is itself a reason to suspect a failure may be underway, and so if a failure repeats itself too often, an event describing this repetition is generated.

The events are collected together from the different detection modules in the collector/integrator component. Given a set of events $E_1,...,E_k$, with corresponding weights $W_1,...,W_k$ and certainties $C_1,....,C_k$, for specificity i, the alarm level A_i is calculated as follows:

$$A_i = \sum_{i=1}^{k} W_i C_i$$

Once alarm levels are raised above threshold, the system reasons about the possible failures, verifying and possibly recovering from the failures. The recovery process lowers the alarm levels appropriately.

The three current failure-detection modules in IFDARS are: (a) a social comparison module, implementing SOCFAD, (b) a condition-monitoring module, and (c) an activity measurement module. The three modules utilize different input sources for detecting failures. The condition monitoring module monitors the currently running reactive plans, via designer-supplied conditions. The activity measurement module attempts to detect when the agent is unreasonably idle (i.e., stuck). The social comparison module is the basis for SOCFAD. We have found all three modules to be useful in detecting failures in the agent's behavior, but as condition-monitoring approaches and activity measurement monitoring are already common techniques in failure detection, we will focus on the social comparison process in the next section.

4 Social Comparison for Failure Detection: SOCFAD

SOCFAD is inspired by Social Comparison Theory [4], a theory from social psychology, developed to explain cognitive processes in groups of humans. Newell [9] presents the first three axioms of this theory as follows (pg. 497):

1. Every agent has a drive to evaluate its opinions and abilities.
2. If the agent can't evaluate its opinions and abilities objectively, then it compares them against the opinions and abilities of others.
3. Comparing against others decreases as the difference with others increases.

The numerous reports of failures we have collected demonstrate the very real need of agents in dynamic, unpredictable domains to evaluate themselves by monitoring their execution. This empirically verifies the importance of the first axiom. Approaches emphasizing the designer as a source of information against which to compare the agent's performance fit naturally under the title of objective sources for the agent's self-evaluation. SOCFAD focuses on the remaining parts of the axioms - allowing the agent to compare its own abilities and opinions (i.e., behavior, beliefs, operators, and goals) to those of others (second axiom), and considering the weight put on the results of such comparison (third axiom).

Although Social Comparison Theory is descriptive, we have begun to operationalize it for monitoring (see Algorithm 1). The abstract version of our algorithm accepts inputs representing the states of agents being compared - their beliefs, goals, behavior, etc. The agents' states are then compared by *Find-Difference* to detect possible failures, and a social similarity metric is used in the function *Similarity* to produce a level of certainty in the detected failure.

```
Social-Failure-Detect(myself, other-agents)  {
        1.Difference ← Find-Difference(my-self, other-agents)
        2.If Difference = NIL then goto 5
        3.Failure-Certainty ← Similarity(Difference)
        4.If Failure-Certainty > 0 then return Difference as a detected
          failure, with certainty Failure-Certainty.
        5.No failure was detected.  Return NIL.

}
```

Algorithm 1. Social Failure Detection (Abstract Version).

The interesting issues in this algorithm are hidden in the two functions *Find-Difference* and *Similarity*. Different capabilities and performance result by changing the information being compared by *Find-Difference*, (e.g., internal beliefs and goals vs. observable behavior). In *Find-Difference*, it is useful to (i) limit agent states compared for efficiency, and (ii) use information that captures the control processes of the agents. Agent's plan hierarchies usually satisfy both constraints, but potentially other aspects of states could be used. The *Similarity* function reasons about the social similarity of agents being compared, and translates the differences to a certainty that indeed a failure has occurred. These algorithms will be incrementally developed through the rest of this section.

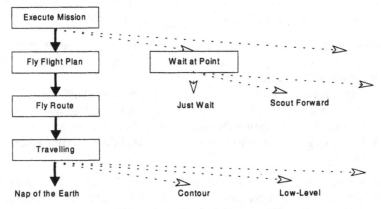

Figure 2. An Example Operator Hierarchy

Our agents' design is based on reactive plans (operators) ([5], [9], [11]), which form a hierarchy that controls each agent (Figure 2). The design implements the *Joint Intention Framework* [7]. Following this framework, operators may be team operators (shared by the team) or individual (specific to one agent). Boxed operator names signify team operators, which achieve and maintain joint goals, while the other operators are individual. Team operators require coordination with the other members of the team as part of their application ([13], [14]). Figure 2 presents a small portion of the hierarchy. The filled arrows signify the operator hierarchy currently in control, while dotted arrows point to alternative operators which may be used. In the figure, the agent is currently executing the execute-mission team operator as its highest-level team plan, and has chosen to execute the fly-flight-plan operator, for flying the agent team through the different locations specified in its mission.

Operator hierarchies form the basic structure of our agent's reasoning process, and were natural objects for comparison. To operationalize SOCFAD we require a way of acquiring knowledge of the operator hierarchies of other agents (so that we have something to compare against), a definition for *Find-Difference* (a procedure for comparing hierarchies), and a definition for *Similarity* as well.

In theory, knowledge of other agents can be communicated. However, such communication is often highly impractical given significant communication costs, risk in communicating in hostile environments, and unreliability in dynamic and uncertain settings. Instead our implementation of SOCFAD relies on agent modeling (plan recognition) techniques that infer an agent's beliefs, goals, and plans from its observable behavior and surrounding.

We use the RESC$_{team}$ [13] method in modeling other agents, but different techniques may be used interchangeably, as long as they provide the needed information and representation. RESC$_{team}$ will be briefly described here (see [13] for more detail). RESC$_{team}$ represents other agents' plans by building additional operator hierarchies in the agent's memory which correspond to the other agents' inferred reactive plans currently executed. Thus, the monitoring agent has unified access not only to its own original operator hierarchy, but also to the inferred operator hierarchies of other team members (Figure 3).

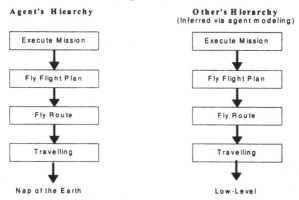

Figure 3. An Example of Two Hierarchies in the Agent's Memory.

Based on the representation of the other agents' plans by operator hierarchies, the *Find-Difference* function can be easily implemented (Algorithm 2) as the simple process of comparing the chosen operators in equal depths of the hierarchies. Hierarchies of different lengths are also considered different.

```
Find-Difference(my-operator-hierarchy, other-hierarchies) {
    1.Depth ← 0
    2.Compare operators in hierarchies at depth Depth
    3.If a difference is found, return it.
    4.Else, are the operators leaves of the hierarchies?
        4.1 No. Increase Depth. Goto 2.
        4.2 Yes. Return NIL.

}
```

Algorithm 2. Find-Difference.

As implied by the third axiom of social comparison theory, differences with other agents are meaningful only to the extent that the other agents are *socially similar*. Other agents may not be executing plans that are relevant to the agent's goals, and therefore may not be able to contribute relevant information towards the monitoring of the agents own plans and goals. Worse yet, other agents may intentionally want to use deception in order to influence the agent's decision making to advance their own agendas.

Fortunately, a team context provides an initial solution. Team members tend to work on joint goals and sub-plans related to the one the agent should be executing, and can be assumed to be non-hostile (therefore not intentionally deceiving the agent in question). The comparison process in Find-Difference therefore considers team members only.

4.1 Team Operator Differences

Our agents use the Joint Intentions framework [7] as the basis for their coordination of team activities. In this framework, explicit team operators form the basis for teamwork, requiring mutual belief (MB) on the part of the team members as a condition for the establishment, and termination (based on achievement, unachieveability, or irrelevancy), of explicit team operators. Team operators must therefore be identical for all team members. A difference in team operators is therefore a certain sign of failure, regardless of its cause.

In one example above, one agent has failed to detect a key landmark position and continued execution of the "fly-flight-plan" team operator. However, its teammates correctly detected the landmark and terminated execution of that operator. They then switched to executing "wait-at-point" team operator, in which two agents are to land while the *scout* is to go forward and scout the enemy position. Through agent modeling, the miscoordinating agent infers the operators the other agents are executing. It realizes that they could potentially be executing the "wait-at-point" operator and detects a discrepancy with its own team operator of "fly flight plan". At this point it does not know which side is correct – either itself is at fault or its teammates. Regardless, the agent can conclude that a failure has occurred with the team and the coordination among its members.

The purpose of utilizing the joint intentions framework is to benefit from the domain-independent guarantees it provides for team coordination. As the agents are designed to follow the framework, it would appear at first that the above failures of miscoordination cannot occur. However, given the well recognized difficulty of establishing mutual belief *in practice*, differences in team operators do occur. In the example motivating this discussion, since the landmark that was to signal termination of the "fly-flight-plan" operator is in the external environment, it was assumed to be visible to all agents. Thus, mutual belief that the landmark was detected was assumed by the agent that successfully detected it, and it correctly abandoned the team operator (this assumption is motivated by the inefficiency of continuous communications). The second agent, which had missed detection of the landmark was true to the joint intentions framework as well: It didn't abandon one team operator without establishing mutual belief that it was achieved, unachievable, or irrelevant. The key point is that while both agents have correctly followed the joint intentions framework, a failure in sensing, coupled with a practical assumption about establishment of mutual belief caused the joint-goals of both agents to differ. And no matter which agent is right, a failure has certainly occurred, since the team is no longer coordinated.

```
Similarity (Operator-Difference) {
        If Operator-Difference is between team operators then
                return maximum certainty
}
```

Algorithm 3a. Similarity, Version 1.

To operationalize this discussion, we can now define an initial version of the Similarity function used in the social failure detection algorithm (Algorithm 1). The key idea is that at the team level, agents have identical team operators, and so are maximally socially similar.

4.2 Individual Operator Differences

The previous section discussed differences between agents that are maximally similar--agents that have joint goals and together form a team. However, in service of team operators different agents may work on different individual operators. These individual operators do not necessarily carry with them the responsibilities for mutual belief that team operators do, and so differences in individual operators are not sure signs of failure, but at best indications of the possibility.

We therefore require additional information about the agents causing the difference which can help in determining whether the difference is justified or not. For instance, agents working towards similar goals have similar *social roles:* For example, in a soccer game there are field players and a goalie which have different roles within the team. Agents with similar roles would serve as better sources of information for plan-execution monitoring than other agents. Related to the social role is *social status*, which may also justify differences in individual operators among team members. For instance, in the military domain agents of different ranks may follow different individual operators to guide their behavior.

The example where a failing agent was stuck in place while its team-members have taken off and were flying away serves to illustrate this distinct type of discrepancy. Here, a comparison of the agent's own chosen method-of-flight operator to the methods of flight chosen by its comrades indicates to the agent that it is not acting like the rest of the team - that in fact a failure may have occurred (see leaf operators in Figure 3).

We have provided our agent with the means to explicitly utilize the social similarity of team-members in their reasoning. The agent explicitly considers the parameter of the social role of other agents within the team in filtering and assigning weights to the information inferred about them. For example, if the agent is an *attacker*, which is one of the roles in a team in our domain, it will assign more weight to other agents which are *attackers*. For efficiency, the agent may completely ignore agents which it decides, based on their role, are not relevant as information sources.

Even after filtering irrelevant differences with agents of differing social roles, there remain individual differences which are justifiable and do not constitute a failure, simply because agents may not necessarily find themselves in identical external and internal states. For instance, in the real world, no two agents can share the exact same physical space. We therefore require more techniques which can raise our confidence that indeed a failure has occurred, when a discrepancy in individual operators is found.

The above discussion brings us to an updated version of the Similarity function, incorporating the heuristics discussed above: social role and social status. The exact definition of role and status, and the weights by which they modify the certainty (3.1-3.2 in Algorithm 3b below) are domain dependent, as are the default certainties that a failure has occurred.

Similarity (Operator-Difference) {
    1. Certainty ← Default /* or a-priori certainty */
    2. If Operator-Difference is between team operators then
       Certainty←Maximum Certainty /* From version 1 */
    3. Else /* difference between individual operators */
         3.1 If Operator-Difference is between agents with same Role, then increase
            Certainty, else decrease it.
         3.2 If Operator-Difference is between agents with same Status, then
            increase Certainty, else decrease it.
    4. Return Certainty.
}

Algorithm 3b. Similarity, Version 2.

4.3 Towards Recovery Based on Social Comparison

In general, to recover from a failure, a process of diagnosis is required. Here again social comparison raises novel issues. First, it does not make the *model-correctness assumption* made in previous approaches. Second, it allows the process of diagnosis and recovery to utilize social sources of information which were not utilized before.

Model-correctness assumption. In recovering from a failure detected by social comparison, the agent must reason explicitly about the differences in beliefs that exist between itself and the other members of the team. From the fact that other agents are executing a different plan, the agent can infer by abduction that the preconditions necessary for selection and execution of that plan were satisfied by the other agents. It can then reason about the relevance of these preconditions to its own selected plan. For instance, in the example of the agent's failure to detect a key landmark, it appears that the other agents are carrying out the wait-at-point operator (one agent lands, while the other one which is known to be the scout goes forward). Once this discrepancy is noted ("I am executing fly-flight-plan, they are executing wait-at-point"), the agents makes an abductive inference that the other agents believe that the team has indeed reached the landmark. However, the agent does not necessarily adapt the team-members' view - it does not assume the model (other agents) to be correct.

Socially-based recovery. As the model-correctness assumption is made explicit, social information sources can be utilized for diagnosis and recovery. If the agent believes it is at fault, it can alter its own beliefs by adopting the preconditions which it inferred are satisfied for the other agents' operators. In particular, team operator's preconditions require mutual belief, and so by adopting them the agent allows the correct team plan to be selected, therefore synchronizing itself with the rest of the team. For example, the agent in the landmark example fixed its own beliefs regarding the landmark based on this abduction. This fulfills the preconditions of its own "wait-at-point" operator, which is now selected and allows the agent to recover gracefully from the failure.

5 Results and Evaluation

Our agent, including IFDARS, is implemented completely in Soar [9]. Approximately 1200 rules are used in the implementation of the agent, which includes the military procedures, as well as the teamwork and agent-modeling capabilities. Additional 60 rules implement IFDARS, forming an add-on layer on top of the procedures making up the agent.

The social comparison approach to failure detection complements the condition-monitoring detection methods, being able to detect different types of failures. In general, the condition-monitoring approaches cannot detect failures where a feature of the environment is not detected, and are limited in their abilities to detect failures where the inputs to the agent (as perceived by the sensors) are incorrect. Model-based approaches in particular use the agent's own inputs to generate an ideal output which is compared to the actual output to detect problems in the process converting inputs to outputs. However, failures may occur in the inputs to the agent due to sensory problems, resulting either in incorrect readings or in missing perceptions. A model-based approach cannot detect these failures as it uses the erroneous inputs. However, the social comparison approach can detect such failures and correct them as demonstrated in the example of the undetected landmark.

In contrast, social comparison methods will encounter problems in single-agent situations, or if all team members encounter identical failures simultaneously (which we hypothesize to occur very infrequently in complex multi-agent settings). There a process of comparison would not generate any differences if the execution of the plan is incorrect, as the agents would all display the same incorrect behavior.

Here a model-based or condition-monitoring approach is very suitable for detecting failures.

Our explicit choice to prefer agent-modeling to communications for acquiring the information for comparison from the other agent stems from practical constraints common to many multi-agent domains. However, in general, using the following decision tree, an agent can decide whether to use agent modeling for acquiring the information, or to have (by request or by design) the other agents communicate back their beliefs, plans and goals:

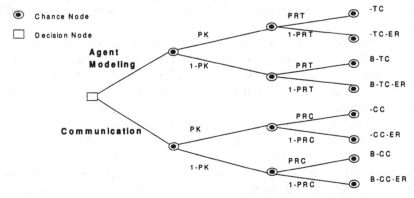

Figure 4. Decision Tree for Information-Acquiring Method.

The purpose of acquiring information about the other agents (by either modeling or communications) is to detect possible failures. In the decision tree above, the agent seeks to maximize its expected utility from the process of acquisition. Thus, a bonus B is rewarded in the decision tree above if the agent indeed acquires new information. This bonus is not awarded if the information does not differ in any way from what the agent already knew. TC and CC are the costs for modeling and communicating, respectively (CC is the total cost incurred by sender and receiver). PK is the probability that the information is already known (so no difference is detected), PRT the probability that the modeling process was reliable, and PRC the probability that communications were reliable (for both modeling and communication, reliability implies that the information was acquired correctly). ER is the penalty for making a mistake - for example for incorrect inference made by modeling, or for receiving an unreliable message.

By following the tree, it is clear that the agent should rely on agent modeling rather on communications from other agents whenever TC+(1-PRT)*ER < CC+(1-PRC)*ER. In our domain, the cost of communications is very high, as the agents operate in a hostile environment and expose themselves by communicating with each other. On the other hand, the cost of agent modeling is relatively low, being mostly a computational cost rather than a survival risk. In addition, in a team context, modeling is often reliable, in contrast to communications, which are unreliable quite often. Our estimation of reliability and the cost of error make agent modeling an attractive choice for acquiring knowledge of others. For simplicity, one may choose to assume reliable communications and agent-modeling, and then the agent's choice is dictated solely by the cost of modeling vs. communications.

6 Related Work

Social comparison is related to work on multi-agent coordination and teamwork, although in general, social comparison generalizes to also detect failures in execution of individual operators, which are outside the scope of coordination. Particularly relevant are *observation-based* methods, which utilize agent modeling rather than communications for coordination (e.g., [6], [14]). Work on teamwork [14] concentrates on maintaining identical joint goals to prevent miscoordination, while the focus of SOCFAD is on detecting when the goals do differ. Indeed, social comparison can be useful for recovering from failures in teamwork. The recovery from the undetected landmark failure mentioned earlier can be construed as an example of active coordination on the part of the team. Huber and Durfee [6] do not assume joint goals but instead look at coordination as emergent from opportunistic agents, which coordinate with others when it suits their individual goals. As these agents do not have team goals, they cannot assume maximal social similarity at the team coordination level, and so would not be able to detect team failure. Also, while Huber and Durfee demonstrate the benefits of using plan-recognition rather than explicit communications in a dynamic domain, they do not discuss the qualities of the domain which make plan-recognition beneficial. The decision-tree provided in the previous section presents a first step towards this direction.

Atkins et al. [2] attacks a similar problem of detecting states for which the agent does not have a plan ready. They offer a classification of these states, and provide planning algorithms that build tests for these states. However, their approach considers only the individual agents and not teams. It also suffers from the same limitations as condition monitoring approaches in not being able to detect modeled states which have not been sensed correctly. For instance, their approach cannot detect states which were not planned-for by the planner, but are still "safe" [2] such as the example of the undetected landmark.

Social comparison is also related to imitation [2]. In fact, imitation can be shown to be a special case of the general social comparison algorithm (Algorithm 1). By choosing to compare itself against the observable behavior of other agents, rather than their internal goals, the social comparison approach leads to imitation. In the example of the agent failing to detect a landmark and land, a simple imitation of the scout would be clearly inadequate. Alternatively, imitation of the other *attacker* would lead to failure later on as the agent is still executing the wrong team-operator and follows the wrong sequence of actions.

To illustrate this point further, consider a similar case, where the failing agent is actually the scout that is supposed to go forward. Upon reaching the landmark, its two team-members land waiting for it to go forward. Since it didn't detect the landmark the agent is still executing the flying-in-formation plan. If it were to imitate its team-mates, it would simply land or hover near them while they are waiting for it to go forward. Instead, with SOCFAD the agent would compare the plan that it is executing with those of its team-mates, and realize that they are now executing a different plan, based on detecting a landmark which it has failed to detect. It could thus recover from such an error.

Mataric [8] used socially similar agents (*next of kin*) to investigate generation of group behavior from local interactions, while the focus of SOCFAD is on failure detection. By restricting group members to be socially similar, Mataric showed little communication is necessary as the agents can make correct predictions on the behavior of their peers, and this allows coherent group behavior to emerge. Although SOCFAD emphasizes the importance of social similarity for the individual, we do not assume it. In fact, a core issue in SOCFAD is the search for socially similar agents which can be used for comparison among all agents.

7 Summary and Future Work

This paper presents a novel approach to failure detection, an important problem plaguing multi-agent systems in large-scale, dynamic, complex domains. Existing approaches often face difficulty in addressing this problem in such domains. The key novelties of our approach are: (a) a new failure detection method, utilizing other agents in the environment as information sources for comparison, (b) a general heuristic for team-based comparison, (c) a detection and repair method for (previously undetectable) information failures using abductive inference based on other agents' beliefs, and (d) a decision-theoretic approach to selecting the information acquisition medium.

Several issues are open for future work. One important issue is in techniques and biases useful for deciding which side is correct where a difference is encountered with another agent, but no information is known to support either side. Previous approaches have arbitrarily chosen to bias their decision by making the model correctness assumption implicitly. IFDARS allows to explicitly handle this state by other biases and heuristics to be used. A simple techniques that may be used is to follow the majority, so that if a majority of agents agree with one agent, its beliefs and behavior is taken to be correct. Such a technique has clear limitations, but initial experiments show it to be quite useful. Another technique is to bias the agent detecting the failure towards accepting responsibility for the failure (low self-confidence) or for rejecting it, possibly attributing it to the other agent. This bias can be easily parameterized, and can result in very different behaviors on the part of the failure-detecting agent. An additional option enabled by IFDARS is to utilize evidence supplied by other failure-detection modules to provide additional evidence.

Another important issue left for future work is the integration of learning into the detection and recovery process, whereby the agent should be able to learn not only how to respond to detected failures, but also the settings in which they are likely to arise, how to prevent them from happening, etc. A key object for learning is social similarity, where the agent would learn which agents are socially similar, or otherwise serve as good source of information for failure-detection purposes (good role-models).

References

1. Atkins, E. M.; Durfee, E. H.; and Shin, K. G. 1996. Detecting and reacting to unplanned-for world states, in *Proceedings of the AAAI-96 Fall symposium on Plan Execution*. pp. 1-7.
2. Bakker, P.; and Kuniyoshi, Y. 1996. Robot see, robot do: An overview of robot imitation. *AISB Workshop on Learning in Robots and Animals*, Brighton, UK.
3. Doyle R. J., Atkinson D. J., Doshi R. S., Generating perception requests and expectations to verify the execution of plans, in *Proceedings of AAAI-86*, Philadelphia, PA (1986).
4. Festinger, L. 1954. A theory of social comparison processes. *Human Relations*, 7, pp. 117-140.
5. Firby, J. 1987. An investigation into reactive planning in complex domains. In *Proceedings of the National Conference on Artificial Intelligence (AAAI-87)*.
6. Huber, M. J.; and Durfee, E. H. 1996. An Initial Assessment of Plan-Recognition-Based Coordination for Multi-Agent Teams. In *Proceedings of the Second International Conference on Multi-Agent Systems (ICMAS-96)*. Kyoto, Japan. pp. 126-133.
7. Levesque, H. J.; Cohen, P. R.; Nunes, J. 1990. On acting together, in *Proceedings of the National Conference on Artificial Intelligence (AAAI-1990)*, Menlo Park, California, AAAI Press.
8. Mataric, M. J. 1993. Kin Recognition, Similarity, and Group Behavior. In *Proceedings of the Fifteenth Annual Cognitive Science Society Conference*. Boulder, Colorado. Pp. 705-710.
9. Newell A., 1990. *Unified Theories of Cognition*. Harvard University Press.
10. Reece, G. A.; and Tate, A. Synthesizing protection monitors from causal structure, in *Proceedings of AIPS-94*, Chicago, Illinois (1994).
11. Rao, A. S.; Lucas, A.; Morley, D., Selvestrel, M.; and Murray, G. 1993. Agent-oriented architecture for air-combat simulation. Technical Report: Technical Note 42, The Australian Artificial Intelligence Institute.
12. Tambe, M.; Johnson W. L.; Jones, R.; Koss, F.; Laird, J. E.; Rosenbloom, P. S.; and Schwamb, K. 1995. Intelligent Agents for interactive simulation environments. *AI Magazine*, 16(1) (Spring).
13. Tambe, M. 1996. Tracking Dynamic Team Activity, in *Proceedings of the National Conference on Artificial Intelligence (AAAI-96)*, Portland, Oregon.
14. Tambe, M. 1997. Agent Architectures for Flexible, Practical Teamwork, in *Proceedings of the National Conference on Artificial Intelligence*, Providence, Rhode Island (To appear).
15. Williams, B. C.; and Nayak, P. P. 1996. A Model-Based Approach to Reactive Self-Configuring Systems. In *Proceedings of the Thirteenth National Conference on Artificial Intelligence (AAAI-96)*, Portland, Oregon.

Multi-Agent Coordination through Coalition Formation *

Onn M. Shehory, Katia Sycara and Somesh Jha

The Robotics Institute
Carnegie Mellon University
Pittsburgh, PA 15213, U.S.A.
onn,katia,sjha@cs.cmu.edu
www.cs.cmu.edu/~softagents

Abstract. Incorporating coalition formation algorithms into agent systems shall be advantageous due to the consequent increase in the overall quality of task performance. Coalition formation was addressed in game theory, however the game theoretic approach is centralized and computationally intractable. Recent work in DAI has resulted in distributed algorithms with computational tractability. This paper addresses the implementation of distributed coalition formation algorithms within a real-world multi-agent system. We present the problems that arise when attempting to utilize the theoretical coalition formation algorithms for a real-world system, demonstrate how some of their restrictive assumptions can be relaxed, and discuss the resulting benefits. In addition, we analyze the modifications, the complexity and the quality of the cooperation mechanisms. The task domain of our multi-agent system is information gathering, filtering and decision support within the WWW.

1   Introduction

Theories of cooperation among computational intelligent agents have been developed in the last decade, providing methods which enable, theoretically, low complexity of the cooperation mechanisms as well as high performance of the multi-agent systems. Although they seem promising, most of these mechanisms were not tested in a *real-world* multi-agent environment.

Cooperating groups of agents, referred to as coalitions, were thoroughly investigated within game theory (e.g., in [11]). There, issues of solution stability, fairness and payoff disbursements were discussed and analyzed. The formal analysis provided there can be used to compute multi-agent coalitions, however only in a centralized manner and with exponential complexity. DAI researchers have adopted some of the game-theoretical concepts and upon them developed coalition formation algorithms, to be used by agents within a multi-agent system (e.g., [19, 6]). These algorithms concentrate on distribution of the computations, complexity reduction, efficient task allocation and communication issues. Nevertheless, some of the underlying assumptions of the coalition formation algorithms, which are essential for their implementation, do not hold in real-world multi-agent systems.

---

* This material is based upon work supported in part by ARPA Grant #F33615-93-1-1330, by ONR Grant #N00014-96-1-1222, and by NSF Grant #IRI-9508191.

In this paper we report on coalition formation as a means for coordinating agents. The coalition formation method we present is appropriate for dozens of agents[2]. We begin with a brief overview of the multi-agent system into which the algorithms are applied in section 2. We continue by presenting the theoretical coalition formation method, in section 3. We then present the implementation requirements (section 4) and relaxation of theoretical assumptions (section 5). In section 6 we analyze the properties and modifications of the implemented method, both theoretically and via simulations. Finally we conclude in section 7.

2   The Information Multi-agent System

The problem of locating information sources, accessing, filtering, and integrating information, as well as interleaving information retrieval and problem solving has become a very critical task, due to the increasing amount of distributed, dynamically changing information.

Most work in intelligent software agents that gather information from Internet-based sources, e.g., [8, 9, 1] focussed on a single agent with simple knowledge and problem solving capabilities whose main task is information filtering to alleviate the user's cognitive overload. Another type of agent is the *Softbot* ([4]), a single agent with general knowledge that performs a wide range of user-delegated information-finding tasks. A single general agent would need an enormous amount of knowledge to effectively deal with user information requests that cover a variety of tasks. In addition, a centralized system constitutes a processing bottleneck and a "single point of failure". Finally, because of the complexity of the information finding and filtering task and the large amount of information, the required processing would overwhelm a single agent. To resolve the above problems, a multi-agent system is necessary.

We have developed a multi-agent system named RETSINA (REusable Task-based System of Intelligent Networked Agents) [16, 15, 14] to integrate information gathering from web-based sources and decision support tasks. The agents in RETSINA compartmentalize specialized task knowledge, organize themselves to avoid processing bottlenecks, and can be constructed specifically to deal with dynamic changes in information, tasks, number of agents and their capabilities.

2.1   The System Infrastructure

In RETSINA, the agents are distributed and run across different machines. Based on models of users, agents and tasks, the agents decide how to decompose tasks and whether to pass them to others, what information is needed at each decision point, and when to cooperate with other agents. The agents communicate with each other to delegate tasks, request or provide information, find information sources, filter or integrate information, and negotiate to resolve inconsistencies in information and task models. The system consists of three classes of agents (see Figure 1): *interface* agents, *task* agents and

---

[2] For hundreds of agents, coalition formation methods are usually too complex. However, several cooperation methods were developed for such cases (e.g., market oriented solutions [17]).

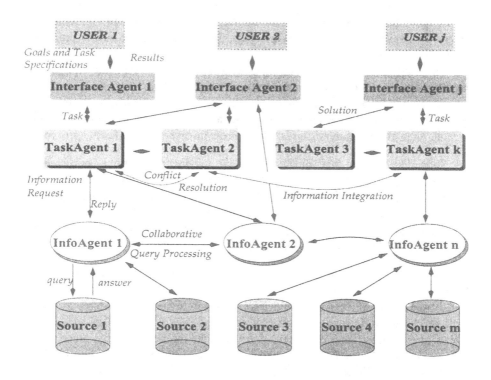

Fig. 1. Illustration of the infrastructure of the agent system

information agents. Note that a similar infrastructure is used in InfoSleuth, and the communication protocol used is similar as well [10].

Interface agents interact with users receiving their specifications and delivering results. They acquire, model and utilize user preferences. Task agents formulate plans and carry them out. They have knowledge of the task domain, and which other task agents or information agents are relevant to performing various parts of the task. In addition, task agents have strategies for resolving conflicts and fusing information retrieved by information agents. They decompose plans and cooperate with appropriate task agents or information agents for plan execution, monitoring and results composition. Information agents provide intelligent access to a heterogeneous collection of information sources. They have models of the information resources and strategies for source selection, information access, conflict resolution and information fusion. Information agents are active, in the sense that they actively monitor information sources and *proactively* deliver the information.

2.2 Agent Matchmaking

One of the basic design problems of cooperative, *open*, multi-agent systems for the Internet is the connection problem [2]. That is, each agent must be able to locate the other agents who might have capabilities which are necessary for the execution of tasks, either locally or via coalition formation. The fact that the system is open (participating agent may dynamically enter and leave) and distributed over the entire Internet precludes broadcast communication solutions.

The solution to this problem in our system relies, instead, on some well-known agents and some basic interactions with them – matchmaking [7, 3]. In general, the process of matchmaking allows an agent with some tasks, the requester, to learn the contact information and capabilities of another agent, the server, who may be able to execute some of the requester's tasks. This process involves three different agent roles:

- Requester: an agent that holds a set of tasks and wants them to be performed (at least partially) by other agents who possess relevant capabilities.
- Matchmaker: an agent that knows the contact information, capabilities, and other service characteristics (e.g. cost, availability, reliability) of other agents.
- Server: an agent that has committed to the execution of a task or at least part of a task delegated to it by a requester.

During the operation of the multi-agent system, agents that join the system advertise themselves and their capabilities to a matchmaker, and when they leave the agent society, they un-advertise (for more details, see [14]). Requesters, in search of agents with which they may possibly form coalitions, approach a matchmaker and ask for names of relevant servers. After having acquired the information about other agents they can directly contact these agents and initiate cooperation as needed. Note that there may be several matchmaker agents to relax the problem of unavailable or overwhelmed single matchmaker.

3 Cooperation via Coalition Formation

Coalition formation methods among multiple agents (e.g., in [19, 12, 6, 13]) refer to cases in which groups of agents work jointly in order to accomplish their tasks. The RETSINA system can receive several tasks from several users. Our hypothesis is that incorporation of a coalition formation mechanism increases the efficiency of groupwise task execution, resulting in near-optimal task performance. We report such results in section 6. In addition, this mechanism will enable agents to decide upon the importance (and thus – the order) of tasks to be performed. Such decision making is important in real-world domains, where there may be situations in which a system cannot fulfill all of its tasks.

We provide below a brief description of the coalition formation model presented in [13], which we later modify to enable its implementation and take into consideration additional requirements of an open and dynamic agent environment. There is a set of n autonomous, cooperative agents, $\{A_1, A_2, \ldots, A_n\}$. Each agent A_i has a vector of real non-negative capabilities $B_i = \langle b_1^i, \ldots, b_r^i \rangle$. Each capability[3] is a property of an agent that quantifies its ability to perform a specific type of action[4]. In order to enable the

---

[3] In the context of information agents, an example of a capability is the type and the amount of information that an agent can provide.

[4] Action is the most fundamental task, virtually indivisible.

assessment of coalitions and task-execution, an evaluation function should be attached to each type of capability. There is a set of $|T|$ independent tasks $T = \{t_1, t_2, \ldots, t_m\}$. For the satisfaction of each task t_j, a vector of capabilities $B_j = \langle b_1^j, \ldots, b_r^j \rangle$ is necessary. The benefits gained from performing the task depend on the capabilities that are required for its performance. Benefits are measured from the whole system viewpoint, however task-execution is distributed and there is no central authority that distributes the tasks or coordinates among the agents.

A coalition is defined as a group of agents who have decided to cooperate in order to perform a common task. The model assumes that a coalition can work on a single task at a time, and that agents may be members of more than one coalition. A coalition C has a vector of capabilities B_c which is the sum of the capabilities that the coalition members contribute to this specific coalition. C has a value V which is the joint benefits of the members of C when cooperatively satisfying a specific task.

The model assumes that the agents are group-rational. That is, they join a coalition only if they (jointly) benefit as a coalition at least as much as the sum of their personal benefits outside of it [5, 11]. Group rationality is necessary to ensure that whenever agents form a coalition, they always increase the system's global benefits, which is the sum of the coalitional values. It is also assumed that the agent-population does not change during the coalition formation; all of the agents must know about all of the tasks and the other agents[5]; the details of intra-coalitional activity are not necessary for agents outside of the coalition; there is no clock synchronization among the agents. The coalition formation algorithm consists of two main stages[6]:

1. A preliminary stage – all possible coalitions are distributively calculated. This distribution is achieved by having each agent A_i compute only coalitions in which it is a member (put these in a list L_i).
2. A main stage – an iterative greedy procedure in which two sub-stages occur:
   - The coalitional values are calculated[7] such that for each task, all of the coalitions that can satisfy it are considered. The distribution of these calculations is done by having each agent A_i approach the agents which are members of the coalitions in L_i and commit to the calculation of the values of coalitions in which they are both members. Consequently, each coalition value calculation will be committed to only once (this distribution depends on the communication order).
   - The agents decide upon the preferred coalition (according to its maximal calculated value with respect to a specific task) and form it, and perform the respective task.

Since the number of the possible coalitions is exponential (2^n), such is the complexity of the algorithm. This is reduced by limiting the permitted coalitions. Such heuristics were implemented in the algorithm by using an integer k which denotes the highest coalitional

---

[5] Since RETSINA operates in an open, dynamic environment, it does not satisfy these two assumptions (see section 5).

[6] For additional details with respect to the algorithm see [13].

[7] Note that the value calculation must be repeated on every iteration, since the execution of tasks may change these values.

size allowed. This restriction limits the number of coalitions to $O(n^k)$ (polynomial in n). We later explain why such a limitation is justified.

As shown in [13], the algorithm has a logarithmically increasing ratio bound, $\rho = \frac{c_{tot}}{c_{tot}^*} \leq \sum_{i=1}^{max(|C_j|)} \frac{1}{i}$, where c_{tot} denotes the total cost[8] of all coalitions derived by the algorithm, c_{tot}^* denotes the optimal total cost, and $max(|C_j|)$ is the maximal coalition size. The ratio bound ρ is the worst case bound and, as shown in section 6, the average case is significantly better. The two processes of calculating coalitional values and choosing coalitions may be repeated up to $|T|$ times. Therefore, the worst case complexity per agent is $O(n^{k-1} \cdot |T|)$ computations and $O(n \cdot |T|)$ communication operations.

4 The Cooperation Component

The architecture of each agent in the RETSINA framework includes a generic cooperation component. We shall elaborate on the architecture, the functionality and the advantages of this component. The role of the cooperation component is to enable close cooperation among agents. An agent should consider cooperation if one of the following holds:

- The agent cannot perform a specific task by itself.
- The agent can perform a specific task, but other agents are more efficient in performing this task (e.g., they require less resources or perform faster).
- The agent can perform a specific task, but working on it collaboratively will increase the benefits from the task (or reduce the costs).

The last two conditions are not necessarily easy for an agent to perceive, especially in cases of incomplete information with regard to the capabilities of other agents and the expected benefits from task execution by them. Nevertheless, reasoning about the global utility of cooperation and the application of cooperation strategies strongly relies on such expected benefits. Measurable expected benefits can be compared to decide upon the preferable ones and the cooperation activities that may achieve them. Benefits are commonly assessed and expressed by utility functions[9]. We are interested only in the payoff gained by the whole agent-system as the result of agent activity, and not in the individual payoff of an agent. While the other parts of the cooperation component of the agent are reusable[10], the utility functions must be determined and implemented specifically for each task domain.

Cooperation strategies mainly depend on two parameters: the environment type with respect to payoffs (super-additive vs. non-super-additive) and the agent rationality (self-rationality vs. group-rationality). Each of the four combination of these requires

---

[8] Note that the notion of cost (and not value) is used here, however the translation of the first to the latter is rather simple. In our system costs, which are part of an agent's advertisement to a match maker, stem from the computation and communication efforts associated with the agent activity.

[9] Utility functions are frequently referred to as cost functions or payoff functions.

[10] That is, they can be used for various domains with no modifications.

different cooperation strategies to increase the payoffs, either of single agents in the self-rationality case or of the whole system in the group-rationality case. However, since they do not depend on the specific task domain, cooperation strategies can be formulated in a generic manner, and instantiated by the agents for each specific task domain.

5 Coalition Re-design

In RETSINA we implement coalition formation mechanisms for group-rationality cases. We rely on the theoretical methods presented in [13] as a basis for the algorithms implemented, however modify them due to fundamental differences between the agent-systems discussed there (see section 3) and those discussed here:

- The number of goals and agents in [13] is fixed, while RETSINA is a dynamic system where agents appear and disappear and tasks vary constantly.
- The size of coalitions in [13] is bounded by a pre-defined constant k, independent of the n and $|T|$. k has a significant effect on the complexity of the solution. Such an artificial constraint may prohibit solutions even in cases where these not only exist but are also feasible and beneficial.
- The algorithm in [13] does not discuss the effect of two cases which are typical in our system: how to choose from among two agents (or more) that can provide the same service with the same expected payoff; how to deal with the case of reusable or non-depleting capabilities.
- Tasks with complex time dependencies, such as partial overlapping use of a resource, which are typical in our dynamic system, are not referred to in [13].
- The method in which the information with regards to the existence of tasks and their details is distributed in not discussed in the original algorithm.

To resolve the above restrictions, we made various modifications to the algorithm.

Since the communication- and computation-time for value calculation and coalition design (section 3) are significantly small as compared to the task execution time, and tasks can dynamically appear, the modified algorithm includes a re-design process. When a new task is received by the system, we require:

- When an agent receives a new task, it finds through matchmaking relevant agents that can execute the task.
- If tasks that were assigned to coalitions have not been performed yet within the current iteration of the coalition formation algorithm, the agents will re-calculate the coalitional values to take into consideration the arrival of the new task.
  - If inclusion of the newly arrived task in coalition recalculations in the current iteration raises the value of a coalition, then the agents shall re-design coalitions, selecting again the best among the actual, re-designed, coalitions[11].
  - Otherwise, the agents shall avoid coalition re-design, and consider the new task for inclusion in coalitions at the next iteration.

---

[11] Note re-design may not be allowed if the expected task flow is rapid, lest the system will constantly re-design and not perform its tasks.

- If all previous tasks are in process, the new task will be added to the group of tasks T and be dealt with in the next coalition formation iteration.
- In case of a rapid high-frequency stream of new tasks, the re-design process may be dis-enabled. If such a rate of new tasks is expected in advance, or the agents statistically infer such a rate by sampling the task stream and interpolating the statistical data, the re-design process shall be avoided.

The dynamic addition of tasks to the agent system does not change the overall order of complexity of the algorithm, it however adds a factor to it. This is since the complexity is linear in $|T|$, and the maximal number of re-design processes is bounded by the number of the dynamically received tasks $|T_d|$, and $|T_d| < |T|$. Hence, the worst case complexity will be less than twice the non-dynamic complexity.

The communication requirements of the original algorithm are in the worst case $O(n)$ per agent per task (however the average is $O(1)$). In the new algorithm, however, there is an additional complexity due to the dynamic task advertisement. Hence, while the worst case remains unchanged, the average case becomes $O(|T_d| \cdot k)$. Yet this is a low linear complexity. Nevertheless, in WWW information gathering (in which our agent system operates), the high network latency causes the computation time for coalition formation to be dwarfed by comparison. This was observed in the course of our experiments.

6 Algorithm Modification and Analysis

6.1 Computational Complexity

In section 3, the number of agents n was assumed to be constant. However, in our agent system, n may dynamically change. Given this difference, the analysis of the complexity must be modified. We introduce[12] $N = max(n)$. Using N, the complexity can be expressed by a similar expression as in section 3, where n is substituted by N, resulting in $O(N^{k-1} \cdot |T|)$. Since $N = const \cdot n$, the complexity will remain of the same order. The k limitation, that enable polynomial complexity is disturbing. The limitation it represents with respect to the size of coalitions must either be justified and adjusted to our system or omitted. We show that some restrictions can be applied in our system, without reduction in its functionality, as described below.

An important property of a RETSINA agent is its ability to perform task reductions [18]. In practice, the internal complexity of a sub-task is determined within the plan library. The plan library is domain-specific, hence the designers of the domain-specific components have control over the complexity of sub-tasks. In the information domain of RETSINA sub-tasks, each sub-task can typically be performed by a small number of agents. This implies that the coalition formation procedure will concentrate on the formation of small coalitions of agents with particular expertise to perform a task.

For example, one of the domains in which RETSINA was implemented is satellite tracking. One of the tasks that the agents can cooperatively perform is finding if and

---

[12] Since $max(n)$ may be unknown, N shall be decided upon according to the expectations of the designers with regards to their agent system.

when a specific satellite will be observable in a specific location. For this, up to 4 information agents are involved in the information gathering, and up to 4 other agents are involved in other related tasks. This means that the maximal coalition size for this task type is 8. Since other tasks of the system are of same order of complexity, the sizes of coalitions are limited as well. The system may include other active agents, however these will be involved in other tasks or be idle.

Each agent in our system is specialized in a specific type of task-performance. We do not incorporate complex, multi-purpose agents, since most of the capabilities of such agents may remain unused most of the time, while their size and complexity consume computational resources, reducing the system's performance. This specialization results in the incorporation of agents into coalitions according to their specialty/capability (necessarily, when more than one agent with the same specialty are present, their utility functions enables comparison which results in the choice of the one with the highest payoff). Thus, a coalition size is limited to the number of different specialties which are necessary for the execution of the task that this coalition performs. The number of specialties which are necessary for a given task execution is small and hence such is also the size of coalitions. Denoting the maximal number of specialties necessary for sub-task execution by k, we obtain the required restriction on the size of coalitions[13]. However, since different decompositions of tasks along different specialty dimensions are possible, a specific agent system may have several k's. Among them, the maximal will determine the worst case complexity. There is a trade-off between the complexity of sub-tasks and the complexity of task reduction: a more complex task reduction will result in simpler sub-tasks thus reducing their complexity, and vice versa.

6.2 Quality Analysis

Recall the theoretical ratio bound $\rho = \frac{c_{tot}^*}{c_{tot}} \leq \sum_{i=1}^{max(|C_j|)} \frac{1}{i}$ in [13]. This is a logarithmically increasing expression with respect to $max(|C_j|)$, i.e., $\rho \sim \log k$. A logarithmically increasing cost (c_{tot}) entails a logarithmically decreasing value. This means that according to the ratio bound analysis the overall payoff from task execution may be less than half of the optimal payoff of the system. This is far from being satisfactory. We have shown via simulations that the average case is close to the optimal case (see figure 2)[14].

The figure shows that the average performance (in terms of task allocation and execution) reached via simulation, depicted by the solid line, is around 0.9 of the optimal performance[15], while the worst case (the ratio bound), depicted by the broken line, declines fast to less than 0.5 of the optimal performance. Since the ratio bound depends on k, and in our system k does not depend on n or N, the logarithmic expression holds, and its magnitude can be determined by the designers. Thus the worst case performance can be traded-off with the computational complexity of task reduction. For instance,

---

[13] The k restriction can be further relaxed e.g., by designing task decomposition that avoids $k \sim n/2$.

[14] In order to get statistically significant results, we performed controlled experiments through simulation.

[15] We calculated the optimal performance explicitly, off line, when a small number of agents are involved in coalition formation. Small here means up to 20.

by simplifying the task reduction process, the reduced tasks remain rather complicated and will probably require more agents to perform each (since each involves more capabilities). Coalitions will therefore have to be larger. Hence, while the computational complexity for task reduction was reduced, the coalition formation complexity increased. The analysis of this trade-off may allow to further improve the performance of the system.

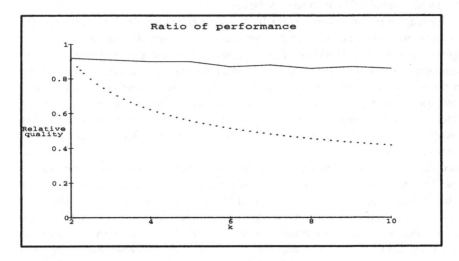

Fig. 2. The average performance with respect to the worst case

The simulations performed for checking the performance of the implemented algorithm were done as follows. A dynamic set of agents which included up to 20 agents ($N = 20$), where each provided with a vector of capabilities $B_j = \langle b_1^j, \ldots, b_r^j \rangle$. The agents received an initial set of tasks T, and additional tasks were provided dynamically in a random manner (i.e., the frequency of tasks, their type and the required capabilities were randomly chosen). Each task was associated with a vector of capabilities necessary for its execution[16] and a payoff function for calculating the value of the task. During the simulation, coalitions of agents were formed, where a task was allocated to each, and the value of its execution by this coalition was calculated. The sum of these values was calculated to find the total payoff. When new tasks arrived, the re-design procedure was followed. We have performed this simulation several hundreds of times, and compared the total payoffs to the optimal payoffs (calculated off-line) and to the theoretical ratio bound, as depicted above.

7 Discussion

In this research we have utilized coalition formation methods to improve multi-agent coordination (in terms of the joint payoff) of a real-world, information multi-agent

---

[16] Note that in the simulation we avoided the planning phase of task reduction. This simplification does not affect the properties of the coalition formation mechanism.

system. The coalition formation algorithm takes into consideration requirements and constraints arising from the dynamic nature of the environment in which the system operates. We have shown through simulation that the obtained efficiency and quality of the allocation of groups of agents for task execution is close to the optimal. In addition, the incorporation of coalition formation algorithms into an open, multi-agent system creates a decision mechanism for cases in which a subset of the tasks cannot be performed, allowing the choice of the more beneficial ones for execution. To enable the implementation of the coalition formation methods within a working, real-world agent system, we had to relax several binding assumptions and limitations which are common in the theoretical coalition formation theory, and provide solution to problems arising from these relaxations and from the dynamics and uncertainty to which our system is subject. We have analyzed the complexity and the quality, and shown that the incorporation of the coalition formation method induces a near-optimal task allocation while not significantly increasing the execution time. The algorithm implementation described in the paper is most appropriate for group-rationality cases. We currently work on the implementation of coalition formation methods for self-rationality cases.

References

1. Robert Armstrong, Dayne Freitag, Thorsten Joachims, and Tom Mitchell. Webwatcher: A learning apprentice for the world wide web. In *Proceedings of AAAI Spring Symposium on Information Gathering from Heterogenous Distributed Environments*, 1995.
2. R. Davis and R. G. Smith. Negotiation as a metaphor for distributed problem solving. *Artificial Intelligence*, 20(1):63–109, January 1983.
3. K. Decker, K. Sycara, and M. Williamson. Middle-agents for the internet. In *Proceeding of IJCAI-97*, Nagoya, Japan, 1997.
4. Oren Etzioni and Daniel Weld. A softbot-based interface to the internet. *Communications of the ACM*, 37(7), July 1994.
5. J. C. Harsanyi. *Rational Behavior and Bargaining Equilibrium in Games and Social Situations*. Cambridge University Press, 1977.
6. S. P. Ketchpel. Forming coalitions in the face of uncertain rewards. In *Proc. of AAAI94*, pages 414–419, Seattle, Washington, 1994.
7. D. Kuokka and L. Harada. On using KQML for matchmaking. In *Proceedings of the First International Conference on Multi-Agent Systems*, pages 239–245, San Francisco, June 1995. AAAI Press.
8. K. Lang. Learning to filter netnews. In *Proceedings of the Machine Learning Conference 1995*, 1995.
9. P. Maes. Agents that reduce work and information overload. *Communications of the ACM*, 37(7):31–40, 1994.
10. M. Nodine and A. Unruh. Facilitating open communication in agent systems: the infosleuth infrastructure. In this volume.
11. A. Rapoport. *N-Person Game Theory*. University of Michigan, 1970.
12. T. W. Sandholm and V. R. Lesser. Coalition formation among bounded rational agents. In *Proc. of IJCAI-95*, pages 662–669, Montrèal, 1995.
13. O. Shehory and S. Kraus. Formation of overlapping coalitions for precedence-ordered task-execution among autonomous agents. In *Proc. of ICMAS-96*, pages 330–337, Kyoto, Japan, 1996.

14. K. Sycara, K. Decker, A. Pannu, and M. Williamson. Designing behaviors for information agents. In *Proceeding of Agents-97*, pages 404–412, Los Angeles, 1997.

15. K. Sycara, K. Decker, A. Pannu, M. Williamson, and D. Zeng. Distributed intelligent agents. *IEEE Expert – Inteligent Systems and Their Applications*, 11(6):36–45, 1996.

16. K. Sycara and D. Zeng. Coordination of multiple intelligent software agents. *International Journal of Intelligent and Cooperative Information Systems*, 1996.

17. M. P. Wellman. A market-oriented programming environment and its application to distributed multicommodity flow problems. *Journal of Artificial Intelligence Research*, 1:1–23, 1993.

18. M. Williamson, K. Decker, and K. Sycara. Unified information and control flow in hierarchical task networks. In *Proceedings of the AAAI-96 workshop on Theories of Planning, Action, and Control*, 1996.

19. G. Zlotkin and J. S. Rosenschein. Coalition, cryptography, and stability: Mechanisms for coalition formation in task oriented domains. In *Proc. of AAAI94*, pages 432–437, Seattle, Washington, 1994.

A Formal Specification of dMARS

Mark d'Inverno*   David Kinny†   Michael Luck‡   Michael Wooldridge‖

* Cavendish School of Computer Science, Westminster University, London W1M 8JS, UK
dinverm@westminster.ac.uk

† Australian Artificial Intelligence Institute, Melbourne, Australia
dnk@aaii.oz.au

‡ Department of Computer Science, University of Warwick, CV4 7AL, UK
mikeluck@dcs.warwick.ac.uk

‖ Dept. of Electronic Engineering, Queen Mary & Westfield College, London E1 4NS, UK
M.J.Wooldridge@qmw.ac.uk

Abstract. The Procedural Reasoning System (PRS) is the best established agent architecture currently available. It has been deployed in many major industrial applications, ranging from fault diagnosis on the space shuttle to air traffic management and business process control. The theory of PRS-like systems has also been widely studied: within the intelligent agents research community, the belief-desire-intention (BDI) model of practical reasoning that underpins PRS is arguably the dominant force in the theoretical foundations of rational agency. Despite the interest in PRS and BDI agents, no complete attempt has yet been made to precisely specify the behaviour of real PRS systems. This has led to the development of a range of systems that claim to conform to the PRS model, but which differ from it in many important respects. Our aim in this paper is to rectify this omission. We provide an abstract formal model of an idealised dMARS system (the most recent implementation of the PRS architecture), which precisely defines the key data structures present within the architecture and the operations that manipulate these structures. We focus in particular on dMARS plans, since these are the key tool for programming dMARS agents. The specification we present will enable other implementations of PRS to be easily developed, and will serve as a benchmark against which future architectural enhancements can be evaluated.

1   Introduction

Since the mid 1980s, many control architectures for practical reasoning agents have been proposed [19]. Most of these have been deployed only in limited artificial environments; very few have been applied to realistic problems, and even fewer have led to the development of useful field-tested applications. The most notable exception is the Procedural Reasoning System (PRS). Originally described in 1987 [7], this architecture has progressed from an experimental LISP version to a fully fledged C++ implementation known as the distributed Multi-Agent Reasoning System (dMARS), which has been applied in perhaps the most significant multi-agent applications to date [8]. The PRS architecture has its conceptual roots in the belief-desire-intention (BDI) model of practical reasoning developed by Michael Bratman and colleagues [1], and in tandem with the evolution of the PRS architecture into an industrial-strength production architecture, the theoretical foundations of the BDI model have also been closely investigated (see, e.g., [12] for a survey).

Despite the success of the PRS architecture, in terms of both its demonstrable applicability to real-world problems and its theoretical foundations, there has to date been no systematic attempt to unambiguously define its operation. There have, however, been several attempts in this direction. For example, in [14], Rao and Georgeff give an abstract specification of the architecture, and informally discuss the extent to which an embodiment of it could be said to satisfy various possible axioms of BDI theory [12]. However, that specification is (quite deliberately) at a high level, and does not lend itself to direct implementation. Another related attempt is embodied by the AgentSpeak(L) language developed by Rao [11]. AgentSpeak(L) is a programming language based on an abstraction of the PRS architecture; irrelevant implementation detail is removed, and PRS is stripped to its bare essentials. Building on this work, d'Inverno and Luck have constructed a formal specification (in Z [17]) of AgentSpeak(L) [3]. This specification reformalises Rao's original description so that it is couched in terms of state and operations on state that can be easily refined into an implemented system. In addition, being based on a simplified version of dMARS, the specification provides a starting point for actual specifications of these more sophisticated systems.

In this paper, we continue and extend that work, by giving an abstract formal specification of dMARS: the system upon which AgentSpeak(L) is based. In so doing, we provide an operational semantics for dMARS, and thus provide a benchmark against which future BDI systems and PRS-like implementations can be compared. The specification is *abstract* in that important aspects of the dMARS system are included, but unnecessary implementation-specific details are omitted. This approach is very similar to that of [18], in which a formal specification of the MYWORLD architecture was developed using VDM, a formal specification language closely related to Z.

The remainder of this paper is structured as follows. First, in Section 2 we present an overview of the dMARS system. In Section 3, we describe the basic types and primitive components of the system, and in Section 4 we proceed to specify more complex components including plans. The next section specifies the dMARS agent and its state, followed by a description of its cycle of operation. At the end of the paper we summarise the contribution made by this specification, its relation to previous work, and prospects for the future.

Notation The specification below is presented using the Z language [17]. Z is a model-oriented formal specification language based on set theory and first-order logic. The key components of a Z specification are definitions of the *state space* of a system and the possible *operations* that transform it from one state to another. Because of space constraints, some auxiliary function definitions are omitted, and only a very brief account of binding is given. A more complete account of a related system can be found in [3], which provides both an introduction to Z and more explanation of several of the aspects not covered here. The full dMARS specification is available on request from the first author.

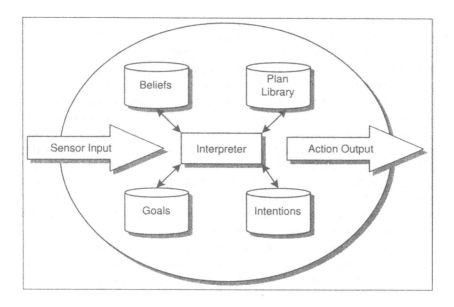

Fig. 1. A BDI Agent Architecture: PRS

2 An Overview of dMARS

The *Procedural Reasoning System (PRS)* developed by Georgeff and Lansky [7] is perhaps the best-known agent architecture. Both PRS and its successor *dMARS* are examples of a currently popular paradigm known as the *belief-desire-intention* (BDI) approach [1]. As Figure 1 shows, a BDI architecture typically contains four key data structures: beliefs, goals, intentions and a plan library.

An agent's *beliefs* correspond to information the agent has about the world, which may be incomplete or incorrect. Beliefs may be as simple as variables (in the sense of, e.g., PASCAL programs) but implemented BDI agents typically represent beliefs symbolically (e.g., as PROLOG-like facts [7]). An agent's *desires* (or goals, in the system) intuitively correspond to the tasks allocated to it. (Implemented BDI agents require that desires be logically consistent, although *human* desires often fail in this respect.) The intuition with BDI systems is that an agent will not, in general, be able to achieve *all* its desires, even if these desires *are* consistent. Agents must therefore fix upon some subset of available desires and commit resources to achieving them. These chosen desires are *intentions*, and an agent will typically continue to try to achieve an intention until either it believes the intention is satisfied, or it believes the intention is no longer achievable [2]. The BDI model is operationalised in dMARS agents by *plans*. Each agent has a *plan library*, which is a set of plans, or *recipes*, specifying courses of action that may be undertaken by an agent in order to achieve its intentions. An agent's plan library represents its *procedural knowledge*, or *know-how*: knowledge about how to bring about states of affairs.

Each plan contains several components. The *trigger* or *invocation condition* for a plan specifies the circumstances under which the plan should be considered, usually specified in terms of events. For example, the plan "make tea" may be triggered by the event "thirsty". In addition, a plan has a *context*, or *pre-condition*, specifying the circumstances under which the execution of the plan may commence. For example, the plan "make tea" might have the context "have tea-bags". A plan may also have a *maintenance condition*, which characterises the circumstances that must remain true while the plan is executing. Finally, a plan has a *body*, defining a potentially quite complex course of action, which may consist of both goals (or subgoals) and primitive actions. Our "tea" plan might have the body *get boiling water; add tea-bag to cup; add water to cup*. Here, *get boiling water* is a subgoal, (something that must be achieved when plan execution reaches this point in the plan), whereas *add tea-bag to cup* and *add water to cup* are primitive actions, i.e., actions that can be performed directly by the agent. Primitive actions can be thought of as procedure calls.

dMARS agents monitor both the world and their own internal state, and any events that are perceived are placed on an *event queue*. The *interpreter* in Figure 1 is responsible for managing the overall operation of the agent. It continually executes the following cycle:

- observe the world and the agent's internal state, and update the event queue to reflect the events that have been observed;
- generate new possible desires (tasks), by finding plans whose trigger event matches an event in the event queue;
- select from this set of matching plans one for execution (an *intended means*);
- push the intended means onto an existing or new intention stack, according to whether or not the event is a subgoal; and
- select an intention stack, take the topmost plan (intended means), and execute the next step of this current plan: if the step is an action, perform it; otherwise, if it is a subgoal, post this subgoal on the event queue.

In this way, when a plan starts executing, its subgoals will be posted on the event queue which, in turn, will cause plans that achieve this subgoal to become active, and so on. This is the basic execution model of dMARS agents. Note that agents do no first-principles planning at all, as all plans must be generated by the agent programmer at design time. The planning done by agents consists entirely of context-sensitive subgoal expansion, which is deferred until a point in time at which the subgoal is selected for execution.

Other efforts to give a formal semantics to BDI architectures include a range of *BDI logics* that have been developed by Rao and Georgeff [12]. These logics are extensions to the branching time logic CTL* [5], which also contain normal modal connectives for representing beliefs, desires, and intentions. Most work on BDI logics has focussed on possible relationships between the three 'mental states' [13] and, more recently, on developing proof methods for restricted forms of the logics [15]. In future work we will investigate the relationship between this work and the operational semantics described in this paper.

3 Beliefs, Goals, and Actions

We begin our specification by defining the allowable *beliefs* of an agent. Beliefs in dMARS are rather like PROLOG facts: they are essentially ground literals of classical first-order logic (i.e., positive or negative atomic formulae containing no variables). In order to define atomic formulae, we need a stock of variables, function and predicate symbols. We are not concerned with the contents of these sets, and hence we parachute them into our specification.

$[Var, FunSym, PredSym]$

A *term* is either a variable or a function symbol applied to a (possibly empty) sequence of terms.

$Term ::= var \langle\!\langle Var \rangle\!\rangle \mid functor \langle\!\langle FunSym \times \text{seq } Term \rangle\!\rangle$

An *atom* is a predicate symbol applied to a (possibly empty) sequence of terms.

```
┌─ Atom ──────────────────────────────
│ head : PredSym
│ terms : seq Term
└─────────────────────────────────────
```

A *belief formula* is then either an atom or the negation of an atom.

$BeliefFormula ::= pos \langle\!\langle Atom \rangle\!\rangle \mid not \langle\!\langle Atom \rangle\!\rangle$

The set of *beliefs* is the set of all ground belief formulae (i.e. those containing no variables).

$Belief == \{b : BeliefFormula \mid belvars\ b = \varnothing \bullet b\}$

An auxiliary function *belvars* is assumed which, given a belief formula, returns the set of variables it contains.

dMARS allows an agent's *goals* to be specified in terms of a simple temporal modal language with two unary connectives in addition to the connectives of classical logic. The operators are "!" and "?", for "achieve" and "query" respectively, so that a formula $!\phi$ in dMARS is read "achieve ϕ". Thus an agent with goal $!\phi$ has a goal of performing some (possibly empty) sequence of actions, such that after these actions are performed, ϕ will be true. Similarly, a formula "$?\phi$" means "query ϕ". Thus an agent with goal $?\phi$ has a goal of performing some (possibly empty) sequence of actions, such that after it performs these actions, it will know whether or not ϕ is true. In order to define these additional connectives, we must first define *situation formulae*: these are expressions whose truth can be evaluated with respect to a set of beliefs, and are thus not temporal.

$SituationFormula ::= belform \langle\!\langle BeliefFormula \rangle\!\rangle$
$\qquad\qquad\qquad\ \mid\ and \langle\!\langle SituationFormula \times SituationFormula \rangle\!\rangle$
$\qquad\qquad\qquad\ \mid\ or \langle\!\langle SituationFormula \times SituationFormula \rangle\!\rangle$
$\qquad\qquad\qquad\ \mid\ true$
$\qquad\qquad\qquad\ \mid\ false$

A *temporal formula*, known as a *goal* is then a belief formula prefixed with an achieve operator or a situation formula prefixed with a query operator. Thus an agent can have a goal either of achieving a state of affairs or of determining whether the state of affairs holds.

$$Goal ::= \; achieve \langle\!\langle BeliefFormula \rangle\!\rangle \; | \; query \langle\!\langle SituationFormula \rangle\!\rangle$$

The types of action that agents can perform may be classified as either *external* (in which case the domain of the action is the environment outside the agent) or *internal* (in which case the domain of the action is the agent itself). External actions are specified as if they are procedure calls or method invocations (and in reality, from the agent programmer's perspective, they usually are). An external action thus comprises an external action symbol (cf. the procedure name) taken from the set [*ActionSym*], and a sequence of terms (cf. the parameters of the procedure).

```
 __ ExtAction _____
 |   name : ActionSym
 |   terms : seq Term
 |_____
```

Internal actions may be one of two types: add or remove a belief from the data base (cf. the PROLOG `assert` and `retract` clauses). Note that it is not possible to add or remove an atom that contains variables.

$$IntAction ::= \; add \langle\!\langle BeliefFormula \rangle\!\rangle \; | \; remove \langle\!\langle BeliefFormula \rangle\!\rangle$$

4 Plans

Plans are *adopted* by agents, in the way we describe below. Once adopted, plans constrain an agent's behaviour and act as *intentions*. Plans consists of six components: an *invocation condition* (or *triggering event*); an optional *context* (a situation formula) that defines the pre-conditions of the plan, i.e., what must be believed by the agent for a plan to be executable; the *plan body*, which is a tree representing a kind of flow-graph of actions to perform; a *maintenance condition* that must be true for the plan to continue executing; a set of *internal actions* that are performed if the plan succeeds; and finally, a set of *internal actions* that are performed if the plan fails. The tree representing the body has states as nodes, and arcs (branches) representing either a goal, an internal action or an external action as defined below. Executing a plan successfully involves traversing the tree from the root to any leaf node.

First, we define trigger events. A trigger event is one that causes a plan to be adopted. Four types of events are allowable as triggers: the acquisition of a new belief; the removal of a belief; the receipt of a message; or the acquisition of a new goal. This last type of trigger event allows goal-driven as well as event-driven processing.

$$
\begin{aligned}
TriggerEvent ::= \; & addbelevent \langle\!\langle Belief \rangle\!\rangle \\
| \; & rembelevent \langle\!\langle Belief \rangle\!\rangle \\
| \; & toldevent \langle\!\langle Atom \rangle\!\rangle \\
| \; & goalevent \langle\!\langle Goal \rangle\!\rangle
\end{aligned}
$$

As we noted above, plan bodies are trees in which arcs are labelled with either goals or actions and states are place holders. Since states are not important in themselves, we define them using the given set [*State*]. An arc (branch) within a plan body may be labelled with either an internal or external action, or a subgoal.

$$Branch ::= \; extaction \langle\!\langle ExtAction \rangle\!\rangle$$
$$| \quad intaction \langle\!\langle IntAction \rangle\!\rangle$$
$$| \quad subgoal \langle\!\langle Goal \rangle\!\rangle$$

Next, we define plan bodies. A dMARS plan body is either an *end tip* containing a state, or a *fork* containing a state and a non-empty set of branches each leading to another tree.

$$Body ::= \; End \langle\!\langle State \rangle\!\rangle \; | \; Fork \langle\!\langle \mathbb{P}_1 (State \times Branch \times Body) \rangle\!\rangle$$

We can bring these components together into the definition of a plan. The formal definition of the *optional* type and related components, which are non-standard Z, can be found in Appendix A.

```
┌─ Plan ─────────────────────────────────────────
│ inv : TriggerEvent
│ context : optional[SituationFormula]
│ body : Body
│ maint : SituationFormula
│ succ : seq IntAction
│ fail : seq IntAction
└────────────────────────────────────────────────
```

Plans with no body are called *primitive plans*.

$$PrimitivePlan == \{p : Plan \mid p.body \in (\text{ran } End) \bullet p\}$$

4.1 Instantiating Plans

The basic execution mechanism for dMARS agents, described in Section 2, involves an agent matching the trigger and context of each plan against the chosen event in the event queue and the current set of beliefs, respectively, and then generating a set of candidate, matching plans, selecting one, and making a *plan instance* for it. A plan instance contains a copy of the original plan and, in addition: the *environment* of the plan (i.e., any bindings that have been generated in the course of executing the plan); the current state reached in the plan (initially the root of the plan body); the set of branches it can attempt to traverse from this state; the branch it *is* attempting to traverse; an identifier to uniquely identify the plan instance to the agent owner from the set [*PlanInstanceId*] of all such identifiers; and finally, the *status* of the plan (either "active", indicating that the plan is part of an intention, or "inactive", indicating that the plan has temporarily been suspended).

When a branch cannot be traversed (e.g., because an action or subgoal fails), then the branch itself fails and is removed from the set of possible branches. If the branch that the agent is attempting to traverse is defined, the agent has chosen which branch to attempt next, but if it is undefined, no such choice has been made.

In what follows, the *Substitution* type represents the set of all *substitutions* (i.e., bindings from variables to terms) A function prefixed by AS applies a substitution to a dMARS expression. If s and t are substitutions then $s \ddagger t$ denotes the *composition* of s and t. Finally, a function prefixed by mgu is a function which returns the most general unifier of two expressions. A brief description and some relevant definitions can be found in Appendix B.

A plan instance is thus formally defined as follows.

$Status ::= active \mid suspended$

$\_\_PlanInstance_____$
$origplan : Plan$
$env : Substitution$
$state : State$
$nextbranches : \mathbb{P}\, Branch$
$branch : optional[Branch]$
$status : Status$
$id : PlanInstanceId$

$\rule{4cm}{0.4pt}$

$state \in PlanStates\ origplan$
$state \in \text{dom}\,End \Rightarrow nextbranches = \varnothing$
$nextbranches \subseteq PlanNextBranches\ origplan\ state$
$branch \subseteq nextbranches$

In this schema, we use the auxiliary functions, *PlanNextBranches*, to identify the set of possible next branches from a given state in a plan and *PlanStates*, to give all the states of a plan. The specification that follows also uses the functions, *PlanNextState* and *PlanStartState*, which give the next state in a plan when applied to the current state and the branch traversed, and determine the start state of a plan respectively.

When a plan is first selected, the current state is the first state in the plan. A plan is said to have *succeeded* when it reaches its end state, and it is said to have *failed* if it is not in the end state and there are no available branches (i.e., it has failed if it has tried each branch and none have been successful).

$InitialInstance == \{p : PlanInstance \mid$
$\qquad\qquad p.state = PlanStartState\ p.origplan \wedge p.status = active\}$
$SucceedInstance == \{p : PlanInstance \mid p.state \in (\text{dom}\,End)\}$
$FailedInstance == \{p : PlanInstance \mid$
$\qquad\qquad p.state \notin (\text{dom}\,End) \wedge p.nextbranches = \{\}\}$

4.2 Intentions

An intention in dMARS is just a sequence of plan instances. In response to an external event, an intention is created containing the generated plan instance. If this plan, in turn, creates an internal event to which the agent responds with another plan, the new plan is concatenated to the intention. In this way, the plan at the top of the intention stack is the plan that will be executed first in any intention.

$$Intention == \text{seq } PlanInstance$$

An event consists of the triggering event and, optionally, a plan instance identifier that identifies the event-generating plan, an environment, and a set of plan instances that may already have failed (and may not be retried).

```
┌─ Event ─────────────────────────────────────────────────
│ trig : TriggerEvent
│ id : optional[PlanInstanceId]
│ env : optional[Substitution]
│ failures : optional[ℙ PlanInstance]
└──────────────────────────────────────────────────────────
```

An external event is one that is not associated with an existing plan instance when it first enters the buffer though it will become so when a plan instance is generated for it. By contrast, a subgoal event is an internal event that occurs when the branch of an executing intention is an achieve goal that cannot be achieved immediately. In this case, the variables of the event will all be defined with the constraint that the domain of the environment contains only variables that are contained in the event trigger.

```
┌─ ExternalEvent ─────────────────────────────────────────
│ Event
│ ────────────────
│ trig ∉ ran goalevent
│ undefined env
│ undefined failures
└──────────────────────────────────────────────────────────
```

```
┌─ SubgoalEvent ──────────────────────────────────────────
│ Event
│ ────────────────
│ trig ∈ ran goalevent
│ defined env
│ defined failures
│ dom(the env) ⊆ goalatomvars (goalevent~ trig)
└──────────────────────────────────────────────────────────
```

5 An Operational Semantics for dMARS Agents

The operation of dMARS agents is driven by the interaction of intentions and events. Events, (which may be the addition or deletion of beliefs, or the generation of new goals or subgoals), provide triggers to execute appropriate plans in the agent's plan library. As events are posted on the agent's event queue, so plans are selected from the agent's plan library that are relevant and applicable to the event. Determining whether a plan is relevant and applicable to an event reduces to attempting to unify the invocation condition and context with the event. From the set of applicable plans found by such unification, the agent chooses one plan, and from it generates a plan instance that is then added to the current intentions of the agent. This plan is thus an *intended means*.

Plans in dMARS are sequences of actions and goals with choice points so that, at any point, there may be more than one path to traverse in order to complete the plan. Intentions, which are those plans currently executing, determine which actions the agent takes, and may also give rise to the generation of new subgoals, both of which occur in the course of the agent's efforts to carry out the plan.

The following formal model specifies how relevant and applicable plans are determined initially, how one is chosen, and then how it is used. Essentially, an event generates either a new intention, or adds to an existing one. An agent then selects an intention to execute and, depending on the current component of the plan, different courses of behaviour are required. Actions may be executed directly and may lead to the posting of new events if the database is modified as a result, while goals either lead to the further instantiation of plans, or to the posting of new events (subgoals to be achieved) and the suspension of the currently executing plan.

This section provides a detailed specification of the dMARS agent operation, covering the agent and agent state, the generation of relevant and applicable plans, the way in which events are processed, the execution of intentions, and finally the achievement and failure of plans.

5.1 The dMARS Agent State

As in other BDI architectures, a dMARS agent consists of a plan library, an intention-selection function, an event-selection function and a plan-selection function. It also has a substitution-selection function for choosing between possible alternative bindings, and a function for selecting which branch in a plan should be attempted next.

```
__ dMARSAgent _____
  planlibrary : ℙ Plan
  intentionselect : ℙ₁ Intention ↛ Intention
  planselect : ℙ₁ Plan ↛ Plan
  eventselect : seq₁ Event ↛ Event
  substitutionselect : ℙ₁ Substitution ↛ Substitution
  selectbranch : PlanInstance ↛ Branch
```

In specifying the state of the agent, we indicate which aspects may change over time. These components are the agents' beliefs (which are ground belief formulae), intentions, and events yet to be processed (represented as a sequence).

```
__ dMARSAgentState _____
  dMARSAgent
  beliefs : ℙ Belief
  intentions : ℙ Intention
  events : seq Event
```

An operation only affects the state of the dMARS agent rather than the agent itself.

$$
\begin{array}{|l}
\hline
\_\Delta dMARSAgentState _____ \\
dMARSAgentState \\
dMARSAgentState' \\
\Xi\, dMARSAgentState \\
\hline
\end{array}
$$

Initially, the agent is provided with an event queue and sets of beliefs and intentions that "pump prime" its subsequent intention generation and action.

$$
\begin{array}{|l}
\hline
\_InitdMarsAgentState _____ \\
\Delta dMARSAgentState \\
initBel? : \mathbb{P}\ Belief \\
initInt? : \mathbb{P}\ Intention \\
initEv? : \text{seq}\ Event \\
\hline
beliefs' = initBel? \\
intentions' = initInt? \\
events' = initEv? \\
\hline
\end{array}
$$

Agents can perceive external events which are placed at the end of the event buffer.

$$
\begin{array}{|l}
\hline
\_NewExternalEvent _____ \\
\Delta dMARSAgentState \\
newevent? : Event \\
\hline
events' = events \,^\frown \langle newevent? \rangle \\
\hline
\end{array}
$$

5.2   Relevant and Applicable Plans

A plan is *relevant* with respect to an event if there exists a *most general unifier* (mgu) to bind the triggering events of the plan and the event so that they are equal. This is specified in the function *genrelplans*, which takes an event e and a set of plans ps, and returns a set of plan/substitution pairs, such that if (p, σ) is returned, then p is a relevant plan in ps for the event e, and σ is the most general unifier for p. The signature of the functions defining most general unifiers are given in Appendix B. If the event is a subgoal event and therefore contains a substitution environment, it must be applied to the triggering event before the relevant plans are generated.

$$
\begin{array}{|l}
\hline
genrelplans : Event \to \mathbb{P}\ Plan \to \mathbb{P}(Plan \times Substitution) \\
\hline
\forall\, e : Event;\ lib : \mathbb{P}\ Plan \bullet \\
undefined\ e.env \Rightarrow genrelplans\ e\ lib = \\
\quad \{p : lib;\ \sigma : Substitution \mid mguevents\ (e.trig, p.inv) = \sigma \bullet (p, \sigma)\} \wedge \\
defined\ e.env \Rightarrow genrelplans\ e\ lib = \\
\quad \{p : lib;\ \sigma : Substitution \mid \\
\quad\quad mguevents\ (ASTrigEvent\ (the\ e.env)\ e.trig, p.inv) = \sigma \bullet (p, \sigma)\} \\
\hline
\end{array}
$$

A relevant plan is applicable if its context is a logical consequence of the beliefs of the agent. Thus, we can define a predicate, *dMarsLogCons*, to hold between a situation formula and a belief base if the situation formula is a logical consequence of the belief base.

$$\mid \quad dMarsLogCons\_ : \mathbb{P}(SituationFormula \times \mathbb{P}\ BeliefFormula)$$

Using this logical consequence relation, we define an *applicable plan* relation to hold between a relevant plan, a substitution and a current set of beliefs. This is specified in the function, *genapplplans*, which takes a set of plans (and the substitutions which make them relevant), and the current beliefs, and returns the *applicable* plans and updated substitutions.

$$
\begin{array}{l}
genapplplans : \mathbb{P}(Plan \times Substitution) \rightarrow \\
\qquad\qquad\qquad (\mathbb{P}\ BeliefFormula) \rightarrow \\
\qquad\qquad\qquad\qquad \mathbb{P}(Plan \times Substitution) \\
\hline
\forall\ relsubs : \mathbb{P}(Plan \times Substitution); \\
\qquad bels : \mathbb{P}\ BeliefFormula\ \bullet \\
\quad genapplplans\ relsubs\ bels = \\
\quad \{rel : Plan;\ \sigma, \psi : Substitution \mid \\
\quad (rel, \sigma) \in relsubs\ \wedge \\
\quad dMarsLogCons(ASSitForm\ (\sigma\ \ddagger\ \psi)\ (the\ rel.context),\ bels)\ \bullet \\
\qquad\qquad\qquad\qquad\qquad (rel, \sigma\ \ddagger\ \psi)\}
\end{array}
$$

5.3 Processing Events

With the dMARS agent and its state specified, we can define the dMARS operation cycle. There are two possible modes of operation, depending on whether the event buffer is empty or not. If the event buffer is not empty, an event is selected from it (typically the first element) and relevant plans and, in turn, applicable plans are determined. An applicable plan is selected and used to generate a plan instance.

With an external event, a new intention containing just the plan instance as a singleton sequence is created. With an internal event, the plan instance is pushed onto the intention stack that generated that (subgoal) event. In addition, we specify that a failed plan instance cannot be re-selected for an internal event. The auxiliary function *CreatePlanInstance* takes a plan and a substitution, and creates a plan instance in its initial state. If the event is external then it must be updated to include the id of the new planinstance.

___ *NewPlanInstance* _____
$\Delta dMARSAgentState$
_____

$events \neq \langle\rangle$
Let $event ==$ $eventselect$ $events$ •
 Let $applplans ==$ $genapplplans$ ($genrelplans$ $event$ $planlibrary$) $beliefs$ •
 Let $selectedplan ==$ $planselect$ (dom $applplans$) •
  Let $applunifier ==$ $applplans$ $selectedplan$ • ˙
  Let $instance ==$ $CreatePlanInstance$ $selectedplan$ $applunifier$ •
   $event \in ExternalEvent \Rightarrow$
   $instance \notin$ (the $event.failures$) $\wedge$
   $intentions' = intentions \cup \{\langle instance\rangle\} \wedge$
   $events' = (events \rhd \{event\})\cup$
    $\{(events^\sim event, MakeEvent(event.trig, \{instance.id\}, \varnothing, \varnothing))\} \wedge$
   $event \in SubgoalEvent \Rightarrow$
   (Let $trigint == (\mu\, i : intentions \mid (head\ i).id = (the\ event.id))$ •
   $intentions' = intentions \setminus \{trigint\} \cup \{\langle instance\rangle \frown trigint\})$
_____

5.4 Executing Intentions

The remainder of this section addresses the agent operation when the event buffer is empty. We refer to this as the *intention execution operation*. The variables included in the schema below enable the specification of intention execution to be written more elegantly, but do not define the state, and are reset on every operation cycle. When the event buffer becomes empty, all these variables are set to be undefined.

___ *AgentIntExecutionOperationState* _____
$dMARSAgentState$
_____
$selectedintention : optional[Intention]$
$executingplan : optional[PlanInstance]$
$executingbranch : optional[Branch]$
_____

The first step is to select an intention, *selectedintention'*, identify the executing plan, *executingplan'*, at the top of this intention stack such that the plan is active, and select the branch of the plan to execute, *executingbranch'*.

___ *SelectIntention* _____
$\Delta AgentIntExecutionOperationState$
_____
$events = \langle\rangle$
the $selectedintention' = intentionselect$ $intentions$
the $executingplan' = head(the\ selectedintention')$
(the $executingplan'$).$status = active$
(the $executingbranch'$) $= selectbranch$ (the $executingplan'$)
_____

Before considering the different cases arising from the different types of selected branch, we must introduce two schemas to specify a move to the next state if the branch is successful, and to delete a branch if it fails. The auxiliary function, *AchieveBranch*, takes a plan instance and moves it on to the next state determined by the *branch* variable of the executing plan.

BranchSucceed
$\Delta AgentIntExecutionOperationState$

---
the executingplan' $=$ *AchieveBranch* (*the executingplan*)

BranchFail
$\Delta AgentIntExecutionOperationState$

(*the executingplan'*).*nextbranches* $=$
$\quad$ (*the executingplan*).*nextbranches* $\setminus$ *executingbranch*

There are then four cases, depending on whether the branch is an external action, an internal action, a query goal, or an achieve goal.

External Actions: If the branch is an external action, then it is executed immediately. Its success or failure is modelled by the function *executeaction*, which takes a plan instance with a selected branch that is an external action, and returns the binding that succeeded. If it is not in the domain, the function models the action failing.

$$executeaction : PlanInstance \nrightarrow Substitution$$

With a successful branch, the binding of the action is *composed* with the substitution environment.

BranchExtActionSucceed
$\Delta AgentIntExecutionOperationState$

---
the executingbranch $\in$ ran *extaction*
the executingplan $\in$ dom *executeaction*
(*the executingplan'*).*env* $=$
$\quad$ (*the executingplan*).*env* $\ddagger$ *executeaction* (*the executingplan*)

The branch is then traversed to reach the next state, specified by the *BranchSucceed* schema above. The operation of achieving an external action and so moving onto the next state as defined by the tree is therefore defined as the composition of two operations as follows.

$$BranchExtActionSuceed \fatsemi BranchSuceed$$

An unsuccessful branch fails and there is no state change.

BranchExtActionFail

$\Xi\, AgentIntExecutionOperationState$

---

the executingbranch $\in$ ran *extaction*
the executingplan $\notin$ (dom *executeaction*)

After this occurs the branch must be removed.

$BranchExtActionFail \,\S\, BranchFail$

Internal Actions: If the branch is an internal action (denoted by the local variable *action*), the database is modified according to that action. If this action results in a change to the database, an event is added to the set of events.

$performintaction : (\mathbb{P}\, Belief) \to IntAction \to (\mathbb{P}\, Belief)$

$\forall\, b : Belief;\ i : IntAction;\ bs : \mathbb{P}\, Belief \bullet$
$\quad i = add\ b \Rightarrow performintaction\ bs\ i = bs \cup \{b\}\ \wedge$
$\quad i = remove\ b \Rightarrow performintaction\ bs\ i = bs \setminus \{b\}$

BranchIntAction

$\Delta AgentIntExecutionOperationState$

$(the\ executingbranch) \in (ran\ intaction)$
Let $action == (intaction^{\sim}(the\ executingbranch)) \bullet$
$\quad beliefs' = performintaction\ beliefs\ action\ \wedge$
$\quad action \in (ran\ add) \wedge beliefs' \neq beliefs \Rightarrow$
$\qquad events' = events^{\frown}$
$\qquad\quad \langle MakeEvent(addbelevent\ (add^{\sim}\ action), \varnothing, \varnothing, \varnothing)\rangle\ \wedge$
$\quad action \in (ran\ remove) \wedge beliefs' \neq beliefs \Rightarrow$
$\qquad events' = events^{\frown}$
$\qquad\quad \langle MakeEvent(rembelevent\ (remove^{\sim}\ action), \varnothing, \varnothing, \varnothing)\rangle$

The auxiliary function, *MakeEvent*, in the schema above, simply constructs an event from its constituent components. This operation is then composed with the operation, *BranchSucceed*, as before.

"Query" Goals: In the case of a query goal, *qgoal*, if the environment applied to the goal can be unified with the set of beliefs, the most general unifiers are generated and one is chosen (*sub*). This binding is composed with the substitution environment and the next state is reached. The **unifiquery** relation holds between a goal and a set of beliefs if the goal can be unified with the beliefs.

__ *BranchQueryGoalSucc* _____

$\Delta AgentIntExecutionOperationState$

---

the executingbranch $\in$ ran *subgoal*
subgoal$^\sim$(*the executingbranch*) $\in$ ran *query*
Let *qgoal* $==$ (*subgoal*$^\sim$(*the executingbranch*));
    env $==$ (*the executingplan*).*env* •
$\exists s : Substitution$ • *unifiquery* $(s, (ASGoal\ env\ qgoal, beliefs)) \wedge$
(Let *sub* $==$ *mguquery* $(ASGoal\ env\ qgoal, beliefs)$ •
 (*the executingplan'*).*env* $=$ *env* $\ddagger$ *sub*)

Where no such unification is possible, the branch fails.

__ *BranchQueryGoalFail* _____

$\Delta AgentIntExecutionOperationState$

---

the executingbranch $\in$ ran *subgoal*
subgoal$^\sim$(*the executingbranch*) $\in$ ran *query*
Let *qgoal* $==$ (*subgoal*$^\sim$(*the executingbranch*));
    env $==$ (*the executingplan*).*env* •
$\neg\ (\exists s : Substitution$ • *unifiquery* $(s, (ASGoal\ env\ qgoal, beliefs)))$

"Achieve" Goals: Finally, with an achieve goal, *achievegoal*, that can be unified with
the beliefs, the rest of the executing plan is unified as in the previous case, and the
branch succeeds. If the goal cannot be unified, the goal achieve event is posted, the
executing plan is suspended by setting the status parameter, and the set of tried instances
becomes defined as the set containing the empty set. In addition, the identifier of the
new internal event is set to the current executing plan.

__ *BranchAchieveGoal* _____

$\Delta AgentIntExecutionOperationState$

(*the executingbranch*) $\in$ ran *subgoal*
subgoal$^\sim$(*the executingbranch*) $\in$ ran *achieve*
(*the executingplan'*).*status* $=$ *suspended*
Let *achievegoal* $==$ *subgoal*$^\sim$(*the executingbranch*);
    env $==$ (*the executingplan*).*env* •
    events' $=$ *events* $^\frown$ $\langle MakeEvent$ $((goalevent\ achievegoal),$
                        $\{(the\ executingplan).id\}, \{env\}, \{\emptyset\}))$

Once an achieve goal is posted, the execution cycle can restart, otherwise further
operations are performed as follows.

5.5 Achieving and Failing Plans

A successful branch leads to a new state that is either not an end state, in which case execution of another branch ensues, or is an end state, in which case the plan *succeeds*. In

the latter possibility, the substitution environment, $(the\ executingplan).env$, is applied to the success conditions, $(the\ executingplan).origplan.succ$, to give a sequence of ground internal actions, $groundsuccacts$. Then, the database is updated by performing these ground actions one at a time on the current set of beliefs to give the new set of beliefs, $beliefs'$. The auxiliary definition $fold$ is given in Appendix A.

```
┌─ AchievePlan ────────────────────────────────────────────
│ ΔAgentIntExecutionOperationState
│ ─────────────────────────────────────────────────────────
│ the executingplan ∈ SucceedInstance
│ Let succacts == (the executingplan).origplan.succ;
│     env == (the executingplan).env •
│ Let groundsuccacts == map (ASIntAction env) succacts •
│ beliefs' = fold performintaction beliefs groundsuccacts
└──────────────────────────────────────────────────────────
```

Two further cases arise if a plan succeeds. If there are more plans in the intention, the current substitution environment, $(the\ executingplan).env$, is updated to include the appropriate bindings from both the achieved plan, $executingplan$, and the environment of the next plan in the stack, $secondplan.env$. The successful plan instance is then removed from the top of the selected intention so that the new executing plan, which is re-activated, is the second in the original stack. $TEVars$, returns the set of variables of a trigger event. Also the internal event which generated the completed plan is removed.

```
┌─ AchievePlanOnly ────────────────────────────────────────
│ AchievePlan
│ ─────────────────────────────────────────────────────────
│ #(the selectedintention) > 1
│ Let secondplan == (the selectedintention) 2 •
│ Let newenv ==
│    ((TEVars (the executingplan).origplan.inv) ⊲ secondplan.env ‡
│                   (the executingplan).env) ⊕ secondplan.env •
│ the selectedintention' = tail (the selectedintention) ∧
│ (the executingplan').env = newenv ∧
│ (the executingplan').status = active
│ ran events' = ran events \ {(μ e : SubgoalEvent | e ∈ ran events ∧
│                   the e.id = (the executingplan).id}
└──────────────────────────────────────────────────────────
```

If there are no more plans, the intention has succeeded and can be removed as can the external event which generated it.

```
┌─ AchievePlanAndIntention ────────────────────────────────
│ AchievePlan
│ ─────────────────────────────────────────────────────────
│ #(the selectedintention) = 1
│ intentions' = intentions \ selectedintention
│ ran events' = ran events \ {(μ e : ExternalEvent | e ∈ ran events ∧
│                   the e.id = (the executingplan).id}
└──────────────────────────────────────────────────────────
```

Finally, if a branch fails but more branches remain, these may then be attempted. If there are no further alternatives, however, the plan *fails*. When this is the only plan on the stack, the intention fails completely (which is not specified here), otherwise the substitution environment is applied to the plan's fail conditions, *failacts*, and the ground fail internal actions, *groundfailacts'*, are performed. Since it is not the only plan on the stack, it must have been triggered by an existing *goal* event in the event queue, *origevent*, which is then found and updated to record the failed plan instance so that it is not retried. The status of the second plan remains suspended.

$$
\begin{array}{l}
\underline{\quad FailPlan \underline{\hspace{6cm}}} \\
\Delta AgentIntExecutionOperationState \\
\hline
the\ executingplan \in FailedInstance \\
\text{Let } origevent == (\mu\, e : Event \mid the\ e.id = (the\ executingplan).id); \\
\quad env == (the\ executingplan).env \bullet \\
\text{Let } failacts == (the\ executingplan).origplan.fail \bullet \\
\text{Let } groundfailacts == map\ (ASIntAction\ env)\ failacts \bullet \\
beliefs' = fold\ performintaction\ beliefs\ failacts \wedge \\
\text{ran } events' = (\text{ran } events \setminus \{origevent\}) \cup \\
\qquad \{MakeEvent(origevent.trig,\ origevent.id,\ origevent.env, \\
\qquad\qquad\qquad\qquad (origevent.failures \cup \{executingplan\}))\} \\
the\ selectedintention' = tail(the\ selectedintention)
\end{array}
$$

6 Concluding Remarks

The BDI model that underpins dMARS is similar to other computational models used in agent programming environments. In particular, it is closely related to the Concurrent METATEM programming language, as described in [10]. In Concurrent METATEM, an agent is programmed by giving it an *executable specification* of its behaviour, where such a specification is expressed as a set of temporal logic formulae of the form *past* $\Rightarrow$ *future*. Execution of these rules proceeds by matching the past time antecedents of temporal logic rules against future time consequents; any rules that fire then become *commitments*, which the agent must subsequently attempt to satisfy. Perhaps the main conceptual difference between Concurrent METATEM and the dMARS model is that in dMARS, control structures are explicitly coded in plans; in Concurrent METATEM, a run-time execution algorithm is responsible for determining control, in that it must attempt to find an execution that simultaneously satisfies its commitments. In [10], the relationship between Concurrent METATEM and dMARS is used to encode a dMARS-like interpreter as a set of Concurrent METATEM rules. The same paper also provides an encoding of an abstract BDI interpreter using the DESIRE system (essentially an executable specification framework for knowledge-based systems).

In addition, a new abstract programming language [9] with a well-defined formal semantics in terms of a transition system has been based on the BDI model. This language uses features of both logic programming and imperative programming, and captures some of the features of other BDI-based languages such as AGENT-0 and AgentSpeak(L). The key distinction between this language and the operation of a dMARS agent is that it contains no notion of events and, indeed, the authors suggest that events are not necessary for agent languages that attempt to capture the *intuitions* of the BDI model. However, in comprison with the dMARS formalisation contained in our paper, which provides a strong, computational model of the operation of a dMARS agent (and from which we claim systems can be implemented), it is not clear how such a strong relation between the semantics and a possible implementation might be made in this other work.

As the technology of intelligent agents matures further, we can expect to see a progression from the "scruffiness" of early investigative work to the "neatness" of rigour and formality. In this paper, we have contributed to the growing body of "neat" intelligent agent research, by presenting a complete formal specification of the best-known and most important agent architecture developed to date.

The specification we have presented in this paper is significant for a number of reasons. First, we need to understand clearly how an architecture works in order that we can evaluate it against others. Implementations are too low-level to allow such evaluations to take place. Formal specifications, using standard software engineering tools like the widely used Z language, are an ideal medium through which to communicate the operation of an architecture (e.g. [4]).

Second, there are understood methods for moving from an abstract specification in Z to an implementation, through a systematic process of refinement and reification. Such a process is not possible from a natural language description. Reimplementation and evaluation of the PRS architecture in different languages and environments is therefore a realistic possibility.

Finally, by understanding the model-theoretic foundations of PRS, (through rigorously defining the data structures and operations on those structures that constitute the architecture), we make it possible to develop a proof theory for the architecture. Such a proof theory has been developed for the MYWORLD architecture [18], and also for Rao's AgentSpeak(L) [11], which is itself a restricted version of PRS. Once such an axiomatisation is available, there will exist a straight line from the implementation of PRS to its theory, making it possible to compare the actual behaviour of the architecture against the philosophical idealisations of it that have been developed by BDI theorists [13]. In future work, we hope to investigate such axiomatisations.

Acknowledgements: Many thanks to Michael Georgeff and Anand Rao who provided many illuminations and insights in discussions with the first author during development of the specification contained in this paper. Thanks to the University of Westminster and the Australian Artificial Intelligence Institute, for supporting and hosting the first author during the development of this work. The specification contained in this document has been checked for type correctness using the fuzz package [16]. Thanks also to Sorabain de Lioncourt who identified an error in the original specification.

References

1. M. E. Bratman, D. J. Israel, and M. E. Pollack. Plans and resource-bounded practical reasoning. *Computational Intelligence*, 4:349–355, 1988.

2. P. R. Cohen and H. J. Levesque. Intention is choice with commitment. *Artificial Intelligence*, 42:213–261, 1990.

3. M. d'Inverno and M. Luck. A formal specification of AgentSpeak(L). *Journal of Logic and Computation*, Forthcoming.

4. M. d'Inverno, M. Priestley, and M. Luck. A formal framework for hypertext systems. *IEE Proceedings - Software Engineering Journal*, 144(3):175–184, June, 1997.

5. E. A. Emerson and J. Y. Halpern. 'Sometimes' and 'not never' revisited: on branching time versus linear time temporal logic. *Journal of the ACM*, 33(1):151–178, 1986.

6. M. R. Genesereth and N. Nilsson. *Logical Foundations of Artificial Intelligence*. Morgan Kaufmann Publishers: San Mateo, CA, 1987.

7. M. P. Georgeff and A. L. Lansky. Reactive reasoning and planning. In *Proceedings of the Sixth National Conference on Artificial Intelligence (AAAI-87)*, pages 677–682, Seattle, WA, 1987.

8. M. P. Georgeff and A. S. Rao. A profile of the Australian AI Institute. *IEEE Expert*, 11(6):89–92, December 1996.

9. K. Hindricks, F. de Boer, W. van der Hoek, and J. Meyer, J. Formal semantics for an abstract agent programming language. In this volume.

10. M. Mulder, J. Treur, and M. Fisher. Agent modelling in concurrent METATEM and DESIRE. In this volume.

11. A. S. Rao. AgentSpeak(L): BDI agents speak out in a logical computable language. In W. Van de Velde and J. W. Perram, editors, *Agents Breaking Away: Proceedings of the Seventh European Workshop on Modelling Autonomous Agents in a Multi-Agent World, (LNAI Volume 1038)*, pages 42–55. Springer-Verlag: Heidelberg, Germany, 1996.

12. A. S. Rao and M. Georgeff. BDI Agents: from theory to practice. In *Proceedings of the First International Conference on Multi-Agent Systems (ICMAS-95)*, pages 312–319, San Francisco, CA, June 1995.

13. A. S. Rao and M. P. Georgeff. Modeling rational agents within a BDI-architecture. In R. Fikes and E. Sandewall, editors, *Proceedings of Knowledge Representation and Reasoning (KR&R-91)*, pages 473–484. Morgan Kaufmann Publishers: San Mateo, CA, April 1991.

14. A. S. Rao and M. P. Georgeff. An abstract architecture for rational agents. In C. Rich, W. Swartout, and B. Nebel, editors, *Proceedings of Knowledge Representation and Reasoning (KR&R-92)*, pages 439–449, 1992.

15. A. S. Rao and M. P. Georgeff. Formal models and decision procedures for multi-agent systems. Technical Note 61, Australian AI Institute, Level 6, 171 La Trobe Street, Melbourne, Australia, June 1995.

16. J. M. Spivey. *The ƒUZZ Manual*. Computing Science Consultancy, 2 Willow Close, Garsington, Oxford OX9 9AN, UK, 2nd edition, 1992.

17. M. Spivey. *The Z Notation (second edition)*. Prentice Hall International: Hemel Hempstead, England, 1992.

18. M. Wooldridge. This is MYWORLD: The logic of an agent-oriented testbed for DAI. In M. Wooldridge and N. R. Jennings, editors, *Intelligent Agents: Theories, Architectures, and Languages (LNAI Volume 890)*, pages 160–178. Springer-Verlag: Heidelberg, Germany, January 1995.

19. M. Wooldridge and N. R. Jennings. Intelligent agents: Theory and practice. *The Knowledge Engineering Review*, 10(2):115–152, 1995.

A Auxiliary Z Definitions

The function, *fold*, takes a function, an initial value and a sequence and applies each element in the sequence to the initial value in turn. The function, *map*, takes another function and applies it to every element in a list. Similarly, *mapset*, applies a function to every element in a set.

$$
\begin{array}{l}
\underline{[X, Y]} \\
\quad fold : (X \rightarrow Y \rightarrow X) \rightarrow X \rightarrow (\mathrm{seq}\, Y) \rightarrow X \\
\quad map : (X \rightarrow Y) \rightarrow (\mathrm{seq}\, X) \rightarrow (\mathrm{seq}\, Y) \\
\quad mapset : (X \rightarrow Y) \rightarrow (\mathbb{P}\, X) \rightarrow (\mathbb{P}\, Y) \\
\rule{8cm}{0.4pt} \\
\quad \forall f : (X \rightarrow Y \rightarrow X);\ x : X;\ y : Y;\ ys : \mathrm{seq}\, Y\ \bullet \\
\qquad fold\, f\, x\, \langle\rangle = x\ \wedge \\
\qquad fold\, f\, x\, (\langle y\rangle \frown ys) = fold\, f\, (f\, x\, y)\, ys \\
\quad \forall f : X \rightarrow Y;\ x : X;\ xs : \mathrm{seq}\, X\ \bullet \\
\qquad map\, f\, \langle\rangle = \langle\rangle\ \wedge \\
\qquad map\, f\, \langle x\rangle = \langle f\, x\rangle\ \wedge \\
\qquad map\, f\, (xs \frown ys) = map\, f\, xs \frown map\, f\, ys \\
\quad \forall f : X \rightarrow Y;\ xs : \mathbb{P}\, X\ \bullet \\
\qquad mapset\, f\, xs = \{x : xs \bullet f\, x\}
\end{array}
$$

It is useful to be able to assert that an element is optional. The following definitions provide for a new type, *optional*[*T*], for any existing type, *T*, along with the predicates, *defined* and *undefined*, which test whether an element of *optional*[*T*] is defined or not. The function, *the*, extracts the element from a defined member of *optional*[*T*].

$$optional[X] == \{xs : \mathbb{P}\, X \mid \# xs \leq 1\}$$

$$
\begin{array}{l}
\underline{[X]} \\
\quad defined\_,\ undefined\_ : \mathbb{P}(optional[X]) \\
\quad the : optional[X] \rightarrowtail X \\
\rule{8cm}{0.4pt} \\
\quad \forall xs : optional[X]\ \bullet\ defined\ xs \Leftrightarrow \# xs = 1\ \wedge \\
\qquad\qquad\qquad\qquad\qquad undefined\ xs \Leftrightarrow \# xs = 0 \\
\quad \forall xs : optional[X] \mid defined\ xs\ \bullet \\
\qquad\qquad\qquad the\ xs = (\mu\, x : X \mid x \in xs)
\end{array}
$$

B Binding

The standard definition of a substitution is a mapping from variables to terms such that no variable contained in any of the terms is in the domain of the mapping [6]. This is represented as a partial function between variables and terms since, in general, only some variables will be mapped to a term.

$Substitution ==$
$\quad \{f : Var \nrightarrow Term \mid (\text{dom} f) \cap (\bigcup(mapset\ termvars\ (\text{ran} f))) = \varnothing\}$

The function $ApplySubTerm$ applies either the identity mapping to a variable if the variable is not in the domain of the substitution, or applies the substitution if it is in the domain.

$$ASVar : Substitution \rightarrow Var \rightarrow Term$$
$$\forall \psi : Substitution;\ v : Var \bullet$$
$$ASVar\ \psi\ v = (\{x : Var \bullet (x, var\ x)\} \oplus \psi)\ v$$

We can then define what it means for a substitution to be applied to a term, internal action, a situation formula, a plan, a goal, a belief formula and a trigger event, as given by $ASTerm$, $ASIntAction$, $ASSitForm$, $ASPlan$, $ASGoal$, $ASBeliefFormula$ and $ASTrigEvent$, respectively.

Consider two substitutions τ and σ such that no variable bound in σ appears anywhere in τ. The composition of τ with σ, written $\tau \ddagger \sigma$, is obtained by applying τ to the terms in σ and combining these with the bindings from τ. For example if $\tau = \{x/A, y/B, z/C\}$ and $\sigma = \{u/A, v/F(x, y, z)\}$ then, since none of the variables bound in σ (u, v) appear in τ, it is meaningful to compose τ with σ. In this case $\tau \ddagger \sigma = \{u/A, v/F(A, B, C), x/A, y/B, z/C\}$.

$$=[X, Y]=$$
$$\_ \ddagger \_ : Substitution \times Substitution \rightarrow Substitution$$
$$\forall \tau, \sigma : Substitution \mid$$
$$(\text{dom} \sigma) \cap ((\text{dom} \tau) \cup \bigcup(mapset\ termvars\ (\text{ran} \tau))) = \varnothing \bullet$$
$$\tau \ddagger \sigma = (\tau \cup \{x : Var;\ t : Term \mid (x, t) \in \sigma \bullet (x, ASTerm\ \tau\ t)\})$$

A substitution is a *unifier* for two expressions if the substitution, applied to both of them, makes them equal. A substitution is *more general* than another substitution if there exists a third substitution which, when composed with the first, gives the second. The most general unifier of two expressions is a substitution which unifies the expressions such that there is no other unifier that is more general. Here we define the signatures for the most general unifier of two trigger events, a goal with a set of beliefs, and a trigger event with a goal.

$$mguevents\ :\ (TriggerEvent \times TriggerEvent) \nrightarrow Substitution$$
$$mguquery\ :\ (Goal \times \mathbb{P}\ Belief) \nrightarrow Substitution$$
$$mgugoal\ :\ (TriggerEvent \times Goal) \nrightarrow Substitution$$

A Framework for Argumentation-Based Negotiation

Carles Sierra[‡*], Nick R. Jennings[‡], Pablo Noriega[†**], Simon Parsons[‡]

[‡] Department of Electronic Engineering,
Queen Mary and Westfield College,
University of London, London E1 4NS, UK.
{C.A.Sierra, N.R.Jennings, S.D.Parsons}@qmw.ac.uk

[†] Artificial Intelligence Research Institute, IIIA.
Spanish Scientific Research Council, CSIC.
Campus UAB, 08193 Bellaterra, Barcelona, Spain.
{sierra, pablo}@iiia.csic.es

Abstract. Many autonomous agents operate in domains in which the co-operation of their fellow agents cannot be guaranteed. In such domains negotiation is essential to persuade others of the value of co-operation. This paper describes a general framework for negotiation in which agents exchange proposals backed by arguments which summarise the reasons why the proposals should be accepted. The argumentation is persuasive because the exchanges are able to alter the mental state of the agents involved. The framework is inspired by our work in the domain of business process management and is explained using examples from that domain.

1 Introduction

Negotiation is a key form of interaction in systems composed of multiple autonomous agents. In such environments, agents often have no inherent control over one another and so the only way they can influence one another's behaviour is by persuasion. In some cases, the persuadee may require little or no convincing to act in the way desired by the persuader, for example because the proposed course of action is consistent with their plans. However, in other cases, the persuadee may be unwilling to accept the proposal initially and must be persuaded to change its beliefs, goals or preferences so that the proposal, or some variant thereof, is accepted. In either case, the minimum requirement for negotiation is for the agents to be able to make proposals to one another. These proposals can then either be accepted or rejected as is the case in the contract net protocol [16], for instance. Another level of sophistication occurs when recipients do not just have the choice of accepting or rejecting proposals, but have the option of making counter offers to alter aspects of the proposal which are unsatisfactory [15]. An even more elaborate form of negotiation —argumentation-based— is that in which parties

---

* On sabbatical leave from IIIA[†] thanks to a Spanish MEC grant PR95-313. Research partially supported by the Spanish CICYT project SMASH, TIC96-1038-C04001.

** On leave from *Laboratorio Nacional de Informática Avanzada* —LANIA. Rébsamen, 80; Xalapa, Veracruz, Mexico. Enjoying a Mexican CONACYT grant [69068-7245].

are able to send justifications or arguments along with (counter) proposals indicating why they should be accepted [11, 13, 18]. Arguments such as: "this is my final offer, take it or leave it", "last time this job cost £5, I'm not going to pay £10 now", and "the job will take longer than usual because one of the workers is off sick" may be necessary to change the persuadee's goals or preferences.

This paper deals with argumentation-based negotiation. Because this is a large research topic [9, 19] we limit our scope to argumentation between computational agents where a persuader tries to convince a persuadee to undertake a particular problem solving task (service) on its behalf. We outline the components of a formal model for the process of argumentation-based negotiation which can ultimately be used to build negotiating agents for real world applications. While we draw on our previous work in this area, in this paper we shift our attention from the mechanisms for generating counter proposals [15] and those for generating and interpreting arguments [13] to the social aspects of the negotiation. Moreover, we take advantage of the work on Dialogical Frameworks introduced in [12] to define the static aspects of the negotiation process: shared ontology, social relations, communication language and protocol. We define a minimal notion of the *state* of an agent which captures the evolutionary character of negotiation —enabling the resulting model to recognise different types of arguments that agents can make in support of their proposals. Finally, we indicate how these arguments can be generated and interpreted by agents.

In the paper we discuss three types of illocutions: (i) *threats* —failure to accept this proposal means something negative will happen to the agent; (ii) *rewards* —acceptance of this proposal means something positive will happen to the agent; and (iii) *appeals* —the agent should prefer this option over that alternative for this reason. We realise these are a subset of the illocutions that are involved in persuasive negotiation (see [9] for a list based on psychological research), but our emphasis is in providing an overarching framework in which the key components of argumentation can be described, rather than providing an exhaustive formalisation of all the argument types which can be found in the literature. We illustrate these constructs through a running example introduced in the following section. The main contribution of this work is, therefore, to provide a formal framework in which agents can undertake persuasive negotiation to change each other's beliefs and preferences using an expressive communication language. Moreover, the framework is neutral with respect to the agent's internal architecture and imposes few constraints on its formal resources.

2 Argumentation in Business Process Management

This section describes the scenario which will be used to illustrate the principles and concepts of our model of argumentation. The scenario is motivated by work in the ADEPT project [8] which has developed negotiating agents for business process management applications. In particular, we consider a multi-agent system for managing a British Telecom (BT) business process —namely, providing a quotation for designing a network which offers particular services to a customer (Figure 1). The overall process receives a customer service request as its input and generates as its output a quote specifying how much it would cost to build a network to realise that service. Here we consider a subset of the agents involved in this activity: the customer service division (CSD) agent, the design division (DD) agent, the surveyor department (SD) agent, and the various agents who provide the out-sourced service of vetting customers (VC agents). A full account of all the agents and their negotiations is given in [15].

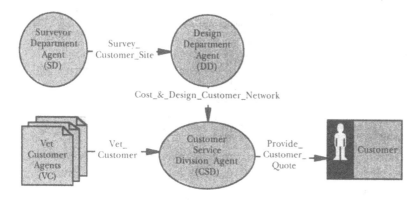

Fig. 1. Agent system for BT's "*Provide_Customer_Quote*" business process. The direction of the arrow indicates who provides the service labelling the arrow to whom.

The first stages of the Provide_Customer_Quote service involve the CSD agent capturing basic information about the customer and vetting the customer in terms of their credit worthiness. The latter service is performed by one of the VC agents and negotiation is used to determine which one is selected. If the customer fails the vetting procedure, then the quote process terminates. Assuming the customer is satisfactory, the CSD agent maps their requirements against a service portfolio. If the requirements can be met by a standard off-the-shelf portfolio item then an immediate quote can be offered based on previous examples. In the case of bespoke services the process is more complex. The CSD agent negotiates with the DD agent for the service of costing and designing the desired network service. To prepare a network design it is usually necessary to have a detailed plan of the existing equipment at the customer's premises. Sometimes such plans might not exist and sometimes they may be out of date. In either case, the DD agent determines whether the customer site(s) should be surveyed. If such a survey is warranted, the DD agent negotiates with the SD agent for the Survey_Customer_Site service. This negotiation differs from the others present in this scenario in that the two agents are part of the same department. Moreover, the DD agent has a degree of authority over SD. Agent negotiation is still required to set the timings of the service, but the SD agent cannot simply refuse to perform the service. On completion of the network design and costing, the DD agent informs the CSD agent which informs the customer of the service quote. The business process then terminates.

The precise nature of the argumentation which can occur in the aforementioned negotiations is determined by three main factors: (i) the negotiation arity —pairwise (1 to 1) negotiations (e.g. the CSD and DD agents for the design network service) differ from 1 to many negotiations (e.g. the CSD and VC agents for the Vet_Customer service); (ii)

Type	Id	Parties	Content	Comments
Threaten	1	CSD-VCs	Match the offer I have from another VC, otherwise I'll break off this negotiation.	Threaten to terminate current negotiation thread.
	2	CSD-VCs	Make sure you get back to me in the specified time period or I won't involve you in future rounds of bidding.	Threaten to terminate all future negotiation threads.
	3	DD-SD	If you cannot complete the service sooner, I'll inform your boss that we missed the deadline because of you.	Threaten to inform outside party of (perceived) poor performance.
Reward	4	CSD-DD	If you produce this design by this time we'll be able to get the quote to our major customer ahead of time.	Indicate positive effect of performing action by specified time.
	5	CSD-VCs	If you vet this customer by this time, I'll make sure you're involved in subsequent rounds of bidding.	Promise future involvement for accepting current proposal.
Appeal	6	CSD-VCs	Last time you vetted this customer, it took this length of time and cost this much.	Appeal to precedent.
	7	CSD-DD	You must complete this design within 48 hours because company policy says customers must be responded to within this time frame.	Appeal to (company's) prevailing practice.
	8	VC-CSD	This customer may be in financial trouble, therefore more time is needed to carry out a higher quality vetting.	Appeal to (CSD's) self interest.
	9	DD-CSD	The design will take longer than normal because one of our surveyors is on holiday this week.	Revealing new information.
	10	SD-DD	Customer has many premises and they all need to be surveyed, thus this service will take longer than normal.	Revealing new information.

Fig. 2. Sample arguments in the BT application.

the power relations [2] between the negotiators —most negotiations are peer-to-peer, but the DD and SD negotiation over the Survey_Customer_Site service is an example of boss-to-subordinate negotiation; and (iii) the organisational relationship of the negotiators —some negotiations are between agents of the same organisation (e.g. the CSD, DD and SD agents), while others are between agents of different organisations (e.g. the CSD and VC agents). Our experience in the domain shows that the argumentation between agents can be captured by the three types of argument mentioned in the Introduction —threats, rewards and appeals. Some examples of such arguments are given in Figure 2.

3 Negotiation Model

Our model describes the process of a single encounter negotiation between multiple agents over a deal. Deals are always between two agents, though an agent may be engaged simultaneously in negotiation with many agents for a given deal. Negotiation is achieved through the exchange of illocutions in a shared communication language CL. The actual exchange of illocutions is driven by the participating agents' *individual* needs and goals —something that will not be part of this negotiation model. Nevertheless, this exchange is subject to some *minimal shared conventions* on the intended usage of the illocutions in CL, and a simple negotiation protocol. These conventions relate to:

1. The elements that are relevant for the negotiation of a deal —in the form of *issues* and *values* that may evolve as negotiation proceeds.

2. The rationality of the participating agents —in terms of some form of preference relationships or utility functions which enable the agents to evaluate and compare different proposals.

3. The deliberation capability of the participating agents —in the form of an internal *state* in which the agent may register the history of the negotiation as well as the evolution of its own theoretical elements on which its decisions are founded.

4. The minimal shared meaning of the acceptable illocutions —this is captured in the way that a *received* illocution should be interpreted when heard by an agent, and by making explicit the conditions that enable an agent to use (or 'generate') a given illocution at a given time.

A minimal set of concepts which are necessary to represent the static components in automated negotiation are presented in Section 3.1, and the dynamic components —the concepts of a negotiation thread and a negotiation state— are introduced in Section 3.2. Social aspects that are relevant for persuasive arguments are dealt with in Section 3.3, and the process of interpreting and generating illocutions is illustrated in Section 3.4.

3.1 A Basic Negotiation Ontology

Negotiation requires communication between the agents and, for it to be unambiguous, each agent must have a unique identifier. We denote the set of identifiers of the agents involved in a negotiation as $Agents$[1]. The agents involved in a negotiation will have a variety of social relationships with one another. These relationships have an important impact upon the persuasion and argumentation process. For instance, prestigious speakers have a large persuasive impact and peers can be persuaded more easily than non-peers [9]. To model this characteristic, we assume that a general and shared social relation is defined between the agents. This relation can be modelled as a binary function over a set of social roles, denoted as $Roles$. In the BT scenario, for example, $Roles$ would be: $\{Customer, Contractor, Boss, Peer\}$. Finally, we assume that agents, when negotiating, interchange illocutions in a common communication language CL defined over a set of illocutionary particles whose propositional content is expressed in a shared logical language L[2]. The precise nature of L is unimportant in our model (e.g. it could be a propositional language or a modal language), however it must contain at least the following:

1. *Variables*. To represent the issues under negotiation. They have to be variables because issues need to be bound to different values during negotiation.

2. *Constants*. To represent values for the issues under negotiation. A special constant '?' is needed to represent the absence of value, and allow for underdefined proposals between agents. (Note this constant does not mean "don't care".)

3. *Equality*. To specify the value of an issue under negotiation.

---

[1] In practice, this set may change dynamically (e.g. new vetting companies may be created and old ones may disappear). However, since this process can be seen as independent from the negotiation process, our model is presented with respect to a fixed set.

[2] In practice, agents often have heterogeneous information models and so need to use one of the variety of techniques for allowing them to interoperate [5, 7]. However, in this work we adopt the simplest solution and assume a common language.

4. *Conjunction*. To define complex sentences.

All of these features are necessary to express the kinds of sentences involved in the negotiation proposals discussed in this paper. An example of such a sentence is:

$$(Price = £10) \wedge (Quality = High) \wedge (Penalty =?)$$

where '*Price*', '*Quality*', and '*Penalty*' are the issues under negotiation and so are represented as variables; '£10', '*High*', and '?' are values for those issues and so are constants; '=' denotes equality; and '$\wedge$' denotes conjunction. However, the language defined so far is not expressive enough to describe everything that is involved in a negotiation. In particular, to 'reason' and 'argue' about offers it is necessary at the very least to have some way of expressing preferences between offers. Offers are formulae in L, hence the most obvious way of representing preferences between formulae would be as a second-order relation in L. However, this would mean that L would be a higher-order logic, with the associated computational problems of such logics [6]. As a result we prefer to express preferences as a meta-language ML with the following minimum requirements:

1. *Quoting functions*. To represent formulae in L as terms in ML.
2. *A preference meta-predicate*. To express preferences between formulae in L.

For example, given the sentences $Price = £10$, and $Price = £20$ in L, we can express a preference for the first over the second as:

$$Pref(equal(\lceil Price \rceil, \lceil £10 \rceil), equal(\lceil Price \rceil, \lceil £20 \rceil))$$

where '*equal*' is the quoting in ML of the predicate '=' in L, and '*Pref*' represents the preference meta-predicate. In the remainder of the paper, instead of writing $equal(\lceil Price \rceil, \lceil £10 \rceil)$ the more compact representation $\lceil Price = £10 \rceil$ is used.

The common communication language, CL, accounts for the set of illocutionary particles necessary to model the set of illocutionary acts we study in this paper. The acts can be divided into two sets, I_{nego} corresponding to negotiation particles (those used to make offers and counter offers) and I_{pers} corresponding to persuasive particles (those used in argumentation). $I_{nego} = \{\text{offer}, \text{request}, \text{accept}, \text{reject}, \text{withdraw}\}$, $I_{pers} = \{\text{appeal}, \text{threaten}, \text{reward}\}$. Other illocutions could conceivably be brought into CL but the present set is sufficient for our purposes.

The negotiation dialogue between two agents consists of a sequence of offers and counter offers containing values for the issues. These offers and counteroffers can be just conjunctions of '*issue = value*' pairs (offer) or can be accompanied by persuasive arguments (threaten, reward, appeal). 'Persuasion' is a general term covering the different illocutionary acts by which agents try to change other agent's beliefs and goals. The selection of three persuasive particles in the set I_{pers} is the result of an analysis of the domain, as explained in Section 2, as well as of the persuasion literature [9, 18]. appeal is a particle with a broad meaning, since there are many different types of appeal. For example, an agent can appeal to authority, to prevailing practice or to self-interest [18]. The structure of the illocutionary act is $\text{appeal}(a, b, \xi, [not]\varphi, t)$, where φ is the argument —a formula in L or in ML, or an illocution in CL— that agent a communicates to b in support of a formula ξ (which may be a formula either in L or ML). All types of appeal adhere to this structure. The differing nature of the appeal is achieved by varying the φ in L or ML or by varying $[not]\varphi$ in CL — $not\ \varphi$ is understood as the fact that action φ does not take place. threaten and reward are simpler because they have a narrower range of interpretations. Their structure, $\text{threaten}(a, b, [not]\psi_1, [not]\psi_2, t)$ and $\text{reward}(a, b, [not]\psi_1, [not]\psi_2, t)$ is recursive since formulae ψ_1 and ψ_2 again may be illocutions in CL. This recursive definition allows for a rich set of possible (illocutionary) actions supporting the persuasion. For instance, agent DD can threaten agent SD that it will inform SD's boss about SD's incompetence if SD does not accept a particular deal:

$$\text{threaten}(DD, SD, not\ \text{accept}(SD, DD, time = 24h, t_2),$$
$$\text{appeal}(DD, Boss\_of\_SD, SD = incompetent,$$
$$not\ \text{accept}(SD, DD, time = 24h, t_2), t_3), t_1)$$

Having introduced all the components, we can now describe our dialogical framework for persuasive negotiation.

Definition 1. A *Dialogical Framework* is a tuple $DF = \langle Agents, Roles, R, L, ML, CL, Time \rangle$, where

1. *Agents* is a set of agent identifiers.
2. *Roles* is a set of role identifiers.
3. $R : Agents \times Agents \to Roles$, assigns a social role to each pair of agents. Social relations can therefore be viewed as a labelled graph.
4. L is a logical language[3] satisfying the requirements mentioned above. $Deals(L)$ denotes the set of all possible conjunctive formulae in L over equalities between issues and values, i.e. $x_1 = v_1 \wedge ... \wedge x_n = v_n$. $Deals_{?-free}(L) \subset Deals(L)$ excludes '?' as an acceptable value in a deal.
5. ML is a metalanguage over L satisfying the requirements mentioned above.
6. CL is the language for communication between agents. Given $a, b \in Agents$ and $t \in Time$ it is defined as:
   (a) if $\delta \in Deals(L)$ then $\text{request}(a, b, \delta, t) \in CL$.
   (b) if $\delta \in Deals_{?-free}(L)$ then $\text{offer}(a, b, \delta, t)$, $\text{accept}(a, b, \delta, t)$, $\text{reject}(a, b, \delta, t) \in CL$.
   (c) $\text{withdraw}(a, b, t) \in CL$.
   (d) if $\psi_1, \psi_2 \in CL$, $\xi \in L \cup ML$, and $\varphi \in L \cup ML \cup CL$ then $\text{threaten}(a, b, [not]\psi_1, [not]\psi_2, t)$, $\text{reward}(a, b, [not]\psi_1, [not]\psi_2, t)$, $\text{appeal}(a, b, \xi, [not]\varphi, t) \in CL$.
7. *Time* is a discrete totally ordered set of instants.

Note that the time stamp, which appears as the last argument in all illocutions, will be omited when there is no ambiguity.

Agents can use the illocutions in CL according to the following negotiation protocol (see Figure 3):

---

[3] In keeping with the spirit of specifying a framework which is neutral with respect to the agent architecture, we do not commit to any specific formal language but note that L could be as simple as a propositional language or as elaborate as a multi-modal BDI logic [10, 14].

1. A negotiation always starts with a *deal proposal*, i.e. an offer or request. In request illocutions the special constant '?' may appear. This is thought of as a petition to an agent to make a detailed proposal by filling the '?'s with defined values.
2. This is followed by an exchange of possibly many counter proposals (that agents may reject) and many persuasive illocutions.
3. Finally, a *closing* illocution is uttered, i.e. an accept or withdraw.

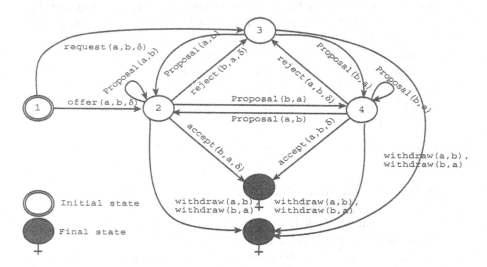

Fig. 3. Negotiation protocol. In accept(x, y, φ) and reject(x, y, φ) illocutions φ always refers to the last proposal. *Proposal*(x, y) stands for any illocution constructed with any of the following particles: offer, threaten, reward, appeal, and between agents x and y. We omit the time stamp in the illocutions.

3.2 Negotiating Agents

The Dialogical Framework described in the previous section represents the static components of the negotiation model — those that are fixed for all negotiations. This section presents the dynamic elements — those that change as a particular negotiation proceeds. Although our model aims to be as neutral as possible about the agent architecture, in order to capture essential aspects of persuasion it is necessary to assume that the agents have memory and are deliberative. Memory is expressed by means of an evolving *negotiation state* which, in turn, requires the notion of a *negotiation thread* [12] to capture the history of the negotiation dialogue between a pair of agents.

Definition 2. A **Negotiation Thread** between agents $a, b \in$ *Agents*, at time $t \in$ *Time*, noted $\vartheta^t_{a \leftrightarrow b}$, is a finite sequence (ordered on *Time*) of the form $\langle x^{t_j}_{d_i \to e_i} : t_j \leq t \rangle$ where:

1. $x^{t_j}_{d_i \to e_i} \in CL$,

2. $d_i, e_i \in \{a, b\}$, the thread contains only illocutions between agents a and b,
3. $d_i \neq e_i$, the illocutions are *between* agents, and
4. if $t_k < t_l$ then $issues(x^{t_k}_{d_i \to e_i}) \subseteq issues(x^{t_l}_{d_j \to e_j})$, where $issues(x)$ represents the set of issues mentioned in illocution x. That is, we assume monotonicity over the set of issues under negotiation, so that once an issue has been brought into the negotiation, it is never supressed. We will use ellipsis whenever useful to make more compact expressions.

We denote the last illocution in a thread as $\breve{\vartheta}$. We say a negotiation thread ϑ is **active** if $\breve{\vartheta}$ is not an `accept` or `withdraw` illocution.

In an extension to our previous work [15], we want to capture the idea that new issues may arise during the negotiation process. This is necessary because we consider that one of the main ways in which an agent may persuade another about the desirability of a particular proposal is to introduce new issues that have hitherto not featured in the thread. This means that we need an explicit representation of the set Ω of issues an agent is aware of. Preferences also evolve. This may be because Ω evolves or because the agent is persuaded to change its preferences. Thus the agent's internal theory T, which includes its preferences in ML and a set of other formulae in L modelling the domain, must be explicitly represented in the agent's state. In this model we do not impose any specific requirements on T. Hence the following definition:

Definition 3. A **Negotiation State** for an agent a at time t is any 3-tuple $s = \langle \Omega, T, H \rangle$, where

- Ω is a finite collection of negotiable issues.
- $T \subseteq L \cup ML$, is a theory in the common languages.
- H, the negotiation history, is the set of all negotiation threads involving agent a. That is, $H = \{\vartheta_{i \leftrightarrow a} | i \in Agents\}$.

All possible negotiation states for agent a will be denoted by S_a. As an illustration of how these notions are used, consider the following example:

Example 4. The CSD agent is negotiating with a VC_i agent for the Vet_Customer service for company A. The CSD agent proposes that the service be completed for £10 and should take 24 hours. VC_i responds that company A is known to be in financial difficulty and therefore a more time consuming and expensive vetting should be undertaken (Figure 2, id 8). Moreover, in order to meet the deadline, VC_i will need to delay the vetting of another BT customer (company B) for which an agreement has already been reached. This dialogue may be represented in CL as the sequence:

1. `offer`$(CSD, VC_i, Company = A \wedge price = £10 \wedge time = 24h, t_1)$
2. `appeal`$(VC_i, CSD, Company = A \wedge price = £20 \wedge time = 48h,$
   $Financial\_Status = bad \wedge Quality\_vetting = high, t_2)$
3. `appeal`$(VC_i, CSD, Company = B \wedge delay = 24h,$
   `accept`$(VC_i, CSD, Company = A \wedge price = £20 \wedge time = 48h, t_2), t_3)$

This example shows how the range of issues Ω involved in the negotiation is extended (the delaying of the vet customer service for company B) and how new information (the fact that company A is known to be in financial difficulty) can be brought to bear. This revelation of information means that the CSD agent extends its domain theory T (to include the fact that A may not be creditworthy). ∎

3.3 Persuasive Agents

As the previous example already showed, the illocutionary acts in CL built from I_{pers} allow arguments to be made in support of a deal. The basic building block for argumentation is $\texttt{appeal}(a, b, \xi, [not]\varphi, t)$ where $a, b \in Agents$, $\xi \in L \cup ML$, and $\varphi \in L \cup ML \cup CL$. This is read as "agent a wants agent b to add ξ to its current theory with argument $[not]\varphi$ supporting it". The other persuasive illocutionary acts, $\texttt{threaten}(a, b, [not]\psi_1, [not]\psi_2, t)$ and $\texttt{reward}(a, b, [not]\psi_1, [not]\psi_2, t)$ with $\psi_1, \psi_2 \in CL$, can contain arguments as long as ψ_1 and/or ψ_2 are appeals, or, recursively, contain appeals.

The interpretation of a persuasive argument for a formula determines whether the hearing agent changes its theory. To make a choice the agent considers the (possibly conflicting) arguments coming from other agents, and from itself, as proofs generated by its own theory. In our domain, and in other work on MAS [2], the social role between the agents is a determining factor in deciding which argument should be preferred. Hence, an authority relation is derived from the social roles and this is then used as the mechanism for comparing arguments. Precisely which social roles correspond to a power relation between the agents depends on the particular domain. In this scenario, for example, the role 'contractor' determines a power relation between the CSD agent and the vetting companies. To build a directed graph representing the authority that one agent has over another, we take the labelled graph associated with the social relation R, remove the links labelled with non-power roles, and add the necessary links to make the relation transitive. Hence the following definition:

Definition 5. Given a Dialogical Framework $DF = \langle Agents, Roles, R, L, ML, CL, Time\rangle$ and a set of authority roles $Power \subseteq Roles$, we define the *authority graph*, $AG \subseteq Agents \times Agents$, for DF as:

1. If $R(a, b) \in Power$ then $(a, b) \in AG$
2. If $(a, b), (b, c) \in AG$ then $(a, c) \in AG$

We say an authority graph is well defined if it is acyclic.

The authority graph encodes the authority relation —or lack of it, since in general AG is not totally connected —between any two agents. Now, our position is that in this domain the 'power' of an argument is determined solely by the authority of the agents which contribute formulae to its construction. Hence, it is necessary to extend the notion of authority from a relation between agents, as captured in the authority graph, to a relation over sets of agents which will be used to establish which arguments to prefer. There are two obvious ways of defining such a relation. We say that a set of agents A has *lower minimum authority* than B, $A \sqsubseteq_{\min} B$, if and only if for all $b \in B$ there exists $a \in A$ such that $(b, a) \in AG$. And that A has *lower maximum authority* than B, $A \sqsubseteq_{\max} B$, if and only if for all $a \in A$ there exists $b \in B$ such that $(b, a) \in AG$.

Thus, intuitively, the order $\sqsubseteq_{\min}$ assumes that if any formula used in the argument was proposed by somebody low in the authority graph the argument is weak, while $\sqsubseteq_{\max}$ assumes that as soon as any formula in the argument is proposed by somebody high in the authority graph the argument is strong. Obviously other authority relations might also be proposed. From now on we refer to any authority relation by the symbol $\sqsubseteq$.

In its most general form an argument is a proof for a formula [1]. We assume that all agents share the same deductive systems for L ($\vdash_L$) and ML ($\vdash_{ML}$). Hence, in this restricted context, a proof can be represented as the conjunction of all the formulae used in it because it can be reconstructed by the agent receiving it. An argument is then a formula $\varphi \in L \cup ML \cup CL$ that might be constructed from atomic formulae present initially in the theory of the agent or obtained in previous negotiation encounters from different agents. Assuming the existence of a function $Support : L \cup ML \cup CL \to 2^{Agents}$ that gives the agents whose formulae are used in the construction of an argument, or the agent that uttered the illocution when $\varphi \in CL$. We can use the social role of those agents to decide how forceful an argument is.

Fundamental to this view of decision making is the idea that one argument may attack another [3]. We represent the fact that an argument Arg supports a formula φ as a pair (Arg, φ) and the fact that the argument pair (Arg_1, φ_1) attacks (Arg_2, φ_2) by $Attacks((Arg_1, \varphi_1), (Arg_2, \varphi_2))$. The precise meaning of $Attacks$ depends strongly on the concrete languages L and ML being used. For the purpose of this paper we follow Dung [3] in assuming that it is a primitive notion, because our focus is on how to resolve the effect of an attack no matter how it is defined.

Definition 6. Given the two argument pairs (Arg_1, φ_1) and (Arg_2, φ_2) such that $Attacks((Arg_1, \varphi_1), (Arg_2, \varphi_2))$ then (Arg_1, φ_1) will be preferred to (Arg_2, φ_2), which we write as $(Arg_2, \varphi_2) \prec (Arg_1, \varphi_1)$, if and only if $Support(Arg_2) \sqsubseteq Support(Arg_1)$. When $(Arg_2, \varphi_2) \not\prec (Arg_1, \varphi_1)$ and $(Arg_1, \varphi_1) \not\prec (Arg_2, \varphi_2)$ we say that an agent is indifferent with respect to the arguments —and denote this by $(Arg_1, \varphi_1) \sim (Arg_2, \varphi_2)$.

The agents use argumentation as the means to decide how to interpret incoming and generate outgoing illocutions. On receiving an argument pair (Arg_1, φ_1) that is not attacked by any argument pair (Arg_2, φ_2) built from its current theory, an open-minded agent may simply add the argument Arg_1 and the formula φ_1 to its theory. In contrast, a more conservative agent may not accept a proposition unless it comes from a higher authority. When $Attacks((Arg_1, \varphi_1), (Arg_2, \varphi_2))$ the most preferred (in the sense defined above) argument pair is kept. If $(Arg_1, \varphi_1) \sim (Arg_2, \varphi_2)$ some additional criteria must be applied to decide which to keep, for instance epistemic entrenchment [4].

Example 7. The DD and SD agents are negotiating over the Survey_Customer_Site service. DD proposes that the service should be completed within 24 hours. SD indicates that one of its surveyors was planning to go on holiday and so the survey will take 48 hours (Figure 2, id 9). DD indicates that it must have the service completed within 24 hours. In CL this is expressed as:

1. offer($DD, SD, time = 24h \wedge service = Survey\_Customer\_Site, t_1$)
2. appeal($SD, DD, time = 48h, surveyor(Smith) \wedge holiday(Smith), t_2$)

3. appeal$(DD, SD, time = 24h, time = 24h, t_3)$

In this example, SD issues an appeal to DD for more time to complete the survey service. DD rejects this argument saying the service must be completed within 24 hours. SD now has two arguments that attack one another: $Attacks((surveyor(Smith) \wedge holiday(Smith), time = 48h), (time = 24h, time = 24h))$. It resolves them by referring to its authority graph which indicates that the authority of DD's argument is more powerful than its own (since DD is its boss, that is, $(DD, SD) \in AG$) and therefore it must do whatever is necessary to ensure the service is completed within 24 hours. That is, $Support(surveyor(Smith) \wedge holiday(Smith)) = \{SD\}$, $Support(time = 24h) = \{DD\}$ and given that $(DD, SD) \in AG$ we have that $(surveyor(Smith) \wedge holiday(Smith), time = 48h) \prec (time = 24h, time = 24h)$ because in our example $\{SD\} \sqsubset \{DD\}$ (using either of the measures mentioned above). ∎

3.4 Interpretation and Generation of Illocutions

For pragmatic reasons, we separate the definition of the semantics of illocutions into two different operations, I and G (see examples 8 and 9). The former implements the negotiation-state transition associated with hearing a given illocution, while the latter determines the illocutionary action to be taken in a particular state.

The underlying idea is that any illocution may introduce new issues into a negotiation, while appeals may, in addition, modify the preference relationships and the agent's theory. However, the actual effect of an illocution depends on the agent's interpretation of the utterances it receives. This interpretation process is highly domain-specific and is also dependent upon the internal structures present in the agent architecture. For this reason, we illustrate how our framework can be used to define a comparatively simple open-minded agent. Naturally this does not prescribe how all agents should behave, but rather exemplifies the concepts of our model which can be used to define many other types of agent.

The illocution interpretation function I for an open-minded agent is based on the following intuitions:

- Every illocution extends the corresponding thread in the negotiation history[4]. In this way, for example, complete illocutionary histories allow agents with total recall to be modelled. Forgetful agents can then be modelled by discarding part of the negotiation thread.
- All illocutions may introduce new issues into the negotiation.
- Appeals may change an agent's preference relationship. They may change the theory as well by extending it with the formulae of the argument in the appeal, provided that the current theory cannot build attacking arguments for the appeal.

---

[4] However, we do not update agents' theories in this minimal semantics because we wish to keep the interpretation of illocutions reasonably neutral with respect to the agents' internal architectures.

Example 8. Open-minded Interpretation. Given a communication language CL, a dialogical framework DF, and the set of all possible negotiation states S_b for an agent b, the interpretation function for an *open-minded agent* is defined by $I : CL \times S_b \times DF \to S_b$ such that —having $s = (\Omega, T, H)$, $H = \{\vartheta_{i \leftrightarrow b} | i \in Agents\}$, and '^' representing concatenation— we have[5]:

1. $I(\iota(a, b, \delta, t), s, df) = (\Omega \cup issues(\delta), T, H - \vartheta_{b \leftrightarrow a} + \vartheta'_{b \leftrightarrow a})$
   with $\iota \in I_{nego}$; $\vartheta'_{b \leftrightarrow a} = \vartheta_{b \leftrightarrow a}{}^\wedge\iota(a, b, \delta, t)$
2. $I(\texttt{threaten}(a, b, [not]\psi_1, [not]\psi_2, t), s, df) =$
   $$(\Omega \cup issues(\psi_1) \cup issues(\psi_2), T, H - \vartheta_{b \leftrightarrow a} + \vartheta'_{b \leftrightarrow a})$$
   with $\vartheta'_{b \leftrightarrow a} = \vartheta_{b \leftrightarrow a}{}^\wedge\texttt{threaten}(a, b, [not]\psi_1, [not]\psi_2, t)$
3. $I(\texttt{reward}(a, b, [not]\psi_1, [not]\psi_2, t), s, df) =$
   $$(\Omega \cup issues(\psi_1) \cup issues(\psi_2), T, H - \vartheta_{b \leftrightarrow a} + \vartheta'_{b \leftrightarrow a})$$
   with $\vartheta'_{b \leftrightarrow a} = \vartheta_{b \leftrightarrow a}{}^\wedge\texttt{reward}(a, b, [not]\psi_1, [not]\psi_2, t)$
4. $I(\texttt{appeal}(a, b, \xi, [not]\varphi, t), s, df) = (\Omega', T', H - \vartheta_{b \leftrightarrow a} + \vartheta'_{b \leftrightarrow a})$
   with $\vartheta'_{b \leftrightarrow a} = \vartheta_{b \leftrightarrow a}{}^\wedge\texttt{appeal}(a, b, \xi, [not]\varphi, t)$;
   if no (Arg, ψ) built from T such that $Attacks(([not]\varphi, \xi), (Arg, \psi))$
   then $\Omega' = \Omega \cup issues(\xi) \cup issues(\varphi)$;
   　　　　if $\varphi \in L \cup ML$ **then** $T' = T + \xi + \varphi$ **else** $T' = T + \xi$
   else $\Omega' = \Omega$; $T' = T$

■

Finally, an agent a's specification must include a way of computing the next illocution to be uttered in the negotiation thread. That is a function $G : S_a \times DF \to CL$ needs to be defined. This function must conform with the protocol depicted in Figure 3 and can conveniently be represented as a collection of condition-action rules, where the action is an illocutionary action. How an agent chooses which illocution to utter depends on many factors: the history of the negotiation, the active goals of the agent, or its theory, and it also depends on the way that particular agent interprets those illocutions. The following example illustrates a simple negotiation dialogue between two agents and contains a fragment of a G function.

Example 9. We use an expanded version of the argument presented in Example 7 to illustrate specific instances of illocution generation and interpretation functions. Given the two initial illocution interchanges:

1. $\texttt{offer}(DD, SD, time = 24h \wedge service = Survey\_Customer\_Site, t_1)$
2. $\texttt{appeal}(SD, DD, time = 48h, surveyor(Smith) \wedge holiday(Smith), t_2)$

We show two decisions taken by two different types of agent; an 'authoritarian' DD agent which exploits its social power (and threatens to inform the company chairman that SD did not agree to complete the task within 24h), and a 'conciliatory' DD agent which resorts to an explanatory appeal (that it is company policy that quotes must be handled within 24h):

3.1 **Authoritarian:** $\texttt{threaten}(DD, SD, not\ accept(SD, DD, time = 24h, t_3),$
$\texttt{appeal}(DD, Chairman, not\ accept(SD, DD, time = 24h, t_3), t_4))$

---

[5] An alternative way of looking at the interpretation of illocutions is as programs that transform one state into another. A natural formalism for that interpretation is Dynamic Logic [12].

3.2 Conciliatory: appeal$(DD, SD, time = 24h, BT\_Policy\_Time = 24h, t_3)$

The G function of an 'obedient' SD agent that, whenever possible, does what it is told could include the following decision rules where 'self' represents the agent interpreting the illocution:

if $\breve{\vartheta}_{x \leftrightarrow self} = \texttt{threaten}(x, self, not~\texttt{accept}(self, x, \delta), \psi_2)$ **and** $(x, self) \in AG$
   and $can\_do(\delta)$ **then** $\texttt{accept}(self, x, \delta)$
if $\breve{\vartheta}_{x \leftrightarrow self} = \texttt{threaten}(x, self, not~\texttt{accept}(self, x, \delta), \psi_2)$ **and** $(x, self) \in AG$
   and not $can\_do(\delta)$ **then** $\delta' = compute\_counter\_offer(s, DF); \texttt{offer}(self, x, \delta')$
if $\breve{\vartheta}_{x \leftrightarrow self} = \texttt{appeal}(x, self, \xi, \varphi)$ **and** $\psi \to \neg\varphi \in T$ **then** $\texttt{appeal}(self, x, \neg\varphi, \psi)$

Assuming that $can\_do(time = 24h \wedge service = Survey\_Customer\_Site)$ is true, by subcontracting the task say, the dialogue with the authoritarian DD ends with:

4.1 accept$(SD, DD, time = 24h \wedge service = Survey\_Customer\_Site, t_4)$

On the other hand, if we assume that the rule $BT\_Policy\_Time = 24h \leftrightarrow Fully\_staffed$ is true and DD utters 3.2, the agent could reply with:

4.2 appeal$(SD, DD, not~(BT\_Policy\_Time = 24h), not~Fully\_staffed)$ ∎

To further illustrate the power of our framework, Figure 4 shows the representation in CL of the arguments presented in Figure 2.

Id	Dialogue
1	$\texttt{appeal}(CSD, VC_i, \texttt{offer}(VC_j, CSD, \delta), true),$ $\texttt{threaten}(CSD, VC_i, not~\texttt{offer}(VC_i, CSD, \delta), \texttt{withdraw}(CSD, VC_i))$
2	$\texttt{threaten}(CSD, VC_i, not~\texttt{offer}(VC_i, CSD, \ldots \wedge time < limit),$ $\quad not~\texttt{request}(CSD, VC_i, Future^a))$ ― [a] *Future* is an universally quantified variable over the future instants in $Time$.
3	$\texttt{threaten}(DD, SD, not~\texttt{acccept}(SD, DD, \ldots \wedge time < limit),$ $\quad \texttt{appeal}(DD, Boss_{SD}, \psi^a, not~\texttt{acccept}(SD, DD, \ldots \wedge time < limit)))$ ― [a] ψ expressing the fact that the deadline has been missed.
4	$\texttt{reward}(CSD, DD, \texttt{accept}(DD, CSD, \delta),$ $\texttt{appeal}(CSD, OurBoss, \psi, \texttt{accept}(DD, CSD, \delta)))^a$ ― [a] $\delta = \ldots Vet = Customer_i \wedge time < limit$. The reward consists of passing the information to our boss. ψ represents the satisfaction of $Customer_i$.
5	$\texttt{reward}(CSD, VC_i, \texttt{accept}(VC_i, CSD, \ldots \wedge time = k \wedge \ldots), \texttt{request}(CSD, VC_i, \Delta, Future))^a$ ― [a] Δ stands for a deal, and *Future* stands for an instant in the future.
6	$\texttt{appeal}(CSD, VC_i, time = t \wedge cost = c, \texttt{accept}(VC_i, CSD, \ldots \wedge time = t \wedge cost = c, Before^a))$ ― [a] *Before* represents a previous instant in $Time$.
7	$\texttt{appeal}(CSD, DD, time = 48h, BT\_policy\_time = 48h)$
8	$\texttt{appeal}(VC_i, CSD, time = high, Financial\_status = trouble \wedge Quality\_vetting = high)$
9	$\texttt{appeal}(DD, CSD, time > t_{normal}, surveyor(Smith) \wedge holiday(Smith))$
10	$\texttt{appeal}(SD, DD, time > t_{normal}, Number\_premises = High)$

Fig. 4. Formalisation of the arguments presented in Figure 2.

4 Related Work

Much of the existing work on agent-based negotiation is rooted in game theory, e.g. [17]. Although this approach has produced significant results, and has been successful in many negotiation domains, it embodies a number of limiting assumptions about the agents' knowledge and utility functions. Even when this approach is extended, as in [11], to cope with conditions that change over time, it does not address the problem of how these changes can be accomplished by one agent influencing another, nor does it cope with the problem of introducing new issues into negotiations. Changing preferences through persuasion, in multi-agent systems, was addressed in Sycara's seminal work on labour negotiation [18], work extended and formalised by Kraus *et al.* [10]. However, this work is set within the context of a particular agent architecture, assumes a fixed and shared domain theory, and deals with five particular types of argument (threats, rewards, appeals to precedent, appeals to prevailing practice, and appeals to self-interest). Furthermore, Kraus *et al.* do not deal with the introduction of new issues or imperfect rationality. In contrast, our model accommodates partial knowledge, imperfect rationality and the introduction of new negotiation issues —which are relevant features in many application domains— while only imposing minimal requirements on agents' internal states and using a general rhetorical language.

We should also acknowledge the differences between our work and the use of argumentation to explain how a single agent reasons. In the former, an agent argues with itself to establish its beliefs. In our work arguments are used by one agent in order to change another agents' beliefs and actions. The other important difference is that the mechanism for resolving conflicts between arguments in single agent argumentation is often built into the logical language in which arguments are constructed and is based upon some intuitive notion of what is correct in the world at large. In contrast, we keep this mechanism at the meta-level and ground it in knowledge about the domain. This has the dual advantage of ensuring that conflicts are resolved in a way that is known to be suitable for our domain whilst allowing new conflict resolution mechanisms to be easily fitted into the model in different domains.

5 Conclusion

This paper has introduced a novel framework for describing persuasive negotiations between autonomous agents. This provides a sound foundation for building specific artificial agents by instantiating the generic components such as L, ML and T. The framework has been strongly influenced by our experience of business process management applications and this makes us confident that it can capture the needs of other real world applications. However, we realise that there are a number of issues which require further investigation. Firstly there is the matter of how expressive CL is required to be. For instance, at the moment an agent can only make threats and promises about illocutionary actions (e.g. to tell somebody about something). It is also desirable for non-illocutionary actions to be the consequence of a threat or promise. Similarly, while appeals could be used to model a wide range of illocutions, it may be useful to characterise subtly different types of illocution through more refined interpretation and generation functions. Secondly, we have reflected an agent's preferences, and the changes in those preferences, simply as sentences and updates in the agent's theory T. Further work is required to tie these preferences to notions of rationality, in particular to standard ideas of expected utility. Finally, we make the simplifying assumption that negotiating agents have a common notion of deduction. This may be inadequate for some domains, in which case it will be necessary for agents to be able to discuss what rules of inference are appropriate.

References

1. S. Benferhat, D. Dubois, and H. Prade. Argumentative inference in uncertain and inconsistent knowledge bases. In *Proc 9th Conf on Uncertainty in AI*, pages 411–419, Washington, USA, 1993.
2. C. Castelfranchi. Social Power: A Point missed in Multi-Agent, DAI and HCI. In Y. Demazeau and J. P. Müller, editors, *Decentralised AI*, pages 49–62. Elsevier, 1990.
3. P. M. Dung. On the acceptability of arguments and its fundamental role in nonmonotonic reasoning, logic programming and n-person games. *Artificial Intelligence*, 77:321–357, 1995.
4. P. Gärdenfors. *Knowledge in Flux*. MIT Press, Cambridge, MA, 1987.
5. F. Giunchiglia and L. Serafini. Multilanguage hierarchical logics (or: How we can do without modal logics). *Artificial Intelligence*, 65:29–70, 1994.
6. W. D. Goldfarb. The undecidability of the second-order unification problem. *Theoretical Computer Science*, 13:225–230, 1981.
7. T. R. Gruber. The role of common ontology in achieving sharable, reusable knowledge bases. In J. A. Allen, R. Fikes, and E. Sandewall, editors, *Proc. of the Second Int. Conf. on Principles of Knowledge Representation and Reasoning*, San Mateo, CA, 1991. Morgan Kaufman.
8. N. R. Jennings, P. Faratin, M. J. Johnson, T. J. Norman, P. O'Brien, and M. E. Wiegand. Agent-based business process management. *International Journal of Cooperative Information Systems*, 5(2&3):105–130, 1996.
9. M. Karlins and H. I. Abelson. *Persuasion*. Crosby Lockwood & Son, London, UK, 1970.
10. S. Kraus, M. Nirkhe, and K. Sycara. Reaching agreements through argumentation: a logical model (preliminary report). In *DAI Workshop'93*, pages 233–247, Pensylvania, USA, 1993.
11. S. Kraus, J. Wilkenfeld, and G. Zlotkin. Multiagent negotiation under time constraints. *Artificial Intelligence*, 75:297–345, 1995.
12. P. Noriega and C. Sierra. Towards layered dialogical agents. In *Proceedings of the ECAI'96 Workshop Agents Theories, Architectures and Languages, ATAL'96*, number 1193 in LNAI, pages 157–171. Springer, 1996.
13. S. Parsons and N. R. Jennings. Negotiation through argumentation—a preliminary report. In *Proc. Second Int. Conf. on Multi-Agent Systems, ICMAS'96*, pages 267–274, Kyoto, Japan, 1996.
14. A. S. Rao and M. P. Georgeff. BDI agents: From Theory to Practice. In *Proc 1st Int Conf on Multi-Agent Systems*, pages 312–319, San Francisco, USA, 1995.
15. C. Sierra, P. Faratin, and N. R. Jennings. A service-oriented negotiation model between autonomous agents. In *MAAMAW'97*, pages 17–35, Ronneby, Sweden, 1997.
16. R. G. Smith and R. Davis. Frameworks for cooperation in distributed problem solving. *IEEE Trans on Systems, Man and Cybernetics*, 11(1):61–70, 1981.
17. J. S.Rosenschein and G. Zlotkin. *Rules of Encounter*. The MIT Press, Cambridge, USA, 1994.
18. K. P. Sycara. Persuasive argumentation in negotiation. *Theory and Decision*, 28:203–242, 1990.
19. D. N. Walton. *Informal Logic*. Cambridge University Press, Cambridge, UK, 1989.

Agent Modelling in METATEM and DESIRE

Marco Mulder*, Jan Treur* and Michael Fisher†

* Department of Mathematics and Computer Science, Vrije Universiteit,
De Boelelaan 1081, 1081 HV Amsterdam, The Netherlands
EMAIL: treur@cs.vu.nl

† Department of Computing, Manchester Metropolitan University,
Chester Street, Manchester M1 5GD, United Kingdom
EMAIL: M.Fisher@doc.mmu.ac.uk

Keywords: modelling, specification, architectures, METATEM, DESIRE

Abstract. In spite of the rapid spread of agent technology, there is, as yet, little evidence of an *engineering* approach to the development of multi-agent systems. For example, both development methods and verification techniques for multi-agent systems are rare. In this paper, we describe a case study aimed at comparing two formal agent modelling languages, namely Concurrent METATEM and DESIRE. A version of the well known PRS architecture is developed and the approaches are compared with respect to this application.

1 Introduction

The majority of existing agent applications have been developed in an ad hoc fashion, following little or no rigorous design methodology and with limited *a priori* specification of either the agents or the system as a whole. This situation is, however, beginning to change. To enable more robust and reliable systems to be developed, researchers are increasingly focusing on the problem of specifying, verifying and validating the behaviour and properties of both the individual agents and the system as a whole. Within this, two broad streams can be identified:

1. those who use logics (often non-classical) to specify their systems (e.g., [19, 8, 6]);
2. those who use modelling techniques originating from standard software and knowledge engineering for specifying their systems (e.g., [5, 16, 18]).

In this paper, examples from these streams are compared: the former is represented by Concurrent METATEM [8, 9], the latter by DESIRE [3, 5]. In order to provide a realistic application upon which this comparison can be made, the Procedural Reasoning System (PRS) [13] is modelled by both approaches. First, in §2, the PRS architecture is described. Next, in §3 Concurrent METATEM is described, followed by a Concurrent METATEM model of PRS in Section 4. In §5 DESIRE is described, followed by a DESIRE model of PRS in §6. Finally, in §7 comparisons and conclusions are provided.

2 The PRS Agent Architecture

The PRS is an agent architecture developed by Georgeff and Lansky [13]. It is designed to function as an embedded reasoning system situated in a dynamic world and operating under real-time constraints and resource limitations. PRS agents have been tested in domains such as the control of mobile robots and malfunction handling in a space shuttle.

An embedded reasoning system is concerned with automating the operation of complex physical systems, for example an automated pilot of an aircraft. On an abstract level, the kind of behaviour that such a system should have is twofold:

1. make plans to achieve a desired goal (e.g. how to get an aircraft at a certain height), and execute them in real-time;
2. react in real-time to events (e.g. a sudden cross wind).

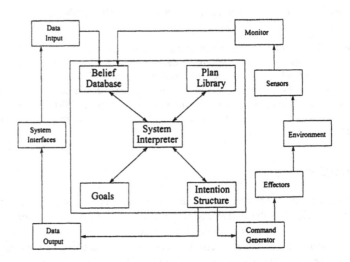

Fig. 1. Basic Structure of the PRS agent

The basic structure of the PRS is shown in Figure 1. A PRS agent has four data structures: a database with the current *beliefs* of the system; a (dynamically changing) set of *goals* to be realized; a set of partially elaborated *plans*, termed Knowledge Areas (KAs); and an *intention structure*, containing tasks that the system has adopted for execution.

The central element of the PRS agent is the *system interpreter*. Its job is to activate plans, place them on the intention structure and execute them. The PRS agent uses *effectors* and *sensors* to interact with the outside world. Changes in the outside world will result in changes in the belief database, and the execution of plans can change the outside world through effectors.

3 Concurrent METATEM

Concurrent METATEM [8, 9] is a language for modelling concurrent and distributed interacting components. The basic elements of Concurrent METATEM are concurrently executing autonomous *objects* (which we consider as agents). Objects communicate by *broadcast* message-passing: information sent by one object can be received by all other objects. The definition of an object has two main components, namely an *interface definition* and an *internal definition*. The interface definition of an object consists of its name together with a definition of which messages it recognizes and which messages it may produce itself. An object's internal definition represents a computation mechanism which recognizes the appropriate incoming messages, computes accordingly, and broadcasts only the prescribed messages. The computation mechanism is provided by a METATEM-like computational engine [2], which is based on the execution of temporal logic formulae.

Temporal logic can be seen as classical logic extended with various modalities representing temporal aspects of the process in logical formulae. The temporal logic used within Concurrent METATEM is called First-Order METATEM Logic (FML). It is based on a linear, discrete model of time, i.e., time is modeled as an infinite sequence of discrete states, with an identified starting point ('the beginning of time'). For every moment in time, the atoms that are true and the future-time constraints that hold are maintained. Classical formulae are used to represent constraints within individual states, while temporal formulae represent constraints *between* states. Rather than provide a detailed description of this logic, we refer the reader to [8, 2, 10] and note that the only temporal operators used here are '$\bullet$' (last time), 'S' (since), '$\bigcirc$' (next time), '$\Diamond$' (sometime), and '$\mathcal{W}$' (unless).

An object's internal definition is given by a set of *rules* of the form "past and present formula" implies "present or future formula". The intuitive interpretation of such a rule is 'on the basis of the past, do the future' [2]. The actual execution of an object is as follows: at every point in time, antecedents of rules are matched against the *history* of incoming messages (predicates named in the input interface) and internal predicates. For those rules that 'fire' (i.e. whose antecedent is satisfied), the present and future-time consequents are executed.

Future-time consequents that are executed introduce indeterministic choices for the execution mechanism. For example, when $\Diamond p$ is executed, the proposition p must *eventually* become true. The execution mechanism will try to satisfy eventualities as soon as possible (i.e., as soon as it does not result in contradiction). The classical operator '$\vee$' also introduces indeterminacy. For example, if '$\bigcirc (a \vee b)$' must be satisfied, the execution can choose to satisfy either a or b in the next state. As an example of a simple METATEM program, consider the following rules:

$$\bullet \, adopt\_goal(G) \Rightarrow \Diamond achieved\_goal(G);$$
$$\neg percept(G) \, S \, adopt\_goal(G) \Rightarrow \neg achieved\_goal(G).$$

Note that 'G' here represents a universally quantified variable. Looking at these rules, we see that whenever *adopt_goal(G)* is true at the last moment in time, a commitment is made to eventually make *achieved_goal(G)* true. However, as long as *percept(G)* does not hold, this commitment will not be fulfilled.

A Concurrent METATEM system consists of a set of objects each executing temporal specifications, as above. All objects are (potentially) concurrently active. They may be asynchronously executing and each object, in executing its temporal formulae, constructs its own sequence of moments independent of other objects.

4 Modelling a PRS Agent in Concurrent METATEM

In this section, a PRS-agent is modelled in Concurrent METATEM. As meta-level activity is involved, an extension of FML. called Meta-METATEM Logic (MML), will be used. In

MML, the domain over which terms range is extended to incorporate the *names* of object-level (temporal) formulae [1].

4.1 Interface and Internal Definitions

The PRS agent's interface definition is prs-agent (percept, goal) [action]. Thus, the agent recognizes two sorts of messages from its environment: messages of the form *percept(P)* represent the percepts of the agent, on which it bases its beliefs; messages of the form *goal(intrinsic, G)* represent goals that are given by the environment to the agent. In a multi-agent situation, the name of the agent that has to achieve the goal may be used instead of *intrinsic*. The agent may itself produce the message *action(A)*, by which it can change its environment. The agent's internal definition consists of representation and maintenance rules for beliefs and goals, representation and execution rules for plans, and rules for representing intentions, for establishing intentions by *plan invocation* and for manipulating the intention structure (*deliberation*). In the following sections, these elements are described in more detail.

4.2 Beliefs — Representation and Maintenance

The belief-database of PRS is represented by a set of ground atoms of the form *belief(B)*, where *B* is a literal, e.g. *belief(¬raining)*. The beliefs of the agent are based on assertions and percepts. For assertions of beliefs by plan execution, the predicate *assert(B)* is used. Percepts of the agent have the form *percept(B)*. The following rules handle the belief maintenance:

$$B1: \qquad (assert(B) \vee percept(B)) \Rightarrow belief(B)$$
$$B2: \qquad \neg(assert(\neg B) \vee percept(\neg B)) \, S \, belief(B) \Rightarrow belief(B)$$

Rule B1 rule states that if the literal *B* is asserted by the agent, or if it is a percept of the agent, it becomes a belief of that agent. For every state where *assert(B)* or *percept(B)* holds, *belief(B)* will also hold. This rule is a *State Rule*: its antecedent and consequence are present-time formulae. Rule B2 states that if the negation of a certain belief held by the agent is neither asserted nor percepted since it established that belief, the belief still holds. In other words: a belief holds until its negation is asserted. Without this rule, beliefs would not be 'remembered' in consecutive states. This rule is a *Temporal Rule*.

4.3 Goals — Representation and Maintenance

Two types of goals are distinguished: *intrinsic goals* and *operational goals* (subgoals). An intrinsic goal is one that originates from outside of the agent, e.g. from another agent. If the agent has plans that are triggered by such a goal, a new intention will be established to achieve that goal (see §4.5). In PRS, intrinsic goals are viewed as the *desires* of the agent. An operational goal *G* is adopted if a plan is executed that has a subgoal *G* in its body. Every plan is executed for a certain intention of the agent. If an operational goal *G* is adopted by a plan that is executed for intention *I*, goal *G* can be seen as a subgoal for intention *I*. Both intrinsic goals and operational goals are represented by the atom *goal(I, G)*. For an intrinsic goal, the argument *I* is the constant *intrinsic*, for an operational goal it is the name of an intention. The argument *G* is the name of the goal. With respect to goals, the PRS agent has the following behaviour: every goal will eventually be either achieved or fail to be achieved. A goal will only be achieved if a plan whose purpose it is to achieve that goal has successfully been executed. In the model, this is indicated by the predicate $achieved(purpose(goal(G)))$. A goal fails if there is no optional plan to achieve that goal left that has not already failed during execution. In the model, the failure of a plan is indicated by $failed(plan(N))$ (see §4.4). The following rules specify the behaviour described above:

G1 : $\bullet goal(I, G) \Rightarrow \Diamond(achieved(goal(G)) \lor failed(goal(G)))$;

G2 : $\neg achieved(purpose(goal(G)))\, S\, goal(I, G) \Rightarrow \neg achieved(goal(G))$;

G3 : $\neg failed(plan(N))\, S\, option(N, I, goal(G), \phi) \Rightarrow \neg failed(goal(G))$.

Rule G1 states that, if $goal(I, G)$ was satisfied in the last state, either $achieved(goal(G))$ or $failed(goal(G))$ will be satisfied in some state in the future. Because of rules G2 and G3, this eventuality cannot immediately be satisfied. If $achieved(purpose(goal(G)))$ was not satisfied since $goal(I, G)$ occurred, rule G2 states that $achieved(goal(G))$ must be false; rule G3 states that if $failed(plan(N))$ has not been satisfied since $option(N, I, goal(G), \phi)$ occurred, $failed(I, G)$ must be false.

4.4   Plans — Representation and Execution

The predicate $plan(Name, Purpose, \phi_{context}, \phi_{body})$ is used to represent plans. Every plan must have a unique $Name$ and a $Purpose$ indicating the event that triggers the plan. There are two types of plans: *reactive* and *goal-achievement* plans. A reactive plan is triggered by a change in the beliefs of the agent; its purpose is to react to a certain event. In a reactive plan, $Purpose$ has the form $react(\phi_{beliefs})$, where $\phi_{beliefs}$ is a first order expression of the beliefs of the agent. For example, if a plan has the $Purpose$ $react(belief(raining) \lor belief(snowing))$, it will be triggered in a state where $belief(raining)$ or $belief(snowing)$ is true, while in the preceding state this is not the case. A goal-achievement plan is triggered by a new goal of the agent; its purpose is to achieve that goal. In a goal-achievement plan, $Purpose$ has the form $goal(G)$, e.g. if a plan has the $Purpose$ $goal(go\text{-}home)$, it will be triggered in a state where the predicate $goal(I, go\text{-}home)$ is true for a certain intention I.

    The context of a plan, $\phi_{context}$ is, just like $\phi_{beliefs}$, a first order expression of the beliefs of an agent. The expression must be true for a plan to be triggered. Unlike $\phi_{beliefs}$, this is not interpreted as a *change* in the beliefs of an agent. For example, if the $Purpose$ of a plan is $react(belief(raining))$ and $\phi_{context}$ is $belief(\neg at\_home)$, then the plan is triggered if in the last state it was not raining, in the current state it is raining and the agent is not at home. It does not matter whether or not the agent was at home in the last state.

    In PRS, the bodies of plans are represented as plan graphs of which each arc is labeled with a plan expression. They provide a temporal description of desired behaviours of an agent. In the Concurrent METATEM model of PRS, plan-bodies are represented as temporal logic formulae (ϕ_{body}). These formulae are not meant to be executed directly by Concurrent METATEM, but by a specific *meta-interpreter*, outlined below. In this way it is possible to have control over the execution of plans, e.g. to suspend the execution of one plan in favour of a more urgent plan. While we will not describe plan structures in detail, we note that a simple plan which achieves subgoal b, tests for the truth of c, and then if d is true carries out *e* and terminates, else carries out *f* then terminates, is represented by the formula

$$\phi_{body} = goal(b) \,\wedge\, \Diamond(achieved(goal(b)) \,\wedge\, \bigcirc(test(c) \wedge$$
$$\bigcirc((belief(d) \Rightarrow \bigcirc(action(e) \wedge \bigcirc end)) \,\wedge$$
$$(\neg belief(d) \Rightarrow \bigcirc(action(f) \wedge \bigcirc end)))))$$

As plan bodies are executed by a meta interpreter (outlined below), the next-time operator in a plan body can be interpreted as *the next state where this plan is being executed*.

Plan Execution The predicate *exec_plan(Name, Intention, Purpose, ϕ_{body})* is used for the execution of the temporal logic plan bodies described above and effectively characterises a meta-interpreter for formulae comprising those bodies. Its arguments are the *Name* of the plan, the *Intention* for which the plan is executed, the *Purpose* of the plan, and the remaining body of the plan that is yet to be executed. Rules describing this meta-interpreter can be characterised as either *Temporal Rules*, which are used to 'move' plan execution forward, and *State Rules*, which define conditions on the current state. Temporal rules are used to interpret the temporal operators that occur in a plan and state rules are used to interpret conjunctions etc. Rather than providing a full description of these rules (see [17]), we simply consider

$$\bullet \; (exec\_plan(N,I,P,\bigcirc\phi) \,\wedge\, \neg failed(plan(N))) \Rightarrow \Diamond exec\_plan(N,I,P,\phi)$$

This is a temporal rule that interprets the next-time operator. It states that if in the last state plan N did not fail (e.g. because it performed a test that failed, or a subgoal could not be achieved), and in the next state where plan N is being executed, ϕ must be executed, then sometime in the future ϕ will be executed. Assuming that Concurrent METATEM satisfies eventualities as soon as possible, $exec\_plan(N,I,P,\phi)$ will immediately be satisfied unless the deliberation rules (§4.5) specify that another plan must be executed first.

4.5 Intentions — Representation, Plan Invocation, Deliberation

In PRS, the *intention structure* contains all those tasks that the system has adopted for execution, either immediately or at some later time. The invocation of a plan by a change in the beliefs of the system or by the adoption of an intrinsic goal results in the establishment of a new intention. A single intention consists of its top-level plan(s), together with all the various (sub-) plans that are currently being used to fulfill the requirements of the top-level plan(s). At any given moment, the intention structure may contain a number of such intentions. Usually, only one of them is *active* (for that intention, plans are currently being executed) and the rest are *suspended* (because plans for a more urgent intention are being executed).

In the Concurrent METATEM model, a new intention is created by asserting the predicate *new_intention(I)*, e.g. *new_intention(react(belief(raining)))*. Every intention will eventually be *done*: it either *succeeds* or *fails*. An intention succeeds if one of its top-level plans succeeds. If all such plans fail, the intention fails. Because of the way plans are invoked (see below), *achieved(intention(I))* can only be satisfied if a top-level plan for the intention has successfully been executed, and *failed(intention(I))* can only be satisfied if all such plans failed. Note that if intention I is adopted, the predicate *new_intention(I)* will only be true in the state where it is adopted. In the later states where the agent still has the intention the eventuality $\Diamond(done(intention(I)))$ holds. If an intention is not *done* (succeeded or failed), it is a *current_intention* of the agent. If in a certain state a plan is being executed for intention I, intention I is an *active intention*. If for intention I no plan is active (e.g. because a plan for a more urgent intention is being executed), it is a *suspended intention*. This is reflected by the following rules:

P3 : $\neg done(intention(I))\ S\ new\_intention(I) \Rightarrow current\_intention(I)$;
P4 : $exec\_plan(name(N), intention(I), goal(G), \phi_{body}) \Rightarrow active\_intention(I)$;
P5 : $current\_intention(I) \wedge \neg active\_intention(I) \Rightarrow suspended\_intention(I)$.

Plan invocation Three types of plan invocation are distinguished:

1. The invocation of a reactive plan by a change in the beliefs of an agent.
2. The invocation of a goal-achievement plan by an intrinsic goal.
3. The invocation of a goal-achievement play a subgoal of another plan.

In the first two cases, a new intention is established, and the invoked plan becomes a top-level plan for the new intention. While lack of space again precludes the description in full of these three rules, we will outline the second of these. A goal-achievement plan is triggered by an intrinsic goal with the following rule:

$$\bullet\ \left(plan(name(N), goal(G), \phi_{context}, \phi_{body}) \wedge goal(intrinsic, G) \wedge \phi_{context} \right) \Rightarrow$$
$$\left(\begin{array}{c} option(name(N), intention(goal(G)), goal(G), \phi_{body}) \wedge\ new\_intention(goal(G)) \\ \wedge\ \neg achieved(intention(goal(G)))\ W\ achieved(goal(G)) \\ \wedge \neg failed(intention(goal(G)))\ W\ failed(goal(G)) \end{array} \right)$$

If, in the last state, the intrinsic goal G was adopted, and $\phi_{context}$ was believed by the agent, the plan becomes an *option*. More than one plan can be triggered to achieve the same goal. If execution of one of these plans succeeds, the others will not be executed. To make this behaviour possible, a triggered goal-achievement plan becomes an *option*, not an eventuality.

Deliberation If there is more than one optional plan for a certain goal, only one of them must be executed at a time (and if one of them succeeds, the others will not be executed). For every two plans for the same goal, the predicate *preferred_option* states which of them has to be tried first. The following rule prevents execution of a plan unless all preferable plans for a certain goal have failed:

$$\bullet\ (option(N, I, goal(G), \phi_1) \wedge option(M, I, goal(G), \phi_2) \wedge preferred\_option(N, M))$$
$$\Rightarrow \neg exec\_plan(M, I, goal(G), \phi_1)\ W\ failed(plan(N))$$

Again, we must omit discussion of the further rules relating to deliberation (see [17]).

Thus, the representation of PRS in Concurrent METATEM is achieved through a large set of temporal rules and implementation is carried out by directly executing these rules. This execution deals with basic maintenance and manipulation of beliefs, goals and intentions, while a meta-interpreter actually executes the selected plans.

5 DESIRE

DESIRE (which stands for framework for DEsign and Specification of Interacting REasoning components) is a framework for the design and formal specification of compositional multi-agent systems [4]. In DESIRE, a model is hierarchically composed of components that specify (sub)tasks. Because a system is viewed as a series of interacting components, DESIRE is suited to the specification of the dynamics and interactions in multi-agent systems. The current design environment based on DESIRE contains a graphical editor and tools to support implementation [3]. In DESIRE, task composition, information exchange, sequencing of tasks, task delegation and knowledge structures, are all modelled and specified.

Tasks are structured in a task hierarchy and mapped into DESIRE components. Two sorts of components are distinguished: *primitive* and *composed* components. A primitive component represents a primitive task (i.e., without subtasks) in a task hierarchy and a composed component represents a composed task. The functionality of a primitive component is specified by a *knowledge base*. A composed component contains subcomponents, which can be primitive or composed themselves. The different roles information can play within reasoning can be distinguished by different (meta-)levels. In a two-level situation, the lowest level is termed *object-level* and the second level is termed *meta-level*. Every component has a leveled *input* and *output interface*.

Between the output interface of one component and the input interface of another and between the (input/output) interfaces of a component and its subcomponents, information exchange is specified by *information links*. In information links, it is specified how truth values of one interface atom are linked to truth values of another interface atom.

Task sequencing is explicitly modelled as *task control knowledge*. Every composed component contains a task control knowledge base that specifies how and when its subcomponents and information links must be activated, based on the evaluation of its subcomponents' processes. For every component, the following information is maintained that is used for task control: *task control foci* that state to which targets a component's reasoning is focussed (a component's focus can be changed dynamically); the *extent* to which a component tries to achieve its goals — all possible, every, any or any new; *evaluation criteria* by which the success or failure of the process of a component is measured; an *activation type*: idle, active or awake — a component that is made *active* will become idle when it has finished the process it was activated for (it has to be activated again explicitly when needed), while an *awake* component stays awake and processes information as soon as it arrives. Like components, information links also have activation types: *idle*, *uptodate* and *awake*. If a link gets the status uptodate, it transfers information and becomes idle again. Once a link is awake, it stays awake and transfers information as soon as it arrives.

During knowledge analysis a task as a whole is modelled. In the course of the modelling process decisions are made as to which tasks are (to be) performed by which agent. This process, which may also be performed at run-time, results in the delegation of tasks to the parties involved in tasks execution. In addition to these specific tasks, often generic agent tasks, such as interaction with the world (observation, execution of actions) and other agents (communication and cooperation) are assigned.

The structures used to express (domain) knowledge are specified by *signatures*. A signature consists of hierarchically ordered sorts, predicate symbols (relations), function symbols and constants (objects). Units of information are represented by the (ground; i.e. instantiated) *atoms* defined by the signature. Three valued logic is used: every atom can be either true, false or unknown. Truth values of atoms are maintained in the input/output interfaces of all components and in internal *information states* of primitive components. The inference relation *chaining* is used to derive values of output atoms of a primitive component based on its input atoms and knowledge base.

6 Modelling a PRS Agent in DESIRE

In this section, the PRS-agent together with its environment is modelled in DESIRE, and is instantiated with a Blocksworld example: the environment consists of a table with several blocks on it and actions are defined to move blocks around. The agent can plan how to achieve certain configurations the blocks and can react to changes in the configuration. The model of the agent and its environment are general in the sense that only the knowledge structures in the environment and the plans of the agent are specific to the Blocksworld example.

6.1 Top Level

In Figure 2, the composition and information exchange of the Top Level component of the model are shown. Here, two roles are distinguished: the composed component prs_agent models the PRS-agent and the composed component environment models the environment in which the agent is embedded. The link environment_percepts transfers information about the state of the environment to *percepts* of the agent. The link goals_to_agent transfers *intrinsic goals* from environment to agent, while actions_to_environment transfers *actions* by which the agent can change the state of its environment.

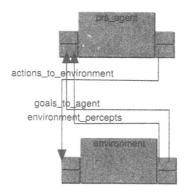

Fig. 2. Top Level: The PRS agent and its environment

6.2 PRS-agent

Figure 3 shows how the PRS agent is composed of its five main components and the information exchange between these components. First the components are briefly described, then a more extensive description is provided.

- In belief_database, beliefs of the agent are maintained. These beliefs are based on perceptions from the environment and assertions made by the agent.
- In maintain_goals, intrinsic goals and subgoals are maintained. It is determined which goals have already been achieved and which goals should trigger new plans.
- In plan_library, plans are triggered by changes in the goals and the beliefs of the agent. If the *context* of a triggered plan is fulfilled by the current beliefs of the agent, it becomes an *optional plan*.
- In intention_structure it is chosen which intention is *active* at each point in time. It also selects which of the optional plans should be executed for an intention.
- In plan_execution, plans are executed.

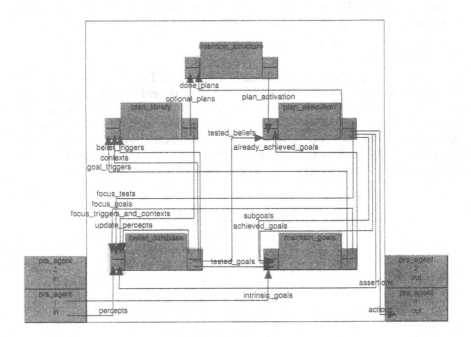

Fig. 3. PRS agent

In PRS, the *system interpreter* runs the entire system: it invokes plans, places them in the intention structure, and selects plans for execution. The other components are merely used for data storage. The components in the DESIRE model described in this section are active components. Every component contains the knowledge that is associated with its role in the agent. Thus, while plan_library invokes plans, intention_structure selects plans and intentions and plan_execution executes plans.

The *information exchange* between the subcomponents of prs_agent will first be described by short description of all its information links. The most important knowledge structures and information links will then be described in more detail.

The link `percepts` transfers percepts from the input signature of the agent to the input signature of `belief_database`. In this component, *current* and *previous* percepts are distinguished. The link `update_percepts` updates the previous percepts: they are made equal to he current percepts. The link `assertions` transfers assertions that are executed by plans; `focus_tests`, `focus_goals` and `focus_triggers_and_contexts` are used to target `belief_database` to derive all (currently) relevant beliefs. Beliefs used for plan invocation are transferred to `plan_library` by the links `belief_triggers` and `contexts`. The link `tested_goals` transfers beliefs that are used to test if a goal has already been achieved. Beliefs used for tests that are executed by plans are transferred by `tested_beliefs`. The link `intrinsic_goals` transfers intrinsic goals from the input interface of the agent to `maintain_goals`. The link `subgoals` transfers subgoals from `plan_execution` to `maintain goals`. Goals that have been achieved by executing plans are removed by the link `achieved_goals`. The `goal_triggers` link transfers goals that will trigger plans in `plan_library`. Plans that are invoked are transferred to `intention_structure` by the link `optional_plans`. The currently active intention and plans that are chosen for execution are transferred by `plan_activation`. Information about the failure or success of plan execution is transferred by `done_plans`. Actions that are chosen by plan execution are transferred to the output interface by the link `actions`.

The component `belief_database` is primitive, meaning that its functionality is not specified by subcomponents but by a knowledge base. In the component, the relation between (current and previous) percepts, assertions and beliefs is defined. In the knowledge base it is stated that current percepts and asserted beliefs become *current* beliefs of the agent. If the truth value of an atom that is used to describe the world changes, a *new* belief is established. An agent believes all conjunctions and disjunctions of its current and new beliefs.

The component `maintain_goals` is a primitive component in which goals are maintained. Goals are added by the links `intrinsic_goals` and `subgoals`, goals are removed by the link `achieved_goals`. It is possible that a subgoal is executed for a world-state that is already satisfied. For example, if the agent has the intention to make a pile of blocks on a table, the first goal that is executed can be to place the lowest block on the table. If the block is already on the table, no plan should be invoked to achieve the subgoal. Therefore, `maintain_goals` first targets the belief database to test if the goal was already achieved by the link `focus_goals`. The result is transferred as a `current_belief` by the link `tested_goals`. Intrinsic goals and subgoals not yet achieved are transferred to the plan library by the link `goal_triggers` (they will trigger plans); achieved goals are transferred to `plan_execution` by the `already_achieved_goals` link, so that `plan_execution` knows that a subgoal of a plan has successfully been executed.

The component `maintain_goals` contains the following knowledge base which reflects the above described behaviour:

```
if      subgoal_of(GOAL:WORLD_ATOM, I:INTENTION)
then    to_test_goal(GOAL:WORLD_ATOM);

if      subgoal_of(GOAL:WORLD_ATOM, I:INTENTION)
and     current_belief(GOAL:WORLD_ATOM)
then    achieved_goal_for(GOAL:WORLD_ATOM, I:INTENTION);

if      subgoal_of(GOAL:WORLD_ATOM, I:INTENTION)
and     current_belief(not_(GOAL:WORLD_ATOM))
```

```
then     new_subgoal_of(GOAL:WORLD_ATOM, I:INTENTION);
```

The plan library is modelled as a primitive component. Based on changes in the beliefs of the agent and goals that it has adopted (the *triggers* of plans), the component determines for which plans it should test the *context* (which has to be a current belief of the agent). If it has been derived in the belief database that the context of such a triggered plan is a current belief of the agent, the triggered plan becomes an *optional plan* and is transferred to the component that represents the intention structure. The new beliefs and the tested contexts come from `belief_database` through the links `belief_triggers` and `contexts`. The new subgoals and intrinsic goals come from `maintain_goals` through the link `goal_triggers`.

The component `intention_structure` is a composed component. Based on the optional plans that have been invoked in the component `plan_library` (transferred via `optional_plans_is`) and the results of the execution of plans that are established in `plan_execution` (transferred via `done_plans_is`), the component selects the optional plans that should be executed. For every purpose (to achieve a goal or to react to a change in beliefs), one plan must be chosen. The component also determines all the current intentions and which intentions have been achieved. Based on this information, the component selects the *active intention*, which is the intention for which plans are currently executed.

The component `plan_execution` is a composed component whose task is to determine which plan-expression should be executed next, based on the currently active intention and the status of the plans that have to be executed, and to execute plan expressions.

7   Comparing Concurrent METATEM and DESIRE

Representation of dynamic behaviour   The use of temporal logic for the internal definition of Concurrent METATEM objects has the advantage that information within an agent is encapsulated with its associated behaviour. In DESIRE, static and dynamic aspects of an agent are encapsulated within a component, but they are specified separately. Consider, for example, the way optional plans are dealt with in the two models of the PRS-agent. In Concurrent METATEM, for any optional plan to achieve a certain goal, *eventually* (at an unspecified future point in time) either the plan is executed or the goal has already been achieved:

$$\bullet\, option(name(N), intention(I), goal(G), \phi_{body}) \Rightarrow$$
$$\Diamond\,(\,achieved(goal(G)) \,\vee\, exec\_plan(name(N), intention(I), goal(G), \phi_{body})\,)$$

Also, if there is more than one optional plan to achieve the same goal, the less preferable plan must not be executed before the more preferable plan has failed execution.

In DESIRE, this behaviour is modelled by using the fact that atoms in a primitive component are by default *persistent*. Once an atom is true, it stays true until its truth value changes by updating an information link (or the truth value of an atom on which its value depends by means of a knowledge base changes). In the component `select_options`, the predicate `optional_plan_for` is true for an option as long as it is not retracted explicitly by the link `reset_options`, which retracts options for which `to_retract_option` is true.

It is stated that an option that is invoked for a certain purpose (e.g. to achieve a certain goal) must be retracted when a plan for the same purpose has successfully been executed, or when the plan itself has failed execution. The dynamic behaviour of the system is specified in *task control knowledge*. For example, it is stated that if an option has failed execution, the link reset_options must be updated to retract the option and the component select_options must determine the new set of postponed options:

```
if evaluation(select_options,failed_option,any_new,succeeded) then
    next_task_control_focus(select_options,determine_postponed) and
    next_extent(select_options,all_p) and
    next_link_state(reset_options,uptodate);
```

In the task control knowledge of a DESIRE component, temporal behaviour of its subcomponents is specified. This is a more coarse grained approach than Concurrent METATEM.

Representation of knowledge In DESIRE, the knowledge structures that are used in the knowledge bases and for the input and output interfaces of components are defined in terms of *signatures*, in which sort hierarchies can be defined. Signatures define sets of ground *atoms*. An assignment of truth values (true, false or unknown) to atoms is called an *information state*. Every primitive component has an internal information state, and all input- and output interfaces have information states. Information states evolve over time. Atoms are persistent in the sense that an atom in a certain information state is assigned to the same truth value as in the previous information state, unless its truth value has changed because of updating an information link. In a knowledge base, the antecedent and consequent of a rule are conjunctions of literals. A knowledge base only defines *refinements* of an information state: the reasoning of a primitive component can only result in a change of the truth value for an atom from unknown to true or false.

Structure of the multi-agent model In a DESIRE specification of a multi-agent system, the agents are (usually) subcomponents of the top-level component that represents the whole (multi-agent) system, together with one or more components that represent the rest of the environment. A component that represents an agent can be a composed component: an agent task hierarchy is mapped into a hierarchy of components. All (sub-)components (and information links) have their own time scale.

In a Concurrent METATEM model, agents are modelled as objects that have no further structure. Every object has its own time-scale and all its tasks are modelled with one set of rules. However, if larger specifications are considered, it may be convenient to decompose the agent itself into a group of communicating objects, each with its temporal specification.

The communication between agents in DESIRE is defined by the information links between them: communication is based on *point-to-point* message passing. All possible communication between agents is specified in advance. Communication between agents in Concurrent METATEM is achieved by *broadcast* message passing. When an object sends a message, it can be received by all other objects. On top of this, both multi-cast and point-to-point message passing can be defined.

Meta-level reasoning In DESIRE, meta-reasoning is modelled by using separate components for the object and the meta-level. For example, one component can reason about the reasoning process and information state of another component. This can be iterated.

For meta-reasoning in Concurrent METATEM, the logic MML has been developed [1]. In MML, the domain over which terms range has been extended to incorporate the *names* of object-level formulae. Execution of temporal formulae can be controlled by executing them by a meta-interpreter, such as that given in the PRS model. However, the extensive use of meta-level capabilities in this way is not always desirable and one of the side-effects of this work has been the development of an extension of Concurrent METATEM targetted specifically at PRS-like architectures [12].

Representing and verifying properties of agents In the Concurrent METATEM model of the PRS agent, high-level temporal properties are expressed, like 'if a goal has been adopted, sometime in the future either it will be achieved or it will be established that the agent can not achieve the goal'. Furthermore, restrictions on when such a commitment is fulfilled are expressed, like 'if no plan whose purpose it is to achieve goal G has successfully been executed since goal G was adopted, goal G has not been achieved' and 'if a certain plan N has not failed execution since it was invoked to achieve goal G, goal G has not failed to be achieved'. In the DESIRE model, such properties are not represented in the specification itself. The behaviour of the model is that as long as the agent tries to achieve a certain goal, the goal is maintained in the component `maintain_goals`. The properties can be defined as properties of the specification and verified by an external proof process (see [7]).

8 Conclusions and Further Work

The general conclusion of this case study is that both Concurrent METATEM and DESIRE can be used to model the PRS. However, it is clear that each approach has different strengths and weaknesses. In particular, Concurrent METATEM is concerned with specifying the detailed behaviour of an agent and consequently, when an agent is as complex as the PRS is, the temporal specification can become unwieldy. (One mechanism of avoiding this is to split the specification of a large agent into a group of smaller ones.) On the other hand, DESIRE is designed with large structures in mind, being based upon experiences from traditional software and knowledge engineering. However, it is consequently less easy to represent the core dynamic behaviour of a small, yet powerful, agent in a concise manner.

Because Concurrent METATEM agents are close to temporal logic theories, verification can be performed in a rather direct manner [11]. Especially if the agents are relatively small this has advantages. For DESIRE a compositional verification method has been developed that structures the verification process according to the component hierarchy, thus taking advantage of the structured form of DESIRE models [7, 15]. If agents have a more complex structure this has advantages. Concurrent METATEM is intented to be directly executable and, indeed, is particularly useful for prototyping multi-agent systems. However, the implementations produced have not yet been rigourously tested and are still under development. This stems from the fact that the specification/execution technology is still in the research domain. DESIRE, on the other hand, has been widely tested and has been used on a number of large multi-agent systems, e.g. [5], reflecting the maturity of the techniques it uses.

Finally, our future work will include comparisons of both these approaches with the refined Concurrent METATEM described in [12], and the agent language defined in [14]. Although the aims of the latter are similar to ours, the logical basis for their language is much more complex than either of the approaches considered here.

References

1. Barringer, H., Fisher, M., Gabbay, D., Hunter, A. Meta-Reasoning in Executable Logic. In Proceedings of Second International Conference on Principles of Knowledge Representation and Reasoning, Morgan Kaufmann Publishers, San Mateo, 1991.
2. Barringer, H., Fisher, M., Gabbay, D., Owens, R., and Reynolds, M. (editors). The Imperative Future — Principles of Executable Temporal Logic. Research Studies Press, UK, 1995.
3. Brazier, F. M. T., Treur, J., Wijngaards, N. J. E. and Willems, M., Formal specification of Hierarchically (De)Composed Tasks, Data and Knowledge Engineering, 1996.
4. Brazier, F. M. T., Treur, J., Wijngaards, N. J. E. and Willems, M., Temporal semantics of complex reasoning tasks In Proceedings of the 10th Banff Knowledge Acquisition for Knowledge-based Systems workshop, KAW'96, Calgary. Extended version to appear in: Data and Knowledge Engineering, 1997
5. Brazier, F. M. T., Dunin-Keplicz, B. M., Jennings, N. R. and Treur, J., DESIRE: Modelling multi-agent systems in a compositional formal framework, In *International Journal of Cooperative Information Systems*, 6(1):67-94, 1997.
6. Burkhard, H. D., Liveness and Fairness Properties in Multi-Agent systems. In *Proceedings 13th International Joint Conference on AI*, Chambery, France, 1993.
7. Cornelissen, F., Jonker, C., Treur, J., Compositional verification of knowledge based systems: a case study in diagnosis. In *Proc. European Knowledge Acquisition Workshop*, Lecture Notes in AI, Springer-Verlag, 1997.
8. Fisher, M., Concurrent METATEM - A Language for Modelling Reactive Systems. In Parallel Architectures and Languages, Europe (PARLE), Munich, Germany, June 1993.
9. Fisher M., A survey of Concurrent METATEM - The language and its applications. In *Proceedings of the First International Conference on Temporal Logic*. Springer Verlag, July 1994.
10. Fisher, M., A Normal Form for Temporal Logic and its Application in Theorem-Proving and Execution. In *Journal of Logic and Computation*, 7(4), 1997.
11. Fisher, M., and Wooldridge, M., On the Formal Specification and Verification of Multi-Agent Systems. In *International Journal of Cooperative Information Systems*, 6(1), 1997.
12. Fisher, M. Implementing BDI Systems by Direct Execution. In *Proceedings 15th International Joint Conference on AI*, 1997.
13. Georgeff, M. P. and Lansky, A. L. Reactive Reasoning and Planning. In *Proceedings of the American Association for Artificial Intelligence (AAAI)*, Morgan Kaufmann, 1987.
14. Hindricks, K., de Boer, F., van der Hoek, W., and Meyer, J-J. Ch. Formal Semantics of an Abstract Agent Programming Language. In this volume.
15. Jonker, C.M. and Treur, J. Compositional Verification of Multi-Agent Systems: a Formal Analysis of Pro-activeness and Reactiveness. In *Proceedings of the International Symposium on Compositionality (COMPOS97)*, Springer Verlag, to appear.
16. Luck, M., d'Inverno, M. A Formal Framework for Agency and Autonomy. In Proceedings First International Conference on Multi-Agent Systems, AAAI Press/The MIT Press, 1995.
17. Mulder, M. Comparing Agent Models in Concurrent METATEM and DESIRE. MSc Thesis, Department of Mathematics & Computer Science, Vrije Universiteit Amsterdam, 1997.
18. O'Hare, G. M. P. Agent Factory: An Environment for the Fabrication of Multi-Agent Systems. In: Foundations of Distributed Artificial Intelligence Wiley Interscience, 1996.
19. A. S. Rao and M. P. Georgeff. Modeling rational agents within a BDI-architecture. In Proceedings of the Second International Conference on Principles of Knowledge Representation and Reasoning. Morgan Kaufmann Publishers, San Mateo, 1991.

Semantics for an Agent Communication Language

Yannis Labrou, and Tim Finin

Computer Science and Electrical Engineering Department
University of Maryland Baltimore County
Baltimore MD 21250 USA
{jklabrou,finin}@cs.umbc.edu

Abstract. We address the issue of semantics for an *agent communication language*. In particular, the semantics of Knowledge Query Manipulation Language (KQML) is investigated. KQML is a language and protocol to support communication between software agents. We present a semantic description for KQML that associates states of the agent with the use of the language's primitives (performatives). We have used this approach to describe the semantics for the whole set of *reserved* KQML performatives. Our research offers a method for a speech act theory-based semantic description of a language of communication acts.

1 Introduction

This research is concerned with communication between software agents. We see software agents as a paradigm that suggests a new way to view existing technologies as tools to build software applications that dynamically interact and communicate with their immediate environment (user, local resources and computer system) and/or the world, in an autonomous (or semi-autonomous), task-oriented fashion.

A crucial component of this paradigm is the communication language, which is the medium through which the attitudes regarding the content of an exchange between software agents are communicated; the communication language suggests whether the content of the communication is an assertion, a request, some form of query *etc*. Knowledge Query and Manipulation Language (KQML) is an agent communication language that consists of primitives (called *performatives*) which allow agents to communicate such attitudes to other agents and find other agents suitable to process their requests. Our research provides semantics for KQML along with a framework for the semantic description of KQML-like languages for agent communication. We do so, avoiding commitments to agent models and inter-agent interaction protocols.

2 KQML and the Problem of Its Semantics

This is an example of a KQML message:

```
(ask-if :sender   A   :receiver   B   :language   prolog
        :ontology foo :reply-with id1 :content   ''bar(a,b)'' )
```

In KQML terminology, *ask-if* is a *performative*. The value of the :content is an expression in some language (in this case in Prolog) or another KQML message and represents the content of the communication (illocutionary) act. The other parameters (*keywords*) introduce values that provide a context for the interpretation of the :content and hold information to facilitate the processing of the message.

There is no such thing as an *implementation* of KQML, *per se*, meaning that KQML is not an *interpreted* or *compiled* language that is offered in some hardware platform or an abstract machine. Agents *speak* KQML in the sense that they use those primitives, this *library of communication acts*, with their reserved *meaning*. The application programmer is expected to provide code that processes each one of the performatives for the agent's language or knowledge representation framework.

KQML semantics have not been formally defined. Our goal is to provide a semantic description for the language, in a way that captures all the intuitions about the language, expressed in its existing documentation [1] without making commitments to specific agent models and coordination protocols in order to ensure the widest possible applicability of the language. There is good reason to supplement KQML with formal semantics. The lack of semantics for KQML has often been a source of criticism for KQML. Also, although various agent systems implementations that use KQML have appeared (such as the one described in the chapter entitled *"Facilitating Open Communication in Agent Systems: the Infosleuth Infrastructure"*, in this volume), there seems to be neither an agreement regarding the exact meaning of the used performatives nor a framework for defining the meaning of new performatives; these are problems that our semantic approach addresses. Moreover, agents can use the semantic definitions of performatives in order to make inferences resulting from the use of the KQML communication primitives.

The semantic approach we propose uses expressions, that suggest the minimum set of preconditions and postconditions that govern the use of a performative, along with conditions that suggest the final state for the successful performance of the speech act (performative); these expressions describe the relevant to the exchange agents' states and use propositional attitudes like *belief, knowledge, desire, etc.* (this *intentional description* of an agent is only intended as a way of viewing the agent).

3   A Framework for the Semantics of Performatives

3.1   What Constitutes the Semantic Description

The following constitutes the semantic description for each of the performatives: **(1)** A natural language description of the performative's intuitive meaning; **(2)** An expression that describes the content of the communication act and serves as a formalization of the natural language description; **(3)** Preconditions that indicate what can be assumed to be (in part) the state of an agent when it sends a performative (**Pre(A)**) and what should be the state of the receiver in order to accept it and successfully process it (**Pre(B)**); **(4)** Postconditions that describe what can be assumed to be the (relevant to this message exchange) states of both interlocutors after the *successful* utterance of a performative (by the sender) and after the receipt and processing (but before a counter utterance) of a message (by the receiver). The postconditions (**Post(A)** and **Post(B)**, respectively) hold unless a *sorry* or an *error* is sent as a *response* in order to suggest the unsuccessful processing of the message; **(5)** A completion condition for the performative (**Completion**) that indicates the final state, after possibly a conversation has taken place and the intention suggested by the performative that started the conversation, has been fulfilled; and **(6)** Any comments that we might find suitable to enhance the understanding of the performative.

3.2 Describing Agents' States

We use expressions in a meta-language to formally define (cognitive) states for agents and use them to describe the performative, the preconditions, postconditions and completion conditions associated with the use of a particular performative. In these expressions we use operators that stand for propositional attitudes and have a reserved meaning: **(1)** BEL, as in BEL(A,P), which has the meaning that P is (or can be proven) true for A; P is an expression in the native language of agent A; **(2)** KNOW, as in KNOW(A,S), expresses knowledge for S, where S is a state description (the same holds for the following two operators); **(3)** WANT, as in WANT(A,S), to mean that agent A desires the cognitive state (or action) described by S, to occur in the future; and **(4)** INT, as in INT(A,S), to mean that A has every intention of doing S and thus is committed to a course of action towards achieving S in the future. We also introduce two instances of actions: **(1)** PROC(A,M) refers to the action of A processing the KQML message M, meaning that the *received* and valid KQML message M is handled by the piece of code designated with processing the performative for the application (PROC(A,M) guarantees neither the proper processing of the message nor the conformance of the code with the semantic description); and **(2)** SENDMSG(A,B,M) refers to the action of A sending the KQML message **M** to B.

The argument of BEL is an expression P in the agent's implementation language. BEL(A,P) if and only if P is true for agent A; we do not assume any axioms for BEL. Roughly, KNOW, WANT and INT stand for the psychological states of knowledge, desire and intention, respectively. All three take an agent's state description (either a cognitive state or an action) as their arguments. An agent can KNOW an expression that refers to the agent's own state or some other agent's state description if it has been communicated to it. So, KNOW(A,BEL(A,"foo(a,b))) is a valid agent's state, as is KNOW(A,BEL(B,"foo(a,b)")), if BEL(B,"foo(a,b)") has been communicated to A with some message, but KNOW(A,"foo(a,b)") is not valid because "foo(A,B)" stands for an expression in the agent's knowledge store and not for a state description. Researchers have grappled for years with the problem of formally capturing the notions of *desire* and *intention* (the chapter entitled *"Intentional Agents and Goal Formation"*, in this volume, is just one such example). Various formalizations exist but none is considered a definitive one. We do not adopt a particular one neither we offer a formalization of our own. It is our belief that any of the existing formalizations would accommodate the modest use of WANT and INT in our framework.

3.3 A Language and Notation for Agents' States

For a KQML message **performative(A,B,X)**, **A** is the :sender, **B** is the :receiver and **X** is the :content of the performative (KQML message). We will use capital-case letters from the beginning of the alphabet (*e.g.*, *A*, *B*, *etc.*) for agents' names and letters towards the end of the alphabet (*e.g.*, *X,Y,Z*) for propositional contents of performatives. We also use *S* to refer to an agent's state and **M** for an instance of a KQML message.

All expressions in our language denote agents' states. Agents' states are either actions that have occurred (PROC and SENDMSG) or agents' mental states (BEL, KNOW, WANT or INT). We allow conjunctions (∧) and disjunctions (∨) of expressions that stand for agents' states (the resulting expressions represent agents' states, also), but we do not allow ∧ and ∨ in the scope of KNOW, WANT and INT. Propositions in the agent's native language can only appear in the scope of BEL and BEL can only take such a proposition as its argument. BEL, KNOW, WANT, INT and actions can be used as arguments for KNOW (actions should then be interpreted as actions that have already happened). WANT and INT can only use KNOW or an action as arguments. When actions are arguments of WANT or INT, they are actions to take place in the future.

A negation of a mental state is taken to mean that the mental state does not hold in the sense that it should not be inferred (we will use the symbol not). When ¬ qualifies BEL, *e.g.*, ¬ (BEL(A,X)), it is taken to mean that the :content expression *X* is not true for agent *A*, *i.e.*, it is not provable in *A*'s knowledge base. Obviously, what "not provable" means is going to depend on the details of the particular agent system, for which we want to make no assumptions.

4 Semantics for three KQML Performatives

We present the semantics for three KQML performatives (*ask-if*, *tell* and *sorry*) in order to illustrate our approach. [1]

- **ask-if(A,B,X)**
  1. A wants to know what B believes regarding the truth status of the content *X*.
  2. WANT(A,KNOW(A,S))
     where *S* may be any of BEL(B,X), or ¬(BEL(B,X)).
  3. **Pre(A)**: WANT(A,KNOW(A,S)) ∧ KNOW(A,INT(B,PROC(B,M)))
     where *M* is **ask-if(A,B,X)**
     Pre(B): INT(B,PROC(B,M))
  4. **Post(A)**: INT(A,KNOW(A,S))
     Post(B): KNOW(B,WANT(A,KNOW(A,S)))
  5. **Completion**: KNOW(A,S'))
     where *S'* is either BEL(B,X) or ¬(BEL(B,X)), but not necessarily the same instantiation of *S* that appears in *Post*(*A*), for example.
  6. Not believing something is not necessarily the same with believing its negation (assuming that the language of *B* provides logical negation), although this may be the case for certain systems. The **Pre(A)** and **Pre(B)** suggest that a proper advertisement is needed to establish them.

---

[1] A more detailed account can be found in [4] and the semantics for the complete set in [3].

– **tell(A,B,X)**
   1. A states to B that A believes the content to be true.
   2. BEL(A,X)
   3. **Pre(A)**: BEL(A,X) $\wedge$ KNOW(A,WANT(B,KNOW(B,S)))
      Pre(B): INT(B,KNOW(B,S))
      where S may be any of BEL(B,X), or $\neg$(BEL(B,X)).
   4. **Post(A)**: KNOW(A,KNOW(B,BEL(A,X)))
      Post(B): KNOW(B,BEL(A,X))
   5. **Completion**: KNOW(B,BEL(A,X))
   6. The completion condition holds, unless a *sorry* or *error* suggests B's inability to acknowledge the *tell* properly, as is the case with any other performative.
– **sorry(A,B,Id)**
   1. A states to B that although it processed the message, it has no response to provide to the KQML message M identified by the :reply-with value **Id** (some message identifier).
   2. PROC(A,M)
   3. **Pre(A)**: PROC(A,M)
      Pre(B): SENDMSG(B,A,M)
   4. **Post(A)**: KNOW(A,KNOW(B,PROC(A,M))) $\wedge$ not($Post_M(A)$),
      where $Post_M(A)$ is the **Post(A)** for message M.
      Post(B): KNOW(B,PROC(A,M)) $\wedge$ not($Post_M(B)$)
   5. **Completion**: KNOW(B,PROC(A,M))
   6. The postconditions for M, as a result of message M do not hold. The not should be taken to mean that the mental state it qualifies should not be inferred to be true as a *result* of this particular message. This does not mean that for example $Post_M(B)$ does not hold if it has already been established by a previous message; it is up to B to decide (perhaps after using additional information) if and how it wants to alter its internal state with respect to the *sorry*.

5 Discussion

The communication language has been an integral part of numerous multi-agent systems. But more often than not, the communication language is customized to the application environment and its assumptions. Whether it is the underlying agent theory, or the esoteric interaction protocols the agents follow, or the subtleties of the domain, such communication languages have primitives whose meaning is confined within the boundaries of the particular multi-agent system. The issue of semantics for the communication acts of such languages has received a fair share of attention in current research (such as [2], [7], [6], or [5]). We perceive two problems with such approaches when used to describe the semantics of a *common ACL*: (1) they are tied to a specific agent theory that might not be applicable to all agents that want to use the ACL (as a matter fact, the aforementioned references suggest differing agent theories), and (2) they introduce complex formalisms that have no bearing to the implementation of agent systems.

As a way to address these concerns, we do not provide formal semantics (in a *possible-worlds* formalism or some similar framework) for the modal operators, in our approach, but we restrict the scope and use of these operators, so that they can be subsumed by similar modalities whose semantics could be provided by an intentional theory of agency. By attempting a semantics for communication acts without a theory of agency, *i.e.*, formal semantics for the propositional attitudes (operators), we certainly give up interesting inferencing. For example, if an agent sends **tell(A,B,X)** and later **tell(A,B,X → Y)**, B will not be able to infer that BEL(A,Y) (since we do not even assume a universal *weak S4* model for BEL) based on the KQML semantics alone. But, if B has additional information about A, which can be easily supplied as part of the KQML exchange (*e.g.*, in the :ontology value of a KQML message), such information may be inferred. Similar observations can be made about the other modalities. In the end, we trade a formal semantics for the propositional attitudes, which inevitably define a *model of agency* that is unlikely to be universal for all agents, for a simpler formalism and agent theory independence.

6 Conclusions

KQML is a language for agent communication whose semantics have not been specified thus far. First attempts have been made but no complete semantic description for the full set of KQML performatives has appeared yet in the literature. We have devised a semantic framework for the semantic description of KQML-like languages, *i.e.*, languages of attitude-expressing communication primitives, for the communication between software agents. Our semantic framework separates the communication language from the agent model and the coordination protocol. We have used our approach to provide semantics for the full set of KQML primitives and we have presented the framework and the semantic description for three performatives.

References

1. ARPA Knowledge Sharing Initiative. Specification of the KQML agent-communication language. ARPA Knowledge Sharing Initiative, External Interfaces Working Group, July 1993.
2. Philip R. Cohen and H.J. Levesque. Communicative actions for artificial agents. In *Proceedings of the 1st International Conference on Multi-Agent Systems (ICMAS'95)*. AAAI Press, June 1995.
3. Yannis Labrou. *Semantics for an Agent Communication Language*. PhD thesis, University of Maryland, Baltimore County, August 1996.
4. Yannis Labrou and Timothy Finin. Semantics and conversations for an agent communication language. In *Proceedings of the Fifteenth International Joint Conference on Artificial Intelligence (IJCAI-97)*, Nagoya, Japan, August 1997.
5. M.D. Sadek. A study in the logic of intention. In *Proceedings of the 3rd Conference on Principles of Knowledge Representation and Reasoning (KR'92)*, pages 462–473, Cambridge, MA, 1992.
6. M.P. Singh. A logic of intentions and beliefs. *Journal of Philosophical Logic*, 22:513–544, 1993.
7. Ira A. Smith and Philip R. Cohen. Toward a semantics for an agent communications language based on speech-acts. In *Proceedings of the 13th National Conference on Artificial Intelligence*. AAAI/MIT Press, August 1996.

Formal Semantics for an Abstract Agent Programming Language *

Koen V. Hindriks, Frank S. de Boer,
Wiebe van der Hoek, John-Jules Ch. Meyer

Universiteit Utrecht, Department of Computer Science
P.O. Box 80.089, 3508 TB Utrecht, The Netherlands
{koenh,frankb,wiebe,jj}@cs.ruu.nl

Abstract. In this article we investigate agent-oriented programming both from a theoretical and a practical view. We propose an abstract agent programming language with a clear and formally defined semantics. The semantics of our language is defined in terms of a transition system. Our language combines features of both logic programming, i.e. it is rule-based, and imperative programming, i.e. it includes the full range of conventional programming constructs. These features are well-understood and provide a solid basis for a structured agent programming language. On the more practical side we investigate the different properties of agents usually attributed to them, i.e. agents have a complex mental state, act pro-actively and reactively, and have reflective capabilites. We illustrate how these properties of agents are implemented in our programming language. In particalur, we propose general rules, called practical reasoning rules, which are used to define the reflective capabilities of agents and provide a mechanism for goal revision. The combination of the theoretical and practical perspective contributes, we hope, to filling the gap between theory and practice.

keywords: formal semantics, agent programming, self-modification, practical reasoning, reflective capabilites

1 Introduction

Research on intelligent agents ranges from theoretical, logical investigations to more practical, implemented applications. The issues that are being solved on each side of the spectrum, in general, are very different. On the logical side, much research goes into deriving formal properties of logical systems, like completeness or decidability ([16,18,20]). On the other side, architectures, issues like scheduling, and other design and implementation issues are investigated ([11]).

Quite a number of researchers have made proposals for agent programming languages or agent design frameworks, e.g. [4,13–15,17]. Some of these languages, however, lack a clear and formally defined semantics, and therefore it is difficult to formalize the design, specification and verification of programs. Other types of languages are based directly on logic ([7,8,6,21]).

* This research is partially supported by the Human Capital and Mobility Network EXPRESS

In contrast to these existing approaches, our approach is based on the combination of existing programming concepts from various known paradigms in order to model agent-oriented features. The clear advantage of this approach is that these concepts are well-understood, both from a theoretical and practical perspective.

More precisely, the programming language we propose is based on a combination of features of logic programming and imperative programming, which allows for an elegant description of many agent-oriented features. In particular, concepts from imperative programming are used to describe the *execution* of the goals of an agent. Whereas the *reflective* capabilities of an agent, on the other hand, are described by a rule-based reasoning which is driven by the pattern-matching from logic programming. The operational semantics of the agent programming language is defined in terms of a transition system. This is a simple and lucid formalism for specifying the meaning of programs.

2 Programming BDI-agents

In the DAI community the concept of BDI-agents is nowadays a well-known notion. A lot of theory and practical investigation has gone into making this notion both better understood and applicable to real-world problems. The design and programming of BDI-agents, however, is still somewhat disconnected from theory. One of our aims is to construct a more unifying language which covers a relatively large part of the current research into programming agents. We thereby hope to clarify also part of the essence of AOP. The programming language we propose captures the main features of both AGENT-0 ([15]) and AgentSpeak(L) ([14]). Although, at first sight, these languages seem very different in nature, they incorporate a few basic principles which are unified in the language we propose. The basic differences reside in the particular *control structure* chosen in each of these languages from which we abstract.

An important question which must be answered first is which features a general agent programming language should include. Most researchers seem to agree on the following characteristics of BDI-agents:

- agents have a complex internal mental state which is made up of beliefs, desires, plans, and intentions, and which may change over time;
- agents act pro-actively, i.e. goal-directed, and reactively, i.e. respond to changes in their environment in a timely manner;
- agents have reflective or meta-level reasoning capabilities.

From this list we derive that intelligent agents are *goal-directed, belief-transforming* entities, i.e. agents have a set of goals which guide their behaviour and keep up with the world by maintaining a belief base with information about the (current) situation they find themselves in. To realise their goals, agents need to find the means for their ends, i.e. agents try to realise their goals by *means-end reasoning* or *practical reasoning* (cf. [2]). Plans are recipes for achieving the goals of the agent, and therefore play a crucial role in this reasoning. A reflective agent also needs to have the ability to *monitor* its success or failure, and the reasoning mechanisms for responding to failure.

A minimal requirement for an agent programming language, therefore, is that it has features for dealing with these different notions. At the least, this means such a language must have features for:

- *belief updating*, for dealing with newly observed data, communication, and the derivation of new facts,
- *goal updating*, for goal revision in the light of (new) information and requests of other agents, and
- *practical reasoning*, for finding the means to achieve a goal.

A more practical concern is related to the choice of programming constructs. In our language we include all the familiar constructs from imperative programming like sequential composition, tests, parallel execution, etc.

3 An Abstract Agent Programming Language

We now define an agent language corresponding to the three components outlined above: belief updating, goal updating, and practical reasoning. First, we define a first-order language in which to express the beliefs of agents. Next we define a goal language: goals are taken to be programs. The agent's practical reasoning capabilities are defined by practical reasoning rules. Thus, our language is a rule-based language.

3.1 Beliefs

The beliefs of an agent are simply first-order formulae from a language $\mathcal{L}$. The basic elements of the language are given by a *signature* Σ, which is a quadruple $\langle P, F, C, A \rangle$ where P is a set of *predicate symbols*, F is a set of *function symbols*, C is a set of *constants*, and A is a set of *action symbols*. *Terms* and *first-order formulae* of a language $\mathcal{L}$ are defined as usual from a signature Σ and an infinite set of variables TVar. (The action symbols are not used in this definition.) The set of *atoms* is denoted by At.

Example 1. (robot Greedy)
The running example in this paper concerns a robot called Greedy. Imagine robot Greedy wandering around in a two-dimensional grid world. In this fictitious world, diamonds pop up and disappear at random. The only obstacles in the world are rocks. Robot Greedy cannot move rocks and has to go around them. The basic predicates which describe this world are: `diam(X,Y)` for 'there is a diamond at coordinates X,Y'; `greedy(X,Y)` for 'robot Greedy is at coordinates X,Y'; `rock(X,Y)` for 'there is a rock at coordinates X,Y'.

For this example, we assume that Greedy has perfect knowledge of its environment, i.e. it knows at any moment its own position, and the location of the rocks and diamonds.

3.2 Goals and Actions

The goals of an agent set objectives the agent tries to achieve. We distinguish two kinds of goals: goals to do some action and goals to achieve some state of affairs. We also allow different kinds of composition of these types of goals.

Definition 2. *(basic actions, goal language)*
Let $\Sigma = \langle P, F, C, A \rangle$ be a signature, and Gvar an infinite set of goal variables ranging over goals.

- The set of *goals* $\mathcal{L}^g$ is inductively defined by:

  [Syn-5] $A \subseteq \mathcal{L}^g$, called *basic actions*,

  [Syn-6] $At \subseteq \mathcal{L}^g$,

  [Syn-7] If $\varphi \in \mathcal{L}$, then $\varphi? \in \mathcal{L}^g$,

  [Syn-8] $Gvar \subseteq \mathcal{L}^g$,

  [Syn-9] If $\pi_1, \pi_2 \in \mathcal{L}^g$, then $\pi_1; \pi_2, \pi_1 + \pi_2, \pi_1 \| \pi_2 \in \mathcal{L}^g$.

Basic actions $a \in A$, achievement goals $P(t) \in At$, and test goals $\varphi?$ are the basic goals in our language. Basic actions in our language are *update actions* or *update operators* on the belief base of an agent. For example, an action pickup deletes from the belief base of Greedy the belief that there is a diamond at the current position of Greedy. Achievement goals $P(t)$ are goals to achieve a state where $P(t)$ holds. Test goals $\varphi?$ are checks performed on the belief base to see if a proposition φ holds.

It is also possible to build more complex compositions of basic goals, by using the program constructs for sequential composition, nondeterministic choice, and parallel composition. This allows us to specify disjunctive goals $\pi_1 + \pi_2$ by means of nondeterministic choice, i.e. do either π_1 or π_2, and conjunctive goals $\pi_1 \| \pi_2$ by means of parallel composition, i.e. do both π_1 and π_2.

Furthermore, the language includes variables which range over goals. These variables serve several purposes. First of all, they can be used for reflective reasoning. This will become clear in the next paragraph, where these variables are also allowed in the head of practical reasoning rules. Secondly, they might be used in communication. For example, an agent might receive in a goal variable a request to establish some goal.

Example 3. The robot Greedy is capable of performing the following basic actions: west for moving west, east for moving east, north for moving north, south for moving south, and pickup for 'robot Greedy picks up a diamond'.

The *goal* of robot Greedy is to collect diamonds. This goal is denoted by the predicate collect_diam, which is a user-defined predicate and is in fact given below as a (usual) procedure definition.

Remark 4. A note on terminology:

We speak about goals, and use this term rather than the term 'intention', since we think that a goal in the goal base of an agent does reflect a choice an agent has made, but does not specify the level of commitment made to that goal. Intentions are sometimes defined in the literature as choice + commitment ([1]). Since the commitment made to a goal remains implicit in the practical reasoning rules, we use the more neutral term 'goal' for the proattitudes of agents. The practical reasoning rules determine how easily an agent will revise its goals, and thereby the level of commitment made to a goal.

3.3 Practical Reasoning Rules

To achieve its goals an agent has to find the means for achieving them, and sometimes may have to revise its goals. This kind of reasoning is called *practical reasoning*. To perform this type of reasoning an agent uses a set of practical reasoning rules:

Definition 5. *(rule language)*
The set of *practical reasoning rules* $\mathcal{L}^p$ is defined by:

[Syn-10] If $\varphi \in \mathcal{L}$, $\pi, \pi' \in \mathcal{L}^g$, then $\pi \leftarrow \varphi | \pi' \in \mathcal{L}^p$.

A practical reasoning rule consists of the following components:

Definition 6. *(head, body, guard, global and local variables)*
Let $\pi \leftarrow \varphi | \pi'$ be a practical reasoning rule. Then:

- π is called the *head* of the rule,
- π' is called the *body* of the rule,
- φ is called the *guard* of the rule,
- the free variables in the head of a rule are called the *global variables* of the rule,
- all variables in a rule which are not global are called *local variables*.

The guard of a rule serves two functions. First, the guard can be used to specify the context in which the rule might be applied. For example, Greedy might want to pick up a diamond in case there is a diamond at its feet. Secondly, the guard can be used to retrieve data from the set of beliefs. This is done by unifying some of the parameters in the guard and head with beliefs in the belief base (see below). For example, the current position of Greedy needs to be retrieved for deciding which way to go.

The distinction between global and local variables is made to separate the specific local data-processing in the body which uses a local set of variables from the global variables which are also used in other parts of the program (i.e. goal) and which can be used to 'communicate with the rest of the goal' (return values, etc.).

A practical reasoning rule also serves two functions.

First, a rule can specify the *means* to achieve a particular goal. In this case the head of the rule is a basic goal $P(t)$ and the body of the rule is a *plan* or *recipe* for achieving the goal. So, achievement goals $P(t)$ may be viewed as procedure calls to plans specifying the means to achieve the goal. A plan is a program which may contain parallel actions and nondeterministic choice. These type of rules are also called *plan rules*. A plan rule encodes the *procedural knowledge* of an agent. Thus, an agent has a plan library it consults to find the means to execute (high-level) actions. The agents performs a kind of dynamic planning during execution. This is quite different from more static planning systems like STRIPS ([5]).

Example 7. Greedy wants to collect the diamonds in his world. A plan rule which specifies how to achieve this goal is the following:

```
collect_diam <- greedy(X0,Y0) /\ nearest_diam(X0,Y0,X,Y) |
greedy(X,Y);diam(X,Y)?;pickup;collect_diam
```

This rule specifies a plan to achieve `collect_diam`. The plan is to go to the nearest place where a diamond can be found, pick up that diamond, and then recursively start collecting diamonds again. The guard retrieves the current position of Greedy, and the position of (one of) the nearest diamond(s).

A plan for getting Greedy at a specific position is the following:

```
greedy(X,Y) <- greedy(X0,Y0) | (X=X0 /\ Y=Y0)? +
[(X<X0)?;west+(X0<X)?;east+(Y<Y0)?;south+(Y0<Y)?;north];
greedy(X,Y)
```

The plan (i.e. body) states that to get at position (X,Y) one should repeat making a move in the right direction until that position is reached (X=X0,Y=Y0). The rule also illustrates how to program while or repeat-until loops.

This rule illustrates the two uses of predicates in our language. The predicate greedy(X,Y) in the head denotes a possible (sub)*goal* of the agent, while the predicate greedy(X0,Y0) in the guard denotes a test on the belief base. By using a predicate both in the head (as a goal) and in the guard (as a belief) in a practical reasoning rule an interface between the belief and goal bases is established. Thus, predicates in goals are not just procedurally defined, but can be related to their logical interpretation as beliefs via practical reasoning rules.

The second purpose practical reasoning rules can be used for is the *revision of goals*. In this case practical reasoning rules encode the *reflective capabilities* of an agent, and arbitrary programs (including goal variables) may be used as the head of a rule. Basically, there are two types of situations in which a rational agent might wish to revise one of his goals, namely, in case a more optimal strategy can be followed, or in case of failure. We show an instance of each of these cases of goal revision, also illustrating the use of goal variables.

Example 8. Assume that Greedy has a goal to go west to collect a diamond, but suddenly a new diamond pops up nearer to his current position. In this unpredictable fictitious world where diamonds may pop up and disappear at random a more optimal strategy for Greedy probably is to revise its current goal and go after the new diamond. The following rule makes this type of goal-revision possible:

```
G;greedy(X,Y) <-
greedy(X0,Y0)/\nearest_diam(X0,Y0,X1,Y1)/\not(X=X1/\Y=Y1) |
greedy(X1,Y1)
```

The rule applies when robot Greedy has a goal of doing some (possibly empty) list of actions G, for example going west, and after that get at position (X,Y), but at the same time there also is a diamond nearer to robot Greedy's current position than the target-position (X,Y). In that case the rule makes it possible to revise the old goal by replacing it with a new goal of going to the nearest diamond.

In another situation, where Greedy still has the goal of going west, Greedy might encounter the following problem. Assume this time that a rock is in the way and Greedy cannot move west. So, if Greedy tries to move west, it fails. Since Greedy is assumed to have perfect knowledge Greedy immediately detects the failure and knows that it is still at its old position. To avoid such failure Greedy might use the following rule:

```
west;greedy(X,Y) <- greedy(X0,Y0)/\rock(X0-1,Y0) |
[(Y0<=Y)?;north + (Y0>=Y)?;south];greedy(X,Y)
```

This rule detects the failure and makes it possible to revise the goal and employ a strategy to go around the rock. (Not a very adequate one.)

Summarizing, our approach distinguishes three levels of agent programming. At the most basic level, basic actions act upon the belief bases of agents. At the second level, goals are executed. Note that goals *are* somewhat generalized programs, i.e. goals are programs built from the regular programming constructs *and* goal variables. The goal base of an agent in fact represents the program an agent is executing at the moment. Agents, however, also have reflective capabilities for revising their goals. Therefore, agents are not just programs (goals), but are *self-modifying* programs. This concept of self-modification is built into the practical reasoning rules, the third level of our agent programming language. By means of practical reasoning the agent can transform a program to another program (as in the examples above), not just by execution or procedure calls, but by more general revision rules (i.e. the practical reasoning rules with general head). This is a distinguishing feature of agents.

Substitutions and variables We need a number of technical definitions in order to proceed. The *scope of a quantifier*, a *bound occurrence* of a variable x in an expression e, i.e. a term, formula, or program, and a *free variable* are defined in the usual way. The set of free variables in an expression e is denoted by $\mathrm{Free}(e)$. The notions of *variable substitution*, *unifier*, *most general unifier*, and *variant* are defined as usual (cf. [9]).

4 Agent Programs

Agents are goal-directed, belief-transforming entities, which are capable of means-end reasoning and have reflective capabilities. We assume that beliefs are updated by basic actions, and goals are updated by execution and revision. This cleanly seperates the two different types of updating. The practical reasoning component is encoded in practical reasoning rules.

In this picture, the only components of an agent that change are its beliefs and goals (thus, we assume the set of practical reasoning rules and basic actions are fixed). Beliefs and goals make up the mental state of an agent. Therefore, we define:

Definition 9. *(mental state)*
A *mental state* is a pair $\langle \Pi, \sigma \rangle$, where

- $\Pi \subseteq \mathcal{L}^g$ is a *goal base*, i.e. a set of goals, and
- $\sigma \subseteq \mathcal{L}$ is a *belief base*, i.e. a set of beliefs.

We use Π to denote a goal base, and σ (possibly indexed) to denote a belief base. The set of belief bases is denoted by $\mathcal{B}$. We use Γ to denote a PR-base, i.e. a set of practical reasoning rules.

The dynamics or behaviour of an agent, therefore, is fully specified if the semantics of basic actions is given and the mechanisms for executing goals and applying rules are defined. We assume that a transition function for basic actions is given. Basic actions define the basic skills of agents. The treatment of the mechanisms for executing goals is postponed to the next section.

Since basic actions only change belief bases, and have no effect on the goal base or PR-base, the effect of basic actions is fully specified by giving their effect on belief bases.

Definition 10. *(basic action transitions)*

The semantics of basic actions A is given by a transition function $\mathcal{T}$ of type : $\mathcal{B} \times \mathcal{B} \rightarrow \wp(\text{A})$. Let $a \in \text{A}$. We use the following notational convention, and write: $\langle \sigma, \sigma' \rangle a$ for $a \in \mathcal{T}(\sigma, \sigma')$.

Example 11. Robot Greedy is capable of performing five basic actions. The operational semantics of these actions is given by:

- $\langle \{\ldots, \text{greedy}(X,Y), \text{not}(\text{rock}(X-1,Y),\ldots\},$
  $\{\ldots, \text{greedy}(X-1,Y), \text{not}(\text{rock}(X-1,Y),\ldots\}\rangle \text{west};$
  similar definitions apply to actions east, north, and south.
- $\langle \{\ldots, \text{diam}(X,Y), \text{greedy}(X,Y),\ldots\},$
  $\{\ldots, \text{greedy}(X,Y), \text{not}(\text{diam}(X,Y),,\ldots\}\rangle \text{pickup},$

The intended reading of these definitions is that, for example, action west can be performed if Greedy believes it is at coordinates (X,Y), and afterwards its beliefs have changed such that Greedy believes he is at coordinates (X-1,Y) after performing the action west.

Note that in the case there is a rock blocking the way to the west but Greedy doesn't *believe* there is a rock to the west, although the west action will fail in the real world Greedy will still *believe* he has made a move to the west. Only by observing the environment Greedy will notice that his action of moving west has failed. Similar remarks apply to the other actions. (The issue of failure is not discussed any further in this paper, however, since we assumed perfect knowledge this type of failure cannot occur.)

Now, to program an agent is to specify its initial mental state, the semantics of the basic actions the agent can perform, and to write a set of practical reasoning rules. This is formally stated in the next definition.

Definition 12. *(agent program)*

An *agent program* is a quadruple $\langle \mathcal{T}, \Pi_0, \sigma_0, \Gamma \rangle$ where

- $\mathcal{T}$ is a basic action transition function, specifying the effect of basic actions,
- Π_0 is the initial goal base,
- σ_0 is the initial belief base, and
- Γ is a PR-base.

Example 13. The agent program for Greedy is the following:

- $\mathcal{T}$ is defined for the basic actions in example 11,
- the initial goal base is given by: $\{\text{collect\_diam}\}$,
- the initial belief base is given by:
  $\{\text{greedy}(0,0), \text{rock}(1,5), \text{rock}(3,3), \text{rock}(2,1), \text{diam}(2,2)\}$.
- the PR-base contains the PR-rules as defined in examples 7 and 8. We add two other rules, to illustrate two other features:
  - If at the target-position, Greedy should pick up a diamond. However, since diamonds may disappear at random, the diamond may not be there anymore. Greedy tests before picking up a diamond if there is one; in case there is none,

however, Greedy will fail the test, and the goal becomes infeasible. A rule for dropping such a goal is an example of the first feature which is that we allow an *empty body* in rules:

```
diam(X,Y)?;pickup <- not(diam(X,Y))|
```

- In case Greedy happens to be at a position of a diamond, Greedy should pick it up, regardless of what other goals Greedy has at that moment. This can be achieved by the following rule, an example of the second feature which is that we also allow *empty heads* in rules:

```
<- greedy(X,Y) /\ diam(X,Y) |pickup.
```

We call this type of rules *data-directed*.

Data-directed rules create new goals on the basis of beliefs only. These rules are a distinguishing feature of agents, although they do resemble interrupts. Data-directed rules could be used to make agents reactive to their environment (like interrupts), however, the level of reactiveness accomplished also highly depends on the underlying control structure of the language.

5 Operational Semantics

We define the operational semantics of our language in this section. First, we explain what a transition system is. Next we give the transition rules which define the semantics.

5.1 Transition System

Transition systems can be used to define the operational semantics of programming languages ([12]). For example, specifying the operational semantics of an imperative programming language means specifying how a program can transform the state of a system. This is done by specifying how an assignment changes the state, and by giving rules for all the other programming constructs.

Formally, a transition system is a deductive system which allows to *derive* the transitions of a program. A transition system consists of a set of *transition rules* that specify the meaning of each programming construct in the language. Transition rules transform *configurations*. In imperative programming a configuration is a pair $\langle \pi, \sigma \rangle$ with π a program and σ a variable assignment. In our framework a configuration is the same as a mental state, i.e. a pair $\langle \Pi, \sigma \rangle$ of goals and beliefs. Thus, a transition rule maps a configuration to another configuration by executing a goal or matching the head of a practical reasoning rule with a goal. For example, there is a rule which fixes the meaning of sequential composition, a rule for parallel composition, etc. A single transition models the execution of a simple instruction (assignment in the case of imperative programming, basic actions and tests in our case).

5.2 Practical Reasoning Rule

In the rest of this paragraph and the next, let σ, σ' be belief bases, θ a variable substitution, and V a set of variables. In the examples, we have already seen a number of practical reasoning rules. In the following definition the application of these rules is formally defined.

Definition 14. *(PR-rule application)*
Let θ be a most general unifier for π and π', and γ a substitution.

$$\frac{\pi' \leftarrow \varphi|\pi'' \in' \Gamma \text{ and } \sigma \models \forall(\varphi\theta\gamma)}{\langle \pi, \sigma \rangle_V \longrightarrow_{\theta\gamma} \langle \pi''\theta\gamma, \sigma \rangle} \qquad \text{where}$$

- $\pi' \leftarrow \varphi|\pi'' \in' \Gamma$ means that $\pi' \leftarrow \varphi|\pi''$ is a variant of a PR-rule in Γ with fresh variables not occurring in V, and
- γ is a substitution such that for no variable x: $\gamma(x) \in V$

Pattern-matching of logic programming is used to unify the head of a practical reasoning rule with a goal in the goal base. First, the substitution θ unifies the head of the practical reasoning rule with a goal in the goal base to get the parameter values which are part of the agent's current goal to instantiate (some of) the global variables. Next, γ retrieves parameter values from the current belief base. This explains the order of application of the substitutions θ and γ. A variant of the plan is used to avoid interference between local and global variables. In the set V the global variables of the goal base are recorded. Local variables are chosen such that no interference occurs. The additional information (the substitution $\theta\gamma$) attached to the transition-relation ($\longrightarrow$) is used below in the execution rules.

Example 15. Suppose that the goal base is $\{\texttt{west};\texttt{greedy(3,4)}\}$ and the belief base is the initial belief base from example 13. In this case, the revision rule of example 8 is applicable, since Greedy's current goal is not leading to any diamond at all.

The most general unifier $\theta = \{G/\texttt{west}, X/3, Y/4\}$. Using this substitution the guard becomes:
`greedy(X0,Y0)/\nearest_diam(X0,Y0,X1,Y1)/\not(3=X1/\4=Y1).`
Matching with the belief base yields a substitution $\gamma=\{\texttt{X0/0,Y0/0,X1/2,Y1/2}\}$. Now we can substitute the original goal with the new goal, using substitution $\theta\gamma$, which evaluates to: `greedy(2,2)`.

It is important that the local variables in the body of a rule are changed to new variables not yet occurring in the goal base (recorded in the set V) to avoid undesired communication between subgoals. For example, in a goal
`greedy(X,Y);greedy(X0,Y0)?;greedy(X0+1,Y0)`
the global variables $X0$ and $Y0$ are the same as the local variables of the practical reasoning rule for `greedy(X,Y)` for getting at a specific position (cf. example 8). Without renaming the local variables the application of the practical reasoning rule leads to undesired parameter passing. This explains the conditions in the definition.

5.3 Execution Rules

In this paragraph we define the meaning of the basic actions and conventional programming constructs. We use E to denote termination, and identify $E;\pi$ with π and $E\|\pi$ with π. Specifying the meaning of a basic action a is simple, since we have assumed that a transition function $\mathcal{T}$ is given for these actions. Executing a basic action means changing the state according to the transition function and after that stop execution. The identity substitution $\emptyset$ is attached to the transition for basic actions.

Definition 16. *(execution rule 1; basic actions)*

$$\frac{\langle \sigma, \sigma' \rangle a}{\langle a, \sigma \rangle_V \longrightarrow_{\emptyset} \langle E, \sigma' \rangle}$$

Tests are actions to check if some condition follows from the belief base. Free variables in tests may be used to retrieve data from the belief base. The values retrieved are recorded in a substitution θ; this substitution is a parameter of the transition, which can be applied in other transitions again.

Definition 17. *(execution rule 2; first-order tests)*

$$\frac{\sigma \models \forall(\varphi\theta)}{\langle \varphi?, \sigma \rangle_V \longrightarrow_{\theta} \langle E, \sigma \rangle}$$

For example, the test
```
(greedy(X0,Y0)/\nearest_diam(X0,Y0,X,Y))?
```
executed in the initial state of example 13 yields the substitution:
$\theta = \{X0/0, Y0/0, X/2, Y/2\}$.

These values can be passed to the rest of the goal. For example, by executing a sequential goal
```
(greedy(X0,Y0)/\nearest_diam(X0,Y0,X,Y))?;greedy(X,Y)
```
the test is first executed, and then the values are passed onto the subgoal `greedy(X,Y)` by application of the substitutions to the remaining goal. More formally, this is stated in the next rule for sequential composition:

Definition 18. *(execution rule 3; sequential composition)*

$$\frac{\langle \pi_1, \sigma \rangle_V \longrightarrow_{\theta} \langle \pi_1', \sigma' \rangle}{\langle \pi_1; \pi_2, \sigma \rangle_V \longrightarrow_{\theta} \langle \pi_1'; \pi_2\theta, \sigma' \rangle}$$

Applying the rule to the example yields a new mental state with goal component `greedy(2,2)`.

To execute a nondeterministic choice goal, just pick one of the subgoals that is enabled, i.e. can be executed, and execute this goal.

Definition 19. *(execution rule 4; non-determinimistic choice)*

$$\frac{\langle \pi_1, \sigma \rangle_V \longrightarrow_{\theta} \langle \pi_1', \sigma' \rangle}{\langle \pi_1 + \pi_2, \sigma \rangle_V \longrightarrow_{\theta} \langle \pi_1', \sigma' \rangle}$$

(A similar rule can be given for right choice.)

For example,
```
(2<0)?;west+(0<2)?;east+(2<0)?;south+(0<2)?;north
```
can be executed by executing `(0<2)?;east` or `(0<2)?;north`.

Parallel execution is modelled by interleaving. The parallel subgoals may communicate with each other through shared variables: If one of the subgoals retrieves data from the belief base, the substitution so obtained is also applied to the other parallel subgoal. (Note that θ does not have to be applied to π_1'.)

Definition 20. *(execution rule 5; parallel composition)*

$$\frac{\langle \pi_1, \sigma \rangle_V \longrightarrow_\theta \langle \pi_1', \sigma' \rangle}{\langle \pi_1 \| \pi_2, \sigma \rangle_V \longrightarrow_\theta \langle \pi_1' \| \pi_2 \theta, \sigma' \rangle}$$

(A similar rule can be given for the right branch.)

For example, Greedy might use the following plan for moving:

```
greedy(X0,Y0)?;nearest_diam(X0,Y0,X,Y)?;
([[(X0<X)?;west + (X0>X)?;east]||
[(Y0<Y)?;north + (Y0>Y)?;south]).
```

The left parallel subgoal handles horizontal movement (west, east), the right parallel subgoal handles vertical movement.

Finally, we need one more rule for executing a goal from the goal base in a mental state. We call a mental state the *top level* of execution. At this level, the various goals of the agent are executed in a parallel fashion without communication. This means the top-level goals are independently executing from each other and do not communicate through shared variables (i.e. the substitution obtained is not applied to the other goals).

Definition 21. *(execution rule 6; goal execution)*
Let $\Pi = \{\pi_0, \ldots, \pi_{i-1}, \pi_i, \pi_{i+1}, \ldots\} \subseteq \mathcal{L}^g$, and $V = \mathsf{Free}(\Pi)$. Then:

$$\frac{\langle \pi_i, \sigma \rangle_V \longrightarrow_\theta \langle \pi_i', \sigma' \rangle}{\langle \{\pi_0, \ldots, \pi_{i-1}, \pi_i, \pi_{i+1}, \ldots\}, \sigma \rangle \longrightarrow \langle \{\pi_0, \ldots \pi_{i-1}, \pi_i', \pi_{i+1}, \ldots\}, \sigma' \rangle}$$

Execution rule 6 defines the operational semantics of an agent's mental state. Recall that an agent program was defined as a tuple consisting of the definition of the skills of the agent (basic actions), a PR-base, and its initial belief and goal base. The latter two components determine the initial mental state of the agent which is updated during execution. The former two components define global and fixed properties of the agent.

We have to take one precaution at this level, i.e. we have to make sure the free, global variables at this level do not interact with the local variables of rule-bodies introduced by practical reasoning. To ensure this all the free variables are put in a set V for later reference; the only place this set is used is in the practical reasoning rule, defined in the previous paragraph, which may introduce new local variables.

Note that we distinguish two types of transitions corresponding to goal revision (application of PR-rules) and goal execution (execution rules). The interactions between these transitions are nicely integrated in one system.

Computations and compositionality The transition system defines in a natural way the possible computations of a program. A *computation* of an agent program is a finite or infinite sequence of configurations $\langle \Pi_0, \sigma_0 \rangle, \langle \Pi_1, \sigma_1 \rangle, \langle \Pi_2, \sigma_2 \rangle, \ldots$, i.e. a sequence of mental states, such that for all i we have $\langle \Pi_i, \sigma_i \rangle \longrightarrow \langle \Pi_{i+1}, \sigma_{i+1} \rangle$.

Given the above definition of a computation we can define various notions of *observables*. For example, we might want to observe the sequence of belief bases extracted from a computation, or the sequence of basic action symbols corresponding to single transitions in a computation, for example for planning (cf. [7]). A compositional characterization of these notions does not fall in the scope of this paper, however, it is an important issue for future research. In general a compositional description of the semantics of a programming language allows us to understand a complex program in terms of its (simpler) constituents and thus provides a basis for a better control over the design process.

6 Comparison and Conclusions

We briefly discuss two languages closest to our own, AGENT-0 and AgentSpeak(L), and then comment on some other languages as well.

The basic features of AGENT-0 are commitment-rules and a number of update mechanisms. The programs AGENT-0 agents can execute are restricted to the basic, primitive actions or skills of the agent. In our language the agent can handle much more general programs. Also, the commitment (goal, in our terminology) revision mechanism of AGENT-0 is restricted to removing infeasible commitments and uses a built-in mechanism for this update. In our language, we allow much more general revision rules which are provided by the programmer in the form of practical reasoning rules. AGENT-0 includes primitives for communcation, which our language does not yet provide. However, communication primitives are already extensively investigated in concurrency theory and therefore it should not be to difficult to incorporate communication in our framework in the near future ([19]). The update mechanisms of AGENT-0 are all rule-based and we believe that for all these features we can provide rules in our language which perform the same function.

AgentSpeak(L) is a rule-based language which is quite similar to the language proposed in this paper. Similar remarks as for AGENT-0 apply here. We provide more general and high-level programming constructs, and features for goal revision which AgentSpeak(L) lacks. AgentSpeak(L) incorporates a notion of events which we do not have in our language. It is not quite clear, however, whether or not this is a crucial notion in the language AgentSpeak(L). Actually, we can formally prove that we can simulate every program defined in AgentSpeak(L) in our language (which is discussed more formally in the extended version of this paper).

Although at first sight AGENT-0 and AgentSpeak(L) may seem quite different, we think the main difference resides in the control structure of these languages. This difference is reflected in the different order in which rules in these two languages are applied (cf. the discussion of the interpreters of the languages in resp. [15] and [14]).

Basically, the language dMARS ([3]) adds features for dealing with failure to the language AgentSpeak(L). These features are different from the revision mechanism by practical reasoning rules in our language, which is not incorporated in dMARS. In future research we aim to investigate the use of a revision mechanism for dealing with failures. As to the specifcation method employed in [3] we believe that it should be possible to found a specification in a language like Z on a formal semantics such as the one presented in the present paper. In [10] a comparison between two agent modelling languages, Concurrent METATEM and DESIRE is made. The comparison is not formal, as the comparison of AgentSpeak(L) and our language hinted at above. It is aimed at a comparison from design perspective. In future research we hope to compare these frameworks to ours both from a more formal perspective and practical perspective.

Finally, we make a remark about ConGolog. In [7] a transition system is incorporated into the formalism of the situation calculus. Although the definitions are similar to our execution rules, there remain important differences between ConGolog and our language. First of all, (Con)Golog is a logic-programming language. This differs from our framework since we propose a genuine combination of features of logic programming and imperative programming. ConGolog extracts from a given high-level program a deterministic sequence of primitive actions. This provides for a kind of planning as defined in [7]. This focus also differs from ours since we are more concerned with the execution of programs (goals and plans) and the revision of these goals and plans. In our view we provide a more dynamic perspective contrasting the rather static planning of ConGolog.

In our paper we showed that a transition system is a suitable formalism for specifying the operational semantics of agent programming languages. Transition systems are well-understood and very lucid. A programming language combining features of logic programming and imperative programming was defined. This language includes all the regular programming constructs from imperative programming and the pattern-matching mechanism of logic programming. A number of distinguishing features of agents were identified. In particular, the general heads of practical reasoning rules for goal revision are a unique property of intelligent agents.

In future research we want to investigate extensions of our framework to multiagent systems with communication. We want to exploit the notions of standard concurrency theory (CCS, π-calculus,etc.) as far as possible in modelling agent-oriented features. It remains to be investigated how to incorporate and finetune these notions for agent programming languages. We also want to study more closely the general practical reasoning rule we introduced in our paper, and would like to investigate the role of control structure in the decision mechanisms of agents. On the more theoretical side, we already mentioned as future research the important issue of compositionality of the semantics, and corresponding proof theories and refinement calculi, in order to obtain a method for the design of agents.

References

1. P.R. Cohen and H.J. Levesque. Intention is choice with commitment. *Artificial Intelligence*, 42:213–261, 1990.
2. Frank Dignum and Rosaria Conte. Intentional Agents and Goal Formation. *In this volume.*
3. Mark d'Inverno, David Kinny, Michael Luck, and Michael Wooldridge. A Formal Specification of dMARS. *In this volume.*
4. B. Dunin-Keplicz and J. Treur. Compositional Formal Specification of Multi-Agent Systems. In M.J. Wooldridge and N.R. Jennings, editors, *Intelligent Agents*, pages 102–117. Springer-Verlag, 1995.
5. R.E. Fikes and N.J. Nilson. STRIPS: A new approach to the application of theorem proving to problem solving. *Artificial Intelligence*, 2(3-4):189–208, 1971.
6. M. Fisher. A Survey of Concurrent MetateM - The Language and its Applications. In *Temporal Logic*, pages 480–505. Springer, 1994.

7. G. De Giacomo, Y. Lespérance, and H.J. Levesque. Reasoning about concurrent execution, prioritized interrupts, and exogenous actions in the situation calculus. accepted for IJCAI-97.

8. Y. Lespérance, H.J. Levesque, F. Lin, and D. Marcu. Foundations of a Logical Approach to Agent Programming. In M.J. Wooldridge, J.P. Müller, and M. Tambe, editors, *Intelligent Agents II*, pages 331–346. Springer, 1996.

9. J.W. Lloyd. *Foundations of Logic Programming*. Springer, 1987.

10. Marco Mulder, Jan Treur, and Michael Fisher. Agent Modelling in *MetateM* and DESIRE. *In this volume*.

11. J.P. Müller. *The Design of Intelligent Agents*. Springer, 1996.

12. G. Plotkin. A structural approach to operational semantics. Technical report, Aarhus University, Computer Science Department, 1981.

13. A. Poggi. DAISY: An object-oriented system for distributed artificial intelligence. In M.J. Wooldridge and N.R. Jennings, editors, *Intelligent Agents*, pages 341–354. Springer, 1995.

14. Anand S. Rao. AgentSpeak(L): BDI Agents Speak Out in a Logical Computable Language. In W. van der Velde and J.W. Perram, editors, *Agents Breaking Away*, pages 42–55. Springer, 1996.

15. Yoav Shoham. Agent-oriented programming. *Artificial Intelligence*, 60:51–92, 1993.

16. M.P. Singh. *Multiagent systems*, volume 799 of *LNAI*. Springer, 1994.

17. Sarah Rebecca Thomas. *PLACA, An Agent Oriented Programming Language*. PhD thesis, Department of Computer Science, Stanford University, 1993.

18. W. van der Hoek, B. van Linder, and J.-J. Ch. Meyer. A logic of capabilities. In A. Nerode and Y.V. Matiyasevich, editors, *Proc. of the third int. symposium on the logical foundations of computer science*, pages 366–378. Springer, 1994.

19. R.M. van Eijk, F.S. de Boer, W. van der Hoek, and J.-J. Ch. Meyer. Concurrent programming languages for multi-agent systems. Technical report, Department of Computer Science, University Utrecht, 1997.

20. B. van Linder, W. van der Hoek, and J.-J.Ch. Meyer. Formalising motivational attitudes of agents: On preferences, goals, and commitments. In M.J. Wooldridge, J.P. Müller, and M. Tambe, editors, *Intelligent agents II*, pages 17–32. Springer, 1996.

21. M.J. Wooldridge. A Knowledge-Theoretic Semantics for Concurrent MetateM. In J.P. Müller, M.J. Wooldridge, and N.R. Jennings, editors, *Intelligent Agents III*, pages 357–374. Springer, 1997.

Intentional Agents and Goal Formation

Frank Dignum*   Rosaria Conte[†]

* Faculty of Mathematics & Computer Science, Eindhoven University of Technology
P.O. Box 513, 5600 MB Eindhoven, The Netherlands
dignum@win.tue.nl

[†] Division of AI, Cognitive and Interaction Modelling
PSS (Project on Social Simulation)
IP/Cnr, V.LE Marx 15 - 00137 Roma, Italy
rosaria@pscs2.irmkant.rm.cnr.it

Abstract. This paper is about a fundamental aspect of intentional action, namely the process of goal formation. Existing formal theories of agents are found essentially inadequate to account for the formation of new goals and intentions of the agent; on the other hand, the formation of new goals is often viewed as an essential feature of autonomous agents. Autonomous goal-formation is described thanks to the interplay between existing (built-in) goals and new beliefs. A general rule for goal formation is then formally expressed in terms of a language (FORM) developed for treating properties of autonomous agents. More specific applications of this rule to the social domain are examined, in particular to conformity and help.

1 Introduction

In [16] an answer to the question what actually constitutes an "agent" is given. Although the authors do not provide a comprehensive definition they do provide some characteristics of an agent. The first characteristic is that of autonomy. An agent should operate without the direct intervention of humans and have control over its actions and internal state.

Generally, this feature is integrated into existing agent models. Actually many programs are called agents simply because they exhibit some autonomy. However, Wooldridge and Jennings also mention another characteristic for agents that we find to be crucial. One should be able to ascribe intentional attitudes (like desires, goals, intentions, wants, etc.) to agents. And ,more important, these intentional attitudes should be instrumental to explaining the behaviour of the agent.

In fact the use of intentional attitudes to explain the behaviour of an agent tells us something about the complexity of the agent. If a program or machine is very simple its behaviour can be very well explained without ascribing intentional attitudes to it. However, when a program or machine is very complicated we need to use a higher level of abstraction (like intentional attitudes) to explain its behaviour.

In this paper we will only consider these so-called *intentional agents*.

---

[0] The research is partially supported by ESPRIT BRA 8319 ModelAge.

Of course, if the behaviour of a program is explained by ascribing intentional attitudes to it, the program should also comply to the intuitive characteristics of these intentional attitudes. Otherwise the metaphor would have no use. Therefore much research is done about the characteristics and connections of the intentional attitudes.

A weak point about formal theories of intentions and intended actions is their failure to account for the formation of intentions. This remark may look arbitrary to those readers who are familiar with formal agent theories, e.g. BDI architectures [14] in which intentions are defined as a subset of beliefs and desires (see also [5]).
However, BDI architectures and, more generally, agent theories take for granted the agents choice. Within the logic-based framework, by and large, intentions are a subset of motivations which are chosen for action. Even though Cohen and Levesque [5] and Kinny and Georgeff [12] extensively discuss the abandonment of intentions and goals they do not indicate what the agent should do when a goal is dropped. How does it get a new goal or intention? Do they have a large stack of goals from which they pop a new goal every time?

Of course in many implemented systems some type of goal formation takes place. However, it is usually extremely simple through some rule that relates a perceived external condition with a new goal like in [11] or through a received request (or command) like in [8]. In other frameworks it is something that is done by the user at the start of the system. The agent only decides which goal is active at a certain moment based on the circumstances (see e.g. [10]). We do not intend to disqualify this research, but rather advocate an extension of present research to include the matter of goal formation explicitly in the theories.

This paper does not aim to provide a complete theory of intention formation, but rather clarify some (theoretical) premises for such an ambitious task. The main claim of this paper is that a general notion of goal is a fundamental requirement for a formal theory of intentional action.

A goal will be here defined as a state of the world represented in an agent's mind, which the agent wants to become true; however, a goal should not be intended as chosen by the agent for action ([6]). An agent may have a goal without being oriented to action, neither positive nor negative.
The goal will feed a mental process of goal-dynamics [4], including goal-revision and abandonment, enabling the system to respond to the requirements of the external world by generating goals and checking the conditions and convenience for their achievement. Goals only possibly lead to intentions, and thereby to actions; at the same time, they are necessary for intentions to arise.

The rest of the paper is organized as follows. In section 2 we will describe some related work and indicate the pros and cons of each theory. We will also indicate the open issues with regard to this work. In section 3 we will give an informal description of our theory on goal formation. In section 4 the formal basis for this theory will be sketched. We finish the paper with some conclusions in section 5.

2 Related work

The following two sub-sections discuss some formal attempts to fill the gap between intentional concepts and modalities, and the motivational ones: the BDI architecture worked out by Georgeff and his collaborators and Cohen and Levesque's theory of rational interaction.

2.1 The BDI architecture

The BDI architecture (cf. [14, 15, 9]) describes agents in terms of three primitive modalities: beliefs (B), desires, (D), and intentions (I). The temporal dimension is treated thanks to branching structures. However, the modalities for beliefs, desires, and intentions are defined as usual in terms of possible words semantics. Therefore, possible worlds are defined as belief-, desire-, and intention-accessible worlds, and are represented as time branches, or potential courses of events, which successive actions will prune.

Pros

Among the advantages of this representation, one deserves special mention: the branching structure allows the well-known phenomenon of overcommitment to be avoided. Within uni-linear models of intentional action, goals are closed under consequence; in other words, any believed consequence of one's goals is wanted also. With a branching structure, what is believed to be a consequence on one given path, but is not believed to occur in other paths, is not necessarily intended. In such a way, one can essentially represent different possible scenarios. But what is interesting is that only a subset of such parallel scenarios is represented as following from the agent's intentions. In fact, there is an implication order in the three modalities: the intention-accessible worlds represent a sub-set of both the desire-accessible worlds, and of the belief-accessible worlds.

Cons

Some considerations can be drawn from this model.

1. Somewhat counter-intuitively, intention is here defined as a primitive modality, which is not semantically decomposed into more general notions.
2. Pro-attitudes can be categorised as a subset of desires, that is, endogenous motivations. Apparently, the model rules out the possibility that intentions arise from other inputs (requests, commands, norms, etc.).
3. A selection among desires is presupposed rather than accounted for, despite the complex tests such a selection requires (concerning how likely a given desire is to be realized).
4. It is far from clear whether the model allows for reasoning about instrumental action to be expressed; how to express the notion of a sub-goal which is not yet a subsequence of an intended action ? This is a tricky issue. In fact, before an intention is formed, instrumental reasoning is usually applied even only to test whether a given desire is achievable. Therefore, either the notion of desire is stretched to cover that of goal and sub-goal, or the notion of intention is extended to embrace sub-goals, including those which will be dropped later; which is the case in the model in question?

5. It is not clear how the model in question can express the generation of new goals as means for realizing existing desires: since intention-accessible worlds are a sub-set of desire-accessible worlds, the formation of intentions looks as a mere pruning of existing desires; how is it possible in such a context to account for the generation of new intentions as means for achieving one's desires? Suppose I want to impress my boy-friend showing off on Saturday night in a new silk dress. For this reason, I decide to ingratiate myself with my mother, taking her to a Malaysian restaurant, in order to be able to borrow, later, her beautiful silk dress. In what sense can we say that the intention which I finally execute is a subset of my desire?

To sum up, at least four problems are left open by the model in question:

1. how are realistic desires selected?
2. how are realistic desires selected for action?
3. how are sub-goals generated out of existing desires?
4. how are sub-goals generated out of obligations and other external inputs?

2.2   Goals as chosen desires

One of the most influential theories of intentions, at least in the area of Multi- Agent Systems was developed by Cohen and Levesque (from now on, C&L) ([5]), on the track of Bratman's analysis ([1, 2]).

This theory is aimed at modelling the "rational" properties of action. Intelligent, autonomous, rational agents are designed so as to be capable of producing and dropping intentions under given conditions. But which conditions are relevant for intentions formation and discharge? The authors developed an incremental view of intentions such that, at any step in a goal-driven process leading to intentions, agents are bound to decide, on the grounds of some relevant criterion, whether to keep to or abandon their goals. The language appears as a first-order language with operators for mental attitudes and action. They introduced two modalities for beliefs and goals,

(BEL x p) and (GOAL x p)

defined according to the possible worlds semantics, and therefore through accessibility relations. They implemented two modalities for action

(HAPPENS e) and (DONE a)

expressing, respectively, events taking place in the world independent of the agents' actions and occurrence of actions. Finally, time is represented as an infinite sequence of events.

In such a model, a goal is defined as a belief-compatible desire. (In other words, agents cannot have goals which they believe to be unachievable.) Many notions can be constructed on the grounds of these primitive modalities plus the operators $\Box$ for "always" and $\Diamond$ for "eventually". Among others, the notion of achievement goal,

(A-GOAL x p) $\equiv$ (BEL x ¬p) $\wedge$ (GOAL x (LATER p))

where

(LATER p) ≡ ¬p ∧ ◇p

that is, x has an achievement goal p if x believes that p is not true now but wants x to become eventually true.

Indeed, in this model, an achievement goal is not yet an intention. The process of transforming a goal into an intention has been partially modelled. For example, Cohen and Levesque's theory of persistent goals is an account of a relevant aspect of this process; persistent goals are those that the agents believe to be neither realised nor unachievable:

(P-GOAL x p) ≡ A-GOAL(x p) ∧
        [BEFORE((BEL x p) ∨ (BEL x ¬◇p))
           ¬(GOAL x (LATER p))]

in words, x has a persistent goal p if before giving up trying to achieve it, x believes that p is true or will never be true.

However, even though goals are defined by the authors as both chosen desires and primitives, the process of their choice has not been addressed so far by them.

Finally, Cohen and Levesque have proposed the notion of relativised goal where a goal can be dropped when the "circumstances" relative to which the goal has been formed have changed:

(P-R-GOAL x p q) ≡ A-GOAL(x p) ∧
        [BEFORE((BEL x ¬q) ∨ (BEL x p) ∨ (BEL x ¬◇p))
           ¬(GOAL x (LATER p))]

x has a goal p relativised to q, when x has an achievement goal p, and before ceasing to have p as an achievement goal, x believes either that p is realised or unachievable or that the reason q (for the goal p) does not hold. Essentially, this means that x has p as long as and because he believes that q. Finally, Cohen & Levesque indicate how intentions can be defined as special types of goals, taking action expressions as arguments. We will not describe this step here, because it is not relevant for this paper and it contains many intricate details.

Pros

The above model

1. is somewhat more explicit and richer than what is allowed by the preceding ones;
2. allows for an incremental view of intentions, seen as a special case of goals;
3. sheds some light on the issue of the formation of intentions

Cons

But there are some questions still unsolved:

1. how are desires chosen? Which are the mechanisms responsible for this choice?
2. Should goals be necessarily seen as a subset of desires? In other words, can a goal arise from a non-motivational input? We will get back to this issue in the next section.
3. Some aspects of goal-processing are overlooked, for example, the temporary interruption of goals.
4. Finally, no mechanism of goal-generation is provided: relativised goals can be seen as the outputs, the results of goal-generation, but do not indicate its building blocks.

3   The formation of goals

As can be seen from the previous section, much work has been done about goal achievement. However, not much has been said about goal formation. In this section we describe the rationale behind this process and indicate some rules that could be used for this process.

3.1   Rationale of goal formation

To describe the process of goal formation we will divide the goal formation rules into three categories.

The first category of rules only works on concrete goals. They are used to construct plans that the agent will try to execute. All agents will be endowed with these type of rules. However, they do not really change the behaviour of the agent. Furthermore, if a goal is found unachievable the agent will keep working only if it has some alternatives to reach its overall goal. However, if the overall goal is no longer achievable the agent will come to a halt.

Usually, the goals will therefore be dropped temporarily in circumstances when the agent believes they are not achievable. Somehow they should be re-activated later on, because otherwise the agent would soon run out of goals to pursue and would come to a halt.

Also the overall goals should be some type of maintenance goals. Otherwise the agent would stop as soon as the goal was reached. Usually there are some external events that change the state such that the goal is no longer achieved and the agent has to start pursuing it again. One can think of the search robots on the WWW that have to maintain all information about all Web sites. They have to start again everytime updates are made to the Web to be of real utility. (Of course, to be practical they only operate at certain intervals).

We do not consider agents that are allowed only this kind of goal formation very interesting. They are not flexible and cannot change their behaviour over time under changing circumstances. Actually the goal of the agent is nothing more then the expected result of executing the main program of the agent (one or more times).

The second category of rules is that of "production rules". These production rules can be endogeneous like the ones used for planning. However, we talk about production rules in the case new concrete goals are generated from the overall built-in goals that are abstract. That is, the built-in goal is pursued through the achievement of one or more concrete goals. Often the built-in goal is not really achievable but can be approximated through the concrete goals. E.g. the goal of assembling all information about living creatures on the world. This goal is translated into a number of concrete goals like an extensive search on the WWW, in libraries, etc.

Usually the built-in goals are not made explicit and the goal formation takes place when the agent is implemented. Sometimes, goals can also be added (by the user). In this case the production rules are used to make the agent reactive to its environment. E.g. a user might tell the agent what it wants and this desire is translated into a goal of the agent. Reactive databases can be seen as having this kind of goals. They trigger certain updates on the occurrence of some event. The result of the updates can be seen as the goal generated by the event.

Most agents have these kind of rules and this type of simple goal formation. Usually, however, it is hidden within the implementation and not reflected in the agent architectures or theories.

The last category of rules is that of "instrumental" reasoning. These rules are what we consider to be the only "real" goal formation rules. They form new goals on the basis of a (built-in) goal and some instrumental beliefs. The instrumental beliefs indicate that (and how) a certain condition contributes to achieving the original goal, which can be seen as the reason for the new goal. E.g. the built-in goal can be to obey the law, or avoid the punishment. The instrumental belief is that driving slower than the speed limit is instrumental for obeying the law. Together with the rule the new goal of driving slower than the speed limit is derived.

The connection between the two goals can be of different kinds as we will show in the next subsection. However, the new goal always contributes in some way to achieve the old goal.

From the example above it can be seen that the goals that are derived in this way do not necessarily have to be desires by themselves (I might prefer to drive very fast), which sets them apart from the goals discussed elsewhere.

Using this instrumental reasoning one can start from very abstract, unachievable built-in goals to form goals that might be achievable and at least contribute to the achievement of the built-in goals. E.g. the built-in goal is to be a good person. In order to be a good person one should obey the law. Therefore one should not speed (above the existing limits). Therefore I should not push the gaspedal too much.

Agents that contain instrumental goal formation rules are the most flexible ones. They can start with very abstract goals which will surely remain stable throughout their existence. The concrete goals that they will pursue follow from the instrumental beliefs they have. These beliefs can be changed due to the circumstances or through learning (in any way).

Before we give a formalization for the goal formation process described above we want to make a final remark about the use of the above rules. In the complete process of goal formation all rules above will be used. First the instrumental ones, then the production rules and finally the planning rules. However, besides these rules more is needed to form the final set of goals to be pursued at a certain moment. From one built-in goal many concrete goals may be generated of which many will be alternatives of each other and even may be inconsistent together. Therefore we say that the goals, that are generated with the goal formation rules, are *candidate* goals. Some selection process will choose the actual goals that are pursued by the agent. This selection is based on some type of preference ordering which might be induced by the capabilities of the agent, the costs to reach a goal, an ordering of the built-in goals and the strength of the instrumental beliefs. We will not go into this selection process in this paper but note its importance for further (practical) research.

3.2 The formal rules

We will now describe the goal formation rules in a logic roughly based on [7].
The agents that we consider will be held to have beliefs that conform to the KD45 axiomatisation. We denote the fact that agent x believes q by $BEL_x(q)$.

As in [7], goals are expressed in a conditional form. There are several reasons for this choice. The most important is that the goals that are generated usually depend on the original goal. When the original goal is dropped, the derived goals are also dropped. This looks like the relative goals as defined in [5]. However, there is one major difference. The goals do not disappear but just become unapplicable while the condition upon which they depend is false.

This feature makes it possible to drop goals temporarily and resume the achievement later on. This is not possible with the relative goals described in [5].

We say that an agent x has a candidate goal p in situation q, denoted by $C - GOAL_x(p|q)$, if p is true in all states that the agent x considers desirable when it believes q is true and p is not true in the current state.

An agent x has a goal p in situation q, denoted by $GOAL_x(p|q)$, if p is a candidate goal and x intends to achieve p.

The idea is that an agent can have many candidate goals out of which one or more goals are selected that the agent actually wants to achieve. E.g. to reach work the agent can go by bus or by car. So, from the goal to reach work he might generate two candidate goals: reach the bus and reach the car. Now the agent uses some selection mechanism to determine which of the two candidate goals will become the actual goal.

We say that p is instrumental for q, denoted by $INSTR(p, q)$, if achieving p contributes to achieving q.

This notion of instrumentality can be seen as a generalization of the idea of subgoals. Somehow agent x does not have a plan for q (and cannot directly construct one), but achieving p is a step towards achieving q.

With the above notions we can now define the general goal generation rule:

$$GOAL_x(q|r) \wedge BEL_x(INSTR(p,q)) \supset C - GOAL_x(p|GOAL_x(q|r) \wedge r)$$

I.e. if agent x has a goal q as long as r is true and it believes that p is instrumental in achieving q then agent x has a candidate goal p as long as it has the goal q and r is true. Of course we can also generate a new candidate goal from an existing one:

$$C - GOAL_x(q|r) \wedge BEL_x(INSTR(p,q)) \supset C - GOAL_x(p|C - GOAL_x(q|r) \wedge r)$$

The above rules are completely endogeneous goal formation rules if the beliefs about the instrumentality are given beforehand and do not change. In that case all goals are generated from the built-in goals. The instrumentality rules can then be seen as plan formation rules. An advantage is that the rules are explicit and can be questioned.

However, the goal generation rules can also be used to react to the environment. To effect this, the agent should have some beliefs about the benefits of reacting to other agents. I.e. it should have a theory about how the generation of a goal in response to an event contributes to some overall goal of itself.

We will start with two types of conformity behaviour.

3.3 Goal generation through conformity

The first type of conformity is called *behavioural conformity*. In this case the action of another agent is seen as example for one's own behaviour. This means that whenever an action of agent Y is perceived agent X generates the goal to perform this action as well. To achieve this goal generation we need the following formulas to be true for the agent:

$$GOAL_x(be\_like(x, y)|true)$$
$$BEL_x[DONE(y, \alpha) \supset INSTR(DONE(x, \alpha), be\_like(x, y))]$$

Now, with the goal generation rule, we can derive

$$C - GOAL_x(DONE(x, \alpha)|GOAL_x(be\_like(x, y)))$$

whenever $BEL_x(DONE(y, \alpha))$

Of course we could also describe the action conformity by ascribing the following conditional goal to the agent:

$$GOAL_x(DONE(x, \alpha)|DONE(y, \alpha))$$

This is also correct but not very flexible. This goal only disappears when y does not perform any action anymore or some explicit goal retraction action takes away the goal.
In the first definition of action conformity the reason of the conformity is given by the (built-in) goal "to be like y". In this case we made it unconditional, but it could be defined depending on circumstances, like this goal being beneficial for x. The action conformity would then stop whenever it is no longer beneficial for x.
The action conformity will also stop if the agent no longer believes that the conformity is instrumental to the goal of being like y. I.e. we have made the belief of agent x in action conformity and its purpose explicit.

The second type of conformity is called *goal conformity*. This is a more autonomous type of conformity, where actions are not copied but the reason of the actions (the goal) is adopted. The way goals are generated for goal conformity can be described (like above), with the following two formulas:

$$GOAL_x(be\_like(x, y)|true)$$
$$BEL_x[GOAL_y(p|r) \wedge r \supset INSTR(p, be\_like(x, y))]$$

And again with the general goal generation rule we can derive:

$$C - GOAL_x(p|GOAL_x(be\_like(x, y)))$$

whenever $BEL_x(GOAL_y(p|r) \wedge r)$.

From the above we see that an agent x might keep its goal to be like y, but changes its belief about how to achieve this. In goal conformity the agent believes that adopting the goal of the other agent contributes to being like the other agent.

3.4 Generation of goals through adoption

Goals can also be generated through a process of adoption of norms or goals.
The idea of goal adoption is similar to that of goal conformation. However, the goal is that the other agent obtains its goal. We can write the formulas needed for this type of goal generation as follows:

$$GOAL_x(help(x, y)|true)$$
$$BEL_x[GOAL_y(p|r) \wedge r \supset INSTR(OBT_y(p), help(x, y))]$$

where

$$OBT_y(p) \equiv p \wedge GOAL_y(p|q)UNTILp$$

So, agent y obtained p if p is true and it had the goal p until the moment p became true. Here $qUNTILp$ is defined as follows:

$$qUNTILp \equiv \ll \alpha \gg p \to (\forall \beta : (\beta \neq \gamma; \alpha; \delta) \to [\beta]q)$$

In this definition we translate the temporal operator UNTIL into dynamic logic. The antecedent states that p becomes true only after performing some sequence of actions α. It follows from this antecedent that q should be true until α has been performed completely. That is, it should be true after each sequence of actions that does not include α. We can now derive the following candidate goal for x:

$$C - GOAL_x(OBT_y(p)|GOAL_x(help(x,y)))$$

whenever $BEL_x(GOAL_y(p|r) \wedge r)$.

Notice that the goal for x is not p itself like with goal conformity, but the goal is that agent y obtains the goal p.

The goal generation mechanisms described in this section are more general and flexible than the production rules that are often encountered in agents. For instance the goal conformation could be realized through the following axiom:

$$C - GOAL_x(p|GOAL_y(p))$$

However, in this case agent x would adopt every goal of agent y without discrimination. In our goal generation system agent x might decide to adopt some goals of y, but not all of them, because they will not all serve the goal of helping y. Also the general goal (of helping y) could be made conditional upon the circumstances of agent x. E.g. whether it has enough resources, etc.

4 A sketch of a formalisation

Space limitations prevent us from incorporating the goal formation rules into a complete agent model. The language that we present in this section, however, is based on a language to model complete agents, including actions, communication and norms (see [7]). We will not present the complete range of concepts, because they would distract from the formalisation of the concepts used in this paper. On the other hand, we admit that the concepts used in this paper could be formalised in a simpler way. However, this formalisation could then not so easily be extended to a theory for all aspects of the agents.

The language that we use is a multi-modal, propositional language, based on three denumerable, pairwise disjoint sets: Π, representing the propositional symbols, Ag representing agents, and At containing atomic action expressions. The language $FORM$ is defined in three stages. Starting with a set of propositional formulas ($PFORM$), we define the action expressions, after which $FORM$ can be defined.

The set Act of regular action expressions is built up from the set At of atomic (parameterised) action expressions using the operators ; (sequential composition), + (non-deterministic composition), & (parallel composition), and ‾(action negation). The constant actions **any** and **fail** denote 'don't care what happens' and 'failure' respectively.

Definition 1. The set *Act* of action expressions is defined to be the smallest set closed under:

1. $At \cup \{\textbf{any}, \textbf{fail}\} \subseteq Act$
2. $\alpha_1, \alpha_2 \in Act \Longrightarrow \alpha_1; \alpha_2, \alpha_1 + \alpha_2, \alpha_1 \& \alpha_2, \overline{\alpha_1} \in Act$

The complete language *FORM* is now defined to contain all the constructs informally described in the previous section. That is, there are operators representing informational attitudes, motivational attitudes and aspects of actions. In this paper we leave out the communication aspects due to a lack of space.

Definition 2. The language *FORM* of formulas is defined to be the smallest set closed under:

1. $PFORM \subseteq FORM$
2. $\phi, \phi_1, \phi_2 \in FORM \Longrightarrow \neg\phi, \phi_1 \wedge \phi_2, INSTR(\phi_1, \phi_2) \in FORM$
3. $\phi \in FORM, i \in Ag \Longrightarrow BEL_i(\phi), GOAL_i(\phi), C - GOAL_i(\phi) \in FORM$
4. $\alpha \in Act, \phi \in FORM \Longrightarrow [\alpha]\phi, \ll \alpha \gg \phi \in FORM$
5. $\alpha \in Act, \phi \in FORM \Longrightarrow DONE(\alpha) \in FORM$
6. $\phi, \psi \in FORM, i \in Ag, \alpha, \alpha_1, \alpha_2 \in Act \Longrightarrow INT_i\alpha, O_i(\alpha) \in FORM$

The last rule is only included to show that intentions and norms are also important concepts for agents and related to the goals.

The models used to interpret *FORM* are based on Kripke-style possible worlds models. That is, the backbone of these models is given by a set Σ of states, and a valuation π on propositional symbols relative to a state. Various relations and functions on these states are used to interpret the various (modal) operators. These relations and functions can roughly be classified in four parts, dealing with the informational component, the action component, the motivational component and the social component, respectively. We assume tt and ff to denote the truth values 'true' and 'false', respectively.

Definition 3. A model Mo for *FORM* from the set CMo is a structure $(\Sigma, \pi, Rb, A, M, Dw)$ where

1. Σ is a non-empty set of states and $\pi : \Sigma \times \Pi \rightarrow \{tt, ff\}$.
2. $Rb : Ag \times \Sigma \rightarrow \wp(\Sigma)$ denotes the doxastic alternatives.
3. $A = (Sf, Rprev)$ with $Sf : Ag \times Act \times \Sigma \rightarrow \wp(\Sigma)$ yielding the interpretation of actions and $Rprev : Ag \times \Sigma \rightarrow Act$ yielding the action that has been performed last.
4. $M = (Ri, Ro, G, CG)$ with $Ri : Ag \times \Sigma \rightarrow \wp(Act)$ denoting intended actions, $Ro : Ag \rightarrow \wp(\Sigma \times \Sigma)$ denoting obligations, $CG : Ag \times \Sigma \rightarrow \wp(\Sigma)$ denoting candidate goals and $G : Ag \times \Sigma \rightarrow \wp(\Sigma)$ denoting goals.
5. $Dw : \Sigma \times \Sigma \rightarrow Integers$ yields the "distance" between two worlds. We do not define this any further, but one can think of how many propositions have a different truth value in both worlds together with the difference in beliefs of the agents, etc.

such that the following constraints are validated:

1. $Rb(i, s) \neq \emptyset$, which ensures that belief obeys a KD45 axiomatisation.

2. Sf yields the global state-transition interpretation for regular actions. This function satisfies the usual constraints ensuring an adequate interpretation of composite actions in terms of their constituents.

3. $Ri(i,s) \subseteq \{\alpha \mid Sf(i,\alpha,s) \neq \emptyset\}$ which means that only actions that are possible can be intended.

4. For all $s \in \Sigma$ some $s' \in \Sigma$ exists with $(s,s') \in Ro$, which ensures that all obligations are also permitted (the D-axiom holds).

5. $G(i,s) \subseteq CG(i,s)$

The complete semantics contains an algebraic semantics of action expresses, based on the action semantics of Meyer [13]. In this paper we will abstract from the algebraic interpretation of actions and instead interpret actions as functions on states of affairs.

Definition 4. The binary relation $\models$ between an element of $FORM$ and a pair consisting of a model Mo in CMo and a state s in Mo is for propositional symbols, conjunctions and negations defined as usual. Doxastic formulas $BEL_i\phi$ are interpreted as a necessity operator over Rb respectively. For the other formulas $\models$ is defined as follows:

$$Mo,s \models C - GOAL_i(\phi|\psi) \Longleftrightarrow \text{If } Mo,s \models BEL_i(\psi)$$
$$\text{then } Mo,s' \models \phi \text{ for all } s' \in CG(i,s)$$

$$Mo,s \models GOAL_i(\phi|\psi) \Longleftrightarrow \text{If } Mo,s \models BEL_i(\psi)$$
$$\text{then } Mo,s' \models \phi \text{ for all } s' \in G(i,s)$$

$$Mo,s \models [\alpha(i)]\phi \Longleftrightarrow Mo,s' \models \phi \text{ for all } s' \in Sf(i,\alpha,s)$$

$$Mo,s \models \ll \alpha(i) \gg \phi \Longleftrightarrow Mo,s' \models \phi \text{ for all } s' \in Sf(i,\alpha,s)$$
$$\text{and } Mo,s" \not\models \phi \text{ for all } s" \in Sf(i,\beta,s)$$
$$\text{and } \forall\beta : \alpha = \beta; \gamma$$

$$Mo,s \models DONE(\alpha(i)) \Longleftrightarrow \alpha \in Rprev(i,s)$$

$$Mo,s \models INSTR(\phi,\psi) \Longleftrightarrow \text{for all } s',s" : \pi(s',\phi) = tt \wedge \pi(s",\psi) = tt$$
$$\text{then } Dw(s',s") \leq Dw(s,s")$$

$$Mo,s \models INT_i\alpha \Longleftrightarrow \alpha \in Ri(i,s)$$

$$Mo,s \models O_i(\phi) \Longleftrightarrow Mo,s' \models \phi \text{ for all } s' \text{ with } (s,s') \in Ro(i)$$

$$Mo,s \models O_i(\alpha) \Longleftrightarrow Mo,s \models [\text{any}(i)]O_i(PREV(\alpha(i)))$$

5 Conclusions

In this paper some models of intentional action have been discussed. The main drawback of these models is their tendency to see goals only as a subset of endogenous motivations. This leads to building goals into the agent. This goals are therefore fixed and the agent cannot change its goal in response to events in the environment.

We have provided a general mechanism for goal generation. On the basis of some very general, abstract, built-in goals other goals can be generated thanks to some beliefs on instrumentality. This step of goal generation is a first step towards the forming of intentions. In this paper we have not shown the complete process of intention formation. Some intuitions about the rest of the process can be found in [3].

We have sketched a formalisation of a goal generation mechanism. Some examples of goal generation (through goal conformation, etc.) were given. Space constraints did not allow many details to be fully examined. Also other interesting goal generation rules, like goal generation through norm adoption could for this reason not be included. In a further study the fomalisation will be extended to all stages of intention formation. Finally, an implementation of the mechanism described is planned for future work.

References

1. Bratman, M.E. Intentions, Plans, and Practical Reason. Harvard University Press, 1987.
2. Bratman, M.E. What is intention? In P.R Cohen, J. Morgan, M.A. Pollack (eds), *Intentions in Communication*, 401-15. Cambridge, MA: MIT Press, 1990.
3. Castelfranchi, C. Commitments: From individual intentions to groups and organizations. *Proc. of the 1st International Conference on Multi-Agent Systems, ICMAS-95*, San Francisco, CA. Menlo Park, CA: AAAI Press/ The MIT Press, 1995.
4. Castelfranchi, C. Reasons: Belief support and goal-dynamics. *Journal of Mathware & Soft Computing*, 3(1-2), 233-247, 1996.
5. Cohen, P.R. and H.J. Levesque. Intention is choice with commitment. *Artificial Intelligence*, 42(3), 213-261, 1990.
6. Conte, R. and Castelfranchi, C. Cognitive and social action, London, UCL Press, 1995.
7. F. Dignum. Social interactions of autonomous agents; private and global views on communication. In A. Cesta and P-Y. Schobbens, editors, *Proceedings of the 4th ModelAge workshop on formal models of agents*, pages 99–114, Siena, Italy, 1997.
8. F. Dignum, E. Verharen and S. Bos. Implementation of a Cooperative Agent Architecture based on the Language-Action Perspective. In *this volume*.
9. Georgeff, M.P. and Rao, A.S. The semantics of Intention Maintenance for Rational Agents. *Proceedings of the International Joint Conference of Artificial Intelligence*, 1995.
10. M. d'Inverno, D. Kinny, M. Luck and M. Wooldridge. A Formal Specification of dMARS. In *this volume*.
11. C. Jung and K. Fischer. A Layered Agent Calculus with Concurrent, Continuous Processes. In *this volume*.
12. D. Kinny and M. Georgeff. Commitment and Effectiveness of Situated Agents. In *Proceedings International Joint Conference on Artificial Intel ligence*, Sydney, Australia, pages 82-88.
13. J.-J.Ch. Meyer. A different approach to deontic logic. In *Notre Dame Journal of Formal Logic*, vol.29, pages 109–136, 1988.
14. Rao, A.S. and M.P. Georgeff Modelling rational agents within a BDI architecture. In J. Allen, R. Fikes, E. Sandewall (eds), *Proceedings of the International Conference on Principles of Knowledge Representation and Reasoning*, 473-485. San Mateo, Kaufmann, 1991.
15. Rao, A.S. and Georgeff, M.P. A model-theoretic approach to the verification of situated reasoning systems. *Proceedings of the 13th International Conference of Artificial Intelligence, IJCAI-93*, Chambery, France, 1993.
16. Wooldridge, M.J. and Jennings, N.R. Agent theories, architectures, and languages: A survey, 1994.

A Layered Agent Calculus with Concurrent, Continuous Processes

Christoph G. Jung* and Klaus Fischer†

* GK Kogwiss. & FB Inform., Univ. des Saarlandes
  Im Stadtwald, D-66123 Saarbrücken, Germany
  jung@ags.uni-sb.de

† Multi-Agent Systems Group, DFKI GmbH
  Stuhlsatzenhausweg 3, D-66123 Saarbrücken, Germany
  kuf@dfki.de

Abstract. Current *logical* approaches to describe *intelligent agents* tend to be over-abstract rather than being practical. In contrast, *hybrid* architectures in the software engineering tradition, such as INTERRAP [9], tend to neglect formal methods, leaving a gap between theory and practice. We present the COOP calculus, a language for *concurrent, continuous* inference *processes*, as a means to bridge this gap. COOP presents a *declarative* account of *layered reasoning* in a *rational* and logical setting, but abandons a rigid, *cycle*-oriented view to obtain an operationally *reactive* agent core.

1 Introduction

Due to the increasing complexity of agent applications, especially in global network technology, there is an urgent demand for architectures of open, *intelligent agents* that unify different perspectives from *distributed* [16], *reactive* [1], *deliberative* [12], *cooperative* [6], and *cognitive* [10] systems.

Formal, *logical* approaches to describe intelligent entities originate in high-level *theories of agents*, such as the *Belief, Desire, and Intention* (BDI) tradition of [5, 11, 17], and in *temporal reasoning* [7, 13]. Currently, researchers try to extend the *declarative* foundation to provide more detailed and practical frameworks. Based on abstract notions of rationality, the BDI theory still exhibits a rather artificial relationship to concrete *implementations*. Generally, it is not yet clear, how to make reasonable trade-offs between declarative and *operational* considerations for both *specification* and *verification* purposes.

The *automated loading dock* is a practical *robotics* test bed whose ambitious demands on *situated* fork-lift agents (Fig. 11) go beyond those typically investigated in research with a theoretical background. The fork-lifts are faced with tasks given by a human supervisor to (un-)load boxes of different categories to (from) a truck from (to) the respective shelves. They are equipped with motors for independently controlling the two wheels and an attached gripper. The condition of these devices and data from infrared sensors are available as perception to an agent program. There is a clear need for reactive behaviour: incoming sensory data has to be transformed into *continuous* motor control, following trajectories, avoiding collisions, and manipulating objects. The

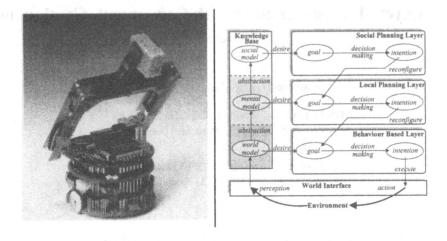

Fig. 1. Khepera Robot and The InteRRaP Architecture

deliberative level handles the (un-)loading tasks, in particular the path planning problems. Because of limited perception and the dynamic environment, in part caused by the agent's own reactive skills, the reasoning is faced with incomplete and changing knowledge. Its processing thus requires sophisticated error-handling facilities. Besides the interaction with the supervisor, forklift agents have to jointly adapt their local deliberation to solve conflict situations, such as the mutual lock caused when two robots block each other's way. Negotiated cooperation can optimise the distribution of tasks locally, such as when two robots exchange the task of delivering particular boxes.

Hybrid architectures, such as INTERRAP [9] (Fig. 1r), that are building on traditions from *software engineering* have been especially designed for domains of this complexity. These approaches reconcile the functionality of separate *components* or *modules* by determining the interactions in a rather pragmatic manner. INTERRAP models the smooth transition from sub-symbolic reactivity to symbolic deliberation and social capabilities by *abstraction* and *meta-reasoning*: the BDI architecture is thus realised with three different *layers*. Applying procedural knowledge, the most concrete, *behaviour-based layer* (BBL) provides short feedback loops with the environment. On top of this, the *local planning layer* (LPL) meta-reasons about how to reconfigure the underlying reactive module to meet more long-term, abstract goals; this is a form of planning. Finally, social decisions (at the *social planning layer* — SPL) that involve communicating and negotiating with other agents about the local inferences also require a form of planning and impose guidelines on the LPL's computation. Two additional components encapsulate the interface to the environment (*world interface* — WIF) and the maintenance of the agent's beliefs (*knowledge base* — KB) for efficiency purposes. Similar to other hybrids, INTERRAP lacks a formal foundation to determine a unique abstract machine. The lack of such a foundation prevents an objective verification of the system and impedes the use of declarative programming techniques, thus restricting its usefulness to program or specify agents.

Contribution and Related Work Our work bridges the gap between theories as in [5, 11, 17, 7, 13] and hybrid architectures as in [9]. We do this by axiomatising an *operational calculus*, COOP (Sec. 2), that defines the notions of *concurrent, continuous processes* and their communication via *signals*. The original, integrative aspects of the INTERRAP layers are still accounted for, although we break with the tradition of *monolithic-cycle agents* and thus refine the granularity of processing. While Sec. 3 gives an overview of the employed reasoning processes, such as knowledge maintenance, goal activation, planning, and execution, their detailed and spacious axiomatisation can be found in, e.g., [4]. There, we describe a similar temporal reasoning mechanism for planning as in [7, 13]. In contrast to their computational model, our approach however makes meta-control, concurrency, and the interaction of reactivity and deliberation explicit. Also we do offer an account of social abilities, an aspect that is often neglected in agent specifications.

The metaphor of processes and signals is common to the design of operating systems and is also found in modern, even logic-based programming languages, such as in Oz's [14] threads and exceptions. COOP expressions thus correspond immediately to a straightforward, mostly declarative implementation. [8] applies similar concepts for controlling continuous real-world activities. As [1], COOP supports *suppression* and *isolation* through the controlling force of components. Parallel research reported in this volume, e.g., [2, 3], also underpins the importance of formal methods in agent design and provides comparable specifications for other well-known theories and architectures.

2 The COOP Calculus

2.1 Concurrent, Continuous Processes

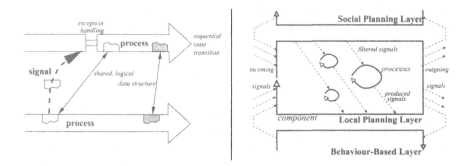

Fig. 2. Processes and Components in COOP

The original description of INTERRAP [9] does not address its embedding in a computational setting. As a straightforward consequence, former implementations either used purely sequential processing strategies or just allowed concurrency between layers. Such coarse control cycles prevent the agent from acting while deliberating. They thus fail to provide continuous, reactive feedback: the crucial parts of, e.g., a fork-lift robot's interface have to migrate into the WIF which deprives them from being controlled. There are, however, more sophisticated design constructs in operating systems and modern programming languages, such as those based on *processes* and *signals* (Fig. 2l). Processes can be seen as *sequential state transitions* that compute continuously in an independent and *concurrent* manner. A critical computation is shielded by a stack of *exception handlers*. Signals indicate explicit, exceptional situations which need immediate reactions and an exception handling mechanism designed for concurrent settings determines an appropriate continuation for the computation. Since signals contain *logical data structures* that can be incorporated into the processes' state, the processes refer to *shared memory* which additionally establishes an implicit, computational form of communication.

In keeping with the INTERRAP architecture, we do not view the agent as an unstructured, heterogeneous mixture of processes that communicate directly with each other. We introduce the concept of a *component* as an additional control structure (Fig. 2r) that encapsulates inferences like a membrane. We require that this membrane controls the activation of fresh, internal computations and serves as a fast relays and filter for every incoming and outgoing signal communication. Components either contain special services, such as the WIF and the KB do, or they represent a certain BDI level, such as BBL, LPL, and SPL, and are therefor called a layer.

We formalise the above concepts using a *term rewriting calculus* $(\mathcal{L}, \equiv, \rightarrow)$ [14], a device suitable to present declarative as well as operational forms of computation. The set $\mathcal{L}$ specifies the *syntax* by enumerating a language. Its *semantics* is described by $\equiv$, an equivalence relation called the *structural congruence* of expressions in $\mathcal{L}$, and the binary $\rightarrow$ relation that contains possible *reduction* steps. We demand $\rightarrow$ to be invariant under congruence, i.e., $(\equiv \circ \rightarrow \circ \equiv) \subseteq \rightarrow$. The transitive closure of $\rightarrow \cup \equiv$ is labelled with $\rightarrow^*$ and links the beginning and the end of a possible *derivation* in the calculus. In the following, we develop the COOP calculus $(A, \equiv_A, \rightarrow_A)$ that describes an agent-environment system in terms of our process-oriented constructs. Sec. 3 afterwards discusses how to instantiate this description to obtain formal and flexible INTERRAP agents.

2.2 Syntax

The grammar of the agent language is presented in Fig. 3. The primitive syntactical elements are *logical* **variables** (V) and **constants** $(C \supseteq \{\exists, ;, \&, \text{ex}, \text{sg}, \text{pr}, \text{co}, \text{ag}, \wedge, \vee, \Rightarrow\})$ [1]. More complex expressions are of type **term** (T) and are recursive combinations of more primitive subexpressions with ϵ being the empty term. The $\exists$ operator hereby allows the *declaration* of variables. & represents the order-independent *composition* of terms expressing *concurrency* or *choice*. An order-dependent, *sequential* composition is denoted by $;$. The standard logical connectives are conjunction $(\wedge)$, disjunction $(\vee)$, and implication $(\Rightarrow)$. As a matter of convenience, $\&, ;, \wedge, \vee$, and $\Rightarrow$ can be used in infix notation.

---

[1] In the following, we use strings beginning with lowercase letters (rob1) as constants and strings beginning with uppercase letters (O) as variables.

Variable	V: *predefined set*
Constant	C: *predefined set*
Term	T: $\epsilon \mid V \mid C \mid C\,(T_1,\dots,T_n)$
Exception	X: $\epsilon \mid \exists(V,X) \mid \text{ex}\,(S^{head},T^{prot},T^{sta})\,\&X$
Exception Stack	Y: $\epsilon \mid \exists(V,Y) \mid X\,;Y$
Signal	S: $\epsilon \mid \exists(V,S) \mid \text{sg}\,(C^{sk},C^{sp},C^{rk},C^{rp},T^{con})\,;S$
Process	P: $\epsilon \mid \exists(V,P) \mid \text{pr}\,(C^{id},C^{cla},S^{in},S^{out},T^{prot},T^{sta},Y)\,\&P$
Component	K: $\epsilon \mid \exists(V,K) \mid \text{co}\,(C^{id},S^{in},S^{out},T^{sta},P)\,\&K$
Environment	E: *predefined set*
Agent	A: $\epsilon \mid \exists(V,A) \mid \text{ag}\,(C^{id},T^{per},T^{act},K)\,;E$

Fig. 3. The COOP Language A (*Backus-Naur-Form*)

The top-level **agent** expression of A is built by the composition of a special agent term and the **environment** state from a set E^2. The agent can be identified by its name (C^{id}, for example rob1). T^{per} represents the current perception: values from infrared sensors, motor registers, and TCP/IP input (per(1.3,7.89,...,sync(rob2))). An action term T^{act} expresses the action to perform next in the environment (for example motor(1,3): set the velocity of the left motor to three units per second). Since an agent is not allowed to give references to its memory to the environment, especially to other agents[3], perception and output are not allowed to contain variables, i.e., they are *ground. Admissible* **agent** expressions should be furthermore *closed*, i.e. all variables are correctly declared and do not occur *free*. The free variables of an expression A build the set $\mathcal{V}(A)$, thus $\mathcal{V}(A) = \{\}$.

The computation of an agent is defined by a concurrent composition of **components** (K) with unique identifiers (C^{id}, for example bb1). A component encapsulates active, dynamic **processes** (P). Because a component serves to control the information flow between the subordinate processes, we enable the processing of incoming **signals** that are queued in S^{in} and that originate from other components or from internal, encapsulated inferences. The reaction to a signal depends on the context stored in the component's dynamic state T^{sta} and is, e.g., able to trigger outgoing communication by signals that will be queued in S^{out}.

Concurrently composed **processes** (P) carry a unique identifier (C^{id}, for example dr9) and a specific *process class* descriptor (C^{cla}, for example drive) that determines the transition of the internal process state T^{sta}. To specify a particular response to a variety of incoming **signals** S^{in}, the **exception stack** Y describes the current mapping of signals to reactions. Proper concurrent exception handling requires the further distinction of an, in contrast to T^{sta}, *un-interruptible* (T^{prot}) part of the process' state. This is to ensure that, e.g., clean-up actions after deactivation of a process, are able to set up a consistent state within the agent. As before, S^{out} stores outgoing signals.

Signals S are queued and processed sequentially within components and processes. Directed communication requires the address of the sending process consisting of its

---

[2] E, V, and C are mutually disjoint.

[3] It is easy to obtain multi-agent variants of the calculus to study simultaneous interactions.

component's and its own identifier (C^{sk}, C^{sp}, for example kb, fc3). The destination is given in the same format (C^{rk}, C^{rp}, for example bb1, dr9). In the special case of signals that originate from or are destined to components, the component and process part of an address can be identical ($C^{rk} = C^{rp}$, $C^{sk} = C^{sp}$). Finally, each signal carries some content (T^{con}, for example deactivate).

The interface to the process-intern computation is constituted by a concurrent exception handling technique that reacts to changing environmental conditions. The exception stack Y constructs nested shells of **exceptions** (X) which in turn relate signals to reactions. An atomic exception ex(sg(...,heading(O)),T^{prot},T^{sta}) replaces the previous state T^{prot}, T^{sta} of a process with $\mu(T^{prot})$, $\mu(T^{sta})$ if facing a signal with content heading(rob2). We use μ as a substitution function that in this case replaces the variable O with rob2. The composition of basic exceptions with the choice operator (&) allows the order-independent handling of several, exceptional situations.

2.3 Semantics

In the following, we describe the congruence $\equiv_A$ and the reduction $\to_A$ by formulating *axioms*. An axiom $\left[\frac{P}{C}\right]$ states that some property C must hold for a relation if all the preconditions P are entailed. A statement $[C]$ is an axiom with empty preconditions, thus C must hold in any case. Because of the hierarchical structure of A, the structural congruence and the reduction decompose into several sub-relations $\equiv_{\{\eta,T\}}$ and $\to_{\{\eta,K,P,Y,X,\phi,\pi\}}$. Since the sub-reductions are context-dependent, they have an arity of ≥ 2. $\equiv_\eta$ and $\to_\eta$ will not be constrained at all, as they capture the domain-specific environment. As aforementioned, the processing of components $\to_\phi$ and processes $\to_\pi$ is outlined in Sec. 3 and axiomatised in detail in, e.g., [4].

Structural Congruence Axiom C1 in Fig. 4 describes equivalent **agent** expressions to have equivalent agent terms and equivalent **environment** subexpressions. The remaining axioms concentrate on defining the general congruence $\equiv_T$ on terms: C2 introduces invariant semantics for the replacement of subexpressions with equivalent ones. C3 and C4 establish the associativity of the composition operators. Especially the & operator is independent of the order of the composed subexpressions (C5). C6 defines the congruence with respect to consistent variable renaming ($=_\alpha$). Furthermore, axioms C7 and C8 describe the properties of locally scoped variables.

Inference In Fig. 5, we define axioms I1 to I5[4] for the reduction down to the process level: derivations can be applied within the scope of a declaration $\exists(V,T)$ and the substitution that arises in a local computation is applied to the whole expression. Axioms I6 to I8 constrain the agent, component, and process levels of $\to_{\{A,K,P\}}$ to interpret the & operator as concurrency: they are able to reduce the first part of the expression, and thus any part due to the congruence. On the top level (I9), the environment uses a domain-specific function $E, T^{act} \to_\eta E^*, T^{per*}$ to consume the output of the agent

---

[4] Fig. 5 uses an abbreviation that easily unfolds into seperate definitions.

C1	$$\left[\dfrac{T \equiv_T T^* \quad E \equiv_\eta E^*}{T\,;E \equiv_A T^*\,;E^*} \right]$$
C2	$$\left[\dfrac{T_1 \equiv_T T_1^* \ldots T_n \equiv_T T_n^*}{C\,(T_1,\ldots,T_n) \equiv_T C\,(T_1^*,\ldots,T_n^*)} \right]$$
C3	$$[T_1\&(T_2\&T_3) \equiv_T (T_1\&T_2)\&T_3]$$
C4	$$[T_1\,;(T_2\,;T_3) \equiv_T (T_1\,;T_2)\,;T_3]$$
C5	$$[T_1\&T_2 \equiv_T T_2\&T_1]$$
C6	$$\left[\dfrac{T_1 =_\alpha T_2}{T_1 \equiv_T T_2} \right]$$
C7	$$[\exists(V_1,\exists(V_2,T)) \equiv_T \exists(V_2,\exists(V_1,T))]$$
C8	$$\left[\dfrac{V \notin \mathcal{V}(T_1) \cup \ldots \cup \mathcal{V}(T_{i-1}) \cup \mathcal{V}(T_{i+1}) \cup \ldots \cup \mathcal{V}(T_n)}{C\,(T_1,\ldots,\exists(V,T_i),\ldots,T_n) \equiv_T \exists(V,C\,(T_1,\ldots,T_i,\ldots,T_n))} \right]$$

Fig. 4. Axioms on Structural Congruence

(T^{act}), to determine a new environment state and to update the agent's perceptions. The agent C^{id} now evolves as one of its concurrent components is rewritten which depends on the new perception T^{per*} and could produce some action T^{act*}. A similar axiom (**I10**) establishes the transition of a component consisting of the transition of any of the active processes. Finally, the process level (**I11, I12**) relies on a change of state $C^{cla} \times T^{sta} \times T^{per*} \times Y_1 \to_\pi T^{sta*} \times T^{act*} \times S^{out*} \times Y_1^*$ that depends on the process class C^{cla} and is outlined in Sec. 3. Besides propagating perception T^{per*} to output T^{act*}, $\to_\pi$ has the ability of manipulating the top of the exception stack Y_1 to Y_1^* and of producing new outgoing signals S^{out*}. Note that this reduction can be applied to both the regular part of the process' state as well as to the protected one. Our definitions ensure, however, that the protected state of the process has priority in reduction as long as it is not empty (ϵ). If both parts of the state are empty, the process has died and **I13** removes its expression.

Signal Routing and Filtering Fig. 6 defines the flow of signals between components and processes. To enable a component to control its sub-processes, every communication that originates (is destined) from (to) a subordinate process has first to pass the component's processing: $\to_K$ can be extended to move the first signal in the outgoing queue of component C_1^{id} to the end of the incoming signals' queue of process C_2^{id} within C_1^{id} (**S1**, see **S2** for the reverse direction). Signals whose destination process has already disappeared are simply removed by **S3**. **S4** introduces the migration of signals between components. Finally, **S5** lets the component handle the signals in the incoming

$$\text{I1}\ldots\text{I5} \quad \left[\frac{\ldots,T,\ldots \to_{\{A,K,P,X,Y\}} \ldots,\mu(T^*),\ldots}{\ldots,\exists(V,T),\ldots \to_{\{A,K,P,Y,X\}} \ldots,\mu(\exists(V,T^*)),\ldots} \right]$$

$$\text{I6}\ldots\text{I8} \quad \left[\frac{\ldots,T_1,\ldots \to_{\{A,K,P\}} \ldots,\mu(T_1^*),\ldots}{\ldots,T_1\&T_2,\ldots \to_{\{A,K,P\}} \ldots,\mu(T_1^*\&T_2),\ldots} \right]$$

$$\text{I9} \quad \left[\frac{E,T^{act} \to_\eta E^*,T^{per*} \quad K,T^{per*} \to_K \mu(K^*),T^{act*}}{\mathsf{ag}\,(C^{id},T^{per},T^{act},K)\,;E \to_A \mu(\mathsf{ag}\,(C^{id},T^{per*},T^{act*},K^*))\,;E^*} \right]$$

$$\text{I10} \quad \left[\frac{P,T^{per*} \to_P \mu(P^*),T^{act*}}{\begin{array}{c}\mathsf{co}\,(C^{id},S^{in},S^{out},T^{sta},P),T^{per*} \\ \to_K \\ \mu(\mathsf{co}(\,(C^{id}(,S^{in}(,S^{out}(,T^{sta}(,P^*)),T^{act*})\end{array}} \right]$$

$$\text{I11} \quad \left[\frac{C^{cla},T^{sta},T^{per*},Y_1 \to_\pi \mu(T^{sta*}),T^{act*},Y_1^*,S^* \quad S^{out*}=S^{out}\,;S^*}{\begin{array}{c}\mathsf{pr}\,(C^{id},C^{cla},S^{in},S^{out},\epsilon,T^{sta},Y_1\,;Y),T^{per*} \\ \to_P \\ \mu(\mathsf{pr}\,(C^{id},C^{cla},S^{in},S^{out*},\epsilon,T^{sta*},Y_1^*\,;Y)),T^{act*}\end{array}} \right]$$

$$\text{I12} \quad \left[\frac{C^{cla},T^{prot},T^{per*},Y_1 \to_\pi \mu(T^{prot*}),T^{act*},Y_1^*,S^* \quad S^{out*}=S^{out}\,;S^*}{\begin{array}{c}\mathsf{pr}\,(C^{id},C^{cla},S^{in},S^{out},T^{prot},T^{sta},Y_1\,;Y),T^{per*} \\ \to_P \\ \mu(\mathsf{pr}\,(C^{id},C^{cla},S^{in},S^{out*},T^{prot*},T^{sta},Y_1^*\,;Y)),T^{act*}\end{array}} \right]$$

$$\text{I13} \quad \left[\mathsf{pr}\,(C^{id},C^{cla},S^{in},S^{out},\epsilon,\epsilon,Y),T^{per*} \to_P \epsilon,\epsilon \right]$$

Fig. 5. Axioms on Inference

queue using the device of a filter function $C^{id} \times T^{sta} \times S \to_\phi T^{sta*} \times S^* \times P^*$. Besides the identifier C^{id} of the component, the filter's output depends on the component's state T^{sta} and the signal S to process. The output consists of a new state T^{sta*}, some freshly activated processes P^*, and new outgoing signals S^*. We do not present $\to_\phi$ in detail here. However, in the most straightforward case, S should be passed to a subordinate process and thus $S = S^*$. Suppressing the output from the sender or isolating the recipient from getting information can be done by setting $S^* = \epsilon$. A common request addressed to the component itself is the activation of a fresh, internal process indicated by $\mathsf{sg}\,(C^{sk},C^{sp},C^{rk},C^{rk},\mathsf{activate}\,(C^{cla},T^{arg},\mathtt{Pid}))$. The state of a component therefore includes class descriptors (C^{cla}) associated with (implicitly) universally quantified argument and initial state terms. By unifying T^{arg} with the argument of a named-apart variant of this class structure, $\to_\phi$ is able to construct a fresh process instance P^* with an instantiated initial state. The variable $\mathtt{Pid}$ reports the address of P^*, a fresh and unique constant, back to the activator.

$$\mathbf{S1}\quad \left[\frac{\dfrac{S = \mathrm{sg}\,(C^{sk}, C^{sp}, C_1^{id}, C_2^{id}, T^{con})}{\mathrm{co}\,(C_1^{id}, S_1^{in}, S; S_1^{out}, T_1^{sta}, \mathrm{pr}\,(C_2^{id}, C^{cla}, S_2^{in}, \ldots)\,\&P), T^{per*}}}{\begin{array}{c}\to_K \\ \mathrm{co}\,(C_1^{id}, S_1^{in}, S_1^{out}, T_1^{sta}, \mathrm{pr}\,(C_2^{id}, C^{cla}, S_2^{in}; S, \ldots)\,\&P), \epsilon\end{array}}\right]$$

$$\mathbf{S2}\quad \left[\frac{\dfrac{S = \mathrm{sg}\,(C_1^{id}, C_2^{id}, C^{rk}, C^{rp}, T^{con})}{\mathrm{co}\,(C_1^{id}, S_1^{in}, S_1^{out}, T_1^{sta}, \mathrm{pr}\,(C_2^{id}, \ldots, S; S_2^{out}, \ldots)\,\&P), T^{per*}}}{\begin{array}{c}\to_K \\ \mathrm{co}\,(C_1^{id}, S_1^{in}; S, S_1^{out}, T_1^{sta}, \mathrm{pr}\,(C_2^{id}, \ldots, S_2^{out}, \ldots)\,\&P), \epsilon\end{array}}\right]$$

$$\mathbf{S3}\quad \left[\frac{S = \mathrm{sg}\,(C^{sk}, C^{sp}, C_1^{id}, C_2^{id}, T^{con}) \quad P_1 \not\equiv_T \mathrm{pr}\,(C_2^{id}, \ldots)\,\&P_2}{\mathrm{co}\,(C_1^{id}, S_1^{in}, S; S_1^{out}, \ldots), T^{per*} \to_K \mathrm{co}\,(C_1^{id}, S_1^{in}, S_1^{out}, \ldots), \epsilon}\right]$$

$$\mathbf{S4}\quad \left[\frac{\dfrac{S = \mathrm{sg}\,(C_1^{id}, C^{sp}, C_2^{id}, C^{rp}, T^{con})}{\mathrm{co}\,(C_1^{id}, S_1^{in}, S; S_1^{out}, \ldots)\,\&\mathrm{co}\,(C_2^{id}, S_2^{in}, S_2^{out}, \ldots), T^{per*}}}{\begin{array}{c}\to_K \\ \mathrm{co}\,(C_1^{id}, S_1^{in}, S_1^{out}, \ldots)\,\&\mathrm{co}\,(C_2^{id}, S_2^{in}; S, S_2^{out}, \ldots), \epsilon\end{array}}\right]$$

$$\mathbf{S5}\quad \left[\frac{\dfrac{S = \mathrm{sg}\,(C^{sk}, C^{sp}, C^{rk}, C^{rp}, T^{con}) \quad C^{id}, T^{sta}, S \to_\phi \mu(T^{sta*}), S^*, P^*}{\mathrm{co}\,(C^{id}, S; S^{in}, S^{out}, T^{sta}, P), T^{per*}}}{\begin{array}{c}\to_K \\ \mu(\mathrm{co}\,(C^{id}, S^{in}, S^{out}; S^*, T^{sta*}, P^*\,\&P)), \epsilon\end{array}}\right]$$

Fig. 6. Axioms on Signal Routing and Filtering

$$\mathbf{E1}\quad \left[\frac{\dfrac{S = \mathrm{sg}\,(C^{sk}, C^{sp}, C^{rk}, C^{id}, T^{con}) \quad S, Y \to_Y \mu(T^{prot*}), \mu(T^{sta*}), Y^*}{\mathrm{pr}\,(C^{id}, C^{cla}, S; S^{in}, S^{out}, \epsilon, T^{sta}, Y), T^{per*}}}{\begin{array}{c}\to_P \\ \mu(\mathrm{pr}\,(C^{id}, C^{cla}, S^{in}, S^{out}, T^{prot*}, T^{sta*}, Y^*)), \epsilon\end{array}}\right]$$

$$\mathbf{E2}\quad \left[\frac{S, X \to_X \mu(T^{prot*}), \mu(T^{sta*})}{S, X; Y \to_Y \mu(T^{prot*}), \mu(T^{sta*}), Y}\right]$$

$$\mathbf{E3}\quad \left[\frac{S, X \not\to_X \ldots \quad S, Y \to_Y \mu(T^{prot*}), \mu(T^{sta*}), Y^*}{S, X; Y \to_Y \mu(T^{prot*}), \mu(T^{sta*}), Y^*}\right]$$

$$\mathbf{E4}\quad \left[\frac{S, X_1 \to_X \mu(T^{prot*}), \mu(T^{sta*})}{S, X_1 \& X_2 \to_X \mu(T^{prot*}), \mu(T^{sta*})}\right]$$

$$\mathbf{E5}\quad \left[\frac{\mu = \mathbf{unify}(S, S^{head})}{S, \mathrm{ex}\,(S^{head}, T^{prot}, T^{sta}) \to_X \mu(T^{prot}), \mu(T^{sta})}\right]$$

Fig. 7. Axioms on Exception Handling

Exception Handling Let us finally model the reactivity of the various process sub-calculi by describing the semantics of exception handling (Fig. 7): provided that the protected state has been processed (ϵ), axiom **E1** puts the current signal S and the exception stack Y into a derivation $S \times Y \rightarrow_Y T^{prot*} \times T^{sta*} \times Y^*$ that computes a reaction $\mu(T^{prot*}), \mu(T^{sta*})$ and a new exception environment Y^*. The top exception X on the stack is responsible for encoding the most specific reaction of the current computation state. If X leads to a successful reaction by $\rightarrow_X$, we adopt its result in the first place (**E2**). If X has no derivation ($S, X \not\rightarrow_X \ldots$), Y probably forces a more general reaction in **E3**. Disjunctive paths in exceptions are passed by non-deterministically choosing one of them that leads to a reaction (**E4**). Finally, the atomic part of the mechanism (**E5**) tries to unify the head of a primitive exception (T^{head}) with the signal. On success, the generated substitution μ is applied to the body of the exception T^{prot}, T^{sta} and the result constitutes the new state of the process. There is a default exception for each fresh process which terminates the process on reception of any signal: $\exists (\text{Def}, \text{ex}(\text{Def}, \epsilon, \epsilon))$. Proper deactivation, however, should be introduced by the signal `deactivate` that can be caught in order to initiate clean-up activities.

2.4 Reduction Strategies

From the definition of derivations in our agent calculus it follows that a computation is subject of non-determinism due to alternatives in the reduction relation. Usually, the requirement of *confluence* constrains the overall result of a computation to be independent of the choices made. Our model prohibits such a strong statement in the first place. We argue that this property is not desirable for our agent calculus: non-confluence rather is a feature of an open framework than it leads to unpredictable behaviour on the conceptual BDI level. Especially, our model is consistent with any implementation that designs a particular *strategy* to deterministically choose a path in derivation: it can be shown that *fair* strategies eventually continue the processing of each subexpression according to the reactive context.

3 INTERRAP and COOP

This section now fills the formal skeleton of $\rightarrow_{\phi,\pi}$ with the concrete components and processes of INTERRAP agents (Fig. 8). INTERRAP agents incorporate five components with the identifiers $C^{id} \in \{\text{kb}, \text{wif}, \text{bbl}, \text{lpl}, \text{spl}\}$. Signals are admissible from `wif` to `kb`, `bbl` to $\{\text{lpl}, \text{kb}, \text{wif}\}$, `lpl` to $\{\text{spl}, \text{kb}, \text{bbl}\}$, `spl` to $\{\text{kb}, \text{lpl}, \text{wif}\}$, and `kb` to $\{\text{spl}, \text{lpl}, \text{bbl}\}$.

3.1 The World Interface

The world interface `wif` is the only component whose internal processes are actually allowed to access perception and action. Continuous, sensoric activities ($C^{cla} = \text{per}$) access parts of the perception term T^{per} ($(1.3, 7.89, \ldots)$) of the agent. Since they memorise the last data, a change in the partial percept (1.3) will be reported as a signal (`update(sensor(1,1.3))`) to the knowledge base `kb`. Actions (`act`) are one-shot processes that copy their state (`motor(1,3)`) into the output T^{act}.

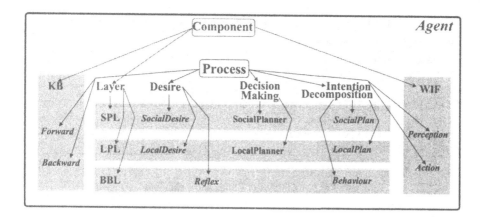

Fig. 8. Processes in INTERRAP

3.2 The Knowledge Base

The kb component organises the belief of the agent ranging from the perceptual world level (sensor(1, 1.3)), the mental level (pos(rob1, (11,22)), colour(boxa, yellow)) to the epistemic level (bel(rob2, area(boxa,truck)). Basic facts are present within the state of the knowledge base. They can be accessed by the signal get (get(colour(boxa,∃(V,V)))). A further kb service registers the sending process to subscribe a proposition. Whenever update causes a change in the appropriate belief, a notification sent by the kb informs the subscribers. Backward reasoning (bc) processes implement typical prolog-style rules[5] ∀̃∃(V3,colour(V1,V3) ∧ colour(V2,V3)) ⇒ compatible(V1,V2) to access the knowledge on demand and produce instantiated conclusions (compatible(boxa,truck)) as their result. Forward reasoning (fc) is used to implement trigger rules often found in production rule systems (∃̃(pos(Me,V1)∧pos(O,V2)∧ahead(V1,V2)⇒ blocked). They are permanently installed upon activation and map a partial situation description to signals that either go into the layers (situation recognition) or cause updates in the kb. In both cases, complex preconditions of rules decompose into simpler bc or fc processes, whereas atomic preconditions use the kb services (get(colour(shelf2,∃(V,V)))), subscribe(pos(Me,∃(V,V)))). Solution substitutions (or changes in belief) will afterwards propagate through the dynamic bc (or fc) net using the orthogonal communication facilities of shared memory (bc) and signals (fc).

3.3 The Behaviour-Based Layer

The behaviour-based layer provides for the reactive instance of the general BDI scheme by running reflexes (ref) and patterns of behaviour (pb). The upper part of Fig. 9

---

[5] The universal quantification can be simulated (see Sec. 2.3).

```
∃avoidcollision(arg(ε),(blocked∧heading(Me,0))⇒ stepaside)
```

```
∃drive(arg(Lgth,Speed,Ini),
ex(deactivate,(P1=act(motor(1,0));P2=act(motor(2,0));
                deactivate(P3);deactivate(P4);
                unlock(motor(1));unlock(motor(2))),ε);
P3=fc(((pos(Me,Pos)∧≥(dist(Pos,Ini),Lgth))⇒deactivate);
P4=fc(blocked(Me)⇒deactivate);
lock(motor(1));lock(motor(2));
P5=act(motor(1,Speed));P6=act(motor(2,Speed)); wait)
```

Fig. 9. Examples of Reflex and Behaviour

describes an example reflex class as found within our forklift agents. Taking no arguments, the body of the reflex installs a `fc` process in the `kb` that triggers as soon as some obstacle appears and moves towards the robot. On notification of the event, the reflex that merges the functionality of desire and decision-making immediately activates a new behaviour process, `stepaside`, forcing the robot to dodge. Goals are thus only implicitly present and associated with the active patterns of behaviour. These patterns of behaviour are routine, but probably complex intentions comparable to continuously computing procedures. The lower part of Fig. 9 shows how they encode, e.g., a straight movement of the robot. The parameters `Lgth` and `Speed` identify the minimal distance and the speed of the robot's desired movement from start position `Ini`. Atomic statements are composed sequentially with the ; operator. First, the `ex` statement pushes protected clean-up actions onto the exception stack to react to any deactivation request. Afterwards, short-cuts for signals are used to activate other, concurrent computations (`P1...P6`) within the knowledge base (`fc`) and the world interface (`act`). Our example installs two situations to be recognised by forward chaining in the `kb`. If the robot has moved the requested distance or an obstacle has been detected ahead, the `deactivation` signal should be reported back. `bbl`-controlled semaphores are implementing a consistent actor (motor) policy: a single process is able to `lock` a semaphore while other candidates are prevented from intervening. Finally, `drive` sets the velocity of both wheels which starts the continuous movement and waits afterwards (`wait`). As soon as some external deactivation signal comes in, the body of the already installed exception stops the motors, properly shuts down the situation recognition, and `unlocks` the semaphores.

3.4 The Local and Social Planning Layers

While goals and decision making have hardwired manifestations on the `bbl`, both upper layers (`lpl`, `spl`) in INTERRAP employ explicit goals as well as reasoning (planning) about those. Therefore, both are using the same classes of processes, but on different levels of abstraction. Desires (`des`) of which reflexes could be seen as a special case link situation recognition to goal activation within the component (`goal(area(boxa,truck))`). Planning processes (`pp`) are triggered to reason (synthesise/modify, analyse/evaluate) about intention structures or plans that will help the agent to satisfy these goals. Any classical planning approach could be plugged into here. We chose an abductive, temporal reasoning calculus [4] because of its flexibility, its formal, logical foundation and the way it enables reactive planning in interaction with changing belief and goals. The primitive plans or actions represent, based on preconditions and effects, process reconfiguration on the subordinate layer which will be induced by signals. The lpl thus controls the (de)activation of reflexes and behaviours. The spl primitives include the (de)activation of communication actions in the world interface and the control of (local) planning and execution processes. Structures of more complex plans are quite similar to the programming constructs found in patterns of behaviour: sequential and concurrent composition, exceptions for protecting causal links, etc.

4 Conclusion

Our framework extends the hybrid INTERRAP approach to agent design towards a formal language. The applied programming methodology ties it tightly to a more practical and flexible implementation than previous descriptions did which is supported by our preliminary experiences both in a simulated as well as a physical version of the loading dock: the very compact code of the agent skeleton consistent with the formal model, the unified way of encoding of domain-specific parts of the forklift agents, the increased planning capabilities, and the performance and robustness of the robots' behaviour confirm our claim. Currently, we are investigating the benefits of adding explicit and resource-based control strategies into the component model.

On the specification side, we try to express COOP in a more standardised fashion, such as by using the Z language [15]. This has been inspired by the work of [2] in this volume. The final connection to some variant of the BDI theory will be made by interpreting COOP as an appropriate proof procedure.

Acknowledgements Alastair Burt and Gero Vierke proof-read and commented various versions of the paper. The work of Jörg Müller on INTERRAP and of the Programming Systems Lab at the Universität des Saarlandes, especially Martin Müller is to mention here, on Oz has been a major source of inspiration. We are grateful for the stimulating discussions with the logic programming section of the Imperial College, London. We would like to thank the reviewers and participants of the ATAL workshop for their help in substantially improving this presentation and research.

References

1. R. A. Brooks. Intelligence without reason. In *Proceedings of the 12th International Joint Conference on Artificial Intelligence (IJCAI-91)*, Sydney, Australia, 1991.
2. M. d'Inverno, D. Kinny, M. Luck, and M. Wooldridge. A Formal Specification of dMARS. In this volume.
3. K. V. Hindricks, F. S. de Boer, W. van der Hoek and J. J. Ch. Meyer. Formal Semantics for an Abstract Agent Programming Language. In this volume.

4. C. G. Jung, K. Fischer, and A. Burt. *Multi-agent Planning using an Abductive Event Calculus*. Number RR-96-4 in DFKI Research Report. DFKI GmbH, Saarbrücken, Germany, 1996.

5. P. R. Cohen and H. J. Levesque. Intention is choice with commitment. *Artificial Intelligence*, 42(3):213—261, 1990.

6. M. N. Huhns, editor. *Distributed Artificical Intelligence*. Research Notes in AI. Morgan Kaufmann, 1987.

7. R. Kowalski and F. Sadri. Towards a unified agent architecture that combines rationality with reactivity. In D. Pedreschi and C. Zaniolo, editors, *Logic in Databases*, volume 1154 of *Lecture Notes in Computer Science*. Springer-Verlag, 1996.

8. D. M. Lyons and A. J. Hendricks. A Practical Approach to Integrating Reaction and Deliberation. In *Proceedings of the 1st International Conference on Artifical Intelligence Planning Systems*, 1992.

9. J. P. Müller. *The Design of Intelligent Agents: A Layered Approach*, volume 1177 of *Lecture Notes in Artificial Intelligence*. Springer-Verlag, December 1996.

10. A. Newell. *Unified theories of cognition*. Harvard University Press, Cambridge, London, 1990.

11. A. S. Rao and M. P. Georgeff. An abstract architecture for rational agents. In *Proc. of the 3rd International Conference on Principles of Knowledge Representation and Reasoning (KR'92)*, pages 439–449. Morgan Kaufmann, October 1992.

12. S J. Russel and P. Norvig. *Artificial Intelligence, A Modern Approach*. Prentice Hall, 1995.

13. M. Shanahan. Robotics and the Common Sense Informatic Situation. In W. Wahlster, editor, *Proceedings of the European Conference on Artificial Intelligence (ECAI'96)*, pages 684—688, 1996.

14. G. Smolka. The Definition of Kernel Oz. In A. Podelski, editor, *Constraints: Basics and Trends*. Springer Verlag, 1995.

15. M. Spivey. *The Z Notation (second edition)*. Prentice Hall International, Hempel Hempstead, England, 1992.

16. The Object Management Group. *Universal Networked Objects*. OMG TC Document. Framingham, September 1994.

17. M. Wooldridge. Practical Reasoning with Procedural Knowledge: A Logic of BDI Agents with Know-How. In *Proceedings of the International Conference on Formal and Applied Practical Reasoning*. Springer-Verlag, 1996.

Approximate Reasoning about Combined Knowledge

Frédéric Koriche

LIRMM, UMR 5506, Université Montpellier II CNRS
161, rue Ada. 34392 Montpellier Cedex 5, France
koriche@lirmm.fr

Abstract. Just as cooperation in multi-agent systems is a central issue for solving complex decision problems, so too is the ability for an intelligent agent to reason about combined knowledge, coming from its background knowledge and the communicated information. Specifically, such an agent is confronted with three main difficulties: the prospect of inconsistency which arises when different beliefs are grouped together, the presence of uncertainty which may occur due to not fully reliable beliefs, and the high computational complexity of reasoning with very large pools of collected information. The purpose of this paper is to define a formal framework which handles these three aspects and which is useful to specify resource bounded agents. Based on the concept of approximate reasoning, our framework includes several major features. First, a model checking approach is advocated, which enables an agent to perform decidable reasoning with a first-order representation language. Second, a stepwise procedure is included for improving approximate answers and allowing their convergence to the correct answer. Third and finally, both sound approximations and complete ones are covered. This method is flexible enough for modeling tractable reasoning in very large, inconsistent and uncertain sets of knowledge.

1 Introduction

In recent years, there has been a great deal of interest in the study of *cooperation* between knowledge-based systems, in both the artificial intelligence community and the database community [2,3,5,8,17,19,25,29,33]. Broadly speaking, cooperation is concerned with how multiple components can work interactively, grouping together their pieces of knowledge in order to solve problems that are beyond their individual capabilities. Such components then are characteristic of intelligent, "knowledge level agents". Their information is expressed declaratively, they are capable of sophisticated reasoning and can work independently. However, in order for these agents to cooperate, it is essential for them to communicate each other. Furthermore, in order for them to solve complex problems, they must be able to reason about *combined knowledge*[1] , that is to manage a very large amount of information coming from their background knowledge as well as the communicated information.

For example, the diagnosis of a hospital patient with a difficult case in a health care knowledge-based system often requires to combine the expertise of different specialists.

---

[1] also called *distributed knowledge* in [12,15].

Protein identification by a biological knowledge based system may also need to merge information from multiple knowledge bases: some may use biochemical knowledge (e.g. the sequence of amino-acids), others may use biophysical knowledge (e.g. x-ray crystallographic imaging), while still others may use pharmacological knowledge (e.g. kinetic analysis of enzymatic properties). Some social activities may also rely on combined beliefs. The classical example is that of a police inspector who question different witnesses [3]. Each witness has its own beliefs concerning the crime and the inspector needs to collect all their evidence in order to find the clue. In such cases, a large pool of information spread over a number of agents must be combined in order to solve a global decision task. As pointed out in [8], this combination is not necessary physical and may remain distributed among the different agents. However, cooperation is performed by "virtually" grouping the pool of information present in the multi-agent system.

Several difficulties arise when attempting to reason about combined knowledge. Probably, the most obvious problem is the prospect of *inconsistency*. Even if the local knowledge of each agent is consistent and trustworthy, it is rather unlikely that the set of combined knowledge will be consistent too. Contradictions may occur due to conflicting viewpoints on a common domain of expertise. For example, in the police inspector scenario, the reports of the witnesses may be in conflict over different points concerning the scene of the crime. Such divergent opinions take the form of inconsistencies in the set of combined knowledge. Another reason is the delocalized management of knowledge-based systems. Since the different components are independently developed and managed, their background knowledge remains locally consistent. However, when knowledge must be combined, the problem of global inconsistency arises.

A secondary, but important, difficulty is the prospect of *uncertainty*. Combined knowledge may be uncertain due to the fact that the different beliefs are not equally reliable. In this case, merging beliefs leads to a preference ordering on the set of combined knowledge, where the level of certainty of the sentences reflects the reliability or relevance of the agent's information. For example, a police inspector can assume that a particular witness is less reliable than the others, since he was standing too far away from the scene of the crime. Such a suspicious attitude is reflected by a preference ordering on the communicated beliefs. Uncertainty may also be associated to a local, preexistent preference ordering inside the beliefs of each agent. This is the case when the background knowledge includes defeasible facts and rules which are ranked according to their level of certainty. Provided that these different local orderings are commensurate, the combination of beliefs leads to a pool of uncertain information.

Finally, we have to deal with a problem of *computational complexity*. Even if an agent is able to process information from its background knowledge, it might run out of computing resources for reasoning efficiently within a very large pool of combined information. This problem is exacerbated still further when the agents need at least the expressiveness of first-order logic in order to adequately represent their domain of expertise. For example, "software agents" use a first-order language, the KIF interlingua, for representing and reasoning about the knowledge embedded in software applications [14]. In such circumstances, most of the decisions tasks which are interesting in multi-agents systems are computationally infeasible (polynomially intractable) or even undecidable.

The present paper investigates these three problems; we are interested in defining a formal framework which handles the aspects of consistency, reliability and tractability. In addition, the framework will be used to specify *resource bounded agents* capable of reasoning efficiently about combined knowledge. In order to achieve this goal, the method we present relies on the notion of *approximate reasoning* which integrates three major features.

- The framework is based on the *model checking* approach. This strategy suggested by Halpern and Vardi in [18] offers an elegant compromise to the computational dilemma of knowledge representation. On the one hand, an agent's knowledge can be represented using a very expressive language such as first order logic, and, on the other, the agent can always "check" whether a queried sentence follows from its knowledge. This aspect of *decidability* constitutes here the prime requirement of reasoning about combined knowledge.
- The framework includes *anytime reasoning*. This method is inspired from the idea of "limited inference" proposed by Levesque [21] and recommended in [19,20] among others. In particular, the authors argue that an agent should be able to distinguish what is *explicit* or evident in what he knows, and what is *implicit* and can be inferred provided enough resources. In this study, we expand this idea in model checking approach, using a stepwise method in the sense of Cadoli and Schaerf [6,27] which returns a good approximation to the intended answer at any step, and which guarantees that the approximation gets better with time. In other words, when the agent is faced with simple queries that only involve explicit knowledge, the inference process is guaranteed to terminate quickly. On the other hand, when the agent is confronted with more complex queries, it progressively infers what is implicit in the pool of combined knowledge. So, the appropriateness of inferences is improvable and depends on the computational effort that has been spent.
- The framework covers *dual reasoning*. Specifically, both sound and complete answers are returned at any step; they respectively correspond to the lower and upper bounds of the range of possible conclusions that approximate the correct answer.

The paper is organized as follows. In section 2, we present a functional approach of resource bounded agents that will be used to guide their formal specification. We notably introduce a first-order language and a four-valued semantics for representing combined knowledge. The main contribution of this paper lies in the next two sections, where the concept of approximate reasoning is integrated to the framework. In section 3, we begin to examine the case of consistent and reliable knowledge, and next, we integrate in section 4 the aspects of inconsistency and uncertainty. Related work and future extensions of are discussed in the concluding section.

2 The approach

Before exploring in detail the approach, we explicit several points of terminology. Following [15], a *knowledge level agent* consists of three components: (1) a knowledge base used to store knowledge in a declarative way, (2) an *agent program*, used for logical information processing, and (3) an *architecture*, used to physically interact with the other agents. The collection of all the knowledge bases accessible to an agents via the communication network is called the *combined knowledge base*. This notion is intended to capture the information directly available from the background knowledge of the agent, together with the information accessible by means of communications. Finally, we define a *resource bounded agent* as an agent whose program is constrained by a finite amount of computational resources.

A well known methodology in computer science is to separate what a program computes from how it computes it. On the one hand, the program is specified *functionally* in terms of its input/output behavior, and on the other, it is described *structurally* in terms of internal processes and data structures. In this study, we focus on what an agent program infers from a combined knowledge base, that is its functional representation. Thus, the task of specifying the agent program comes down to defining two components: (1) a *representation language* for describing input information present in knowledge bases, and (2) a systematic input/output relation between what is accessible to the agent and what is inferable given the available computational resources. As usual, this input/output relation is called *entailment*.

In the remaining section, we start the formal treatment by defining a representation language and a suitable semantics. Specifically, we concentrate on a first-order language based on a finite alphabet without function symbols. We notably omit them because their introduction leads to severe difficulties for model checking. Fortunately, they are not required for most of the current formalizations of databases and knowledge bases (see e.g. [1]). Furthermore, the practical purpose of this language is quite different from the use of epistemic logics in multi-agent systems [9,12,15]. In the setting suggested by our approach, this language is to be thought of as directly representing the information conveyed by the knowledge bases and processed by the agent programs. So, the notions of "quantifying-in" and "introspection" related to meta-knowledge are not examined here; their issue is deferred to the forthcoming sequel.

2.1 Syntax

We consider a first order language $\mathcal{L}_W$ constructed from a *workspace* $W = (C, R)$ consisting of a finite set C of constants, and a finite set R of relations. In particular, R is provided a distinguished binary relation $=$ which will function for us as equality. Additionally, the language contains a countable set of variables. Given the usual notions of terms and atoms, a ground atom is an atom where all terms are constants. The finite collection of all ground atoms is denoted $\mathcal{G}_W$. The formulae of $\mathcal{L}_W$ are built up in the classical way from the atoms, the connectives $\wedge, \vee, \neg$ and the quantifiers $\forall, \exists$. As usual, a *sentence* is a closed formula. A *knowledge base* is a finite set of sentences, identified with the conjunction of formulae it contains. A *combined knowledge base* is a finite union of knowledge bases, identified by the conjunction of these bases.

In the remaining paper, ground atoms are denoted by lowercase Latin letters and sentences are denoted by Greek letters. Uppercase Latin letters stand for knowledge bases (possibly combined). The *size* of a sentence ϕ, denoted $|\phi|$, is defined by counting all ground atoms in all ground instantiations of ϕ, and the size of a knowledge base A, denoted $|A|$, is defined as the sum over the sizes of its sentences.

Example 1. The police investigation example [3] will be used, in several variants, as the running example throughout the paper. The scenario consists of a police inspector questioning two witnesses, Bill and John, who have contradictory beliefs concerning the crime. Three people are suspected, Ed, Fred and Tom. The inspector possesses some hypothesis concerning the possible murderer. In addition, he is provided integrity constraints for performing inferences and detecting contradictions. We assume that the knowledge bases specified below are parts of very large belief sets containing information about the suspects and the surrounding situation. The bases use a small workspace $W = (C, R)$, which we also assume to be part of a larger universe of discourse.

$$C \quad = \{Car, Coat, Hat, Ed, Fred, Tom\};$$
$$R \quad = \{black, hascar, hascoat, hashat, murderer, white, =\};$$

$$A_{Bill} \quad = \begin{cases} white(Car), \\ \neg black(Coat), \\ white(Car) \vee \neg hascar(Fred, Car), \\ \neg black(Car) \vee \neg hascar(Ed, Car) \vee \neg hascar(Tom, Car), \\ \neg black(Coat) \vee hascoat(Fred, Coat) \vee hascoat(Tom, Coat). \end{cases}$$

$$A_{John} \quad = \begin{cases} black(Car), \\ black(Coat), \\ \neg black(Car) \vee hascar(Ed, Car), \\ \neg black(Coat) \vee \neg hascoat(Fred, Coat), \\ white(Hat) \vee \neg hashat(Ed, Hat). \end{cases}$$

$$A_{Inspector} = \begin{cases} Car = Car, \\ murderer(Ed) \vee murderer(Fred) \vee murderer(Tom), \\ (\forall x)(\forall y) \neg white(x) \vee \neg black(y) \vee \neg(x = y), \\ (\forall x) hascar(x, Car) \vee \neg murderer(x), \\ (\forall x) hascoat(x, Coat) \vee \neg murderer(x). \end{cases}$$

2.2 Semantics

The basic building block of the semantics is a domain T of truth values which determines the interpretation of sentences and the properties of entailment relations. In the context of limited reasoning, the four valued semantics proposed by Dunn [10] and Belnap [4], and more recently studied in [19–21], meets our needs. It is a simple modification of classical interpretation in which sentences take as truth-values subsets of $\{0, 1\}$, instead simply either 0 or 1 alone.

To be precise, the starting point of the semantics may be defined by a algebraic structure $(T, \leq_t, \leq_i)$, where T is the power-set of $\{0, 1\}$, and $\leq_t, \leq_i$ are partial orderings giving T the structure of a bilattice. In what follows, the truth values $\emptyset$, $\{0\}$, $\{1\}$ and $\{0, 1\}$ are respectively denoted $\bot$, 0, 1 and $\top$. The relations $\leq_t$ and $\leq_i$ are called *truth ordering* and *information ordering*. Their bottom elements are respectively given by 0 and $\bot$. Meet and join under the truth-ordering are denoted $\wedge$ and $\vee$, and directly provide a four valued interpretation for conjunction and disjunction. Negation can also be defined directly by an idempotent operation ¬ which reverses $\leq_t$ and leaves unchanged $\leq_i$. A key characteristic of this structure is that the operations ∧, ∨ and ¬ are *monotone* with respect to $\leq_i$. As we shall see in the next sections, this property plays an important role in the specification of approximate reasoning.

Based on this structure, we define an *interpretation* as a total function v form $\mathcal{G}_W$ to T. Intuitively, interpretations can be seen as generalizations of classical Herbrand interpretations. Namely, the truth values assigned to an atom and its negation are not necessarily complementary. The finite set of interpretations generated from the collection of all ground atoms $\mathcal{G}_W$ is denoted $\mathcal{V}_W$. We remark that this set inherits the structure of a bilattice under the pointwise orderings $\leq_t$ and $\leq_i$. A standard or *Herbrand interpretation* is an interpretation which maps every ground atom $p \in \mathcal{G}_W$ into 1 or 0. The set of all Herbrand interpretations is denoted $\mathcal{H}_W$. Now we can provide a four-valued semantics to our representation language.

Definition 2. Given an interpretation v, an *extended interpretation* is a function, also denoted v, from sentences of $\mathcal{L}_W$ to T, defined inductively by the following clauses:

$$v(\neg\phi) = \neg v(\phi), \tag{1}$$

$$v(\phi \vee \psi) = v(\phi) \vee v(\psi), \tag{2}$$

$$v(\phi \wedge \psi) = v(\phi) \wedge v(\psi), \tag{3}$$

$$v((\exists x)\phi(x)) = \bigvee \{v(\phi(c)) : c \in C\}, \tag{4}$$

$$v((\forall x)\phi(x)) = \bigwedge \{v(\phi(c)) : c \in C\}. \tag{5}$$

3 Reasoning about consistent and reliable knowledge

In this section, we restrict attention to consistent and certain sets of combined knowledge. The motivation here is to understand and to model the ability of resource bounded agents to perform useful inferences within very large pools of communicated sentences. Efficient reasoning relies on two important notions, namely, decidability and tractability. We first examine decidable reasoning, and next, we introduce the concept of approximation for assessing tractability.

3.1 Decidable reasoning

As stated in introduction, decidability constitutes the prime characteristic of the properties of knowledge. Specifically, an agent knows a given sentence if its program can determine whether this sentence is a logical consequence of its knowledge base. This notion of logical consequence corresponds here to the standard "tarskian entailment" relation, which allows an agent to recognize what is implicit in its pool of combined knowledge. At this very point, the classical proposal in literature is to specify tarskian entailment using a theorem-proving approach. Unfortunately, it is known that there exists no algorithm at all which generally decides logical consequence in first-order logic, and this remains true even when languages with finite workspaces, such as $\mathcal{L}_W$, are taken into consideration [31].

An alternative to this problem is to adopt the model-checking approach stressed by Halpern and Vardi [18]. Here an agent knows a particular sentence if its program can check whether all standard interpretations which satisfy the knowledge base also satisfy the sentence. Since in the present study the set of Herbrand interpretations $\mathcal{H}_W$ is finite, the model checking algorithm is guaranteed to terminate in finite time. Following this approach, we first review the notion of standard satisfiability. A sentence ϕ is *satisfiable* if there exists an Herbrand interpretation v such that $v(\phi) = 1$. Now, we can formally specify agent programs which are capable of decidable reasoning.

Definition 3. A *decidable agent program* is a structure $(\mathcal{L}_W, \models)$ where $\mathcal{L}_W$ is a representation language and $\models$ is a binary relation from knowledge bases of $\mathcal{L}_W$ to sentences of $\mathcal{L}_W$, defined by the following condition:

$$A \models \phi \text{ iff } A \wedge \neg\phi \text{ is unsatisfiable.}$$

3.2 Approximate reasoning

A second important aspect in the specification of resource-bounded agents is tractability. Clearly, decidability is a necessary but not sufficient condition for tractable reasoning. In fact, first-order model checking is known to be solvable in polynomial space [7,32]; hence this problem, although decidable, is still very hard to solve for real agents. Since the model checking approach does not take into account the computational resources of an agent, it is essential to make formal steps in this direction.

Our motivation is to provide a systematic method to control exploration in the large space of possibilities $\mathcal{H}_W$. Essentially, the method we present relies on the definition of smaller sets of interpretations which correspond to a limited exploration. These sets are determined by a *resource parameter* S, a subset of $\mathcal{G}_W$, which captures the computational resources of an agent. Furthermore, anytime reasoning is incorporated by including "sequences" of these sets which gradually approximate the space $\mathcal{H}_W$. The quality of the approximation improves with larger resource parameters, and eventually converges to the correct answer. Finally, since both sound approximations and complete ones are covered, two sequences of sets of interpretations are included, the first ones being correct and the second ones being complete wrt standard entailment. To sum up, the stepwise method consists in generating two sequences of increasing search spaces, which can be interrupted at any time, and which return both approximations "from above" and "from below".

Based on these considerations, we include the following additional definitions. A S^+ *interpretation* is an interpretation which maps every ground atom p of S into 1 or 0. Furthermore, it maps every ground atom p not in S into $\top$. The notion of extended S^+ interpretation is defined by means of the five clauses presented in definition 2. Dually, a S^- *interpretation* is an interpretation which maps every ground atom p of S into 1 or 0. Moreover, it maps every ground atom p not in S into $\bot$. Let $C(S)$ denotes the set of all constants which appear in atoms of S. We define extended S^- interpretations by means of the first four clauses used in definition 2 and the following:

$$v((\forall x)\phi(x)) = \begin{cases} \bot & \text{if } S = \emptyset, \\ \bigwedge\{v(\phi(c)) : c \in C(S)\} & \text{otherwise.} \end{cases} \tag{5'}$$

The notion of "approximate satisfiability" is defined as follows. A sentence ϕ is S^+ *satisfiable* if there exists a S^+ interpretation v such that $v(\phi) \geq_i 1$. Finally, ϕ is S^- *satisfiable* if there exists a S^- interpretation v such that $v(\phi) \geq_i 1$. Now we can specify approximate reasoning with consistent and reliable sets of knowledge.

Definition 4. An *approximate agent program* is a structure $(\mathcal{L}_W, \models_S^+, \models_S^-)$ consisting of a language $\mathcal{L}_W$ and two binary relations $\models_S^+$ and $\models_S^-$ from finite sets of sentences of $\mathcal{L}_W$ to sentences of $\mathcal{L}_W$, respectively defined as follows:

$$A \models_S^+ \phi \text{ iff } A \wedge \neg\phi \text{ is } S^+ \text{unsatisfiable, and}$$
$$A \models_S^- \phi \text{ iff } A \wedge \neg\phi \text{ is } S^- \text{unsatisfiable.}$$

The reasoning process of a resource-bounded agent is performed in an incremental fashion by gradually accumulating implicit information. Specifically, the process is defined by an increasing sequence of resource parameters:

$$\langle S_0 = \emptyset \cdots \subset S_i \cdots \subset S_n = \mathcal{G}_W \rangle,$$

which approximates the set $\mathcal{H}_W$ by means of two dual families of sets:

$$\mathcal{V}_i^+ = \{v : v \text{ is a } S^+ \text{interpretation}\} \text{ and } \mathcal{V}_i^- = \{v : v \text{ is a } S^- \text{interpretation}\}.$$

In algebraic terms, the interpretations generated by these sets are dual with respect to the information ordering $\leq_i$. The first ones gradually "loose information" while the second ones progressively "gain information". The three following properties clarify the interest of the method.

Proposition 5 (Monotonicity). *For any S and S' such that $S \subseteq S' \subseteq \mathcal{G}_W$, if $A \models_S^+ \phi$, then $A \models_{S'}^+ \phi$. Furthermore, if $A \not\models_S^- \phi$, then $A \not\models_{S'}^- \phi$.*

Proof. Let ψ denotes the sentence $A \wedge \neg\phi$. We split the proof into two parts. We first prove that if ψ is S^+ unsatisfiable then ψ is S'^+ unsatisfiable. Next, we prove that if ψ is S^- satisfiable then ψ is S'^- satisfiable.

– Let us examine the first part. ψ is S^+ unsatisfiable iff for each S^+ interpretation v, $v(\psi) <_i 1$. Furthermore, it is easy to notice that if $S \subseteq S'$ then for each S'^+ interpretation v', there must exist a S^+ interpretation v such that $v' \leq_i v$. Taking into account the monotonicity property of the bilattice $\mathcal{V}_W$, it is always the case that $v' \leq_i v$ iff $v'(\psi) \leq_i v(\psi)$. Therefore, if $v(\psi) <_i 1$ then it follows that $v'(\psi) <_i 1$.
– Now we turn to the second part. Dual considerations hold here, and the only nontrivial case is when ψ contains a sentence of the form $(\forall x)\psi'(x)$. Assume that ψ is S^- satisfiable and ψ is S'^- unsatisfiable. Therefore, there must exist a constant c such that $c \notin C(S)$, $c \in C(S')$ and $\psi'(c)$ is S'^- unsatisfiable. So, both $\psi'(c)$ and $\neg\psi'(c)$ must occur in the sentence ψ. However $(\forall x)\psi'(x)$ cannot be inconsistent because it would be S^- unsatisfiable, so either $\psi'(c)$ or $\neg\psi'(c)$ must belong to the remaining sentence ψ. But in this case $c \in C(S)$, hence contradiction.

Proposition 6 (Convergence). *If $A \models \phi$, then there exists an $S \subseteq \mathcal{G}_W$ such that $A \models_S^+ \phi$. Furthermore, if $A \not\models \phi$, then there exists an $S \subseteq \mathcal{G}_W$ such that $A \not\models_S^- \phi$.*

Proposition 7 (Complexity). *There exists an algorithm for deciding whether the sentence ϕ is S^+ satisfiable and ϕ is S^- satisfiable which runs in $O(|\phi| \cdot 2^{|S|})$ time.*

Proof. For each interpretation $v \in \mathcal{V}_W$, the truth value $v(\phi)$ can be determined in $O(|\phi|)$ time. Since a set S generates $2^{|S|}$ possible interpretations, S^+ satisfiability and S^- satisfiability of a sentence ϕ can be checked in $O(|\phi| \cdot 2^{|S|})$ time.

It is important to emphasize that the parameter S plays a key part in the formalization of resource-bounded agents. The underlying idea is that only some of the ground atoms are examined while others are ignored. Such an intuition is widespread in the metareasoning literature (see e.g. [6,22,27,30]). In particular, similar deductive strategies may be applied for choosing a parameter for which we have high expectation of having correct answers. For a combined knowledge base in a clausal form A and a given query ϕ, S^+ satisfiability models a backward chaining technique which is used in resolution-based algorithms. Namely, we try to prove unsatisfiability of the sentence $A \wedge \neg\phi$ by deriving in a stepwise way the empty clause ; for a given step i, we resolve only clauses having literals whose ground atoms belong to S_i. Dually, S^- satisfiability models a search strategy which is used in enumeration-based algorithms. We try here to prove satisfiability of the sentence $A \wedge \neg\phi$ by generating in an iterative way an interpretation which satisfy this sentence ; for a given step i, we assign to the sentence an interpretation that is consistent with clauses having literals whose atoms belong to S_i.

Such stepwise procedures model a local form of reasoning in which part of the set of knowledge is ignored on purpose. They have an important advantage that the computation may be stopped when a correct answer is obtained for a small size of S. This yields a potentially drastic reduction of computational costs. In the following, we show an example in which the notion of S^- satisfiability is used.

Example 8. Let us consider the police investigation scenario of example 1. Suppose that only Bill is questioned by the inspector. So, the combined knowledge base C is given by $A_{Inspector} \wedge A_{Bill}$. Assume further that the inspector want to prove that Ed "is not" the murderer. In other words, we want to verify that $C \not\models murderer(Ed)$ holds. The goal is thus to determine a resource parameter S such that $C \not\models_S^- murderer(Ed)$ holds. Using the instantiations of the relations $black$ and $murderer$ over the atoms Car, $Coat$ and Ed, together with the ground atoms $Car = Car$, $white(Car)$, $hascar(Ed, Car)$ and $hascoat(Ed, Coat)$ we obtain a set S of size 10, and such that $C \not\models_S^- murderer(Ed)$ holds. Notice that this value is very small compared to $|\mathcal{G}_W| = 162$.

4 Reasoning about inconsistent and uncertain knowledge

In this section, we extend the concepts developed so far to the generalized case of inconsistent and possibly uncertain pools of combined knowledge. In particular, we are interested in analyzing not what is directly accessible in the multi-agent system, but "what the set of combined knowledge would be like if contradictions where removed". As previously, we begin to focus on decidable reasoning, and next, we examine approximate reasoning.

4.1 Decidable reasoning

A central issue in formal representations of combined knowledge is the choice of an appropriate semantics for inconsistent theories. We recall that classical logic is clearly inappropriate in this setting since it entails everything, if indeed there is a contradiction in the theory. However, a more plausible principle may use the following strategy: first, find all maximal consistent subsets of the inconsistent theory; next, take the closure of each subset under the classical entailment, and then, conclude only the sentences which are in the intersection of all the closures. Many semantics use this *cautious* principle. This includes notably the framework of Rescher and Manor [26] which has been recommended in the areas of belief update [13], belief base revision [16,24], and combined knowledge [2,17]. If all pieces of information in the environment are equally reliable, this principle can be specified by a mapping $\triangle$, which we call *cautious scheme*, from finite sets of sentences of $\mathcal{L}_W$ to sentences of $\mathcal{L}_W$ and defined as follows:

$$\triangle(A) = \bigcap max(\{B \subseteq A : B \text{ is satisfiable}\}, \subseteq).$$

However, in most applications, agents need to distinguish the relevance or level of certainty of communicated information (see e.g. [3,5,8,25,33]). This idea of assigning different priorities to sentences can be formalized by employing an ordering over the formulae in the set of combined knowledge. Since we consider only finite bases, this can be done by partitioning a combined knowledge base C into a finite number n of priority classes C_i, with the understanding that, for $i \leq j \leq n$, the sentences in class C_i are less reliable or relevant than the sentences in class C_j. Additionally, the priority class of any sub-base A of C is given by the smaller priority class of its elements. The associated strict partial order defined by $B <_p A$ if and only if the priority class of B is smaller than A's, is called *priority order*. This relation can be refined to extend set containment in a straightforward way by setting $B \preceq_p A$ if and only if $B <_p A$ or $B \subseteq A$. The resulting partial preorder $\preceq_p$ is called *priority preorder*. With these definitions in hand, we can define a *prioritized cautious scheme* $\triangle_p$ as follows:

$$\triangle_p(A) = \bigcap max(\{B \preceq_p A : B \text{ is satisfiable}\}, \preceq_p).$$

Based on these sophistications, we can specify in a formal setting decidable reasoning in presence of inconsistency and uncertainty.

Definition 9. A *decidable prioritized cautious agent program* is a structure $(\mathcal{L}_W, \models_p)$ where $\mathcal{L}_W$ is a representation language, and $\models_p$ is a binary relation from finite sets of sentences of $\mathcal{L}_W$ to sentences of $\mathcal{L}_W$ defined as follows:

$$A \models_p \phi \text{ iff } \triangle_p(A) \models \phi.$$

4.2 Approximate reasoning

Now, we turn to the formalization of approximate reasoning. From this point of view, it is interesting to notice that cautious reasoning, possibly prioritized, corresponds neatly to revising a knowledge base, in the sence of [16,24], with the sentence "true", which indeed eliminates inconsistency. However, it has been recently proved that deciding whether a sentence belongs to such a revised knowledge base is a Π_2^P complete problem in the propositional case [11]. In other words, it seems impossible to solve it by a polynomial number of entailment checks. Actually, the cautious principle advocated for removing contradictions has two independent sources of complexity. Roughly speaking, the first source is caused by the complexity of deciding entailment (exponential), while the second is caused by the very large number of choices that we have in general in order to make a combined knowledge base consistent.

The key idea for approximating such a decision problem is to reduce both sources of complexity. Since in section 3 we have introduced a method for approximating standard entailment, we concentrate here on a suitable way to limit the combinatorial explosion of maximal consistent subsets. This can be done by parameterizing the set $\triangle_p(A)$ by the means of two families of sets $\triangle_{p \cdot S}^-(A)$ and $\triangle_{p \cdot S}^+(A)$, the first one being sound, while the second one being complete wrt prioritized cautious reasoning. The corresponding "approximation schemes" are defined as follows:

$$\triangle_{p \cdot S}^-(A) = \bigcap max(\{B \preceq_p A : B \text{ is } S^- \text{satisfiable}\}, \preceq_p), \text{ and}$$

$$\triangle_{p \cdot S}^+(A) = \bigcap max(\{B \preceq_p A : B \text{ is } S^+ \text{satisfiable}\}, \preceq_p).$$

The resource parameter S controls the quality of the generated knowledge bases. Notice that the signs are reversed here. Specifically, $\triangle_{p \cdot S}^+(A)$ is a superset of $\triangle_p(A)$, since S^+ satisfiability is "weaker" than standard satisfiability. As far as $\triangle_{p \cdot S}^-(A)$ is concerned, dual considerations hold ; $\triangle_{p \cdot S}^-(A)$ is a subset of $\triangle_p(A)$, since S^- satisfiability is "stronger" than standard satisfiability. The two families of schemes correspond to the so called dual forms of nonmonotonic reasoning. For a given parameter S, the scheme $\triangle_{p \cdot S}^+(A)$ accounts for credulous reasoner, while the scheme $\triangle_{p \cdot S}^-(A)$ accounts for a skeptical one. Now we have the formal tools for specifying approximate reasoning in presence of inconsistent and uncertain knowledge.

Definition 10. An *approximate prioritized cautious agent program* consists of a structure $(\mathcal{L}_W, \models_{p \cdot S}^+, \models_{p \cdot S}^-)$ where $\mathcal{L}_W$ is a representation language, and $\models_{p \cdot S}^+$ and $\models_{p \cdot S}^-$ are two binary relations from finite sets of sentences of $\mathcal{L}_W$ to sentences of $\mathcal{L}_W$, respectively defined as follows:

$$A \models_{p \cdot S}^+ \phi \text{ iff } \triangle_{p \cdot S}^-(A) \models_S^+ \phi, \text{ and}$$

$$A \models_{p \cdot S}^- \phi \text{ iff } \triangle_{p \cdot S}^+(A) \models_S^- \phi.$$

Based on this definition, we extend the results examined in the preceding section. The next two propositions claim that the properties of monotonicity and convergence are preserved in the case of prioritized cautious entailment. As shown in the proof, this directly follows from the monotonicity of approximate satisfiability. Furthermore, the complexity result presented in the third proposition states that the number of maximal consistent subsets generated from the approximation schemes is bounded by $2^{|S|}$. Since the computational cost of checking entailment is also bounded by $2^{|S|}$, both sources of complexity are bounded by the resource parameter S. This captures in a single notation the epistemic properties of resource bounded agents.

Proposition 11 (Monotonicity). *For any S and S' such that $S \subseteq S' \subseteq \mathcal{G}_W$, if $A \models^+_{p \cdot S} \phi$, then $A \models^+_{p \cdot S'} \phi$. Furthermore, if $A \not\models^-_{p \cdot S} \phi$, then $A \not\models^-_{p \cdot S'} \phi$.*

Proof. We divide the proof into two parts. First of all we prove, at the same time, that (i) if $S \subseteq S'$ then $\triangle^+_{p \cdot S}(A) \supseteq \triangle^+_{p \cdot S'}(A)$, and (ii) if $S \subseteq S'$ then $\triangle^-_{p \cdot S}(A) \subseteq \triangle^-_{p \cdot S'}(A)$. In the second part we prove, at the same time, that (iii) if $S \subseteq S'$ and $A \subseteq A'$ then A is S^+unsatisfiable implies A' is S'^+unsatisfiable, and (iv) if $S \subseteq S'$ and $A \supseteq A'$ then A is S^-satisfiable implies A' is S'^-satisfiable. The first part of the proposition follows from the lemmas (ii) and (iii), while the second part follows from the lemmas (i) and (iv).

- We begin to prove lemma (i). A knowledge base B belongs to $\triangle^+_{p \cdot S}(A)$ iff B is a maximal subset such that $B \preceq_p A$ and B is S^+satisfiable. Since the preorder $\preceq_p$ is the same for the approximate schemes, $\triangle^+_{p \cdot S}(A) \supseteq \triangle^+_{p \cdot S'}(A)$ holds iff B is S'^+satisfiable implies B is S^+satisfiable. By using contraposition, this directly follows from proposition 5. A dual argument applies to lemma (ii).
- We now prove lemma (iii). A knowledge base A is S^+unsatisfiable iff for each S^+interpretation v, we have $v(A) = 0$. Since $A' \supseteq A$, for any sentence $\psi \in A'$, we have $v(A \wedge \psi) = 0$. So, A' is S^+unsatisfiable, and from proposition 5 it follows that A' is S'^+unsatisfiable. Dual considerations hold for lemma (iv).

Proposition 12 (Convergence). *If $A \models_p \phi$, then there exists an $S \subseteq \mathcal{G}_W$ such that $A \models^+_{p \cdot S} \phi$. Further if $A \not\models_p \phi$, then there exists an $S \subseteq \mathcal{G}_W$ such that $A \not\models^-_{p \cdot S} \phi$.*

Proposition 13 (Complexity). *There exists an algorithm for computing $\triangle^-_{p \cdot S}(A)$ and $\triangle^+_{p \cdot S}(A)$ which runs in $O(|A| \cdot 2^{|S|})$ time.*

Proof. We split the proof into two parts. First, we prove that for a given knowledge base A, it is always the case that $\triangle^+_{p \cdot S}(A) \subseteq \triangle^+_S(A)$, and $\triangle^-_{p \cdot S}(A) \subseteq \triangle^-_S(A)$. Second, we prove that $\triangle^+_S(A)$ and $\triangle^-_S(A)$ have at most $2^{|S|}$ sets of sentences.

- Let us consider the first part. Suppose that there is a S^+satisfiable base B such that $B \in \triangle^+_{p \cdot S}(A)$ but $B \notin \triangle^+_S(A)$. Notice that if $B \in \triangle^+_{p \cdot S}(A)$ then there is no S^+satisfiable base B' such that $B \subset B'$ or $B <_p B'$. However if $B \notin \triangle^+_S(A)$ then there exists a S^+satisfiable base B'' such that $B \subset B''$, hence contradiction. The same argument applies to $\triangle^-_{p \cdot S}(A)$ and $\triangle^-_S(A)$.
- Now we turn to the second part. First of all, given two knowledge bases B and B' such that $B, B' \in \triangle^+_S(A)$, then it is easy to show that their union $B \cup B'$ is S^+unsatisfiable. Let $M^+_S(B)$ and $M^+_S(B')$ denote the S^+interpretations satisfying B and B'. $B \cup B'$ is S^+unsatisfiable iff $M^+_S(B) \cap M^+_S(B') = \emptyset$. Since there exists $2^{|S|}$ S^+interpretations, the maximum number of bases being locally S^+satisfiable and pairwise S^+unsatisfiable is $2^{|S|}$. The proof is the same for $\triangle^-_S(A)$.

Example 14. Consider again the scenario of example 1. We now suppose that both witnesses are talking to the inspector. So, the combined knowledge base C is given by $A_{Bill} \wedge A_{John} \wedge A_{Inspector}$. Suppose further that the inspector possesses some extra-information about the reliability of witnesses. For instance, he knows that the crime was committed on a foggy day and Bill was standing too far away from the scene of the crime. So Bill is less reliable than John. This can be done by assigning a smaller certainty level to the facts $white(Car)$ and $\neg black(Coat)$. Using the instantiations of the relation $murderer$ over the atoms Car, $Coat$, Ed, $Fred$ and Tom, together with the ground atoms $black(Car)$, $black(Coat)$, $hascar(Ed, Car)$, $hascar(Tom, Car)$, $hascoat(Ed, Coat)$ and $hascoat(Fred, Coat)$, we obtain a set S of size 11, and such that $C \models^+_{p \cdot S} murderer(Ed)$ holds.

5 Conclusion

In this paper, we have dealt with the problem of reasoning about combined knowledge in multi-agent systems by focusing on three central difficulties. The first is the prospect of inconsistency, which arises when different beliefs are merged together. The second is the occurrence of uncertainty which may arises due to not fully reliable beliefs. The third is the high computational complexity of logical reasoning about very large pools of combined information. Our aim was to provide a formal, logic oriented framework which treats suitably these aspects and that enables us to specify resource bounded agents. Based on the concept of approximate reasoning, we have illustrated that our framework integrates several major features: expressiveness, decidability, improvability and dual reasoning. We have first examined reasoning about consistent and reliable knowledge, and next, we have extended the framework for both aspects of inconsistency and uncertainty. For each problem category, we have integrated a reasonable way to reason accurately and efficiently with combined information.

In the context of related work, our study was mainly inspired from two currently disjoint research fields. The first is concerned by tractable approaches of knowledge representation. Standard techniques such as language restriction (e.g. [23]) or knowledge compilation (e.g. [28]) are ill-suited in this setting. Notably, they use classical logic and thus become fragile when contradictions appear within a pool of combined information. Furthermore, the technique of language restriction is not adequate for modeling agents that need at least the expressiveness of first-order logic for representing knowledge [14]. In this study, we have used the paradigm of limited reasoning suggested by Levesque [21]. We have notably stressed on anytime algorithms based on the model checking approach [18] which expands in several directions the framework proposed by Cadoli and Schaerf in [6,27].

The second field is concerned by the problem of reasoning with inconsistent knowledge. In this setting, the standard proposal in literature is to preserve classical logic but to eliminate contradictions in order not to collapse. Most of the proposed techniques privilege maximal consistent subsets [2,17]; they notably extend this conflict-resolution principle by using "extra-logical" information such as integrity constraints [3], degrees of priority [5,25], preference orderings [33] and reliability orderings of sources [8]. The present study adopts an integrated approach, notably inspired from techniques of belief base update and revision [13,16,24].

We believe that the results reported here are interesting and worth of further investigations. We outline some of them. A first extension is to incorporate more complex forms of knowledge in our framework. One of these are *quantifying-in* which allows an agent to make distinctions such as "knowing that" versus "knowing who" (see e.g. [15,20]). *Introspection* is another important property of intelligent agents which enables them to be aware of what they know and what they do not know. An important issue here is the problem of combining such pieces of knowledge in a multi-agent setting and reasoning efficiently with them. In this setting, an interesting starting point is the study presented in [9] which examines the computational properties of reasoners using epistemic logics. A second extension concerns the "heuristic" analysis of resource-bounded agents. The parameter S is reminiscent to anytime algorithms based on limited reasoning [6,19,27,30]. Intelligent control strategies inspired from commonsense reasoning and logic programming will certainly help for an appropriate choice of this parameter. A third possible extension is to consider *coordination* and *negotiation* between resource-bounded agents. These notions should play an important role in decision making tasks by allocating some agents to specific resource parameters, exchanging approximate results and negotiating conflicting conclusions.

References

1. S. Abiteboul, R. Hull, and V. Vianu. *Foundations of Databases*. Addison-Wesley, Reading, Mass., 1995.

2. C. Baral, S. Kraus, and J. Minker. Combining multiple knowledge bases. *IEEE Transactions on Knowledge and Data Engineering*, 3(2):208–220, 1991.

3. C. Baral, S. Kraus, J. Minker, and V. S. Subrahmanian. Combining knowledge bases consisting of first order theories. *Computational Intelligence*, 8(1):45–71, 1992.

4. N. D. Belnap. A useful four-valued logic. In J. M. Dunn and G. Epstein, editors, *Modern Uses of Multiple-valued Logic*, pages 8–37. Reidel, Dordrecht, 1977.

5. S. Benferhat, D. Dubois, and H. Prade. How to infer form inconsistent beliefs without revising ? In *Proceedings of the 14th International Joint Conference on Artificial Intelligence (IJCAI-95)*, pages 1449–1455, Toronto, Canada, 1995. Morgan Kaufmann.

6. M. Cadoli and M. Schaerf. Approximate inference in default reasoning and circumscription. In B. Neumann, editor, *Proceedings 10th European Conference on Artificial Intelligence (ECAI-92)*, pages 319–323, Vienna, Austria, 1992. John Wiley & Sons.

7. A. K. Chandra and P. M. Merlin. Optimal implementation of conjunctive queries in relational databases. In *Proceedings 9th Annual ACM Symposium on the Theory of Computing*, pages 77–90, New York, 1977.

8. L. Cholvy. Proving theorems in a multi-source environment. In *Proceedings 13th International Joint Conference on Artificial Intelligence (IJCAI-93)*, pages 66–71, Chambéry, France, 1993. Morgan Kaufmann.

9. H. N. Duc. On the epistemic foundations of agent theories. In *this volume*.

10. J. M. Dunn. Intuitive semantics for first-degree entailments and coupled trees. *Philosophical Studies*, 29:149–168, 1976.

11. T. Eiter and G. Gottlob. On the complexity of propositional knowledge base revision, updates, and counterfactuals. *Artificial Intelligence*, 57(2-3):227–270, 1992.

12. R. Fagin, J. Y. Halpern, Y. Moses, and M. Y. Vardi. *Reasoning About Knowledge*. MIT-Press, Cambridge (MA), 1995.

13. R. Fagin, J. D. Ullman, and M. Y. Vardi. On the semantics of updates in databases. In *Proceedings of the Second ACM SIGACT-SIGMOD Symposium on Principles of Database Systems*, pages 352–365, Atlanta, (GA), 1983.

14. M. R. Genesereth and S. P. Ketchpel. Software agents. *Communications of the ACM*, 37(7):49–53, 1994.

15. M. R. Genesereth and N. J. Nilsson. *Logical Foundations of Artificial Intelligence*. Morgan Kaufmann, Palo Alto (CA), 1987.

16. M. L. Ginsberg. Counterfactuals. *Artificial Intelligence*, 30(1):35–79, 1986.

17. J. Grant and V. S. Subrahmanian. Reasoning in inconsistent knowledge bases. Technical Report UMIACS-TR-90-118, Department of Computer Science, University of Maryland, 1990.

18. J. Y. Halpern and M. Y. Vardi. Model checking vs. theorem proving: A manifesto. In J. Allen, R. Fikes, and E. Sandewall, editors, *Proceedings of the 2nd International Conference on Principles of Knowledge Representation and Reasoning*, pages 325–334, San Mateo, CA, USA, 1991. Morgan Kaufmann Publishers.

19. F. Koriche. Fault-tolerant and approximate reasoning in multi-source environments. In A. L. P. Chen, W. Klas, and M. P. Singh, editors, *Proceedings of the Second IFCIS International Conference on Cooperative Information Systems (CoopIS-97)*, pages 66–72, Kiawah Island (SC), 1997. IEEE Computer Society.

20. G. Lakemeyer. Limited reasoning in first-order knowledge bases. *Artificial Intelligence*, 71:213–255, 1994.

21. H. J. Levesque. A logic of implicit and explicit belief. In R. J. Brachman, editor, *Proceedings of the 6th National Conference on Artificial Intelligence*, pages 198–202, Austin, Texas, 1984. William Kaufmann.

22. H. J. Levesque. A knowledge-level account of abduction. In N. S. Sridharan, editor, *Proceedings of the 11th International Joint Conference on Artificial Intelligence*, pages 1061–1067, Detroit (MI), 1989. Morgan Kaufmann.

23. H. J. Levesque and R. J. Brachman. Expressiveness and tractability in knowledge representation and reasoning. *Computational Intelligence*, 3(2):78–93, 1987.

24. B. Nebel. Belief revision and default reasoning: Syntax-based approaches. In J. Allen, R. Fikes, and E. Sandewall, editors, *Proceedings of the 2nd International Conference on Principles of Knowledge Representation and Reasoning*, pages 417–428, San Mateo (CA), 1991. Morgan Kaufmann.

25. S. Pradhan and J. Minker. Using priorities to combine knowledge bases. *International Journal of Cooperative Information Systems*, 5(2–3):333–364, 1996.

26. N. Rescher and R. Manor. On inference from inconsistent premises. *Theory and Decision*, 1:179–217, 1970.

27. M. Schaerf and M. Cadoli. Tractable reasoning via approximation. *Artificial Intelligence*, 74:249–310, 1995.

28. B. Selman and H. Kautz. Knowledge compilation and theory approximation. *Journal of the ACM*, 43(2):193–224, 1996.

29. V. S. Subrahmanian. Amalgamating knowledge bases. *ACM Transactions on Database Systems*, 19(2):291–331, 1994.

30. A. ten Teije and F. van Harmelen. Computing approximate diagnoses by using approximate entailment. In L. C. Aiello, J. Doyle, and S. Shapiro, editors, *Proceedings of the Fifth International Conference on Principles of Knowledge Representation and Reasoning*, pages 256–267, San Francisco (CA), 1996. Morgan Kaufmann.

31. B. A. Trahtenbrot. Impossibility of an algorithm for the decision problem in finite classes. *American Mathematical Society Translation Series*, 23(2):1–5, 1963.

32. M. Y. Vardi. The complexity of relational query languages. In *ACM Symposion on Theory of Computation*, pages 137–146, Baltimore, (MA), 1982. ACM Press.

33. S. T. C. Wong. Preference-based decision making for cooperative knowledge-based systems. *ACM Transactions on Information Systems*, 12(4):407–435, 1994.

On the Epistemic Foundations of Agent Theories

Ho Ngoc Duc

Institute of Informatics, University of Leipzig
Augustusplatz 10-11, D-04009 Leipzig, Germany
duc@informatik.uni-leipzig.de

Abstract. We argue that existing epistemic logics are not able to account for resource-bounded reasoning and therefore cannot serve the needs of agent theories adequately. We propose a new approach to reasoning about resource-bounded agents which combines epistemic logic with complexity analysis.

1 Introduction

In recent years a number of approaches have been proposed in (Distributed) Artificial Intelligence to specify rational agents in terms of mental qualities like knowledge, belief, want, goal, commitment, and intention. (See [7] for an overview of some recent agent theories.) There is no clear consensus in the DAI community about precisely which combination of mental attitudes is best suited to characterizing agents, yet it seems to be an agreement that belief (or knowledge[1]) should be taken as one of the basic notions of the agent theory (see, e.g., [1], [4], [5], [6], [7].)

From the viewpoint of agent theories, what agents explicitly know is clearly more important than what is only implicitly represented in their information states: it is the former kind of knowledge that agents can act upon, but not the latter. The mere implicit knowledge that some path connecting all towns in a region is the shortest one is useless for a traveling salesman who seeks to maximize his profit — he must make this implicit knowledge explicit in order to choose what path to travel. The mere implicit knowledge that a certain strategy leads to victory is useless for a chess player who must make the next move within a short time. An information agent whose knowledge is represented as a knowledge base must normally make complex and time-consuming inferences before he can answer a query. Since agents need to act upon what they *actually* (or explicitly) know, and not what they merely *possibly* (or implicitly) know, agent theories must be based on logics that can capture what agents actually know. Moreover, as the resources available to the agents are limited, agent theories have to take resource-boundedness into account.

We have argued elsewhere ([2]) that the existing epistemic logics cannot account for rational, yet non-omniscient agents. Moreover, they do not provide a way to deal with resource-bounded agents. Therefore they are hardly suited to formalizing realistic agents. In the sequel I shall present a novel approach to epistemic logic which overcomes the weaknesses of the existing formalisms. The main idea is to combine

---

[1] For the purposes of the paper the distinction between knowledge and belief is irrelevant. We use the two terms interchangeably.

epistemic logic with a complexity analysis: we consider how long an agent will need to compute the answer to a certain query. We shall show that our approach is suited to describe realistic agents. In particular, it can account for the resource-boundedness of agents and offer an intuitive solution to the logical omniscience problem while preserving the intuition that agents are rational.

2 Knowledge, Reasoning, and Time

An agent's action depends not only on what he knows *now*, but also on what he can infer within some specific amount of time (intuitively, the time within which a decision must be made — a classical example being the time available to make the next move in chess.) An agent may not know a sentence *now*, but he may possess a procedure to 'prove' that sentence within a certain amount of time, where the amount of time needed depends on the complexity of the sentence, the agent's reasoning power, etc. If an agent knows that he cannot know the optimal solution to a certain problem within some time limit, he may try to find a near-optimal solution instead. If an agent knows that another agent must act under some time constraint, he may infer what the second agent can or cannot know within this constraint and predict his action accordingly. Therefore, it is worth considering what the agents can know within $1, 2, 3, \ldots$ time units, and not just what they currently know, i.e., what they know within 0 unit of time.

We want to represent not only *what* agents know or can know, but also *how long* they need to know what they can know. The first question is answered by specifying the logic used by agents in their reasoning, and the second by a complexity analysis. What time structure do we need in modeling that kind of knowledge? Temporal logics have been dealing with linear and branching, point-based and interval-based, qualitative and quantitative time structures. Our obvious choice is a point-based, linear structure with a metric defined on it, because temporal constraints are usually given in quantitative terms and over a linear time line. For simplicity we assume time to be isomorphic to the natural numbers (with the usual ordering and metric.)

The language we consider extends the usual language of the propositional calculus by n two-place knowledge operators $K_1, \ldots, K_n$, each for one agent, such that $K_i^x \alpha$ is a formula whenever x is a natural number and α is a formula. The formula $K_i^x \alpha$ can be read "agent i knows α within x units of time" and is interpreted: "if agent i chooses to 'derive' α from his current knowledge, then after at most x time units he will succeed", or alternatively, "if asked about α, i is able to derive reliably the answer 'yes' within x units of time". That is, we require not only that i has at least one procedure to 'prove' α, but also that i be able to choose the correct procedure leading to α under the given time constraint, namely, to arrive at the conclusion α after at most x time units[2]. The word 'prove' (or 'derive') should not be interpreted too narrowly as 'deductive proof': the procedure to gain the knowledge of α may be any acceptable method.

Formally, our language is defined as follows:

---

[2] This reading does not imply that agent i *will* know α at time $t_{now} + n$, where t_{now} is the current time. If the agent is not asked to provide the information α, then she has no reason to waste her resources in order to find a useless answer: The aspect of goal-directedness is implicit in our concept of knowledge.

Definition 1. Let $\mathbb{N}$ be the set of natural numbers and Var be a set of number variables. Let $Agent$ be a finite set of agents and At be a countably infinite set of atomic formulae.

1. The set of temporal terms is the least set $Term$ such that $\mathbb{N} \subseteq Term$, $Var \subseteq Term$, and $t_1, t_2 \in Term$ implies $t_1 + t_2 \in Term$
2. The set of formulae is the least set Fml such that $At \subseteq Fml$, $\{\alpha, \beta\} \subseteq Fml$ implies $\{\neg\alpha, \alpha \wedge \beta\} \subseteq Fml$, $x \in Var$ and $\alpha \in Fml$ imply $\forall x\alpha \in Fml$, and $i \in Agent, t \in Term, \alpha \in Fml$ imply $K_i^t\alpha \in Fml$.

The rationality of agents is expressed through two capacities: first, the ability to draw logical consequences from what is already known, and second, the ability to compute the complexities of certain reasoning problems in order to infer when something can be known. Note that these too capacities are implementable. It turns out that we can develop quite rich theories of the notion of knowledge we have introduced. We shall take classical logic as our basis logic. As we assume the natural numbers as our time structure, we shall also assume some laws of number theory. For our purposes it suffices to assume Presburger arithmetic (i.e., additive number theory.) Our epistemic systems will be obtained by adding (proper) epistemic laws to this basis. Now let us see how such laws may look like.

Suppose that an agent i knows α within x units of time, i.e., he needs x time units to infer α if needed. Then it is plausible to assume that he is able to do it when even more time is available. So we can take as axiom all ground instances of the formula $K_i^x\alpha \rightarrow K_i^y\alpha$, where $x < y$. Note that this axiom *does not* say that knowledge is persistent in the sense that once established it will be available henceforth.

Now let us assume that β follows logically from the premises $\alpha_1, \ldots, \alpha_n$ (i.e., $\alpha_1 \wedge \ldots \wedge \alpha_n \rightarrow \beta$ is valid.) Suppose further that an agent i can reliably infer those premises, i.e., $K_i^{x_1}\alpha_1, \ldots, K_i^{x_n}\alpha_n$ for some $x_1, \ldots, x_n$. What can be said about agent i's information state? Because $x_j < x_1 + \ldots + x_n$ for all $j = 1, \ldots, n$ we may assume that i can derive every premise within $x_1 + \ldots + x_n$ units of time. Once the premises are available they can be used to infer the conclusion β. Thus, it is plausible to adopt the principle $\exists x_1 K_i^{x_1}\alpha_1, \ldots, \exists x_n K_i^{x_n}\alpha_n \rightarrow \exists y K_i^y\beta$, provided that $\alpha_1 \wedge \ldots \wedge \alpha_n \rightarrow \beta$ is valid. We shall use some instances of that rule to axiomatize our basic logic.

Definition 2. The logic **RB0** consists of all propositional tautologies (in the language Fml), the theory of Presburger arithmetic (with respect to the numerical part of the language), and the following axioms and rules of inference:

KA1. $\exists x K_i^x\alpha \wedge \exists y K_i^y(\alpha \rightarrow \beta) \rightarrow \exists z K_i^z\beta$
KA2. $K_i^x\alpha \rightarrow K_i^y\alpha$, for all pairs x, y such that $x < y$.
KR. From α infer $\exists x K_i^x\alpha$
MP. From α and $\alpha \rightarrow \beta$ infer β

It is easy to see that **RB0** is consistent and that it solves all variants of the logical omniscience problem. For example, it is easy to see that what an agent explicitly knows (i.e., what she knows in 0 unit of time) needs not be closed under logical consequences or even under any logical law, e.g., $K_i^0\alpha \wedge K_i^0(\alpha \rightarrow \beta) \wedge \neg K_i^0\beta$ is perfectly **RB0**-consistent. On the other hand, agents described by our logic are rational: they can draw all logical consequences of their knowledge if the necessary resources are available, as the following lemma shows.

Lemma 3. *The following rule of inference is valid:*

$$\frac{\alpha \to \beta}{\exists x K_i^x \alpha \to \exists y K_i^y \beta}$$

In particular, from $\alpha \to \beta$ one can infer $K_i^0 \alpha \to \exists x K_i^x \beta$.

Proof. Suppose that $\alpha \to \beta$ is a theorem. By **(KR)** we can infer $\exists z K_i^z (\alpha \to \beta)$. The formula $\exists z K_i^z (\alpha \to \beta) \to (\exists x K_i^x \alpha \to \exists y K_i^y \beta)$ is equivalent to **(KA1)** and is therefore a theorem of **RB0**. Applying modus ponens we get the desired result.

3 Knowledge and Complexity

Now we have developed **RB0**, a basic logic for resource-bounded reasoning which can account for rational, but not hyper-rational agents. The set of **RB0**-theorems is recursively enumerable and so can be generated algorithmically. If β follows from α and an agent i knows α then he can employ a theorem prover (or a more efficient special-purpose problem solver) for **RB0** to deduce β, so he will know β after some time.

But how long will the agent need to infer a formula which follows logically from his knowledge base? Recall that our aim is to represent not only *what* agents know or can know, but also *how long* they need to know what they can know. Our analyses up to now can only answer the first question. To answer the the second question, a complexity analysis is needed. With the help of complexity theory we can obtain epistemic principles for specific problem classes. The underlying idea is simple: if an agent i receives a query α of length l and if α belongs to a class C of problems whose complexities are known to be a function f_C of the input, then after at most $t = c_i f_C(l)$ units of time agent i is expected to have the answer, where c_i is a number that measures the computation speed of i. So the formulae $\{K_i^t \alpha : \alpha \in C\}$ can be adopted as axioms.

Interestingly, the previous analysis can be used by an agent within the system in order to reason about himself or about other agents, provided that he has a built-in mechanism to calculate the complexity of reasoning problems. They can be given knowledge of the complexities for different problem classes. Then an agent k can recognize relatively easily that a certain problem α belongs to a class C, so he can reason about agent i exactly like we did before to expect i to know α within t time units. But to estimate the time i would need to derive α, k does not have to actually derive it. He has only to calculate the complexity of α, which can be accomplished in a short time. So $K_k^d K_i^t \alpha$ is a plausible postulate, where d is a small number and $t = c_i f(m, l)$ as before. In particular, if i and k are identical then the axiom $K_i^d K_i^t \alpha$ can be adopted.

It is sometimes important to know not only what an agent knows, but also what he does not know within a certain time limit. The expectation that something cannot be known within some limit is based on the complexity of the reasoning required: we use lower complexity bounds to estimate the least amount of time that an agent would need to infer some sentence, and so to infer what he cannot reliably know within some given limit of time.

Adding to the basic system **RB0** epistemic principles that are found through complexity analysis will yield more powerful logics. An example how such an extension of **RB0** could be used is as follows: an agent i has to solve a problem α. First, he checks if α belongs to a known problem class $\mathcal{C}$. If not, a "universal problem solver" (for any problem describable in the language) is activated, and i can only hope to find the solution quickly. But if $\alpha \in \mathcal{C}$, i may estimate its complexity and then decide if the optimal solution can be obtained in time or if some heuristics is needed. Based on that information he can then choose a procedure to solve α^3. Other agents can also reason about i and about the problems he has to solve to explain or predict his actions accordingly.

4 Conclusions

Currently there still exists a wide gap between agent theories and agents existing in practice. Our work is an attempt to bridge this gap. We are trying to develop theories of mental concepts that make much more realistic assumptions about agents than other theories. Our work is guided by the principle that the capacities attributed to agents must be implementable. The main idea is to combine epistemic logic with a complexity analysis: we consider how long an agent will need to compute the answer to a certain query. It is shown that our approach is suited to formalizing resource-bounded agents. Much remains to be done to develop our framework further. But we firmly believe that our framework is a very useful one, which can be used to represent the kind of knowledge needed by agent theories better than any other existing logic of knowledge.

References

1. P. R. Cohen and H. J. Levesque. Intention is choice with commitment. *Artificial Intelligence*, 42:213–261, 1990.
2. Ho N. Duc. Reasoning about rational, but not logically omniscient agents. *Journal of Logic and Computation*, 7, 1997.
3. F. Koriche. Approximate Reasoning about Combined Knowledge. In this volume.
4. A. S. Rao and M. P. Georgeff. Modeling rational agents within a BDI-architecture. In R. Fikes and E. Sandewall, editors, *Proceedings of Knowledge Representation and Reasoning (KR&R-91)*, pages 473–484. Morgan Kaufmann Publishers, 1991.
5. Y. Shoham. Agent-oriented programming. *Artificial Intelligence*, 60(1):51–92, 1993.
6. M. P. Singh. *Multiagent Systems: A Theoretical Framework for Intentions, Know-How, and Communications*, volume 799 of *LNAI*. Springer-Verlag, Heidelberg, 1994.
7. M. Wooldridge and N. R. Jennings. Intelligent agents: Theory and practice. *Knowledge Engineering Review*, 10(2):115–152, 1995.

---

[3] Our work is complementary to other approaches to resource-bounded agents (e.g., [3]) in the following sense: instead of trying to find near-optimal solutions to some specific problem (or class of problems) we try to model the control mechanism used by an agent to select a suitable action sequence for the given situation.

Facilitating Open Communication in Agent Systems: The InfoSleuth Infrastructure

Marian H. Nodine* and Amy Unruh*,†

* MCC, 3500 West Balcones Center Drive, Austin, TX 78759
{nodine,unruh}@mcc.com

† Systems and Software Lab, DSPS RDC, Texas Instruments
PO Box 655303, MS 8378, Dallas, TX, 75265

Abstract. This paper addresses issues in developing open multiagent systems, in which it is easy to expand the functionality by adding new agents with new capabilities, and which facilitate interoperability with other agent systems. We argue that an open multiagent system should define the following support elements for agent communication:

1. A common set of *speech acts* to define the types of messages that an agent might send to another agent.
2. A common *service ontology* by which the agents can describe their capabilities to each other, and reason about which agents have the capabilities needed to execute specific tasks.
3. A common set of *prescriptive conversation policies* to define the acceptable exchanges of messages between agents.

In addition to the above, we also discuss the utility of having a matchmaking agent that can reason over agent capabilities to recommend agents for specific tasks, where the capabilities and requirements are defined using a common service ontology. This ensures that the semantics of matching agent capabilities to task requirements remains the same across the multiagent system.

1   Introduction

Autonomous, intelligent agents are currently being developed in many different application areas. In a multiagent system, each agent executes specific types of tasks, and serves a specific purpose. No agent does an entire job. Rather, it does what it can, then delegates tasks to other agents. No one agent has control over how a task is executed or who executes it, other than controlling the execution of its own specific subtasks.

Because of their modular, cooperative and distributed nature, it should be easy to expand the functionality of a multiagent system by adding new agents that have different capabilities. Ideally, these agents should be able to be added by constructing them independently of the multiagent system, then providing some means by which the multiagent system can find out about the agent and its capabilities. Another attractive option with respect to agent systems is to allow different but related multiagent systems, developed independently, to interoperate.

An open agent architecture is designed to facilitate the addition of new agents to a multiagent system, and to facilitate the interoperation of related multiagent systems. In an open agent system, the agents operate within a common infrastructure that governs how the agents advertise their capabilities and services, how they select which agent is appropriate for executing a given task at a given time, and how they communicate with one another during the execution of a task. This means providing all agents not only with a common understanding of specific messages and message types, but also a common understanding of the dialogs that can occur between pairs of agents, and among subgroups of agents that were specifically designed to work together. Furthermore, if agents are self-describing over some common service ontology that can be assimilated by other agents, this facilitates the integration of agents with new capabilities. In this paper, we specifically address issues involving inter-agent communication that impact the openness of a given multiagent system.

2 Keys to Open Communication

In a multiagent system, the need for agents to communicate is obvious. Several loose standards for agent communication have been proposed (e.g., KQML [7], FIPA [22], and even in some cases, CORBA). Furthermore, at least in the information integration area, several multiagent systems with sufficiently similar communication paradigms have evolved to the point where it is reasonable to start to attempt interoperation. Our agent system, InfoSleuth, is one of these. InfoSleuth supports a dynamic set of agents, spread out across a network, that collaborate to do information retrieval and integration.

Our experience so far has led us to appreciate the need for standard, open agent architectures to allow for the easy integration of new agents into an existing multiagent system, and to allow for the easy interoperation of related multiagent systems. Many multiagent systems are "closed", either because they communicate using their own protocols, or they assume that each agent has specific, built-in knowledge of most other agents in their system. In this paper, we address several overall requirements that openness imposes on the architecture of a multiagent system. We will use our experiences with InfoSleuth to illustrate these issues.

We propose that keys to communication in open systems include a shared set of *speech acts* ("verbs") to provide a structure to the discourse among agents, a common service ontology (a shared set of "nouns" and "adjectives") which provides a dictionary of meta-information about agent capabilities, and a shared set of prescriptive conversation policies to provide a structure for basic agent dialog. The greater the extent to which this shared information is supported, the easier agent integration and interoperation will be. Also, these requirements are separate from the communication issues involved in the use of a shared domain ontology and domain communication language to execute domain-specific tasks.

2.1 Speech acts, or "verbs"

The concept of *speech acts*, or *illocutionary acts*, has grown out of philosophy and linguistics research [5]. These actions include requesting, promising, offering, acknowledging, asserting, etc. It is suggested that human utterances are the observable byproduct of such actions.

Speech act theory has been proposed recently as the foundation for inter-agent communication. The use of a standard set of speech acts in open systems provides a structure to agent discourse in which the intended meaning of the content of the speech act (what is being said) can be interpreted more easily, and provides a semantic structure to the messages intuitive to the human users of a system.

It has been observed [17] that the speech acts in existing agent systems fall primarily into two general categories: *requests* and *assertions*. This suggests — and has been borne out by our own observations – that there is a strong overlap in the speech acts required by many agent systems, and that a small comprehensive set would be sufficient for many multiagent systems. Currently, there are several efforts towards defining this standard, comprehensive set of speech acts, but these efforts have not reached the point of agreement. The more complete the effort for standardizing a set of speech act types, and the greater the adherence to the standard, the more "open" an agent system will be.

However, in an open system, one can't assume that all agents will be able to implement a formal specification of the semantics behind a set of message types, since the agents may implement a wide spectrum of capabilities. This can lead to semantic mismatches (e.g., does TELL imply that the contents must be remembered by the agent being told, or not? Does it imply that the contents must be true or not?). Nevertheless, we believe that a standard set of speech acts, with at least a semi-formal specification of their semantics used to describe their intended meaning (e.g. [13]), provides an important *heuristic* in support of openness. Of course, the greater the extend to which agents do follow a formal specification, the more "open" the agent system will be.

2.2 Service ontologies, or "nouns" and "adjectives"

One fundamental aspect of openness is that an agent should not have *a priori* knowledge of (most) other agents in the system. Rather, if a task requires an agent with a specific capability, it must be able to locate such an agent. In a fairly stable system, perhaps the agent information can then be cached; however, in a fully flexible system where agents may enter and leave the multiagent system, this location information may need to be generated frequently.

For this to occur, a common means of representing and exchanging service and capability information is important. The exchange of this information can be done either in the form of an advertisement or in answer to a query. This advertisement or query must be specified in terms of a predefined set of common semantic concepts, which we call a "service ontology". The service ontology may contain the "nouns" indicating *what* it can do, and the "adjectives" limiting or further describing these capabilities.

Once the capabilities of an agent are expressed in terms of this common service ontology, the current requirements of a task may be formulated in terms of the same ontology, making it possible to deduce whether or not the agent is a good match for the task. Thus, a multiagent system's matchmaking and brokering capabilities contribute to its openness.

2.3 Prescriptive conversations

A set of standard messages representing the available speech acts, and a common service ontology, serve as a basis for very simple communication among agents. However, messages do not get sent in isolation; rather, there are often ongoing dialogs among two or more agents. Within a dialog, the interpretation of an individual message may depend on the *context* of the dialog in which they are participating. Take, for example, a SUBSCRIBE message. This message makes sense if it is received out of the blue by some agent that has the knowledge requested, and has the capability of returning and noticing changes in that knowledge. However, if this message is received in reply to a transmitted ASK-ONE message, it should be an error.

A "conversation" is a partially-ordered set of messages transmitted among a fixed set of agents, all of which relate conceptually to an initiating speech act. A "conversation policy" is the formal and deterministic specification of the ordering of speech acts exchanged between two agents during a conversation. A "prescriptive conversation policy" is one that is defined *a priori*, as opposed to one that evolves during the course of a specific conversation.

Open agent communication requires that any two agents that communicate share a common set of conversation policies. When an agent initiates a conversation or receives an incoming conversation request, it needs to know what types of replies are appropriate. If the conversation can be interrupted (e.g., if the remote agent is sending a stream of responses to the SUBSCRIBE), then each agent must know how and when it can correctly interrupt the conversation.

We believe that all agents in an open system must support a default set of prescriptive conversation policies. These policies must be prescriptive because we can make no assumptions that two agents will reason about conversational responses in the same way, nor can we assume that all agents have the capability to do this kind of reasoning. Clearly, the more such policies that are shared among a group of agents, the richer the agent interaction will be.

3 Overview of InfoSleuth

The InfoSleuth project at MCC [3, 11, 18, 19] is investigating and developing technologies to support a robust and extensible agent architecture for heterogeneous information gathering and discovery in a dynamic environment. InfoSleuth views an information source at the level of its relevant semantic concepts, thus preserving the autonomy of its data. Information requests to InfoSleuth are specified generically, independent of the structure, location, or even existence of the requested information. InfoSleuth filters these requests, specified at the semantic level, flexibly matching them to the information resources that are relevant at the time the request is processed.

Key components supporting our approach include:

- the representation and use of common ontologies with which all agents communicate;
- the use of a *broker* agent with deductive reasoning capabilities, to which all other agents advertise their capabilities and to which the agents then can can formulate queries about desired requirements;

- the use of task scenarios to support different types of high-level queries; and
- techniques for query decomposition over dynamically located relevant resources.

In the remainder of this paper, we discuss each key to open communication, proposed in Section 2, in the context of the InfoSleuth implementation. Section 7 then discusses related issues and concludes.

4 Speech Acts and KQML

The use of a standard set of speech acts in open systems provides a structure to agent discourse in which the intended meaning of the *content* of the speech act (*what* is being said) can be more easily interpreted. In InfoSleuth, we have chosen to build on KQML to define the set of speech acts used in our system. KQML [12, 7] is an effort to define standard useful set of speech acts, or *performatives*, that agents can use to exchange information; as well as the (semi-formal) semantics behind the performatives. The performatives each have a number of fields, or parameters associated with them — in addition to the *content* of the performative, other *contextual* parameters specify e.g., the language and ontology of the message. Routing parameters specify the sender and receiver.

By factoring the contextual and routing information out of the content of the message in a standard manner, the goal is that agents receiving a message will be able to analyze and possibly route the message, independent of whether or not they can understand the content itself. An important research issue is the question of how *much* content information should be pushed to the level of the performative. As an example, consider the general category of *requesting* performatives. In KQML, the SUBSCRIBE and ASK-* performatives both fall into this category. Both ask for information, but differ in what they expect in return. The semantics of this expectation could conceivably be pushed down to the content of the message (which could then be wrapped in a more general REQUEST performative). However, offloading this semantics to the performative level, and making an explicit distinction between a SUBSCRIBE and an ASK, is useful because it enables the agents to obtain important information about the request without having to parse the content. On the other hand, too much complexity at the performative level, especially with those performatives that are not commonly used, will inhibit its utility as an open standard.

Though KQML is not yet stable as a standard, we believe it is a useful vehicle to drive community-wide research in defining a commonly used set of performatives, as well as research into what the structure and fields of those performatives should be. In practice, the InfoSleuth group has found the need to use only a subset of the existing performatives, while finding it useful to define new performatives as well. One performative in particular, ADVERTISE, is particularly pertinent to the exchange of capability information in open systems, and we discuss it in more detail in Section 5.

5 Agent Services and Capabilities

In an open system, no a priori knowledge of most other agents is assumed. For this reason, a common means of exchanging service and capability information is crucial to open communication: for agents to effectively and robustly interoperate in a dynamic system, there needs to be some way for the agents to identify each other's roles and capabilities. The greater the extent to which this is achievable, the more effective the agents' communication and interoperation will be.

In this section, we discuss several aspects of use of capability information in an open system: the content of the service vocabulary, the representation of the service information, and the necessity for a means to formulate requirements about agent capabilities as well as the existence of semantic matchmaking functionality to reason about the requirements.

5.1 Service Ontology as Support for Open Communication

Service and capability information needs to be communicated between agents using a common *ontology* and shared representation rich enough to support it. The contents of a service ontology will contain both domain-independent and domain-dependent components, where the domain-independent portion describes information needed for any type of agent task, such as availability of an agent, or the performatives the agent understands. The domain-dependent portion may describe aspects of an agent's functionality relevant to a certain class of tasks (such as information gathering or design). An agent in an open system must be able to understand both a standardized common ontology describing domain-independent capability information, as well as the ontology describing capability information for its task domain[1].

The InfoSleuth service ontology is driven by the needs of agents in *information-gathering* domains. It includes the following information, which we believe describes a minimum set of concepts for effective agent interoperation in an information-gathering domain. Currently, the domain-independent capabilities are not yet factored out. Research is ongoing to determine what extensions to the ontology are useful, and to identify the subset of the following which should be understood by agents engaged in other types of tasks as well.

- An agent's unique ID
- The type of agent functionality (e.g., *user agent, resource agent*, etc., in InfoSleuth)
- Supported ontologies
- Supported content languages
- Supported conversations
- Access cost
- Access time
- Reliability
- Transactional capabilities
- Notification capabilities
- Meta-information about the classes of objects an agent has information about, with respect to an ontology (e.g., schema information).

---

[1] By "task domain", we do not refer to an application domain, which for InfoSleuth may range from healthcare administration to wafer processing. Rather, we refer to the class of activity, such as information-gathering and discovery, towards which the agents are employed.

– Constraints on the *contents* of the objects an agent knows about, with respect to an ontology.

In [6], a strikingly similar set of capabilities is described. This suggests that our eventual goal of an inter-system service ontology is feasible.

5.2 Representation of Service Information

Agent service information has the potential to be represented in a number of different ways, with respect to the semantic level at which it is encoded. Specifically at issue is the question of what service information should be encoded at the speech-act level, and what should be encoded as the *content* of speech acts. Existing approaches range along this spectrum.

The KQML specification [12] suggests that an ADVERTISE performative should be used to exchange service information, where embedded in an ADVERTISE is a performative (such as an ASK-ALL) that the agent supports. Thus, KQML pushes the capability description entirely into the speech-act syntax. However, we found that the KQML ADVERTISE, with an embedded performative, was not sufficient as a mechanism for exchange of the capability information in the InfoSleuth ontology. As a simple example, many of our agents can answer the same ASK-ALL query. However, each type of agent can have different capabilities with respect to that query. Some agents (*resource* agents) map a query directly to a resource. Some agents (*multi-resource query* agents) perform multi-resource decomposition and joins over a query. And some agents (*task execution* agents) identify and execute a high-level scenario appropriate to answering a query (during which other agents may be identified and queried). Each agent would appear equivalent if another agent had to discriminate based only on the information about the queries they can answer. However, functionally, they are very different, and only one will be appropriate in a given context. Other agents must clearly be able to make this distinction for communication to work in an open environment where a priori information about such functionality is not necessarily available.

One way to make this functionality distinction would be to extend the performatives to make them more expressive. However, in InfoSleuth, we take the approach that speech act communication protocols should not be overloaded to express capability information. Rather, expressions of service capability, and queries on those capabilities, should both be encoded in the content of a performative, consistently with the way that information about and queries on other resources in the system are expressed.

In InfoSleuth, all of the capabilities listed in Section 5.1 are expressed via the content of messages exchanged between agents, using a shared interchange language. The ontological representation and concepts must be standard ones shared by all agents, either directly (as is the case for InfoSleuth) or via a gateway agent that provides interchange translation services.

In [6], the basic insufficiency of the ADVERTISE performative as specified is also recognized, and a similar approach is taken. However, here the representation of the ontology is deliberately tied to KQML. A SERVICE expression is generated for the content of the ADVERTISE, where the representation of the service expression is motivated by a key feature of KQML — that the parameters of the expression may be understood by most other agents even if the content is not. Thus, the SERVICE expression uses KQML syntax and shares some of its field names (such as :ontology and :language) with KQML. However, their approach does not alleviate the need for a common service ontology, as evidenced by the fact that they define other classes of information, both "basic" and that specific to "service", or functionality type. Thus, they mingle service-type information with other standard KQML parameters.

5.3 Name Services

Agent name service (ANS) information and the capability information of Section 5.1 are at different semantic levels in an agent architecture [8, 15]. The name service information is needed to facilitate basic communication, and thus is arguably needed by all agents as a underlying layer upon which the semantic activities needed for open communication can take place.

The name service information should not be confounded with the semantic content of a message; its representation should be factored out, so that implementation of the two layers can be independent. In the community of researchers using speech acts and KQML, at least two different representational approaches exist to do this.

Name Service Information in the Speech-Act Wrapper. The current KQML specification includes routing information — :sender and :receiver parameters — in its wrapper. Because the name service information is very basic, it is feasible that it can be standardized at the speech-act level, in contrast to the more semantically ambiguous agent capability information. For name service information, KQML then serves as the interchange language. An interchange name-service content language is not needed, making it more likely that disparate systems can communicate. This is the approach that InfoSleuth currently uses. Petrie [15] proposes an additional set of KQML "administrative" performatives that further support and extend ANS and routing activities and add additional service specifications at the KQML level.

Name Service Information as a Layer under KQML. A second approach factors out the name service information from the speech act information, allowing the address information to be handled independently by an underlying transport layer. "Classic" KQML [9, 10] facilitates this, by factoring out the routing information from the contextual and content information about the speech act being sent. The benefits of this representation are illustrated, for example, in the exchange of *nomadic transactions*, where the content of a message may be a set of nested performatives to be passed along as a script; the factorization of the address information makes the management of the nested script cleaner. This representation also facilitates using other message routing services, such as CORBA. In this case, the routing information can be omitted, leaving only the semantic information explicitly represented in the message.

5.4 Use of Capability Information

To make use of capability information, agents in an open system must be provided with three supporting functionalities. First, they must be able to exchange the capability information with each other. Second, they need to be able to formulate requirements on those capabilities. Finally, they must have a means for *semantic matchmaking*, or reasoning about whether expressed capabilities match a set of requirements.

In InfoSleuth, all of these activities are supported in the same language: LDL++ [20], a logical deduction language with a semantics similar to Prolog, but which supports transparent access to external databases as well as its own fact base. In InfoSleuth (and similarly in several other agent systems, e.g. [14]), *broker* agents are created to specifically provide semantic matchmaking capabilities. In InfoSleuth, the broker agents use a set of LDL++ deductive rules to support inferences about whether an expression of requirements matches a set of advertised capabilities. All other agents in the system express their capabilities to a broker using a TELL performative[2] (with an LDL++ expression as the content). The broker then accepts matchmaking queries from all agents. These queries to the broker use the ASK-* performatives, consistent with the way agents query other (perhaps domain-specific) resources in the system.

Pragmatically, the use of broker agents means that other agents in the system do not have to implement deductive reasoning capabilities themselves, and do not have to poll a large number of agents to find one which matches the desired capabilities. As long as the agents know the service ontology, and can formulate a query expressing a set of requirements, they can rely on brokers to identify agents which match the requirements.

We suggest that the use of brokers or matchmakers is not only expedient, but a key to the successful operation of an open system. If all other agents work with the same broker(s) to match capabilities, then they are assured of using the same semantics with respect to what it means to match service capabilities. For example, it is possible to use either the closed-world assumption or the open-world assumption when identifying resources that match a certain requirement. It is difficult to enforce that new agents entering a multiagent system are employing matching semantics consistent with what is already in place, and to debug system behavior when they are not. However, if the new agents must use the existing broker(s) in the system to identify resources, consistency of matchmaking semantics is enforced. (The semantic consistency problem remains if new brokers are added to an existing multiagent system, but is reduced in scale).

6 Conversation Policies

While a set of standard performatives and a shared vocabulary for describing agent capabilities provide the foundation for agents in an open system to identify and exchange messages with each other, these capabilities alone are not enough to support open agent communication. The agents need to be able to share a common conversational structure as well. To support open communication, an agent needs to know as best as possible how to interpret responses to performatives it sends out, and needs to know how to respond to incoming performatives such that the receiving agent will interpret the response in the intended way. For example, an agent needs to know that a SORRY is an appropriate response to its ASK-ALL. Conversely, an agent must know what is "expected" of it upon, e.g., receipt of an incoming TELL — is a reply expected by the

---

[2] In [6], ADVERTISE is used for this purpose, as a *commissive* speech act specifically different from TELL. In InfoSleuth, no distinction with respect to commissive semantics is made.

sending agent? If these interpretations are not well-specified across a system of agents, then the behavior of new agents may not be not stable.

6.1 Need for Prescriptive Conversations

The solution we take in InfoSleuth to support open conversations, is to impose the use of a system-wide *prescriptive* conversation policy. We first discuss the difference between *emergent* and prescriptive conversations in a system of agents. Emergent conversations are those in which the agents are not following specific external conversational policies; but rather where the performatives they use are determined by their internal functionality. These actions may be (but are not necessarily) driven by the agent's semantic understanding of the discourse taking place. If agents share the same semantics of discourse, a coherent emergent conversational structure may be generated, e.g. [12, 17]. In particular, intensional semantics for the agents' speech acts can define their conversations.

However, in an open system, one cannot make assumptions about the agents' common understanding of a semantics for discourse. Nor are semantic mismatches easy to debug. Instead, agents need to both expect and provide similar responses in similar contexts. To support interoperation, it becomes necessary to impose structure on at least some functional subset of the agents' conversations to ensure that they are all following the same conversational rules, or policies. The imposition of structure creates a prescriptive conversational policy.

More specifically, we believe that all agents in an open system must support and enforce a default shared set of prescriptive conversational policies. The larger the shared set, the greater the well-defined agent interaction that can occur. Note that the requirement for system-wide default conversational policies does not preclude situations where some subset of the agents in a system support a larger range of conversations. Note also that the use of shared prescriptive conversations does not guarantee semantically consistent actions upon receipt of a message. For example, an agent may "know" that a REPLY needs to follow an ASK-*, but in an open system there is no guarantee (at the requesting agent's end) that the REPLY contains what *it* would consider a semantically reasonable response to its question. Nevertheless, we believe that the use of conversation protocols facilitates consistency in an open system by providing the agent with a definition of which message types it can expect and when; and by providing an implicit semantics for the content of those messages.

6.2 Definition of Conversation Structure

The first step in creating a conversation policy is to define the set of allowable conversations between any two agents in the multiagent system. Any given agent can initiate some subset of these conversations, and can respond to some (possibly different) subset. These subsets can then be used to determine *whether* and *how* any two specific agents can interact with each other.

Because in an open agent architecture, agents should have no real a priori knowledge of each other, conversation types should be uniquely identifiable by the types and/or parameters of the messages that initiate the conversation. For example, in an ASK-ALL

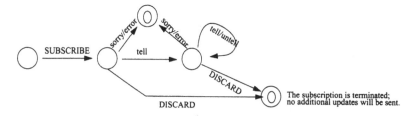

Fig. 1. A finite-state model describing a SUBSCRIBE conversation. The messages from the initiating agent are in uppercase; the messages from the responding agent are in lowercase.

message, the knowledge of its type (ASK-ALL) is sufficient to determine what the response should be. Most multiagent systems handle ASK-ALL consistently. However, some agents acknowledge a TELL message while others do not. It is inappropriate to decide whether or not to expect a response on the basis of which agent you are sending the TELL to, if you wish to maintain an open agent system.

In InfoSleuth, we have used finite-state machines and (in one case) pushdown automata to specify the allowable pairwise conversations between agents in our system. Other work has used a similar approach [4, 12, 21, 22], and [16] presents a prescriptive multi-agent coordination service. Figure 1 shows an example of a conversation type. The transition from the start states in all models correspond to the sending of the conversation-initiating message. The remaining transitions define acceptable message between the two agents at a given time. Final states indicate the end of the conversation.

In InfoSleuth, we currently define conversation policies based on the type of the initial performative. For instance, Figure 1 shows a SUBSCRIBE conversation policy. Other policies we support include TELL, ASK-ONE, ASK-ALL, UPDATE, PERIODIC, and STANDBY (not all of which are "standard" KQML).

Sometimes the agent that receives the initial performative may decide to delegate the conversation to another agent. For example, an agent that plans and executes tasks in InfoSleuth may delegate the processing of certain kind of query to an agent that specializes in that type of query processing. This query processing agent would then take over the responding end of the ASK-* conversation, dealing directly with the agent that sent the query.

6.3 Implementation Approach

To implement prescriptive conversation policies in InfoSleuth, we have incorporated a *conversation layer* into our architecture. The conversation layer defines and enforces the different conversations available to the agents in the InfoSleuth system, and is accessed via a clearly defined API.

The conversation layer sits "on top of" the *generic agent* shell from which all our agents are being built. Thus, all InfoSleuth agents must communicate with other agents by using the conversation layer, which manages both incoming and outgoing conversations, and determines their legality.

However, a key feature of the conversation layer with respect to our development of an open multiagent system, is that it has been cleanly factored from the agent shell. This

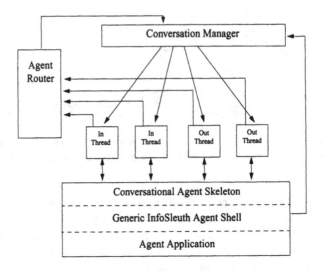

Fig. 2. Implementation of the InfoSleuth conversation layer.

means that it may be used via its API by new agents which do *not* support the shell. In this way conversational policies are enforced without requiring any assumptions about the underlying agent implementation[3].

The conversation layer is implemented by several components:

1. a *router*, which dispatches messages to and receives messages from the KQML implementation layer;
2. a *conversational agent skeleton*, which dispatches messages to and receives messages from the local agent, and
3. a *conversation manager*, which coordinates both incoming and outgoing conversations via "in" and "out" conversation threads.

Each conversation in the multiagent system's conversation policy has an "out thread" class to encode its state machine from the perspective of the initiating agent and an "in thread" class to encode the state machine from the recipient's perspective. Instances of these classes are instantiated as appropriate by the conversation manager. Each thread maintains state, performs error checking, and communicates with the agent for the duration of its conversation. Figure 2 shows the conversation layer architecture.

Thus, the first step in adding a new conversation to the conversation layer is to map its state machine — describing the pairwise conversation — to pairs of state machines which specify a conversation from the point of view of both the initiator and the recipient. Figure 3 shows an example of such a mapping, for simple ASK conversations. Once the incoming and outgoing state machines for a conversation have been specified, new classes are implemented to support the conversation, and are added to the conversation manager's repertoire.

---

[3] The conversation layer is written in Java, so does require a Java wrapper around any agents which utilize it.

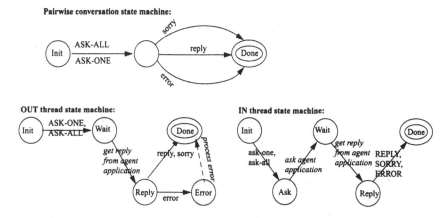

Fig. 3. State machines showing initiator and responder policies for a subset of the performatives.

6.4 Conversation Policies and Core Agent Functionality

Section 6.3 described how the InfoSleuth conversation layer enforces the agents' use of defined conversation policies: it ensures that the performatives output from an agent, and the incoming performatives that it gets, are correct with respect to the defined conversations of the policy. However, the conversation layer itself does not specify whether or not the functionality of the "core" agent matches the conversation layer. For example, the conversation layer ensures that the agent will never send anything but a REPLY (or SORRY or ERROR) in response to an ASK-* performative, but it does not ensure that the core agent "knows" that it needs to REPLY to an ASK. In many cases in our architecture, the correctness of the agents' behavior with respect to the conversation policies remains implicit in the agents' procedural code.

However, some of the InfoSleuth agents employ a rule-based core. These agents use a declarative knowledge base to specify the task plans, or partial ordering of actions, that are carried out in response to an incoming performative of a specific type. The actions, or *operators*, include what might be termed conversational operators. These operators create and send performatives, and process incoming messages. Static analysis of these agents' knowledge bases, and comparison with a declarative specification of the conversation policy, can determine before run-time whether the agents' actions are consistent with the policy[4]. When agents represent their functionality in terms of task plans, the implicit relationship between the conversation layer and the core agent can be made more explicit, increasing the expectation that new agents behave as desired when added to a system.

Some agent systems do not employ a conversation layer, but enforce a conversational policy via rule-based agents which all share the same conversation rules [2, 1]. This approach works very well in a system of agents that all support rule-based reasoning. The InfoSleuth architecture allows agents to exploit rules for conversation when

---

[4] Some operators have procedural attachments. These can not be as easily analyzed, but the effects of each operator can be modularly tested and specified.

they have that ability, but does not require this ability in an open system — the conversation layer enforces conversational consistency even in purely procedural agents.

7 Conclusion

In this paper, we have proposed several keys necessary for openness in a multiagent system, and have discussed the implementation approach that InfoSleuth takes to address them. This approach includes the generation of a service ontology (and the need to push service activities from KQML down to the content of a message), the specification of common prescriptive conversation policies, and the creation of a conversation policy layer in the InfoSleuth architecture. These key issues have emerged from our past and current efforts to expand InfoSleuth by adding new agents with new functionality and with our ongoing efforts to interoperate with several other information-gathering agent systems.

We hint at three orthogonal sets of functionality that an agent communication layer deals with: routing services (including associating reply messages with their request messages), agent capability description, and lastly the content semantics which pertain to a specific task. We believe that there should be a clean factoring of these functions within the communication infrastructure. This would imply, for example, that routing services should be at a separate message layer from capability or task descriptions, and capability descriptions should be specified over a different ontology from task descriptions.

Future work in this area will include KQML interoperability experiments with other multiagent systems, investigation of the issues in using CORBA as a transport layer below KQML, and further investigation and tracking of the relationship between the KQML and FIPA efforts. Future research issues include understanding and increasing the scalability of the InfoSleuth architecture — more specifically, how performance and reliability are affected by the addition of numbers of agents of various types to the multiagent system; and automatic incorporation of new, declaratively-specified conversational policies into an agent system.

Another issue relates to open systems and the modeling of agent state. A conversation policy ensures that the agents in an open system all send the same sequences of speech acts to each other. However, it says nothing about the agents' internal states and how they interpret the semantics of the speech acts — e.g., whether or not they remember the contents of a TELL. An hypothesis of this paper is that the implicit (informally specified) semantics of a standard set of speech acts nevertheless provide heuristics to allow agents in a large, open system to communicate in a way that will be "good enough". We plan experimentation using large open systems to further explore these issues.

References

1. M. Barbuceanu. Coordinating agents by role based social constraints and conversation plans. In *Proceedings of the Fourteenth National Conference on Artificial Intelligence (AAAI '97)*, pages 16–21, 1997.

2. M. Barbuceanu and M. Fox. COOL: A language for describing coordination in multi-agent systems. In *First International Conference on Multi-Agent Systems*, 1995.

3. R. Bayardo, W. Bohrer, R. Brice, A. Cichocki, J. Fowler, A. Helal, V. Kashyap, T. Ksiezyk, G. Martin, M. Nodine, M. Rashid, M. Rusinkiewicz, R. Shea, C. Unnikrishnan, A. Unruh, and D. Woelk. Infosleuth: Agent-based semantic integration of information in open and dynamic environments. In *Proceedings of SIGMOD '97*, 1997.

4. J. Bradshaw, S. Dutfield, P. Benoit, and J. Woolley. KAoS: Toward an industrial-strength open agent architecture. In J.M. Bradshaw, editor, *Software Agents*, chapter 17. AAAI Press, 1997.

5. P. Cohen and H. Levesque. Communicative actions for artificial agents. In *ICMAS-95*, 1995.

6. K. Decker, K. Sycara, and M. Williamson. Modeling information agents: Advertisements, organizational roles, and dynamic behavior. In *Working Notes of the AAAI-96 workshop on "Agent Modeling"*, 1996.

7. T. Finin, Y. Labrou, and J. Mayfield. KQML as an agent communication language. In J.M. Bradshaw, editor, *Software Agents*. AAAI Press, 1997.

8. T. Finin, C. Thirunavukkarasu, A. Potluri, D. McKay, and R McEntire. On agent domains, agent names and proxy agents. In *ACM CIKM Intelligent Information Agents Workshop*, 1995.

9. T. Finin and G. Wiederhold. An overview of KQML: A knowledge query and manipulation language. Technical report, available through the Stanford CS Dept., 1991.

10. D. Geddis, M. Genesereth, A. Keller, and N. Singh. Infomaster: A virtual information system. In *Intelligent Information Agents Workshop at CIKM '95*, 1995.

11. N. Jacobs and R. Shea, "The Role of Java in InfoSleuth: Agent-based Exploitation of Heterogeneous Information Resources", IntraNet96 Java Developers Conference, April, 1996.

12. Y. Labrou. *Semantics for an Agent Communication Language*. PhD thesis, University of Maryland at Baltimore County, 1996.

13. Y. Labrou and T. Finin. Semantics for an agent communication language (working report). 1997. In this volume.

14. McGuire, Kuokka, Weber, Tenenbaum, Gruber, and Olsen. SHADE: Technology for knowledge-based collaborative engineering. *Journal of Concurrent Engineering:Research and Applications*, 1(3), 1993.

15. C. Petrie. http://cdr.stanford.edu/ProcessLink/kqml-proposed.html.

16. M. Singh. A customizable coordination service for autonomous agents. 1997. In this volume.

17. I. Smith and P. Cohen. Toward a semantics for an agent communications language based on speech-acts. In *Proceedings of the Thirteenth National Conference on Artificial Intelligence*, pages 24–31. AAAI, AAAI Press/The MIT Press, 1996.

18. D. Woelk, M. Huhns and C. Tomlinson. "InfoSleuth Agents: The Next Generation of Active Objects", Object Magazine, July/August, 1995.

19. D. Woelk and C. Tomlinson, "The InfoSleuth Project: Intelligent Search Management via Semantic Agents", Second International World Wide Web Conference, October, 1994.

20. C. Zaniolo, "The Logical Data Language (LDL): An Integrated Approach to Logic and Databases", MCC Technical Report STP-LD-328-91, 1991.

21. T. Winograd and F. Flores. *Understanding Computers and Cognition*. Addison-Wesley, 1998.

22. http://www.cselt.stet.it/fipa.

Competition for Attention

Walter Van de Velde*, Sabine Geldof†, and Ronald Schrooten*

* Research Group, Riverland Next Generation
  Excelsiorlaan 40-42, B-1930 Brussels, Belgium
  wvdv@riv.be

† Artificial Intelligence Laboratory, Vrije Universiteit Brussel
  Pleinlaan 2, B-1050 Brussels, Belgium
  sabine@arti.vub.ac.be

* Research Group, Riverland Next Generation
  Excelsiorlaan 40-42, B-1930 Brussels, Belgium
  ronald@riv.be

Abstract. This paper introduces 'Competition for Attention' as a conceptual design paradigm for agent-based multi-media applications. Our aim is to allow for the relative independent development of information services, on the one hand, and value-added agent-based services on the other, and to enable their smooth integration in a particular on-line application. The underlying and long-term objective is to deal in a principled way with the scaling problem, allowing for agent-based applications with hundreds to millions of active agents. Although we have not yet fully realized these objectives, the paper describes three phases of an existing practical application that demonstrates the step that we have taken toward this goal. The application is an on-line WWW service for Brussels summer movie festival Ecran Total. In three consecutive years, three agent-based applications have been developed with increasingly enhanced methodological and technical support for realizing the Competition for Attention paradigm.

1 Introduction

This research is about developing agent-based multi-media applications. Our aim is to advance at the methodological and technical level, such that the development of applications with thousands or millions of agents becomes possible. For the moment, this scale is not really an issue. There are relatively few software agents active and often they are bound to particular applications, assisting the users in working with complex pieces of software (editors, mail programs) [8]. When multiple agents are involved these are carefully designed together to rely on eachother's features (e.g. FireFly) This, however, does not cover the full potential of the notion of software agent and it is, in our opinion, definitely not what future agent-based applications will look like.

The vision that sets the scene for our research is that of a world-wide network, populated with millions of software agents, each of them actively trying to be of interest to a user. So, rather than the users having to take the initiative to pull some information out of the net, it are the software agents that are constantly trying to push information and services toward the user. This 'network turned inside out' works by radical information push. Information push is contrasted with information pull models, in which the user has to take the initiative to pull the information that she thinks she needs. Current information push models provide profile-based pro-active information delivery, such as in customized news filtering and delivery applications (also known as 'publish and subscribe'). Our radical version goes much further as we pursue *context- and situation-based push*: at each moment the information that is deemed relevant for the user's current minute situation is pushed toward her.

Information push has a dubious reputation, as it may easily increase information overload and can be used in unacceptable ways when unwanted, false or misleading information is being pushed, or personal information is being used to manipulate the reader's behavior in subtle ways. However, these problems are not with information push *per se*. They result from lacking dynamic and personal control on push-channels. Our radical version, which is includes not only interest but also context, is aimed at resolving this problem.

Radical information push is an ideal context for software agents. First, it requires *awareness* of what is relevant for the users at each moment in time. Second, it requires *initiative* to act independently of an explicit instruction to do so. Third, it requires a *history* to make sure that the initiatives that are taken are rooted in past experience. These features - awareness, initiative, and history - are core to the agent notion [16, 13]. However, with numerous such agents in the picture one clearly faces a large *scaling* problem: when millions of agents are actively trying 'to do their thing', and are competing to get to potential users, there is a question how this can still behave meaningfully toward the user, or how she will be protected from information overload or pollution.

In a nutshell then, we emphasize that the user's attention is limited and that agents must compete for this attention. The image comes to mind of a bunch of children stretching their necks to be in the viewer of a camera. The camera's field is also limited, and the children must compete for the attention of the photographer: pushing eachother, making faces, waving and so on. With our software agents it is the same. Currently there aren't many and they get all the attention, but in the future they will need to compete for it. The methods are techniques that we are developing center around this idea of "Competition for Attention", and are aimed at achieving this in a scalable way.

The applications that we have in mind rely on rich information contexts, typically derived from on-line multi-media databases. The idea is to augment such sophisticated information services with a variety of agent-based value-added features. In our approach both types of service can be designed relatively independently. The information service can be used without agents at all without changing it, and agents can be added and removed at any time. At each moment, whatever agents are 'present' compete for the attention of the user. In this competition, what plays a role is the context of the user, which is primarily the information that she is looking at, her past behavior, user characteristics (static and dynamic), her goals and intentions (explicitly stated or derived from observing her behavior), and other environmental factors, like the physical location of a client, the time of day, the weather outside, and so on. Our notion of context thus goes much further than user-profile, but includes the minute situation and purpose of using the system. Agents must be aware of this context, take the initiative to get involved, and evolve in the process of doing so.[1]

---

[1] A genuine search agent is a good example: in our view, by the time the user realizes that she is

The real-world application that we will use as an example throughout this paper is the WWW-server for Brussels' major summer movie festival 'Ecran Total'. Three consecutive versions of the Ecran server exhibit qualitative improvements, based on incorporating conceptual ideas on how competition for attention can be exploited in multi-media systems. Through the realization of an *architecture* for competition for attention, the technology tracks the methodology and enables the *structure preserving implementation* of a conceptual design according to the competition for attention approach (Ecran '96). In the most recent version, Ecran'97, we have focussed our effort on dynamic context tracking allowing 6 agents to have greater awareness of the context and thus a better and more dynamic competition for attention. Moreover, we have implemented a feature in which the state of the competition is rendered in natural language meta-texts, giving the user a context-sensitive navigation point to explore the information service from. The following section describes the 3 consecutive versions of the Ecran application in more detail, highlighting the methodological and technological evolution. Section 3 recapitulates at a general level our main methodological and technological and contribution. An evaluation, discussion and preview of future work finishes the paper.

2 A Real-World Experiment: Ecran Total

2.1 Ecran'95: Information, the basis of interaction

The Brussels Ecran Total movie festival is a major yearly cinema-event in the capital of Europe. It features, from july to september around 100 different movies in around 600 showings. The Ecran server is built on top of a traditional information service. It was derived from the textual and graphical material in the festival's printed journal. The Ecran Total server is thus primarily an online journal, featuring the same information as the printed one. In addition a number of functionalities are available that are not possible in the paper-based journal, providing an added value service to the user. These have to do with search (possibility to search for a particular movie in various ways), time-awareness (direct access to program of the day, only future showings mentioned by default), and external linking (cinematographic information is retrieved from other on-line databases, i.c., the Internet Movie Database).

2.2 Ecran'96: Competition for attention

The main feature that distinguishes the second edition from the first one is the addition of several agent-based services. Within the existing context of the festival information, a small set of agents assist users in various ways. The server features an agent that provides personalized advice, one that keeps a personal festival agenda, and one that advertises related events and movies. Compared to our long-term objective this is still a

---

going to need information on something, the search agent is also aware of this, has taken the initiative to do the appropriate search—where the queries are formulated taking into account reactions to previous searches—, and competes for the attention of the user to offer the search results in the concrete context of the interaction. No such search agent exists for the moment.

fairly minimal system, although it was later extended to 6 major agents. For the purpose of this paper it is useful to illustrate one of the key ideas that lead the design of this kind of applications: *competition for attention*.

Competition for attention, in our model, is based on three values that characterize an agent's behavior: a relevance measure, a competence measure and a performance measure. The *relevance measure* captures the relevance of an agent action in a particular (information) context. For example when a user is looking at the time-table of showings for a particular movie, it is relevant for the agenda agent to offer the service of putting a showing on the agenda and making sure the user doesn't forget it. When that same user is looking at a summary of a movie plot, this action would be less relevant. The *competence measure* captures how good an agent is in doing a particular action. We thus take into account that, depending on the situation, an agent may feel more or less competent for doing a particular action. For example, the advice agent works by comparing user profiles, much in the style of HOMER (MIT) and FireFly (Agent Inc., http://www.agents-inc.com/). Depending on the degree of overlap between the current user's profile and those of others, the advice agent can be more or less confident in its advice. Thus, although the action of advice giving may be relevant, the agent may choose not to do it because of lack of competence. In that situation another action may be chosen, for example one from which additional information on user profile may be obtained. The *performance measure*, finally, reflects the accumulated success of an agent's actions over time. A success is, roughly, the case in which the agent manages to capture the user's attention. Currently this is only done by observing clicking-behavior: if the user clicks on an anchor provided by the agent, then it was successful.

Figure 1 shows a screen dump of a page in which an agent manifests itself, meaning that it is allowed to get through to the user based on the outcome of competition for attention. The basic pages that would be browsed when no agents are present are being augmented with speech acts from the agents. In this way the most relevant and competent agents manifests themselves in the context of the ongoing interaction with the user. Whether or not an agent can manifests itself depends on the outcome of the agent competition, which, in turn is a matter of judgment of relevance and competence of its action in the particular information context (the different page-types, in this case). Below we clarify the basis of competition for each of the types of agents. It illustrates the kind of thinking that the application designer must perform in the initial stages of the design (see also Section 3).

Advice agent: The advice agent is one of three agents present in the application. It is also the most 'intelligent' one. It advises the user of a movie she or he may like, or not. The technology used is similar to that of HOMR (MIT) or Firefly (Agents Inc). The agent maintains a large database of user profiles on the basis of which it performs an n-nearest neighbor algorithm to derive recommendations for a movie that a particular user has not seen yet. Thus the advice agent has three types of speech acts: *advice giving*, *profile building*, and *opinion gathering*.

The competence measure for advice giving of the advice agent is derived from the degree of overlap between the current user's profile and the other users' profiles that the agent knows of. With little overlap no confident conclusions can be drawn and the competence measure for advice giving will be low. The competence measure

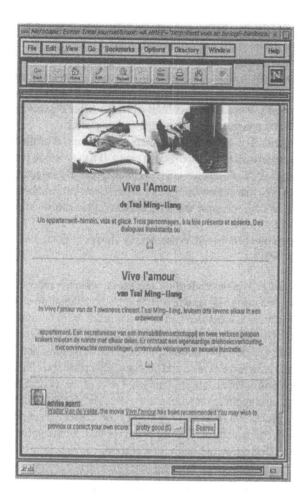

Fig. 1. A journal page with the advise agent. The page is composed of several page fragments, one of which is contributed by the agent that won the competition for attention.

for profile building and opinion gathering, on the other hand, is always high. The relevance measure for advice giving is high if the user is on a page with multiple movie choices. Multiple choices is interpreted as a sign of doubt, so advice would be relevant (but in this implementation the agent does not restrict its advice to the possible choices). The relevance measure for profile building is higher when little profile information is known. The relevance measure for asking a specific opinion (opinion gathering) is high when the user looks at information for a specific movie. With this configuration of relevance and competence measures it is assumed that the performance of the agent (accumulated success) will be high.

Agenda agent: The agenda agent maintains a user's movie agenda, making sure that the relevant movies are on the agenda and that the user is reminded of a showing. The agenda is a list of sessions that the user has selected, while the reminding uses email to the user the day before the session. The agenda agent has thus two types of speech acts: *agenda building* and *notification*.

The competence measure for agenda building of the agenda agent is always high. For notification it depends on whether or not there is something on the agenda. The relevance of agenda building is only high when the user looks at program information. The relevance of notification is high when the time of a session approaches. It is not dependent on page-types since email is being used.

Advertisement agent: The advertisement agent is the simplest of the three. It puts up a publicity on a particular movie or related event. It has only one type of speech act: *advertise*. It has, in its present version, no intelligence for selecting a targeted advertisement, except that it uses things that are relevant in the short run (e.g. today). It could make an alliance with the advice agent but, again, we have not realized this.

The competence measure for advertisement is always high. The relevance measure is also always high.

Note that competence is dependent on the agent, whereas relevance is dependent on the context of interaction. Thus, when changing the navigation structure of an application only the relevance measures had to be reconsidered. The final composition of pages is subject to a choice of speech acts from the agents. For the Ecran'96 version this game is hard-coded: the designer builds a table of information-contexts (page-types) and speech acts, and assigns relevance and competence measures, either as constants or as computable functions. This is an obvious weakness of the system, but the most robust one for this on-line application with many users. The issue of balancing the design is discussed in the Section 3, but the next step in the Ecran Server development was exactly to explore the more careful tracking of the context, allowing for agents dynamic awareness or more effective competition for attention.

2.3 Ecran'97: context sensitive hypertext generation

The main goal of our 1997 Ecran implementation was to investigate how the context of interaction can be captured and rendered within an agent-extended catalog. First we define the notion of context as a multi-dimensional reality, then we explain how a crucial aspect of the context can be modeled for the Ecran application and mapped to competition of agents. Finally, we provide an outlook on how the combination of agent competition and text generation technology can contribute to the information-push model.

We call context the collection of features that determine the desirable content and form of the information. This context is obviously broader than the user alone. It has many aspects, which we can group along 3 dimensions: general user characteristics, situation specific features, and teleological features. In a system where agents evaluate their relevance against such a multi-dimensional context of the interaction, this process easily becomes a complex matter. Most systems that take into account the context of the user to date focus on the least evolving contextual dimension, i.e. general user characteristics (e.g. whether she is a novice or expert user) [9]. However, the more contextual parameters a system can take into account, the more context sensitive it will be. The present experiment focuses on a highly dynamic contextual parameter: the teleological features -the user's topic preferences and goals.

In Ecran'97, the teleological aspect of the context is sensed by observing the user's browsing behaviour. This approach is based on the following assumption: as the user browses the Ecran programme, she expresses straightforwardly what she is interested in, what type of information she is looking for, in other words, for what goal she is consulting the festival's programme. This supposes that the structure of the catalog is interpretable in terms of these teleological features. We us a topic structure to represent and model the possible types of information in an on-line service. A topic structure is a hierarchical structure of topics and subtopics. The topic structure, related to the application ontology, shows the objects of the discourse as the leaves of a tree relating them through higher level concepts. For the Ecran festival, there are 3 main information topics about movies: programmation, production, contents. For instance, the information about when and where a particular movie will be shown belongs to the programmation aspect (particular to this festival), while the plot of the movie or the category to which it belongs pertains to the contents of the movie, what can be told about the movie in a more general way. Details about the director, the year and place in which the movie has been realized constitute the production aspects. The navigation structure of the application can be mapped to the topic structure, indicating which page types relate to which topics or subtopics. See Figure 2. The process of sensing the teleological features of a particular user's interaction context then amounts to attributing weights to the nodes of the topic structure, depending on how frequently she visits a particular page type.

Having designed a way to track the evolving interests of the user, our radical information push can be realized by linking the competition for attention of the different agents with this context awareness. For the Ecran'97 version there are 6 major agents. First there are the three 'task agents' that were previously described. Second there are three 'information agents', each of them related to the major topics of the application: programmation, production and contents. The information agents are, in a way, not so sophisticated as the task agents but they are, on the other hand, more directly linked to information push. Moreover, they can incorporate application goals, like the desire to provide information on the most prestigious showings. For instance, the production agent will be eager to have production related information provided to the user, and as such it is in competition with the programmation agent pushing information on programmation details. Unlike the task agents, their respective competence is equal: in the Ecran interactive programme there is an equal amount of information on each of the three topics. However, they will be able to evaluate their relevance by interpreting the weighted topic structure. Moreover, alliances among information and task agents respectively enrich the competition model. Obviously the agenda and the programmation agent are related and reinforce each other in the competition scheme: whenever the programmation agent is leading the competition -indicating that the user is interested in the programmation details of the festival, the agenda agent's relevance has increased. Alliances between agents thus allow for the task agents to evaluate their relevance indirectly. The basic rational here is that, when a user is interested in information that is also accessed by a task agent, then the relevance of that task agent increases, since the user may be actually interested in that task (rather than 'just' in the information).

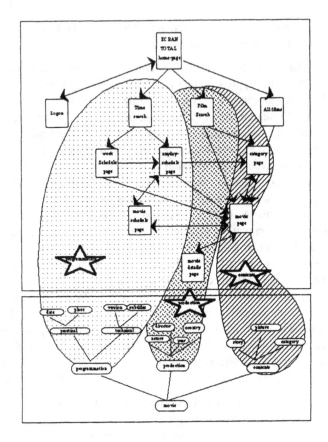

Fig. 2. Mapping of navigation structure to topic structure

By their capability to evaluate their relevance with respect to the context and thus to provide context sensitive information, these agents contribute to the information-push model of the net. In order to make this more concrete for the user, the Ecran catalog has been extended with a so-called context-pane: a summary of the information the user is actually looking at, balanced so that the information deemed contextually most relevant at that point in the interaction is put in evidence. An example is shown in Figures 3. It shows the context pane (upper frame) as generated in case of a winning programmation agent. The context pane is re-generated each time the user clicks on a different movie page and reflects the balance of the weighted topic structure at that particular time. Should the contents agent win the competition for attention, the text would read something like this: "'Le Coeur fantôme' is part of the category Inédits / Onuitgegevenen. The movie tells the story of Philippe, starting a new relationship, but unhappy, since he's missing his 2 children. It's about parenthood and relationship. It was produced by Philippe Garrel. It will be shown at Arenberg Galeries in room 2. You can see some shots here." The underlying text generation technique is template based, using the topic structure as a text plan [5, 6] explains the natural language generation aspects of this approach.

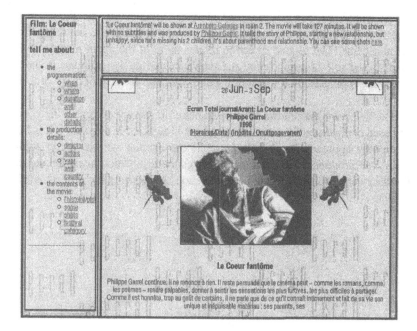

Fig. 3. Upper frame shows the context pane from winning programmation agent.

3 From Methodology to Technology

In this section we recapitulate what are the main methodological and technological contributions that spin-off from the Ecran series of applications.

From a methodological point of view the objective is to conceive information services independently from agent services, and to combine them in a smooth manner. The model of competition for attention should allow for agents to be added and removed without effort: they become players in the competition for the user's attention. Similarly the information and navigation structures can be changed, as long as the relevance measures can be updated. To summarize, from a conceptual design methodological point of view the following steps need to be taken: (i) design the information structure and construct a database that contains the required information, (ii) design the navigation structure, i.e. a global structure of page types that defines the different navigation options for the possible page layouts, (iii) design agent functionalities and competence measure, (iv) connect agents to the application and determine each agent's relevance measure within that application, and (v) design page composition from information and agent-provided page fragments.

Even without any technological support for implementing such a design, the approach has been found useful to conceive and document the relationships between information and agent-based services. When documenting relevance and competence values and relating them to information contexts typically conflicts need to be resolved, simulating in a sense at design time the competition for attention game.

Taking this methodological contribution as a starting point two technical directions have been elaborated. The first proposes an overall architecture that allows for a structure preserving design of any application described according to the competition for attention scheme. The second direction relates more to the agent model itself, making explicit the role of competence and relevance and its dynamic use in the on-line and in-context competition for attention game. We describe each of these contributions below.

The architecture that allows for the structure preserving design of the conceptual agent-based competition for attention paradigm is depicted in Figure 4[2]. It is based on a client server approach where different users can interact with the server application via their web browsers. The client side realizes the application interface and the user profile discovery, while all the other application components are implemented at the server side.

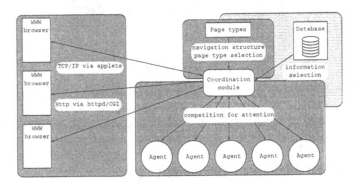

Fig. 4. Architecture of the Ecran Total application. The figure shows the basic architectural components and the interface mechanisms between the components.

The methodology together with the architecture turned out to be very useful as a methodological guide for designing integrated agent- and information-services. However, our objectives, as stated in the introduction, are more ambitious. Competition for attention must be a mechanism that governs the dynamics of agent interaction within the application in real-time, otherwise the vision of a large and open collection of competing software agents will not materialize. The rest of this section focuses on how the individual agents can be designed in order to operate in a competition for attention approach.

The competition model for agents is based on four parameter: relevance, competence, performance and alliances. Measuring each of these parameters can be done in different ways. One approach is to design fixed values into the agent, a more dynamic approach is to let agents accumulate, in a reenforcement learning fashion, estimates for their competition parameters. The first approach, i.e. when measures can be designed, will lead to better performance more rapidly. However, the robustness with respect to unforeseen situations, changes in the information- or navigation structure, and in the

---

[2] A related one is described in [11].

set of agents present in the application may be compromised. On the other hand, the dynamic approach implies that the system may only asymptotically exhibit interesting behavior. Examples of the first approach can be found in the Ecran'96 server. Here the competition parameters for the advertisement agent where design to be always high. There are also situations in which the parameters are not really fixed but an easy computation for them can be designed. For example the competence value of the advice agent depends on the degree of overlap between the current user's profile and the other users' profile. An example of a fixed alliance relation can be found between the programmation agent and the agenda agent.

Exploration of the dynamic approach leads us to the identification of two extra methodological steps for the agents: (vi) design a mechanism to capture the feedback on the actions of the agent, and (vii) design a mechanism that updates the competition values of the agent. An example of how the competence parameters can be calculated in a dynamic fashion follows:

Relevance(R) and Competence(C) A mechanism that allows agents to dynamically derive values for their relevance and competence works via an action-context matrix. Each agent maintains such a matrix. Let AGENTS be the collection of agents in a given location, and Context the context of an encounter. R(agent, action, context) * C(agent, action, context) is an estimate of the usefulness of the action in the context (for the user). Based on this value, or a similar combination, an agent, action is chosen. An action is successful if the next context is compatible with the action. Compatibility, in this case, is determined by hyperlinks or input value from the user.

Now how can the agent update these R and C values? First, let us assume relevance in all or in only this context and update C values accordingly. Then differentiate relevance if it is necessary. So, success is distributed to all contexts (i.e., attributed to the competence), while failure is kept to influence the relevance value for that context only (i.e., attributed to circumstances). This is a typical agent that has a fairly good image of itself, say, a self-confident one. Obviously alternatives exist, leading to different agent 'characters':

1. affirmative: the context is the problem
2. uncertain: the competence is the problem
3. and mixtures - survival based on performance

For example when success is attributed to the context (i.e., attributed to relevance of that context), and failure is attributed to lack of competence, the result is more modest agent, i.e., one that thinks it has been lucky to find the right circumstances.

Performance(P) The performance reflects the accumulated success of an agent, i.e., the extent in which an agent has something useful to say in all contexts. Something is useful if it is being said and appeared to be successful. It is important that this measure is external to the agent. As opposed to competence and performance measures that are updated by the agents themselves, this one is based on observed results of agent activity. The performance measure is used primarily by the coordination module to decide the outcome of the competition for attention. For example an agent that systematically overestimates its competence and relevance, but does not perform well, will not be able to win the competition in the long run, as its performance measure will be low.

Alliances(A) Agents can make alliances with other agents. They can do this by giving away and retrieving competition power. After calculating the three parameter (relevance, competence and performance) an agent knows his initial competition power:

$$Initial\_Competition\_Power = f_{ICP}(R, C, P) \quad and \quad f_{ICP} = R + C + P$$

Now an agent can decide how much of this initial competition power he will use for himself and how much he is going to distribute among the other agents. The alliance function is determined via a parameter α which is high when the agent is selfish and low when the agent is altruistic.

Alliances_Function for agent j, $AF_j(f_{ICP})$:

$$AF_j = \alpha \times f_{ICP} \qquad\qquad altruistic = 0 \leq \alpha \leq 1 = selfish$$

The distribution of the initial competition power is according to the following rule: lookup the alliances that you had with other agents during the previous interactions and then divide your competition power over these other agents in relation to the amount of competition power that you retrieved from them.

The Competition Distribution of agent j at time t to the other agents i:

$$CD_{j,i,t} = \frac{f_{jICP} - AF_j}{\sum_{i=1}^{N} CD_{i,j,t-1}} \times CD_{i,j,t-1} \qquad\qquad i \neq j$$

Summing the values that an agent gets via its alliances with other agents results in a value for its alliance parameter.

The Alliance value for agent j A_j from other agent i is:

$$A_j = \sum_{i=1}^{N} CD_{i,j} \qquad\qquad i \neq j$$

The calculation of the total competition power of one agent becomes:
$$Total\_Competition\_Power = f_{TCP}(f_{ICP}, A)$$
$$and \quad f_{TCP} = R + C + P - CD + A$$

4 Discussion

In designing software systems it is always important to know what the major aim of the system is and to identify the problems. Here the aim of the system is to provide users with relevant information, and the major problem is information overload. This is a problem common to a large number of WWW applications where users need to navigate through a huge amount of information trying to find the information they are looking for. The Ecran total application fits perfectly well in this class of applications and therefore has the same problems. Our solution to this problem is to turn the web inside-out and instead of having the user looking for information it becomes the information that is looking for users. Realizing this idea starts with having a design methodology for these systems. We worked out such a methodology and explored it during the three consecutive versions of the Ecran Total applications. The *fil rouge* of this methodology is the mechanism of "competition for attention" and it covers features that will be criteria for success for the WWW-applications of the future. These features are:

- Information is imposed on the user: shift from information pull towards an information push.
- There is a mixed initiative approach: initiative for interaction lies not only by the user but is inside the system.
- There is a social dynamics among software agents just as there is one among real agent.

The contributions of this paper can be evaluated from various points of view. 1) Scientifically: idea of competition for attention and the developed agent models. 2) Methodologically: a smooth co-design of information and agent services and integration with WWW technology. 3) Technologically: the implementation of an architecture for designing applications around the competition for attention idea. 4) Application: the implementation of the different versions of the Ecran total server has always been implemented with state of the art Internet technology. Together with the integrated agent-based services this resulted in high technological show cases of WWW applications.

From a scientific point of view this research is about understanding social dynamics. Basically, the problem we address is the following: how do agents that are embedded in large societies—hundreds to millions of agents—focus the enormous potential for interaction with others towards the most productive encounters? In this sense our work is similar in spirit to [7]. Competition for attention is one element of our solution. It works within a group of agents that are committed to interact with eachother. A second mechanism, we call it interest-based navigation, is needed to locate the best potential of successful interactions. The broader picture of these developments are being explored within the project COMRIS[3] [14, 2]. Our broader aim in this project is to understand how two loosely coupled parallel societies (a real one and a virtual one) can develop a coherent and useful behavior. The interaction between the two worlds is realized through a wearable computer (the COMRIS parrot) that essentially performs the functions that we have been discussing in this paper: context perception and management of the user's attention. The device is a pure audio approach, using speach output that is based on texts similar to those generated in the most recent Ecran Total version.

From a methodological point of view we have contributed to ongoing work on methodologies for multi-agent systems (e.g. [13] for methodology, or [3] for specifica-

---

[3] Project COMRIS: Co-Habited Mixed Reality Information Spaces (LTR 25500, 97-2000), funded within the EU Long-Term Research initiative Intelligent Information Interfaces (www.i3net.org).

tion work). Our work focuses on designing interactive applications, rather than closed multi-agent systems, and with a fundamental commitment to radical information push models. The idea of competition for attention is obviously an outcome of this bias. We believe that the Ecran series of servers has demonstrated the value of this approach for designing complex and evolving multi-media applications with an open collection of agents active in them (compare [10]. Another contribution is the direction of context-sensitive navigation points, based on natural language, which significantly extends on flexible text generation work [9].

From a technological point of view we have developed a robust framework for incremental and scalable design of agent-based multi-media applications. This architecture has shown broader applicability in the context of agent-based multi-media catalogues [11]. By its use of a simple agent-architecture it does not rely on sophisticated agent-communication technology, à la KQML [4]. On the other hand the technological results are lagging behind the theoretical and methodological wish-list. We are exploring alternatives for working with relevance and competence measures, the context tracking [6] and the formation of alliances [1, 15, 12]. For none of these issues we claim to have conclusive solutions.

The Ecran series of applications is itself an important and highly visible outcome of this work. Reactions of users have been collected by on-line questionnaires, and extensive log-files have been collected for further analysis of user behavior. However, this in itself has proven to be a difficult task, especially in as far as drawing conclusions for better design and usability is concerned. Here an important niche for research remains to be explored. The statistics on usage of the server trace the path that the different users take through a session. The second version of Ecran was most succesful in use. Because of the low performance of the server hardware the more interesting last version was sometimes too slow to use for the occasional user. This should also be remedied by a less server-centered approach, whch is obviously not a good way to deal with the scaling problem at the implementation level. This work, on the other hand, is focusing on conceptual advances that can complement the technological scaling efforts of others.

Acknowledgment

This research was funded by the project MAGICA, 'Electronic Multimedia Catalogues Based on Software Agents', within the EU-Telematics Information Engineering 4th framework program (IE 2069). Additional funding is provided by the project SACEA 'Software Agents for Cooperative Environment Administration' funded by the Belgian Office for Scientific, Technical and Cultural Affairs as project IE/XX/A10, and the project ADIOS 'Advanced Developments in Object-Systems' funded by the Belgian Office for Scientific, Technical and Cultural Affairs as project IF/IT/18. Thanks to Kathleen Van den Abbeele and Brigitte Honig for valuable comments and assistance for preparing the multi-media material. Special thanks to Frank Kresin (Universtiy of Amsterdam) for re-engineering the server in Java, and to Bernard Noel (Cine Libre) for kindly providing the festival related material. The first author is a senior researcher for the Belgian National Science Foundation, FWO.

References

1. S. Brainov. Altruistic cooperation between self-interested agents. In *Proceedings of the European Conference on Artificial Intelligence*, 1996.
2. D. Canamero and W. Van de Velde. Socially emotional: Using emotions to ground social interaction. In *Working Notes of the AAAI'97 Fall Symposium on Socially Intelligent Agents, MIT, MA*, 1997.
3. B. Dunin-Keplicz and J. Treur. Compositional formal specification of multi-agent systems. In M.J. Wooldridge and N. Jennings, editors, *Intelligent Agents: ECAI-94 workshop on agent theories, architectures and languages*, volume 890 of *Lecture Notes in Artificial Intelligence*, pages 102–117, Berlin, 1996. Springer-Verlag.
4. Tim Finin, Rich Fritzson, Don McKay, and Robin McEntire. Kqml - a language and protocol for knowledge and information exchange. Technical Report CS-94-02, Computer Science Department, University of Maryland and Valley Forge Engineering Center, Unisys Corporation, Computer Science Department, University of Maryland, UMBC Baltimore MD 21228, 1994.
5. Sabine Geldof and Walter Van de Velde. An architecture for template-based (hyper)text generation. In W. Hoeppner, editor, *Proceedings of the 6th European Workshop on Natural Language Generation*, pages 28–37, 1997.
6. Sabine Geldof and Walter Van de Velde. Context-sensitive hypertext generation. In K. Mahesh, L. Carlson, S. Nirenburg, A. Ram, and P. Resnik, editors, *Working Notes of the AAAI-97 Spring Symposium on Natural Language Processing for the World Wide Web*, pages 54–61, 1997.
7. Rune Gustavsson. Multi-agent systems as open societies. In this volume.
8. Yezdi Lashkari, Max Metral, and Pattie Maes. Collaborative interface agents. In *Proceedings of AAAI'94*, August 1994.
9. M. Milosavljevic, A. Tulloch, and R. Dale. Text generation in a dynamic hypertext environment. In *Proceedings of the 19th Australasian Computer Science Conference*, Melbourne, Australia, 1996.
10. Van Parunak, John Sauter, and Steve Clark. Specification and design of industrial synthetic ecosystems. In this volume.
11. R. Schrooten and W. Van de Velde. Software agent foundation for dynamic interactive electronic catalogs. *Applied Artificial Intelligence*, 11:459–481, 1997.
12. Onn Shehory, Katia Sycara, and Somesh Jha. Multi-agent coordination through coalition formation. In this volume.
13. Yoav Shoham. Agent-oriented programming. *Artificial Intelligence*, 60(1):51–92, March 1993.
14. W. Van de Velde. Co-habited mixed realities. In *Proceedings of the IJCAI workshop on Social Interaction and Communityware, Nagoya, Japan*, 1997.
15. G. Weiss. Learning to coordinate actions in multi-agent systems. In *Proceedings of the International Joint Conference on Artificial Intelligence*, pages 311–316, 1993.
16. M. Wooldridge and N.R. Jennings. Agent theories, architectures, and languages: A survey. In M. Wooldridge and N.R. Jennings, editors, *Intelligent Agents*, Lecture notes in Artificial Intelligence 890. ECAI-94, Springer-Verlag, August 1994.

Analysis and Design of Multiagent Systems Using MAS-CommonKADS*

Carlos A. Iglesias[†**], Mercedes Garijo[‡],
José C. González[‡] and Juan R. Velasco[‡]

[†] Dep. de Teoría de la Señal, Comunicaciones e Ing. Telemática, E.T.S.I. Telecomunicación,
Univ. de Valladolid. C/ Real de Burgos s/n, 47011 Valladolid, Spain
cif@tel.uva.es

[‡] Dep. de Ingeniería de Sistemas Telemáticos, E.T.S.I. Telecomunicación,
Univ. Politécnica de Madrid. C/ Ciudad Universitaria s/n, 28040 Madrid, Spain
{mga,jcg,juanra}@gsi.dit.upm.es

Abstract. This article proposes an agent-oriented methodology called *MAS-CommonKADS* and develops a case study. This methodology extends the knowledge engineering methodology *CommonKADS* with techniques from object-oriented and protocol engineering methodologies. The methodology consists of the development of seven models: *Agent Model*, that describes the characteristics of each agent; *Task Model*, that describes the tasks that the agents carry out; *Expertise Model*, that describes the knowledge needed by the agents to achieve their goals; *Organisation Model*, that describes the structural relationships between agents (software agents and/or human agents); *Coordination Model*, that describes the dynamic relationships between software agents; *Communication Model*, that describes the dynamic relationships between human agents and their respective personal assistant software agents; and *Design Model*, that refines the previous models and determines the most suitable agent architecture for each agent, and the requirements of the agent network.

1 The MAS-CommonKADS methodology

MAS-CommonKADS [13] extends *CommonKADS* [28], for multiagent systems (MAS) modelling, adding techniques from object oriented (OO) methodologies such as *Object Modelling Technique* (OMT) [26], *Object Oriented Software Engineering* (OOSE) [15] and *Responsibility Driving Design* (RDD) [31] and from protocol engineering for describing the agent protocols, such as *Specification and Description Language* (SDL) [14] and *Message Sequence Charts* (MSC96) [25]). The methodology defines the following models:

---

* This research is funded in part by the Commission of the European Community under the ESPRIT Basic Research Project *MIX: Modular Integration of Connectionist and Symbolic Processing in Knowledge Based Systems*, ESPRIT-9119, and by the Spanish Government under the CICYT projects TIC91-0107 and TIC94-0139.

** This research was partly carried out while the first author was visiting the Dep. Ingeniería de Sistemas Telemáticos (Universidad Politécnica de Madrid).

- *Agent model (AM):* specifies the agent characteristics: reasoning capabilities, skills (sensors/effectors), services, agent groups and hierarchies (both modelled in the organisation model).
- *Task model (TM):* describes the tasks that the agents can carry out: goals, decompositions, ingredients and problem-solving methods, etc.
- *Expertise model (EM):* describes the knowledge needed by the agents to achieve their goals.
- *Organisation model (OM):* describes the organisation into which the MAS is going to be introduced and the social organisation of the agent society.
- *Coordination model (CoM):* describes the conversations between agents: their interactions, protocols and required capabilities.
- *Communication model (CM):* details the human-software agent interactions, and the human factors for developing these user interfaces.
- *Design model (DM):* collects the previous models and consists of three submodels: *network design* for designing the relevant aspects of the agent network infrastructure (required network, knowledge and telematic facilities); *agent design* for dividing or composing the agents of the analysis, according to pragmatic criteria and selecting the most suitable agent architecture for each agent; and *platform design* for selecting the agent development platform for each agent architecture.

The application of the methodology consists of the development of the different models. Each model consists of constituents (the entities to be modelled) and relationships between the constituents. A textual template is defined for each constituent in order to describe it. The states of the constituents describe their development: empty, identified, described or validated.

The software process model of the methodology combines the risk-driven approach with the component-based approach. The general process is risk driven, that is, in every cycle the states of the models to be reached are defined for reducing the perceived risks. When a state consists of identifying components, the developed components (agents, services, knowledge bases, etc.) are candidates for reusing.

In order to illustrate the application of the methodology, we will develop a case study, called *The Travel Agency*. The problem consists of building a system that is consulted by a user for booking a flight, and answers with the cheapest available flights with lowest probability of being delayed. The system will be run by any company, and the information of the flights will be available from the airlines.

2 Conceptualisation

During this phase we will carry out an elicitation task to obtain a preliminary description of the problem. This is carried out following a user-centered approach by determining some use cases (scenarios) which can help us to understand informal requirements and to test the system. Use cases are described using OOSE notation and the interactions are formalised with MSC (Message Sequence Charts) [25, 24].

We can identify one user role: *the traveller*, a person who wishes to travel. The following information should be supplied: departure date (*dd*), arrival date (*ad*) and

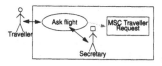

Fig. 1. Use case diagram

destination (*dest*). Two scenarios are identified: the system answers with an available flight (*num_flight*) or with no available flight (and the cause). If there is no available flight, the user can change the flight data. The interaction between the user and the system is represented using the use case notation of OOSE [15] (Fig. 1, notation extended as explained in 3.1). The interactions of the use cases are formalised using MSC as a notation (Fig. 2). In this figure two message interchange alternatives are combined with the alternative (*alt*) operator. A basic MSC contains the description of the asynchronous communication between entities called instances, and has primitives for local actions, timers (set, reset and time-out), process creation, process stop, coregions, and inline operators expressions for composition of event structures (alternative, parallel composition, iteration, exception and optional regions). The purpose in this phase is to get an idea of the interactions, but they will be refined later in the coordination model, specifying the data/knowledge interchanged and the speech-act of each interaction.

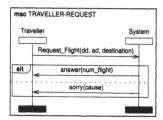

Fig. 2. MSC Traveller request use case diagram

3 Analysis

The results of this phase will be the requirements specification of the MAS through the development of the models previously described, except for the design model. These models are developed in a risk-driven way, and the steps are:

- *Agent modelling:* developing initial instances of the agent model for identifying and describing the agents.

- *Task modelling:* task decomposition and determination of the goals and ingredients of the tasks.
- *Coordination modelling:* developing the coordination model for describing the interactions and coordination protocols between the agents.
- *Knowledge modelling:* modelling of the knowledge on the domain, the agents (knowledge needed to carry out the tasks and their proactive behaviour) and the environment (beliefs and inferences of the world, including the rest of agents).
- *Organisation modelling:* developing the organisation model. Depending on the type of project, it may be necessary to model the organisation of the enterprise in which the MAS is going to be introduced for studying the feasibility of the proposed solution. In this case, two instances of the organisation model are developed: before and after the introduction of the MAS. This model is also used to model the software agent organisation. Another approach to define a social level for MAS extending *CommonKADS* is presented in [11].

3.1 Agent Modelling

Agents can be identified with the following strategies (or a combination of them):

- Analysis of the actors of the use cases defined in the conceptualisation phase. The actors of the use cases delimit the external agents of the system. Several similar roles (actors) can be mapped onto one agent to simplify the communication.
- Analysis of the statement of the problem. The syntactic analysis of the problem statement can help to identify some agents. The candidate agents are the subjects of the sentences, the active objects. The actions carried out by these subjects should be developed by the agents as goals (with initiative) or services (under demand).
- Usage of heuristics. The agents can be identified determining whether there is some *conceptual distance* [3]: knowledge distribution, geographical distribution, logical distribution or organisational distribution.
- An initial task and expertise models can help us to identify the necessary functions and the required knowledge capabilities, resulting in a preliminary definition of the agents. The goals of the tasks will be assigned to the agents.
- Application of the *internal use cases* technique. This technique is based on RDD [31] and its CRC (Class Responsibility Collaboration) cards. Taking as input the use cases of the conceptualisation phase and some initial agents, we can think that each agent "uses" other agent(s), and can use these agents with different roles. The use case notation (Fig. 1 and 3) is extended for showing human agents (with the round head) and software agents (with the squared head). When an agent needs to use an agent for a particular function (for example, evaluate something), we look for such an agent in our agent-library for reusing, combining in this way the top-down and bottom-up approach.
- Application of the enhanced CRC cards. A CRC is filled for each agent, describing its class. Each CRC is divided into five columns: goals assigned, plans for achieving these goals, knowledge needed to carry out the plans, collaborators in these plans, and services used in the collaboration. The back side of the CRC is used for annotations or extended description of the front side.

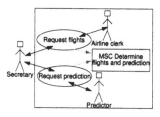

Fig. 3. Internal use case diagram

In the proposed case study, we identify:

- Since there is a user (human agent), as a general rule, we create a user-interface agent derived from an interface agent class for each human agent. In this case, it will be called *Secretary*. The type of interaction (menu-based, etc.) between a human agent and his/her agent assistant should be modelled in the communication model.
- Now we can recognise a knowledge distance (we need an expert in predicting flights without delays), with the role (class) of *Predictor*.
- There is also a geographical distance, the information of the available airlines can only be accessed through *Airlines-Clerk* agents. This information will be requested from *Airlines-Clerk* agents, so it can be useful to define a group for these agents and send multicast messages. This group will be modelled in the organisation model.

We should then fill the textual template of the agent model for each identified agent, that includes its name, type, role, position, a description, offered services, goals, skills (sensors and effectors), reasoning capabilities, general capabilities norms, preferences and permissions.

The approach followed here is quite different from the approach of agent identification in synthetic ecosystems [23], since we suppose that agents will be rather complex (because of their architecture) and we will try to limit the number of agents.

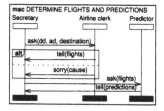

Fig. 4. MSC internal use case diagram

3.2 Task Modelling

Tasks are decomposed following a top-down approach, and described in an and/or tree. The description of a task [8] includes its name, a short description, input and output ingredients, task structure, its control, frequency of application, preconditions and required capabilities of the performers.

The potential benefits of the development of this model are the documentation of the activities of the organisation before and after the introduction of the multiagent system. This documentation serves for supporting the maintenance and management of changes in the organisation and for supporting project feasibility assessment.

3.3 Coordination Modelling

The coordination model has two milestones: (1) definition of the communication channels and building of a prototype; (2) analysis of the interactions and determination of complex interactions (with coordination protocols).

The first phase consists of the following steps:

1. Describe the prototypical scenarios between agents using MSC notation (Fig. 4). The conversations are identified taking as an input the results of the techniques used for identifying agents. During this first stage, we will consider that every conversation consists of just one single interaction and the possible answer.
2. Represent the events (interchanged messages) between agents in event flow diagrams (also called service charts) (Fig. 5). These diagrams collect the relationships between the agents via services.
3. Model the data interchanged in each interaction. The expertise model can help us to define the interchanged knowledge structures. These interchanged data are shown in the event flow diagram between squared brackets.
4. Model each interaction with the state transition diagrams of SDL (Specification and Description Language) [14] specifying speech-acts as inputs/outputs of message events (Fig. 6). These diagrams can be validated with the MSC diagrams.
5. Each state can be further refined in the task or expertise model.
6. Analyse each interaction and determine its synchronisation type: synchronous, asynchronous or future.

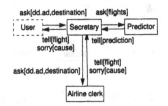

Fig. 5. Event flow diagram

The second phase consists of analysing the interactions for getting more flexibility (relaxing for example the user requirements), taking advantage of the parallelism [7], duplicating tasks using different methods or resolving detected conflicts. When a co-operation protocol is needed, we should consult the library of cooperation protocols and reuse a protocol definition. If there is no protocol suitable for our needs, it is necessary to define a new one. We can use HMSC (High level Message Sequence Charts) [14], which are very useful for this purpose. These diagrams (Fig. 7) show the road map (phases) of the protocol, and how the different phases (specified with MSC) are combined. A phase can be a simple MSC or another HMSC (e.g. *counterp*). The processing of the interactions is described using SDL state diagrams, and it is also necessary to fill in the textual protocol template specifying the required reasoning capabilities of the participants in the protocol. These capabilities can be described using one or several instances of the expertise model. The state diagrams consider three kinds of events: *message events*, events from other agents using message-passing; *external events*, events from the environment perceived through the sensors; and *internal events*, events that arise in an agent because of its proactive attitude.

Fig. 6. SDL state diagram

The potential benefits of the development of this model are:

— The development of the coordination model is a means for specifying the proto-typical interactions between the agents working on the resolution of a problem, together with the interactions with the environment. This model is used to store the decisions of the structure of communications and the protocols associated with these communications. The usage of these descriptions is twofold: the designer can reuse protocols and scenarios and the intelligent agent can select them at run time.
— MSC and SDL are formal description techniques with a well-defined syntax and se-mantics. The usage of these languages for specifying interactions in multiagent sys-tems have been achieved by: (1) defining one signal type for each possible speech-act (message type); (2) associating a logical expression to each state name (using commentaries); and (3) considering internal events (similar to spontaneous trans-itions) for changes in the mental state of the agent motivated because of its proact-ive attitude. In addition, a multicast message has been proposed and requested from the MSC standardisation working group, for simplifying the specification of group

protocols. These languages have been used for supporting the system specification, design, documentation and definition of test cases.
- The development of this model can help in the maintenance and testing of a multiagent system.

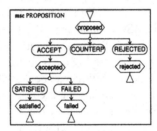

Fig. 7. HMSC diagram

3.4 Knowledge Modelling

The expertise model is used for modelling the reasoning capabilities of the agents to carry out their tasks and achieve their goals. Normally, several instances of the expertise model should be developed: modelling inferences on the domain (i.e. how to predict delays in flights, taxonomies of delays and flights, etc.); modelling the reasoning of the agent (i.e. problem solving methods to achieve a task, character of the agent, etc.) and modelling the inferences of the environment (how an agent can interpret the event it receives from other agents or from the world). When we have to develop the reasoning capabilities of an agent, we will reuse previously developed instances of the expertise model and adapt these instances to the new characteristics of the problem.

The expertise model [30][3] consists of the development of the *application knowledge* (consisting of *domain knowledge*, *inference knowledge* and *task knowledge*) and *problem solving knowledge*.

The usage of this model can take advantage of the work previously developed, for example for developing a planner [2].

Domain Knowledge: represents the declarative knowledge of the problem, modelled as concepts, properties, expressions and relationships using the *Conceptual Modelling Language* (CML) [27] or the graphical notation of the Object Model of OMT.

In our problem, if we are focusing just on the domain, we could identify concepts such as flight, airlines, delay, etc.; properties such as num_flight, ao, dd,.... These concepts are arranged in *domain models* that describe a particular relationship between

---

[3] A very practical approach to the development of this model can be found in [17].

themselves. For example, we could develop a causal model of what events cause a delay; a hierarchy of events, delays, etc. The road map of the developed domain models and their relationships are presented in *model schematas*.

3.5 Organisation Modelling

CommonKADS defines the organisation model for modelling the organisation in which the knowledge based system is going to be introduced. Here the model is extended in the same way as the agent model for modelling the organisation of agents. This model shows the static or structural relationships between the agents, while the coordination model shows the dynamic relationships. The graphical notation of these models is based on the notation of the Object Model of OMT, adding a special symbol for distinguishing between agents and objects. An example of agent hierarchy diagram is shown in Fig. 9. The aggregation symbol is used for expressing agent groups.

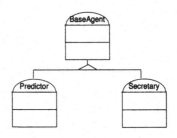

Fig. 9. Class agent diagram

The agent symbol is quite similar to the class symbol proposed in OMT, but has a different meaning. The upper box does not store the defined attributes as in OMT but the mental state and internal attributes of an agent, such as their goals, beliefs, plans, etc. The lower box stores the external attributes of the agents: services, sensors and effectors.

The inheritance relationship between agents is defined as the union of the values of the precedent classes for each attribute. For example, an agent class has its goals and the goals of the precedent agent classes. If an agent defines an attribute as exclusive, the values are overwritten.

The potential benefits of the development of this model is the specification of the structural relationships between human and/or software agents, and the relationship with the environment. The study of the organisation is a tool for the identification of possible impacts of the multiagent system when installed. In the same way, this model can provide information about the functions, workflow, process and structure of the organisation that allows the study of the feasibility of the proposed solutions. This model represents both class agent diagrams and instance agent diagrams, showing the particular relationships with the environment. In contrast with other paradigm (i.e. object oriented), the agent instance diagrams are frequently more relevant than the class agent diagrams.

4 Design

As a result of the analysis phase, an initial set of agents has been determined. During the design phase the design model is developed. This phase is extended for MAS and consists of [13]:

- *Agent network design:* the infrastructure of the MAS-system (so-called *network model* [12]) is determined, and consists of network, knowledge and coordination facilities. The agents (so-called *network agents*) that maintain this infrastructure are also defined, depending on the required facilities. Some of these required facilities can be:
    - *Network facilities:* agent name service, yellow/white pages service, de/registering and subscription service, security level, encryption and authentication, transport/application protocol, accounting service, etc.
    - *Knowledge facilities:* ontology servers, PSM servers, knowledge representation language translators, etc.
    - *Coordination facilities:* available coordination protocols and primitives, protocol servers, group management facilities, facilities for assistance in coordination of shared goals, police agents for detecting misbehaviours and the control of the usage of common resources, etc.

  The result of the common facilities shared by the agents allow the efficient communication between the agents and is expressed in an ontology, in the same way as the service ontology as defined by Nodine [22].
- *Agent design:* the most suitable architecture is determined for each agent, and some agents can be introduced or subdivided according to pragmatic criteria. Each agent is subdivided in modules for user-communication (from communication model), agent communication (from coordination model), deliberation and reaction (from expertise, agent and organisation models), external skills and services (from agent, expertise and task models). The agent design maps the functions defined in these modules onto the selected agent architecture.

  The issue of designing an agent architecture [5] is not addressed in the methodology, since the agent architecture is provided by the agent development platform.
- *Platform design:* selection of the software (multiagent development environment) and hardware that is needed (or available) for the system.

The potential benefits of the development of this model are:

- The decisions on the selection of a multiagent platform and an agent architecture for each agent are documented.
- The design model collects the information of the previously developed models and details how these requirements can be achieved.
- The design model for multiagent systems determines the common resources and needs of the agents and designs a common infrastructure managed by network agents. This facilitates modularity in the design.

5 Related Work

There are several proposals for defining an agent-oriented (AO) methodology.

Here we include a review and the relationship between these approaches and *MAS-CommonKADS*.

Kinny [18] defines a methodology for MAS extending OMT. He proposes two main levels: an external view for modelling the agent relationships (our organisation model) and the interactions (our coordination model). The internal view describes the mental state of a BDI (Belief-Desire-Intention) agent (our expertise and agent models). The modelling of the interactions is elaborated more in our coordination model. The internal view could be an interesting alternative to the our expertise model, though the expertise model offers a very elaborate framework for knowledge modelling.

Burmeister [6] describes an AO methodology, extending OO techniques. Three models are distinguished: agent model (our agent and expertise models), organisational model (our organisation model) and a cooperation model (our coordination model). She proposes a very interesting extension to the CRC cards and a clear development process. Our graphical notation for modelling interactions seems to be more detailed, and the knowledge modelling is elaborated more in the *CommonKADS* framework.

Kendall [16] proposes another AO methodology based on OO and enterprise modelling techniques. The use case model is very similar to our internal use cases. Coordination and knowledge modelling are not so well developed and the process development is not very clear.

MASB [20, 21] proposes an AO methodology that covers analysis and design. The *behaviour diagrams* are similar to the internal use case diagrams, and it proposes a new graphical notation (perhaps too complex) for modelling the agents. The conversation modelling is only mentioned.

CoMoMAS [10] proposes also an extension to *CommonKADS* for MAS. It has a very interesting extension to CML for MAS and a good redefinition of the expertise model. It also defines a new model for cooperation, but is less developed than our coordination model. Our model also proposes different graphical notations instead of just textual templates.

DESIRE [4] is a formal framework for multiagent modelling, that covers mainly our task, agent and expertise models. It could be suitable for specifying the design after the analysis phase.

CoLa [29] is a specification language for task decomposition, transactions and contracts, which are specified in our methodology in the task and coordination models. Our graphical notation could be easily mapped onto this specification language.

COOL [1] and *AgentTalk* [19] are an alternative to our coordination model. Our model takes advantage of the properties of formal description techniques and their standardised textual and graphical notation and semantics.

6 Conclusions and Future Work

The engineering approach [9] to agent-based systems development is a key factor for their introduction into the industry. This principled development will be specially needed as long as the number of agents of the systems increase. The standard advantages of an engineering approach, such as management, testing and reutilisation should be applied in the development of agent-based systems.

This paper presents an agent-oriented methodology that covers the software development life cycle of a multiagent system, through the development of seven models, that can be reused. The software process model combines a risk-driven approach with a component-based approach.

This methodology integrates techniques from a well-known knowledge engineering methodology, *CommonKADS*, with techniques from object-oriented methodologies and protocol engineering. The application of techniques based on well-known techniques is intended to facilitate the learning of the methodology and to provide confidence to the managers with techniques that have been successfully applied.

For each model of the methodology, we have shown the standard development process and the graphical notation. The methodology also defines textual templates for each model, not included here, and some non-standard development processes.

This approach is currently being employed in real applications. The feedback from these applications will help to refine the methodology.

Our main effort has been the development of the new model, the Coordination Model. The rest of the models are subject of further improvement.

Our future work is focused on the development of a workbench for the methodology, since there is no integrated environment available.

Acknowledgements

We would like to thank Amalio F. Nieto, Mark Hallett and two anonymous referees for many suggestions concerning the content and presentation of this paper.

References

1. Mihai Barbuceanu and Mark S. Fox. Capturing and modeling coordination knowledge for multi-agent systems. *Journal on Intelligent and Cooperative Information Systems*, July 1996.
2. V. R. Benjamins, Leliane Nunes de Barros, and Valente Andre. Constructing planners through problem-solving methods. In B. Gaines and M. Musen, editors, *Proceedings of the 10th Banff Knowledge Acquisition for Knowledge-Based Systems Workshop*, volume 1, pages 14–1/20, Banff, Canada, November 1996. KAW.
3. Alan H. Bond and Les Gasser. An analysis of problems and research in DAI. In Alan H. Bond and Les Gasser, editors, *Readings in Distributed Artificial Intelligence*, pages 3–36. Springer-Verlag: Heidelberg, Germany, 1988.
4. F. M. T. Brazier, B. M. Dunin-Keplicz, N. R. Jennings, and Treur J. DESIRE: Modelling multi-agent systems in a compositional formal framework. *Int Journal of Cooperative Information Systems*, 1(6):To appear, January 1997.
5. Joanna Bryson. Agent architecture as object oriented design. (In this volume).
6. Birgit Burmeister. Models and methodology for agent-oriented analysis and design. In K Fischer, editor, *Working Notes of the KI'96 Workshop on Agent-Oriented Programming and Distributed Systems*, 1996. DFKI Document D-96-06.

7. E. H. Durfee, V. R. Lesser, and D. D. Corkill. Trends in cooperative distributed problem solving. *IEEE Transactions on Knowledge and Data Engineering*, 1(1), March 1989.

8. Cuno Duursma, Olle Olsson, and Sundin Ulf. Task model defintion and task analysis process. Technical Report Technical report KADS-II/M5/VUB/TR/004/2.0 ESPRIT Project P5248, Free University Brussels and Swedish Institute of Computer Science, 1994.

9. M. Fisher, J. Müller, M. Schroeder, G. Staniford, and G. Wagne. Methodological foundations for agent-based systems. In *Proceedings of the UK Special Interest Group on Foundations of Multi-Agent Systems (FOMAS). Published in Knowledge Engineering Review (12) 3, 1997.* http://www.dcs.warwick.ac.uk/ fomas/fomas96/abstracts/ker3.ps.

10. Norbert Glaser. *Contribution to Knowledge Modelling in a Multi-Agent Framework (the Co-MoMAS Approach)*. PhD thesis, L'Universtité Henri Poincaré, Nancy I, France, November 1996.

11. Rune E. Gustavsson. Multi agent systems as open societies - a design framework -. (In this volume).

12. C. A. Iglesias, J. C. González, and J. R. Velasco. MIX: A general purpose multiagent architecture. In M. Wooldridge, J. P. Müller, and M. Tambe, editors, *Intelligent Agents II (LNAI 1037)*, pages 251–266. Springer-Verlag: Heidelberg, Germany, 1996.

13. Carlos A. Iglesias, Mercedes Garijo, José C. González, and Juan R. Velasco. A methodological proposal for multiagent systems development extending CommonKADS. In B. Gaines and M. Musen, editors, *Proceedings of the 10th Banff Knowledge Acquisition for Knowledge-Based Systems Workshop*, volume 1, pages 25–1/17, Banff, Canada, November 1996. KAW. Track Agent-Oriented Approaches To Knowledge Engineering.

14. ITU-T. Z100 (1993). CCITT specification and description language (sdl). Technical report, ITU-T, June 1994.

15. I. Jacobson, M. Christerson, P. Jonsson, and Övergaard. *Object-Oriented Software Engineering. A Use Case Driven Approach.* ACM Press, 1992.

16. Elisabeth A. Kendall, Margaret T. Malkoun, and Chong Jiang. A methodology for developing agent based systems for enterprise integration. In D. Luckose and Zhang C., editors, *Proceedings of the First Australian Workshop on DAI*, Lecture Notes on Artificial Intelligence. Springer-Verlag: Heidelberg, Germany, 1996.

17. John Kingston. Building a KBS for health and safety assessment. In *Applications and Innovations in Expert Systems IV, Proceedings of BCS Expert Systems '96*, pages 16–18, Cambridge, December 1996. SBES Publications. Also published as technical report: AIAI-TR-202, Artificial Intelligence Applications Institute, University of Edinburgh.

18. David Kinny, Michael Georgeff, and Anand Rao. A methodology and modelling technique for systems of BDI agents. In W. van der Velde and J. Perram, editors, *Agents Breaking Away: Proceedings of the Seventh European Workshop on Modelling Autonomous Agents in a Multi-Agent World MAAMAW'96, (LNAI Volume 1038)*. Springer-Verlag: Heidelberg, Germany, 1996.

19. Kazushiro Kuwabara, Toru Ishida, and Nobuyasu Osato. AgenTalk: Coordination protocol description for multiagent systems. In *Proceedings of the First International Conference on Multi-Agent Systems (ICMAS-95)*, page 455, San Francisco, CA, June 1995.

20. B. Moulin and L. Cloutier. Collaborative work based on multiagent architectures: A methodological perspective. In Fred Aminzadeh and Mohammad Jamshidi, editors, *Soft Computing: Fuzzy Logic, Neural Networks and Distributed Artificial Intelligence*, pages 261–296. Prentice-Hall, 1994.

21. Bernard Moulin and Mario Brassard. A scenario-based design method and an environment for the development of multiagent systems. In D. Lukose and C. Zhang, editors, *First Australian Workshop on Distributed Artificial Intelligentce, (LNAI volumen 1087)*, pages 216–231. Springer-Verlag: Heidelberg, Germany, 1996.

22. Marian H. Nodine and Amy Unruh. Facilitating open communication in agent systems: the infosleuth infrastructure. (In this volume).
23. Van Parunak, John Sauter, and Steve Clark. Toward the specification and design of industrial synthetic ecosystems. (In this volume).
24. Björn Regnell, Michael Andersson, and Johan Bergstrand. A hierarchical use case model with graphical representation. In *Proceedings of ECBS'96, IEEE International Symposium and Workshop on Engineering of Computer-Based Systems*, March 1996.
25. Ekkart Rudolph, Jens Grabowski, and Peter Graubmann. Tutorial on message sequence charts (MSC). In *Proceedings of FORTE/PSTV'96 Conference*, October 1996.
26. J. Rumbaugh, M.Blaha, W. Premerlani, and V.Lorensen F. Eddy. *Object-Oriented Modeling and Design*. Prentice-Hall, 1991.
27. A. Th. Schreiber, B. J. Wielinga, and J. M. Akkermans W. Van de Velde. CML: The CommonKADS conceptual modelling language. Research report KADS-II/M2/RR/UvA/69/1.0, University of Amsterdam, Netherlands Energy Research Foundation ECN and Free University of Brussels, March 1994. Accepted for EKAW'94.
28. A. Th. Schreiber, B. J. Wielinga, and J. M. Akkermans W. Van de Velde. CommonKADS: A comprehensive methodology for KBS development. Deliverable DM1.2a KADS-II/M1/RR/UvA/70/1.1, University of Amsterdam, Netherlands Energy Research Foundation ECN and Free University of Brussels, 1994.
29. Egon Verharen, Frank Dignum, and Sander Bos. Implementation of a cooperative agent architecture based on the language-action perspective. (In this volume).
30. B. J. Wielinga, W. van de Velde, A. Th. Schreiber, and H. Akkermans. Expertise model definition document. deliverable DM.2a, ESPRIT Project P-5248 /KADS-II/M2/UvA/026/1.1, University of Amsterdam, Free University of Brussels and Netherlands Energy Research Centre ECN, May 1993.
31. R. Wirfs-Brock, B. Wilkerson, and L. Wiener. *Designing Object-Oriented Software*. Prentice-Hall, 1990.

Multi Agent Systems as Open Societies
- A Design Framework

Rune E. Gustavsson

Department of Computer Science and Business Administration,
University of Karlskrona/Ronneby, S-372 25, Ronneby, Sweden.
Rune.Gustavsson@sikt.hk-r.se

Abstract. We propose a Society Level view (SoL) of Multi Agent Systems. The purposes of a SoL approach are to give: Firstly, a basis for a principled design methodology of industry-scale multi agent systems based on, and extending, the CommonKADS methodology. Secondly, a structure-preserving mapping of the Society Level onto emergent technologies for distributed components and network-centric computations. This mapping will provide us with a semantic grounding of concepts at the Society Level. Thirdly, a framework for assessment of techniques and methodologies as well as of foundations of multi agent systems.

1 Overview

The paper gives a background and an introduction to a Society Level (SoL) approach of Multi Agent Systems (MAS) design. We also give pointers to on-going research topics as illustrations of general principles put forward in the paper. The paper is in this form a position paper. In-depth technical investigations are in progress and are partly listed among the references. There are several proposals of system design layers for MAS similar to our SoL proposal. We claim, however, that our proposal has some distinctive advantages, mainly by supporting a natural structure-preserving map-ping onto emerging component-based distributed system architectures.

2 Background

Our research group Societies of Computation (SoC), [H1], is participating in an international R&D project, ISES. ISES stands for Information/Society/Energy/Systems, and is a multi disciplinary R&D project aiming at *Providing information infrastructures for future utilities and their customers*. The ISES project is coordinated by the R&D company EnerSearch AB, [H2].

The goal of the ISES projects is to develop and demonstrate design principles of future key information systems for utilities, their customers, and their system providers. Evaluations of designs are performed in field tests or on an experimental testbed in our laboratory Villa Wega. The field tests are at present a residential area in the town of Ronneby and paper and pulp industry in the same area. Several extensions to other field tests are in the planning phase.

A key business problem for utilities in the emerging deregulated energy market is to change the business model of selling a commodity such as KWh into a business model of customer demanded services and products such as 'comfort of living', 'safe homes', and 'smooth production'. In business management terms, customer intellectual capital is transformed into Intellectual structural capital as an asset for the company. Another key problem in a competitive market is to proper manage the human intellectual capital into a company asset, [14].

We have in the ISES project focused on 'The Interactive Bill' as a way to create a two-way interaction between utilities and their customers. In that project it is clear that appropriate system requirements include much more than implementation spe-cific issues. Another sub-project is 'Active Documents', which aims at transforming human intellectual capital into structural capital of the employing company.

The bottom line here is that, to design appropriate information systems in our applications, we need to describe and design systems at an implementation independent level, taking into account concepts such as knowledge assets, value-added-services, customer satisfaction, market needs and so on. We believe that in order to design, implement and evaluate useful business critical information systems, we need to create a working understanding of business concepts such as those mentioned above as an input to the system design process. We also claim that our design process have to reflect, at a high level, the impacts of basic implementation constraints of distributed systems such as latency and partial failure.

3 Agent Communication Languages

The basic idea behind a multi agent system can be captured in the following equation

$$\text{Task} = \text{Agents} + \text{Communication} \qquad (1)$$

Equation (1) above captures the idea that an Agent Communication Language, ACL, is a concept on the same abstraction level as agents and tasks. There are several attempts to specify appropriate ACLs. We have for instance the standardization efforts KQML by ARPA Knowledge Sharing Effort, the FIPA ACL language by the FIPA consortium, and on-going efforts by the Agent Society. There have been, and is, a rather heated debate concerning those standardization efforts. The main concerns are related to problems with semantics and difficulties to treat, or hide, implementation details.

A common design decision behind several proposals of ACL has been to model ACL using Searle's speech act theory. One should however note that Searle's theory is *speaker oriented*, i.e., it focuses on, essentially, a one-way communication. A huge amount of research has been devoted to build models on top of the speech-act ontology in order to achieve, and to prove, that the listener will understand or act according to the speaker's intention, as expressed in the speech-acts. Of course we encounter a lot of hard semantic problems with this syntax driven approach. Furthermore, the proposed standards often also incorporate implementation specific issues in their ACL. In our view, the speaker oriented approach of an ACL is not fruitful to pursue in a multi agent setting. Agent coordination is, in our opinion, based on the task as well on the context and the competencies or abilities of the agents. Furthermore, the coordination is most naturally seen as dialogues on agreed upon subjects than isolated message sending. This observation, of course, implies that there is no general high-level ACL, but we can hopefully define contexts and agent dependent knowledge sharing mechanisms that are reusable. We believe that the introduction of a Society Level (SoL) in multi agent system design will improve our understanding of these matters as well.

4 The Society Level of Multi-Agent Systems

Following Newell [11], we introduce three abstraction levels for MAS analysis and design. The levels are; the Society Level, the Symbol Level, and the Physical Level. The discussion in this short paper will be on the Society Level aspects of components, composition laws, medium, and, behavior. Finally, we address the issue of open systems in our setting. At the end of the section resource management is used as an illustration of some of our main ideas.

4.1 Components

Components of a MAS at the Society Level are *Agents*, *Contexts* and *Coordination*, compare with the discussion in section 3. Agents have *Competencies* or abilities of two types. Internal competency, corresponding to *knowledge* in the sense of Newell, are modeled in terms of a *cognitive* architecture. In the literature of agents there are nu-merous suggestions of a cognitive architecture of agents, a proposal from our group is [3]. In our presentation we denote a cognitive architecture with the letter C.

The other type of competency is *Social* competency, i.e., knowledge of the social context and the ability to communicate with other agents about certain aspects of the context. We denote the architecture of the social competency with the letter S. In order to act appropriately in response to a message or other event the agent has to evaluate the message according to its competencies. We denote this reasoning component of the agent architecture with the letter E. At the Society Level, the 'head' of an agent can thus be modeled as the triple:

$$A = <C, S, E> \tag{2}$$

We have at least three types of agents. One type is problem solving agents, or just (task specific) agents. The other kind of agents is society agents, for example *sentinels* and *facilitators*. The sentinels see to that the society as such is well-behaved. In a structure-preserving sense facilitators are suitable abstractions of object services at the Symbol Level. Also society support of agents can be modeled by sentinels. We have experienced that introduction of sentinels greatly improves the modularity of a MAS design, [6]. Introduction of sentinels can also serve as a mechanism for society-based learning or adaptation.

The E component of the agent architecture provides, in our case, the *semantic grounding* of SoL concepts by being translated in a structure-preserving way into a Java standard interpreter extended by appropriate context and applets at the Symbol Level.

The *Context* component models organizational aspects, e.g., roles, responsibili-ties, and authorities. The Context also models societal infrastructures, such as norms and conventions guiding behavior and interaction between agents. Parts of the Con-text can sometimes be expressed as so called societal laws. Societal laws could be expressed as high level protocols and thus incorporated into the S component and used by the E component when the agent is engaged in a team work. In our ISES-applications society laws and sentinels implements knowledge management of intellectual capital and support to 'The Interactive Bill' and 'Active Documents' as described in section 2.

Coordination, in different disguises, is at the heart of society behavior and, hence, constitutes the third architectural component of our system at the Society Level. The *Coordination* component models interaction and knowledge sharing mechanisms and has, thus, as a sub component, an appropriate Agent Communication Language (ACL). Messages sent to an agent has to be evaluated by the E component as the message, typically, is part of a dialogue in the context of a contract. The states of the components C and S are changed according to the results of the interpretations by the E component. Proper actions are then executed by the agent.

We believe that coordination, context and agents should be studied in a holistic way, in order to increase our understanding of concepts and interplay between basic con-cepts and relations. Furthermore, this approach will imply natural requirements on appropriate ACLs and classes of ACL can be defined along the route. We summa-rize this point of view by rewriting equation (1) into the following SoL equation for components.

$$\text{Context} = \text{Agents} + \text{Coordination} \qquad (3)$$

As a starting point of our investigations we will use Malone's definitions of basic dependencies in coordination, that is, 'flow', 'sharing', and 'fit', [9]. As an example we can regard 'resource allocation' as a type of 'sharing'. In our applications we have extensively investigated 'computational markets' as a model of 'resource allocation' and hence a possible candidate of a reusable model of sharing-type.

The importance of context in intelligent knowledge sharing has been recognized in contemporary research on natural language understanding. The famous liar's paradox 'This assertion is false' is credited to the ancient philosopher Epimenides and given as an example of paradoxes in self-reference. Recently, 1986, Barwise and Etchemen-dy showed that the root of the paradox was neither self-reference nor truth, but an unacknowledged context. Using formal techniques of situation theory the 'liar's para-dox' was transformed into a theorem. In a couple of books, [4] and [5], Devlin has put forward a very interesting idea of a new 'Theory of Information' based on context or 'infons'. It is our intention to assess those ideas of situation theory in a multi agent context. More exactly, we want to model user-system interactions in 'Active Documents' and 'The Interactive Bill' by using situation theory to capture context and content as well as 'common knowledge' in a dialogue.

4.2 Composition laws

Agents are the active members of the society. They can act alone or form different types of teams for specific purposes. Team formation as well as team work has to be in coherence with the agents' intentions and abilities as well as with the given context. The purpose of a team formation can be referred to as a *social agreement* with a *contract*, defining the rules of the team work. The setting up and closing of social agreements can be seen as tasks in their own right, *articulation work*. It could be preferable to allocate those tasks to sentinels, or facilitators, of the society, instead of incorporating this kind of social knowledge in each agent, [6].

4.3 Medium

The medium models the elements the system processes in order to obtain the intended behavior. As stated in (2), the agent parts of the medium are the two capabilities modeled by the structures C and S and the reasoning components E. The Context models the world, or society, in which the agents live. Of specific interest in the Coordination model are the agent communication languages, high level protocols, and knowledge sharing mechanisms, that we must define in order to model a desired behavior of the agent system.

We have addressed some of those issues in our research on programmable Models of Interactions, [H1].

4.4 Behavior laws - Principle of Rationality

Methods and means to ensure desirable system behavior are crucial parts of system design. Newell introduced his Principle of rationality on the Knowledge Level as a means to specify correct and implementation independent behavior of stand-alone rational agents, [10].

Newell's Principle of Rationality: If an agent has knowledge that one of its actions will lead to one of its goals, then the agent will select that action.

A common understanding today, is that the concepts of rational agents and rational behavior of agents are highly context dependent in accordance with the equation (3) above. Typically, we encounter conflicts between individual goals and desires and societal laws or emerging undesired behavior of the society. In our applications, we might have a conflict between the goals of the tasks 'Save energy' and 'Comfort of living' which then are resolved by the present contract between the customer and the utility. The contract is part of the context and hence a societal law. Other societal laws we are investigating are intended to ensure, for instance, proper knowledge management of intellectual capital, see section 2. In these cases human agents might be forced to use a groupware, such as BSCW, by the rules implemented in an 'Active Document'. The intention is, of course, to electronically capture knowledge of projects and business processes. It is also important that agents, humans and artificial, does not form tasks or teams in violation with company policies.

To summarize: Rational agents and rational behavior in a society are an important part of the design at the Society Level. The behavior in a team work depends on the composition laws, expressed as social agreements with contracts, and the competencies of the agents in the given context. The concepts of rationality and rational behavior are thus highly context-sensitive. Needless to say, much work remains in order to understand the interplay between different types of rational behavior. We hope that our pragmatic structure-preserving semantic grounding principle will shed light on some of the semantic problems at hand.

Our intention is to use the following *Principle of Rationality* in a pragmatic way.

Principle of Rationality: *A team of agents in a multi-agent society have a rational behavior in the sense that they use their capabilities to fulfill the purpose of their social agreement and in co-herence with their contract. The agents act also rational in the team formation and contract ending processes.*

4.5 Open societies

By *open* societies, we mean the plug-and-play capabilities of agents, i.e., smart equipment in a factory or in a smart home. The discussion of rational behavior and the Principle of Rationality in the previous section leads us to qualify the open concept in our Society Level setting as follows. An open society is an infrastructure of contexts, facilitators, and sentinels. The society is open for agents that follow the Principle of Rationality of the society. Again, in our industrial applications it is important to qualify open societies to avoid undesired behaviors. On our Villa Wega testbed we are presently designing and implementing a Home Automation open society.

4.6 An example

We are implementing a load balancing system communicating on the electric grid in hostile environments. In our case we have a very efficient implementation of the resource management task on a distributed system. The system consists of smart components of well defined competencies and a very efficient knowledge sharing mechanism. A redistribution of resources can be settled by exchange of only one message. Furthermore, we also have excellent scaling properties, [15], [16], and [12]. Figure 1 illustrates our Society Level design and a structure-preserving mapping onto a Symbol Level consisting of a distributed system of Echelon LonWorks components. We are at the moment working on adaptations of CommonKADS to support our Society Level approach as well as the structure-preserving mapping, [2], and [13].

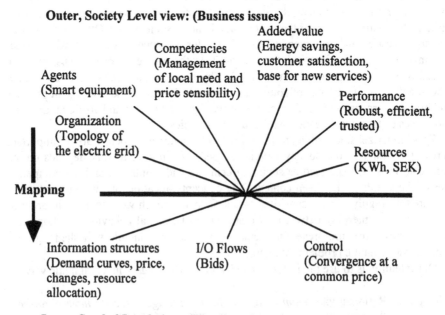

Outer, Society Level view: (Business issues)

Agents (Smart equipment)

Competencies (Management of local need and price sensibility)

Added-value (Energy savings, customer satisfaction, base for new services)

Organization (Topology of the electric grid)

Performance (Robust, efficient, trusted)

Resources (KWh, SEK)

Mapping

Information structures (Demand curves, price, changes, resource allocation)

I/O Flows (Bids)

Control (Convergence at a common price)

Inner, Symbol Level view: (Distributed components, LonWorks)

Fig. 1. Load management modeled at the Society and Symbol Levels

5 Comparisons with Other Approaches

There have been several attempts to define a high modeling level of Multi Agent Systems. In my opinion, the proposals by Aitken-Schmalhofer-Shadbolt [1] and, very recently, by Jennings-Campos, [8], are most similar to ours in spirit and partly in motivation. We agree with most of the motivations provided by the proposers, but we also think that their proposals have some limitations compared to our proposal.

The Aitken-Schmalhofer-Shadbolt proposal aims at investigating coherent behavior of agents in an implementation independent way. They build upon a refinement, by Clancey, of Newell's Principle of rationality and Knowledge Level, in order to investigate systems of agents. Their proposal is as a whole rather incomplete, but they show the benefit from assessing different coordinating principles, such as the contract net and multiple-blackboard, on a high level of abstraction. In essence, however, they use knowledge technologies, similar to CommonKADS, to investigate coordination mechanisms. Society aspects are virtually absent in their model.

The Jennings-Campos proposal introduces a Social Level for multi agent systems. However, they define this level *above* the Newell Knowledge Level. That is, a level above that of individual agents. They introduce a Principle of Social Rationality, based on social utility, which entails the emergent behavior of their system. Based on this model they show that it is possible to discuss and experiment with basic concepts such as acquaintance, influence, and Rights and Duties.

From our perspective, it is somewhat unnatural to define a society level above the Knowledge Level. In effect, it means that there then should exists a mapping between the levels. It seems more natural to introduce hierarchies, as we propose, at the Society Level to address for instance priorities and conflict resolution. In that sense the purpose of Jennings-Campos proposal is different from ours. The mapping of the Social Level onto the Knowledge Level is also not at all clear and is not addressed by Jennings-Campos. In our opinion, the Jennings-Campos Social Level model focuses almost entirely on the S compnent of our Agent model $A = <C, S, E>$, equation (2) in section 4.1.. The Jennings-Campos architecture can thus model social behavior, derived from individuals, in illuminating ways, but it seems not to be suitable to model problem-solving behavior, in the traditional sense. The Aitken-Schmalhofer-Shadbolt proposal, on the other hand, focus on the C component of our agent archi-tecture.

On the surface, our proposal thus combines ideas from the proposals mentioned above. We claim, however, that we have put forward a more comprehensive, yet incomplete, of course, proposal for design of multi agent systems. Highest on the agenda are research aimed at a greater understanding of the society structures, as expressed by sentinels and facilitators, followed by assessments of structurepreserving mappings and their impact on semantics of the Society Level.

Another interesting source of comparison of our approach is emergent methodologies from the Object Management Group (OMG). In a recent proposal on design patterns, [10], a model of architectural levels is proposed. Our Society Level fits nicely in and complements the higher levels of the proposed architecture. The emphasis, in [10], of the horizontal interoperability and metadata flexibility in order to have a balanced software architecture is for instance reflected in the S and C components of our architecture.

In the language of [10] we can state that our Society Level is a 'Design Pattern' at the system and enterprise levels. We think it is important to adapt emerging methodologies of Software Engineering to agent methodologiesin order to approach 'industry-standards' of multi agent system design.

Finally, in this volume Iglesias et. al. give another approach of adapting Common-KADS to a methodology for multi agent system design, [7]. They illustrate their approach by a case study. In their paper Iglesias et. al. also give useful references to other approaches to methodologies of agent systems. Their basic idea is to add techniques from the OO-world to the CommonKADS framework. Basically their approach has the same strengths and weaknesses as ordinary OO approaches, see [10] for a detailed discussion. That is, a vertical application oriented approach which makes it difficult to integrate and maintain applications in systems (societies). Our proposal brings upfront the societal aspects which are also weak in 'pure' CommonKADS.

We are ourselves at the moment members of an EC consortium aiming at adap-ting CommonKADS to a practical tool supporting 'Engineering of Knowledge'. A book on the subject is scheduled to appear 1988.

6 Acknowledgments

Firstly, discussions with professor Akkermans has been invaluable to me in my work. He and the other members of the SoC research team constitute a stimulating environment. Comments on earlier drafts of this paper by the SoC-members Magnus Boman, Paul Davidsson, Staffan Hägg, and Stefan Johansson have been very stimulating and fruitful for me. Last, but not least, most of our efforts could not have happened without the sustained support from Hans Ottosson, CEO of EnerSearch.

7 References

H1 Research group Societies of Computation (SoC):
    http://www.sikt.hk-.se/~soc/
H2 EnerSearch and the ISES project:
    http://www.enersearch.se/

1. Aitken, J. S., Schmalhofer, F., and Shadbolt, N.. A Knowledge Level Characterisation of Multi-Agent Systems. In *Intelligent Agents* (eds. Wooldridge, M. J., and Jennings, N. R.), Springer Verlag, 1995.
2. Akkermans, J.M., Ygge, F., and Gustavsson, R.. HOMEBOTS: Intelligent Decentralized Services for Energy Management. In J.F. Schreinemakers (Ed.) *Knowledge Management: Organization, Competence and Methodology*, Ergon Verlag, Wuerzburg, D, 1996.
3. Davidsson, P.. Linearly Anticipatory Autonomous Agents. In *Proceedings of First International Conference on Autonomous Agents*, ACM Press, 1997.
4. Devlin, K.. *Language at Work*. CSLI Publications, Stanford, USA, 1996.
5. Devlin, K.. *Goodbye, Descartes. The end of logic and a search for a new cosmology of the mind*. John Wiely & Sons, Inc., 1997.
6. Hägg, S.. A Sentinel Approach to Fault Handling in Multi-Agent Systems. In *Proceedings of Fourth Pacific Rim International Conference on Artificial Intelligence*, PRICAI-96, LNAI 1114, Springer Verlag, 1996.

7. Iglesias, C.R., Garijo, M., Gonzalez, J.C., and Velasco, J.R.. Analysis and De-sign of Multiagent Systems using MAS-CommonKADS. In this volume.
8. Jennings, N. R., and Campos, J. R.. Towards a Social Level Characterisation of Socially Responsible Agents. In *IEE Proceedings of Software Engineering*, 144(1), Feb., 1997.
9. Malone, T.W., et. al.. Tools for inventing organizations: Toward a handbook of organizational processes. Center for Coordination Science, MIT, Boston, 1997.
10. Mowbray, T.J., and Malveau, R.C.. Corba Design Patterns. John Wiley, 1997.
11. Newell, A.. The Knowledge Level. Presidential Address, American Association for Artificial Intelligence. *AI Magazine*, Summer 1981.
12. Sandholm, T., and Ygge, F.. On the Gains and Losses of Speculation in Equi-librium. To appear in *Proceedings of IJCAI '97*, Morgan Kaufmann, 1997.
13. Schreiber, A. T., Wielinga, B. J., Akkermans, J. M. , Van de Welde, W, and de Hoog, R.. CommonKADS - A Comprehensive Methodology for KBS Develop-ment. *IEEE Expert* Vol. 9, Nr 6, 1994.
14. Stewart, T.. *Intellectual Capital. The New Wealth of Organizations*. Nicholas Brealey Publishing, London, 1997.
15. Ygge, F., and Akkermans, J. M.. Power Load Management as a Computational Market. In *Proceedings of Second International Conference on Multiagent Sys-tems ICMAS '96*, AAAI Press, 1996.
16. Ygge, F., and Akkermans, J. M.. *Making a Case for MAS*. In *Proceedings of MAAMAW '97*, LNAI 1237, Springer Verlag, 1997.

TKQML: A Scripting Tool for Building Agents

R. Scott Cost, Ian Soboroff, Jeegar Lakhani, Tim Finin, Ethan Miller, and Charles
Nicholas

Computer Science and Electrical Engineering
University of Maryland Baltimore County
Baltimore, Maryland 21250
{rcost1, ian, jlakha1, finin, elm, nicholas}@cs.umbc.edu

Abstract. Tcl/Tk is an attractive language for the design of intelligent agents
because it allows the quick construction of prototypes and user interfaces; new
scripts can easily be bound at runtime to respond to events; and execution state
is encapsulated by the interpreter, which helps in agent migration. However, a
system of intelligent agents must share a common language for communicating requests and knowledge. We have integrated KQML (Knowledge Query Manipulation Language), one such standard language, into Tcl/Tk. The resulting
system, called TKQML, provides several benefits to those building intelligent
agent systems. First, TKQML allows easy integration of existing tools which
have Tcl/Tk interfaces with an agent system by using Tcl to move information
between KQML and the application. Second, TKQML is an excellent language
with which to build agents, allowing on-the-fly specification of message handlers
and construction of graphical interfaces. This paper describes the implementation
of TKQML, and discusses its use in our intelligent agent system for information
retrieval.

1 Introduction

In the past few years, the explosive growth of the Internet has allowed the construction
of "virtual" systems containing hundreds or thousands of individual, relatively inex-
pensive computers. The agent paradigm is well-suited for this environment because it
is based on distributed autonomous computation. Although the definition of a software
agent varies widely, some common features are present in most definitions of agents.
Agents should be autonomous, operating independently of their creators. Agents should
have the ability to move freely about the Internet. Agents should be able to adapt readily
to new information and changes in their environment. Finally, agents should be able to
communicate at a high level, in order to facilitate coordination and cooperation among
groups of agents. These aspects of agency provide a dynamic framework for the design
of distributed systems.

Tcl [7] is an ideal language with which to build agents, because scripts written in
Tcl may be used on any machine that can run Tcl, and because the Tcl language environment itself is highly portable. Additionally, Tcl/Tk greatly facilitates rapid prototyping
and quick development of small applications.

We present TKQML, the integration of an agent communication language, KQML [2]
(Knowledge Query Manipulation Language) into Tcl/Tk. TKQML can be used to build

KQML-speaking agents that run within a TKQML shell. TKQML can also be used to bind together diverse applications into a distributed framework, using KQML as a communication language. Tcl's embeddable nature allows one to easily add agent communication facilities to existing code. As such, TKQML can be used to enhance the functionality of new or existing systems built using a Tcl framework, by allowing easy integration with agent-based systems.

2 Background

KQML is a language for general agent communication. It was developed as part of the Knowledge Sharing Effort [8], a DARPA project exploring agent communication and knowledge reuse. KQML is a language based on speech acts, such as "tell", "ask", and "deny", which describe the nature of a message without reference to its content. Agents communicate application-specific information embedded in general, higher-level KQML messages. A comprehensive semantics [5, 6] for KQML outlines protocols for agent "conversation." Additionally, most implementations provide facilities for message handling, agent naming and resource brokering.

Problems of software agency have not been neglected within the Tcl community. Existing Tcl-based solutions to agent issues, such as AgentTcl [3] and Tacoma [4] have emphasized security and mobility, but fall short with respect to communication. AgentTcl agents, using TCP/IP, exchange bytes strings which have no predefined syntax. In Tacoma, agents must meet in order to communicate. Other projects, such as Tcl-DP [10] provide excellent packages for communication, but lack sufficiently flexible support for higher level languages. TKQML bridges this gap.

3 TKQML

TKQML is an adapter for KATS, a C-based implementation of KQML. It allows Tcl scripts to use existing support for KQML. TKQML usage mirrors that of the KATS API, facilitating easy synchronization with the C version, traditionally the reference implementation.

TKQML is implemented in C as a Tcl application which presents one Tcl command: kqml. The application can be thought of as having two components, the KQML library extensions and the message handler.

3.1 Library Calls

In extending the library, our primary goal was to reflect as closely as possible the usage of the KATS API, through the kqml command. When the kqml command is called, parameters are first translated into an intermediate representation. This allows the representation of complex types at the script level. Next, a call is made to the appropriate function in KATS with the translated parameters. Finally, the return value and resultant parameters are translated back into string representations and, if appropriate, inserted back into the Tcl interpreter environment, simulating call-by-reference.

In TKQML, complex or large objects are kept in memory, and references to these objects are passed up to the Tcl level. These references are merely string representations of the pointers to memory. Script level routines use the kqml commands to access these objects, and are responsible for disposing of them (with a deallocation routine). Since memory pointers have a natural translation to and from string references, no additional memory management is required on the part of TKQML. Note that code could easily be inserted to track allocated memory, facilitating memory management mechanisms.

3.2 Message Handling

An agent will typically deal with each type of incoming message in a different way. KATS provides a pre-emptive solution with the use of a message handler and a router. The router, a separate process, handles the receipt, queuing and transmission of all message traffic. The agent registers message handling routines with a message manager, which is embedded in the agent code. Upon receipt of a message, the router signals the manager, interrupting the current processing. The manager then invokes a routine appropriate for the message.

This process has a natural implementation in Tcl which is much more flexible. Handlers, like the rest of the agent, are written as Tcl scripts, and are registered as strings (or string references to files). Unlike their C counterparts, Tcl handlers do not need to be static objects, compiled and linked before execution. Thus, Tcl handlers can be updated or replaced at any time during execution, making Tcl based agents much more adaptable.

4 CARROT - TKMQL in Action

The CARROT project (Co-operative Agent-based Routing and Retrieval of Text, formerly CAFE) is an ongoing effort at UMBC to develop a distributed architecture for text-based information retrieval [1] that has served as a testbed for TKQML. This project employs a brokered environment of clients and servers. Users make queries through a World-Wide Web-based client, which are routed by a broker agent to an appropriate information source. The broker makes these decisions by gathering information, or metadata, from each source, and deciding which database the query most resembles. A ranked set of results is returned to the client.

A heterogeneous set of text-indexing engines, such as Telltale [9] and mg [11] manage large sets of text data. These engines have been augmented into agents with TKQML. The broker agent communicates transparently with these information servers via KQML. All components consist of C/C++ applications bound to TKQML with a Tcl/Tk shell. One agent, the Agent Control Agent (ACA) is written entirely as a TKQML script. Our experience with CARROT has shown that TKQML can facilitate quick prototyping and rapid development of agents and their GUIs, reducing the time necessary to build large agent-based systems.

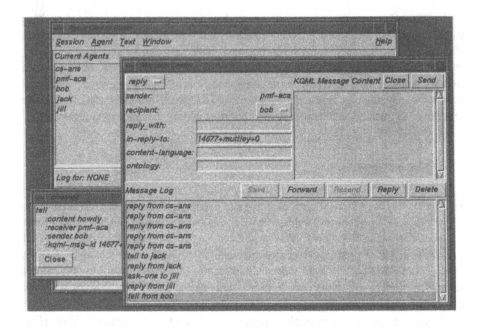

Fig. 1. Agent Control Agent

4.1 The Agent Control Agent

The Agent Control Agent (ACA) was designed to help manage and coordinate the activities of several agents in the CARROT project. It is built entirely from a TKQML shell, and presents a Tk interface panel for controlling agents (see Figure 1).

The ACA provides many facilities for directing agents. It can start or stop agents, and connect to agents which are already running. Arbitrary KQML messages can be sent to agents from the ACA panel. The ACA can monitor the log files of individual agents. A list of currently-known agents is displayed, and appropriate actions apply to the currently highlighted agent in the list.

The ACA, as indicated by its name, is itself a KQML-speaking agent. Almost all control functions are accomplished through the sending and receiving of KQML messages. This makes the ACA independent of individual agent architectures.

The Agent Control Agent has proven itself to be a valuable tool for orchestrating groups of agents. It has been used for managing demonstations, organizing and displaying agent activity, and debugging agent systems in development. Moreover, the flexibility of Tk has allowed us to easily prototype and integrate new functionality on demand.

5 Summary and Conclusions

Both Tcl and KQML are powerful tools in the development of agent-based systems. TKQML combines the two, making it possible to benefit from both the light weight and portability of Tcl scripts and the high-level communication support of KQML with one package. We feel that its power, simplicity and potential for future development make it an ideal platform for the development of agent-based systems.

Resources for TKQML v1.0 can be found at: *http://kqml.org/tkqml/*.

References

1. Grace Crowder and Charles Nicholas. Resource selection in CAFE: An architecture for network information retrieval. In *Proceedings of the Network Information Retrieval Workshop, SIGIR 96*, August 1996.
2. Tim Finin, Yannis Labrou, and James Mayfield. *Software Agents*, chapter KQML as an agent communication language. MIT Press, 1997.
3. Robert Gray. Agent Tcl: A flexible and secure mobile-agent system. In *The Fourth Annual Tcl/Tk Workshop Proceedings*. The USENIX Association, 1996.
4. Dag Johansen, Robbert van Renesse, and Fred B. Schneider. An introduction to the TACOMA distributed system. Technical report, University of Tromso, June 1995.
5. Yannis Labrou. *Semantics for an Agent Communication Language*. PhD thesis, University of Maryland Baltimore County, 1996.
6. Yannis Labrou and Tim Finin. Semantics and conversations for an agent communication language. In *Proceedings of the Fifteenth International Joint Conference on Artificial Intelligence (IJCAI-97)*. Morgan Kaufman, August 1997.
7. John K. Ousterhout. *Tcl and the Tk Toolkit*. Addison-Wesley, 1994.
8. Ramesh S. Patil, Richard E. Fikes, Peter F. Patel-Schneider, Don McKay, Tim Finin, Thomas Gruber, and Robert Neches. The DARPA knowledge sharing effort: Progress report. In Bernhard Nebeld, Charles Rich, and William Swartout, editors, *Principles of Knowledge Representation and Reasoning: Proceedings of the Third International Conference (KR92)*. Morgan Kaufman, 1992.
9. Claudia Pearce and Charles Nicholas. TELLTALE: Experiments in a dynamic hypertext environment for degraded and multilingual data. *Journal of the American Society for Information Science*, June 1994.
10. Brian C. Smith, Lawrence A. Rowe, and Stephen C. Yen. Tcl distributed programming. In *Proceedings of the 1993 Tcl/Tk Workshop*. The USENIX Association, June 1993.
11. Ian H. Witten, Alistair Moffat, and Timothy C. Bell. *Managing Gigabytes: Compressing and Indexing Documents and Images*. Van Nostrand Reinhold, 1994.

Subject Index

A

abstraction 246
"achieve" goals 170
achievement goals 218
achieving plans 170–172
action sequences 17
action transitions 222
actions 217
active documents 330
ADEPT system 178, 35
advertisement agent 300
advice agent 300
agenda 33
agent
- behaviour monitoring 127
- communication languages 330
- connectivity graph (A-graph) 83
- control agent 341
- design 323
- identification 48
- information 145
- interface 144
- model 314
- network design 323
- program 222
- program 261
- skeletons 95
- task 144
- virtual 56
AGENT-0 programming language 172, 216, 227
agent-oriented methodologies 55
agent-oriented paradigm 77
AGENTALK system 104, 324
agents, system 55
agents, watchdog
AGENTSPEAK(L) programming language 156, 216, 227
Aitken, J. S. 333
animal intelligence 16
anytime reasoning 261
appeals 178
applicable plans 165
approximate agent program 266

architecture 261
ARCHON system 50
argumentation 177
assimilation problem 78
atom 159
atoms 200
automated loading dock 245
automated plan synthesis 3

B

battlefield simulation 129
BDI (belief-desire-intention) agents 78, 216
BDI
- architectures 232
- model 155
- theory 245
behaviour based AI 16
behaviour laws 333
behaviour libraries 17
behaviour module 107
behaviour-based layer 256
behavioural conformity 238
behaviours 15
belief 78, 157, 196, 217,
- precedence 83
- recovery process 84
- update event 83
bidding 61–76
- protocol 67
Bratman, M. 155, 234
broadcast message passing 194–195
Brooks, R. 16, 26, 108
Bryson, J. 108
Burmeister, B. 324

C

C++ programming language 13, 24, 155
calculus of communicating systems (CCS) 228
Campos, J. 45, 333
capabilities 146
CARROT project 341
cautious agent program 266

Q-R

S

T

U-Z

Author Index

Lecture Notes in Artificial Intelligence (LNAI)

Lecture Notes in Computer Science